The Faith of Israel

The Faith of Israel

A Theological Survey
of the Old Testament

Second Edition

William J. Dumbrell

Baker Academic

A Division of Baker Book House Co
Grand Rapids, Michigan 49516

© 2002 by William J. Dumbrell

Published by Baker Academic
a division of Baker Book House Company
P.O. Box 6287, Grand Rapids, MI 49516-6287

Printed in the United States of America

Library of Congress Cataloging-in-Publication Data
Dumbrell, William J.
The faith of Israel : a theological survey of the Old Testament / William J. Dumbrell.—2nd ed.
p. cm.
Includes bibliographical references and index.
ISBN 0-8010-2532-X (paper)
1. Bible. O.T.—Theology. I. Title.
BS1192.5 .D86 2002
221.6—dc21   2002023055

For information about Baker Academic, visit our web site:
www.bakeracademic.com

Contents

Abbreviations

ABR	*Australian Biblical Review*
AOAT	Alter Orient und Altes Testament
BA	*Biblical Archaeologist*
BETL	Bibliotheca ephemeridum theologicarum lovaniensium
BHS	*Biblia Hebraica Stuttgartensia.* Edited by K. Elliger and W. Rudolph. Stuttgart, 1983
Bib	*Biblica*
BibSac	*Bibliotheca Sacra*
BTB	*Biblical Theology Bulletin*
BZ	*Biblische Zeitschrift*
BZAW	Beihefte zur Zeitschrift für die alttestamentliche Wissenschaft
CBQ	*Catholic Biblical Quarterly*
ConBOT	Coniectanea biblica: Old Testament Series
EvJ	*Evangelical Journal*
FOTL	Forms of the Old Testament Literature
HSM	Harvard Semitic Monographs
HTR	*Harvard Theological Review*
HUCA	*Hebrew Union College Annual*
IDBSup	*Interpreter's Dictionary of the Bible: Supplementary Volume.* Edited by K. Crim. Nashville, 1976
IEJ	*Israel Exploration Journal*

Int	*Interpretation*
JAAR	*Journal of the American Academy of Religion*
JBL	*Journal of Biblical Literature*
JJS	*Journal of Jewish Studies*
JSOT	*Journal for the Study of the Old Testament*
JSOTSup	Journal for the Study of the Old Testament: Supplement Series
JSS	*Journal of Semitic Studies*
JTS	*Journal of Theological Studies*
NICOT	New International Commentary on the Old Testament
NIGTC	New International Greek Testament Commentary
OTS	Old Testament Studies
OTWSA	*De Ou Testamentiese Werkgemeenskap in Suid-Afrika*
RB	*Revue biblique*
RTR	*Reformed Theological Review*
SBLDS	Society of Biblical Literature Dissertation Series
SBLMS	Society of Biblical Literature Monograph Series
SEÅ	*Svensk exegetisk årsbok*
TynB	*Tyndale Bulletin*
VT	*Vetus Testamentum*
VTSup	*Vetus Testamentum Supplements*
WTJ	*Westminster Theological Journal*
ZAW	*Zeitschrift für die alttestamentliche Wissenschaft*

Introduction

Israel presented her revelation in terms of Law, Prophets, and Writings, the order in which her faith was informed. The Pentateuch—the Law—embraces the first five books of the Old Testament and contains the substance of Israel's gospel. God, who created the world with a New Creation in ultimate view, to be achieved ideally by human cooperation, had given Israel a model in the Eden narrative of what the world was to be. Dominion, in terms of service to God's creation, needed to be exercised over the world outside the garden. Within this dominion, the model of Genesis 2 was extended over all creation. The failure of representative humanity to rise to this task in Genesis 3 meant the call of Israel as the world's evangelist; Israel would be the nation calling the world to the new model of God's government. This was to happen as Israel endorsed kingdom-of-God values in her Promised Land, the new Eden.

The first five books of the Old Testament—the Pentateuch—are intended to highlight this concept. This is the gospel message of the Old Testament, operating the same way within its canon as the Gospels do within the New Testament. Genesis and Exodus document the movement from creation through the fall, to the call of Abraham to Israel and Sinai. Leviticus adds institutions and regulations by which the Promised Land is to be maintained, and within which life within the covenant may continue. Numbers records the journey through the wilderness, the death of one Israel and the birth of another. The incomparable Deuteronomy, by a further covenant in the plains of Moab (Deut. 29–30), regulates the details for life in the Promised Land and also encapsulates the gospel. The gospel is one of national security and God's blessing for Israel in the Promised Land. This makes Deuteronomy a comparable product in the Old Testament to John's Gospel, with its message of life in God's new world in the New Creation.

The Former Prophets (Joshua to 2 Kings) carry forward the message of life in the Land, elaborate the undergirding theology, and inaugurate new theologi-

9

cal movements in view of urbanization and social development that necessitate application of the gospel to a changing Israel. Joshua details the leadership required by Israel to keep the covenant. Judges points to the theocratic government necessary to preserve Israel in spite of her continued attempts to self-destruct. Samuel introduces messiahship and its watchman, the prophet, and Kings unfolds a picture of leadership gone wrong.

The Latter Prophets indicate the shape of Israel's prophetic ministry. As supervisors of covenant performance, the prophets did not, for the most part, start new theological movements. Their understanding of Israel's inevitable dissolution, however, did engender an eschatology. This eschatology looked toward a new beginning for a believing Israel and toward a New Creation (Isa. 65–66). The Christology of the New Testament took this movement further forward in fulfillment.

The Writings contain small books associated with Israel's festivals (Ruth, Songs, Esther, Lamentations); literature of a wisdom movement designed to give guidance for Israel's covenant obedience (Proverbs, Ecclesiastes); and a book such as Job, which raises the vital question of theodicy. Additionally, works of history (Ezra-Nehemiah, Chronicles) that do not reflect on the salvation-historical questions of the Former Prophets, are included. Daniel, which does not fit the prophetic corpus, finds its place, as does the hymnbook of the Second Temple, Psalms. Chronicles, which functions as an addendum to Genesis, detailing the birth, fortunes, demise, and future hopes of Israel, completes the canon.

The Old Testament ends with the prospect of a new covenant. Malachi expects the return of the major covenant figure, Elijah. Chronicles finishes with the decree of Cyrus the Persian, by which the Babylonian rule ended and Israel returned to its land. Chronicles thus raises hopes of the fulfillment of expectations generated by Isaiah 40–66—a return to the Promised Land, which will usher in a new covenant and then a New Creation.

It is undeniable that sources in some form preceded the canonical material we now have. The identification of these sources and of the dates of the completed works is a subjective process and always subject to dispute. Literary criticism provides no assured results, while the vexing question of the relationship of Israel's faith to Israel's history is usually addressed presuppositionally. I attempt to present the theological movement of each book based on the received Masoretic Text and to indicate how each book's content contributes to that book's purpose.

A second edition of a book originally written in the early 1980s has now become necessary. Further work on the text has produced new insights as to the purpose of the canon and how the individual units contribute. Information gleaned from scholarship since the early '80s has been included. Basically, however, if the content has changed somewhat, the thrust of the earlier edition has been maintained. Unless otherwise indicated, scriptural quotations are from the New Revised Standard Version.

Part 1

The Books of the Law

1

Genesis

The Book of Genesis is structured by a recurring formula, "These are the generations of," set before each of ten sections to which it refers. The formula appears at 2:4; 6:9; 11:27; 25:19; 37:2, which begin major sections, and at 5:1; 10:1; 11:10; 25:12; 36:1, where it introduces minor sections within the larger units. Additionally, other genealogical notations demarcate sections (see 4:17–24). Genesis 1–11 presents the account of creation (1:1–2:4) and then moves from Adam to Noah (the tenth from Adam) by interconnecting genealogies, and then from Noah to Abraham (the tenth from Noah), again with interspersed genealogical connections. Chapters 12–50 present a narrative history of the patriarchal period.

Creation and Its Implications (Gen. 1–2)

Genesis 1:1 functions as a heading for the Book of Genesis itself, if not for the OT as a whole. This role is suggested by (1) the elaborate alliteration (in the Hebrew), (2) the reference to the creation of "the heavens and the earth," or the totality of creation, and (3) the lofty theological tone which is struck. By beginning with creation, the biblical account makes it clear that whatever follows in revelation must be understood within this comprehensive first movement of Genesis 1. The effortless way in which the world is brought into being by divine command goes beyond what may be parallels in the Babylonian or Egyptian creation accounts. Indeed, it is possible that such accounts were in the author's mind and that Genesis 1 serves as a polemic against them. If verse 1 is a summary introduction, then it seems best to take verse 3 as referring to the commencement of the work of creation. Verse 2 would then be dependent on verse 3, describing the process by which the world was brought into its present state of order.

Genesis 1:2 requires careful examination. The absolute statement of Genesis 1:1 emphasized God's control over all creation. It was expressed by the Hebrew verb *bara'* 'create', which always has God as its subject and which never takes an accusative of substance from which things are formed. The focus shifts in verse 2 from the universe as a whole (v. 1) to the earth, which is thrown into prominence by its initial position in the sentence. This initial position of "earth" (v. 2) makes it clear that verse 2 is not the logical or natural sequel to verse 1, since this would have required a "converted" form of the Hebrew verb in the initial position. What has been viewed as the "gap" theory, whereby verse 2 documents the Spirit's recovery of the world from the chaos into which the world had supposedly lapsed between verses 1 and 2, is thus eliminated by the Hebrew syntax of verse 2.

The condition of the earth in verse 2 is described as "formless" and "empty" (Heb. *tohu wabohu*). The first of these two nouns is the operative word that the second reinforces. In themselves, the two terms merely point to the condition of the earth, a condition as yet unfit for human habitation. The following clause, however, "darkness was upon the face of the deep," may interpret the first phrase, "the earth was without form and void." The reference then is to the covering of the earth by the primeval waters, whereby the "darkness" of the second clause parallels the "earth" of the first. It is possible that the Hebrew word "deep" (*tehom*) alludes to the detail of the ancient Near Eastern cosmologies (Babylonian and Canaanite), in which a general threat to order comes from the unruly and chaotic sea, which is finally tamed by a warrior god. This god is Baal in Canaan and Marduk in the Babylonian myth of creation, *Enuma Elish,* in which the chaos monster is Ti'amat, cognate with the Hebrew *tehom.*

That Genesis 1:2 reflects something of the chaos/order struggle characteristic of ancient cosmologies is probable in light of correspondence between Genesis 1:2–2:3 and the general events that characterize *Enuma Elish* (Heidel 1961, 129), even if, as is probable, the biblical account is polemical of them. Thus, if Genesis 1:2 is taken in the manner suggested, we have an order like that of the ancient Near Eastern creation narratives of threat, combat, victory, and, as we shall see in Genesis 2:4–25, of resulting temple building. That Genesis 1:2 reflects a chaos/order situation is all the more probable since echoes of a creation conflict are found frequently in later Hebrew poetry (cf. Job 7:12; 26:12; Ps. 74:12–14; 93:3–4; Isa. 51:9–10). We could also think of the invariably pejorative use of "sea" in the Bible, to which reference is made in Revelation 21:1. There, at the advent of the new heavens and earth and with the sweeping away of forces of disorder, it is summarily remarked, "There was no longer any sea."

The force of the first two clauses of verse 2 seems to indicate the provisional character of a creation under threat at that stage. The third clause of verse 2, however, "but (and) the Spirit of God was moving over the face of the waters" (Gibson 1981, 15), seems to attest the power of God to overcome the difficulties posed by the first two statements. "Spirit" in the OT is invariably connected with power and beneficent life (Judg. 6:34; 14:6; Ps. 139:7; Job 33:4; Isa. 61:1). The careful and economical use of vocabulary in Genesis 1:1–2:3, in which, at all points the Hebrew *'elohim* 'God' is an unambiguous reference to the divine name, makes it clear that *'elohim* in verse 2 is not operating as a superlative as some have suggested. The Hebrew word for "spirit" can be translated "wind" and *'elohim* can function as a superlative, thus producing the translation "mighty wind." If the adversarial role of the Spirit (referred to in the translation of Heb. *wa* as "but") is accepted in verse 2, then the presentation is of order imposed on an unruly element in creation. This then is completely congruent with the notion, found in the later biblical poetry, of creation emerging as a result of conflict. We are then forced to deal with the problem of evil as present at the very beginning of creation, a problem that in any case faces us in Genesis 3:1.

On any view, the account of creation presents difficulties. Taking the words "without form and void" of verse 2 as our cue, we have eight creative acts in the first chapter, four on each sequence of the three days, distributed into two sequences of form and content (see fig. 1). The movement in both sequences is from the heavens to the waters to the earth.

Form	Content
Day 1 Light	Day 4 Luminaries
2 Water and sky	5 Fish and birds
3 Land and vegetation	6 Beasts and human beings

Fig. 1. Form and use of the creative acts

It is difficult to be certain whether the presentation of Genesis 1 is chronological or topical. It is possible that it is topical, with the work of days four to six in fact referring in more detail to what happened on days one through three. In this case, the division of creation into its present six days has the primary effect of throwing into clear relief the seventh day of Genesis 2:1–3 as the goal of creation.

The Hebrew word for "day" is used in three senses between Genesis 1:1 and 2:4: for evening and morning taken together (e.g., v. 5), for light as opposed to darkness (v. 5), and in the broader sense of "when" (2:4).

Humankind in the Image (Gen. 1:26–28)

By the distinctive "let us make humankind in our image" (Gen. 1:26), the uniqueness of humankind as a species is suggested. The plural address ("let us") has been variously interpreted—as a piece of fossilized myth, as an address to the heavenly council, or, the most plausible explanation, as a royal plural, and so on. Christian expositors have tended to see the plural address as an address to the Spirit, indicating the distinction within the divine being, or to Wisdom as a divine attribute, on the analogy of Proverbs 8:30. Such an address does not fit the general OT evidence (though in final biblical, trinitarian terms, an address to the Spirit may well be true), however, in which Spirit is God acting powerfully and in which wisdom is, equally, God acting wisely. In any case, the unity of the divine being is reasserted by the singular of Genesis 1:27. The addition of the phrase "after our likeness" in Genesis 1:26 seems designed to exclude the notion of exact copy contained in the word "image," while seeking to convey some resemblance either in nature or function. The connotation of the term "image" is thus weakened by the addition of "likeness," probably in the interests of avoiding the potentially idolatrous idea of an unqualified "in our image."

The Hebrew term *selem* 'image' always conveys visibility in the OT, as beyond it. The Akkadian cognate *salmu* basically refers to a statue in the round and to a representation rather than to a model or a copy. However, even though the term "image" emphasizes externality, we need to remember that humanity in the OT is always a psychic unity. Thus the word refers to the whole of humankind viewed in terms of a representative function in the world. Humankind as a species—humanity—is on view. "Image," therefore, cannot be narrowly understood as rationality, intuitiveness, personal awareness, and so on. The term refers to the whole human being and must include all such characteristics. We should preserve the translation "in our image" but note the implications of the "in." If the "let us make man" of verse 26 is a heavenly self-address by God, then "our image," which, in some sense, man is to reflect and in which he is made, is in heaven and possessed by the Godhead alone (Wenham 1987, 32). Made "in" the image, mankind will thus be simply an image of the heavenly image, a representative of what is divine. Since, as we shall note, Colossians 1:15–20 speaks of the eternal sonship of Christ as the preexistent image of God, some hint is thereby given as to the real character of the image on view here.

Given the nature of humanity as described in the OT, "image" in 1:26 refers to the whole person, but with the major emphasis falling upon function. In both ancient Egypt and Mesopotamia, the notion of humankind as the image of the deity was well known. In Egypt, the Pharaoh of the day was regarded as the image of the creator god, Re, and as the incarnation of Re (Mettinger 1974, 413). In Mesopotamia, the term "image" was commonly used to refer to the statue of a god or king, but when used in priestly or royal designations, the human representative on view was presented as possessing the god's power and authority (Bird 1981). The exact phrase "in the image of God" occurs again in the OT only at Genesis 9:6, although the similar phrase at Genesis 5:3 indicates that being in the image of God is a representative function transmitted by procreation. Additionally, Genesis 1:26c is to be translated as a purpose clause, "in order that they may have dominion." Genesis 1:27a, b recapitulates 1:26, but 1:27c, with the return to the plural and the addition of biological terms for male and female, anticipates and refers to the "male and female he created them" of Genesis 1:28 (Bird 1981, 146–50). On this view, gender distinctions would form no part of the "image." The sexual distinctions referred to in 1:27 are not necessarily a component of what creation conveys in the image. Verse 27b may be more than simply a repetition of verse 27a and may anticipate the blessing conferred in verse 28 (Bird 1981, 134).

"Image" thus appears to refer to humanity as a whole and not to individuals, with humanity then being differentiated by the gender terms. Mesopotamian analogies to which we could appeal indicate that the king as an image of the deity was conceived of as a servant of the gods. "Image" referred to his royal function, as one having a mandate from the gods to rule, and thus as one possessing divine power. In Psalm 8, with clear reference to Genesis 1, humankind is depicted in royal terms. Note that, in Psalm 8:5, man is crowned with "glory and honor"; elsewhere these are divine attributes (see Ps. 29:1, 4; 90:16; 104:1; 111:3; 145:5; Job 40:10). The allusion in Psalm 8:6 to all things being put under the feet of created man refers to an ancient Near Eastern symbol of submission to authority (cf. Josh. 10:24; 1 Kings 5:3; Ps. 110:1). Finally, "have dominion" in Genesis 1:28 refers elsewhere in the OT to the exercise of kingly functions (cf. 1 Kings 4:24; Ps. 72:8; 110:2; Isa. 14:6; Ezek. 34:4). The notion of image as referring to royal authority is attested in both Mesopotamia and Egypt (Schmidt 1973, 137–48).

The creation of humanity in Genesis 1 thus climaxes in the presentation of the species as vice-regent over creation. The account stresses the essential dignity of the image, a dignity not lost as a result of the fall (9:6). Man and woman are created to be rulers in their domain and, in view of their role in the garden in chapter 2, to be priests, as we shall see. Human rule is also clear from the later meditation of Psalm 8 as well as from the language of Genesis 1:26–28 ("have dominion" and "subdue"). If the fall robbed human beings of this function, we would expect the biblical doctrine of redemption to restore it. The presentation of Jesus in the New Testament both as the image of God and as true man points to what individuals will become in Christ.

This first chapter portrays the power of God. We stand in awe as we read this remarkable account of how our world began. In addition, the emphasis of Genesis 1:31 that what was made was "very good" reminds us that creation perfectly corresponded to the divine intention. This need not mean that an absolutely perfect world stemmed from the actions of Genesis 1. It is possible that the world outside of the garden setting of chapter 2, a setting which seems to be so distinct, needed to be brought completely under human control, since it may have contained all the difficulties which we experience in our natural world today. This suggestion raises difficulties, but the direction of biblical eschatology as well as the facts of human experience point to a consummation of history that is more than a mere return to the beginning.

If Genesis 1 transmits the fact of creation, Genesis 2 details the purpose of creation. Genesis 2:1–3 looks back to the work of the six days with 2:1 operating as a bridge ending the creation account. The bridge verse 2:4a sums it up, making the count of the words "create" and "make" (*bara'*, *'asah*) seven each in the section beginning with Genesis 1:1, thus indicating the wholeness and completion of creation. God is now in the condition of one who has rested from his work. Cassuto (1989, 61–62) affirms that the translation of the English pluperfect "had created" (Gen. 2:2–3) is called for. The LXX, Peshitta (an early Syriac version), Samaritan Pentateuch versions, and *Jubilees* 2:1, aware of the difficulty, read the sixth day in verse 2. But the acts of creation have ceased with the work of the sixth, and the tight interrelationship of the first six days, from which the seventh is excluded by form, content, and chapter division, provides a contrast of activity and purpose between Genesis 1 and 2:1–3. The presentation of the seventh day in different terms from the previous six decisively sets off the Genesis 2:1–3 accounts off from 1:1–31.

In 2:1–3, the seventh day is mentioned three times, each time in a sequence of seven words. It is clear that though the noun *shabbaton* 'Sabbath' does not occur, the verb *shabat* is used twice in 2:1–3. It is likely that this creation Sabbath is meant to provide the context in which humankind in Genesis 2 is to operate, since the seventh day, the basis for the later Sabbath, is presented as unending, with no morning or evening and thus as ongoing throughout human history.

The Hebrew verb *shabat* means basically "to stop" or "cease." Sometimes it is translated as "keep Sabbath," which is its later OT-derived meaning. The verb occurs some seventy-three times in the OT and is generally used of persons (Robinson 1980). In none of these basic usages is the idea of "rest" or desisting from work prominent. Thus the seventh day of creation ends the creation week, brings it to completion, and gives point to it. The idea of blessing and hallowing endows the seventh day with the potential to fulfill its purpose in the divine plan and especially sets it apart as a holy day. Blessing refers to the ongoing significance of the seventh day in shaping human development, allowing for the fact that the seventh day acquires special status as a day that belongs to God alone.

Rest for the creating deity is an idea commonly found in many creation texts of the ancient world (Scullion 1984, 16). That this rest gives meaning to the account of creation and explains the purpose of creation is peculiar, as we might expect, to the OT. The seventh-day account flows, after the retrospect of Genesis 2:4–7, into 2:8–25. This rest on the seventh day, into which God enters and, by implication, into which humanity also enters, is given to humankind and cannot be achieved, the narrative implies, by toil or by trial. The Sabbath day provides the ongoing context in which the ideal life of the garden takes place and is to be perpetuated. God's own rest is the divine endorsement of creation, and God's willingness to enter into fellowship with humanity expresses this endorsement. Creation is now fixed and settled, and Genesis 2:8–25 indicates the nature of the fellowship that God and man were to share.

The Garden and the Fall

Following Genesis 2:1–3, verse 2:4a introduces the first *toledot* 'generations' narrative, 2:4b–4:26. Genesis 2:5–7 introduces 2:8–17 by detailing (Futato 1998) the provision of rain (i.e., the "mist" of most translations) and of a cultivator (man) before the Eden narrative, which requires both. Since the note of divine purpose for creation precedes the human fall, creation will clearly continue. One should note the Epistle to the Hebrews 4:9–11, which tells us that there still remains a Sabbath rest, a *sabbatismos* for the people of God. What remains to be experienced is not the Sabbath as such, which, on the evidence of Genesis 2 and the assumption of Hebrews 4, is continuing, but the rest associated with the Sabbath, at least in its complete sense. God's own rest is the divine endorsement of creation and of God's final intention for the New Creation to emerge from this beginning. The rest also indicates God's willingness to enter into fellowship with humanity.

The Garden as Separated from Its World

The Hebrew word *gan* 'garden' refers to a fenced enclosure (Heb. *ganan* 'cover', 'protect', 'enclose') protected by a wall or hedge (Koehler and Baumgartner 1958, 190). Walls surrounding royal gardens are specifically mentioned in the OT (2 Kings 25:4; Jer. 39:4; 52:7; Neh. 3:15). The Garden of Eden is thus a special place separated from the outside world, which presumably is very much like our present world. The Greek OT translates the Hebrew *gan* with *pardes,* itself a loan word from Persian. *Pardes* has the basic sense of "what is walled, what is hedged about" and thus a "pleasure garden surrounded by a stone or earthen wall" (Keil and Delitzsch 1975, 80–81). This information suggests that the garden is a special place, separated from a world that needs to be brought under the dominion of the divine rule, for which Eden is a model. The differentiation of Eden from its world is further advanced by Genesis 3:24, in which the cherubim with flaming swords guard the way to the tree of life. The tree of life seemingly is located at the center of the garden, as is the tree of the knowledge of good and evil. At the end of the canon, however, the new creation is presented in varied symbolism, but lastly and most significantly in Revelation 22:1–5 as a new and universalized Eden.

The Garden as a Sanctuary

Since creation accounts in the ancient world commonly connect creation and temple building (Weinfeld 1981, 502), it is no surprise that Genesis 2:9–17 depicts what seems to have been a sanctuary situation, in which man as priest/king worships in the sanctuary garden, the world center, which is Eden. The presence of God makes the garden the source of world fertility, for the great rivers take their rise there. There are hints, perhaps, at 3:22 of the ancient council of heaven—a motif taken up strongly by later Israelite prophecy—where decrees are issued that affect human relationships.

In the mythical structures of the ancient world, at the center of the earth and controlling it, stood the sacred mountain where the deity of national fortunes presided and where contact with the deity could be made. At this spot it was believed that the upper and lower waters of the cosmos met, and heaven and earth and the netherworld were connected. The important depiction of Eden as the holy mountain of God, a synonym for the temple (cf. Ps. 48:1–3 and Newsom 1984, 161) in Ezekiel 28:13–14, takes us back to a paramount theological point of the ancient Near East. The sacred mountain was the meeting place of heaven and earth, where celestial and mundane reality met. From this place, world decrees, by which creation was to be regulated, were promulgated. From the cosmic mountain there is frequently thought to issue a sacred stream whose water teems with supernatural significance (Levenson 1985, 129–31). There, at the sacred site, the victory that brought creation into being was won and celebrated. Eden is thus presented as the *axis mundi,* the point from which the primal stream radiates to the four quarters (2:10–14). In the center of this center stood the trees of life and of the knowledge of good and evil, the source of life and the manner by which life was to be conducted.

The Garden of Eden in Genesis 2 is best seen as a special sanctuary, quite unlike the rest of the world. The placement of humankind as the image in the garden furthers the association between image and temple, drawing kingship and temple together at the beginning of the Bible. Canaan in the OT is not only paralleled at times to Eden (Isa. 51:3; Ezek. 36:35) but also is fulsomely presented in Deuteronomy as an Israelite correspondence to Eden (see Deut. 8:7–10; 11:8–17). Canaan is, in its totality, presented as divine space (cf. Exod. 15:17; Ps. 78:54). The implication is that Eden is also considered divine space. The walls of the holy place in the later Jerusalem temple are profusely engraved with garden emblems (Beale 1999, 1110–12), and the function of the cherubim as guardians of the divine sanctuary (Gen. 3:24) reappears in the temple's Holy of Holies.

Moreover, since Eden is clearly conceived as a mountain sanctuary in the allusion of Ezekiel 28:13–14, the divine character of the mountain is plain. In Ezekiel 28, "mountain" occurs twice in the phrases "holy mountain of God" (v. 14) and "mountain of God" (v. 16). Ezekiel 28:16, which identifies the king of Tyre as a protecting cherub in the garden of God (cf. Gen. 3:24 and the later tabernacle and temple analogies of the cherubim as sanctuary guardians), speaks of the king as having profaned the holy mountain. Ezekiel 28:1–10 portrays the king of Tyre as saying: "I am El." He is described as being in the seat of the gods, in the heart of the seas, reinforcing the allusion to El, whose dwelling place was the springs of two rivers, amidst the channels of the two deeps. The feature common to Eden and the mountain of Ezekiel 28 is that of holiness (cf. Ezek. 28:14). Genesis 2, where Eden is clearly elevated as the source of living water for the world, confirms Ezekiel's identification of Eden as a holy mountain of God. We may also point to Ezekiel 36:33–36, in which the Garden of Eden is the symbol of fertility and a fitting analogy for the land of Palestine about to be restored.

Eden is thus presented in the narrative as the earthly center where God was to be found. Such presentation is clear from Isaiah 51:3, where Eden/garden of God are paralleled (cf. also Gen. 13:10). The garden is thus sacred space, as the later temple in Israel was to be. Finally, Eden is the representation of what the world is to become—that much becomes clear as divine revelation develops (cf. Rev. 21–22). We are thus, in terms of biblical eschatology, moving from a localized Eden in Genesis 2 to the new creation as a universal Eden in Revelation 22:1–5.

Adam in the Garden

Verses 15–17 conclude the account by focusing on Adam. Reverting to Ezekiel 28, the adornments of the king of Tyre, likened to the original cherub in the garden in Ezekiel 28:13, correspond fairly exactly (in the Greek OT, the

LXX reading) to the precious stones set in the breastplate of the Israelite high priest in Exodus 28:17–20. By all the implications, this gives to the original inhabitant of the garden, Adam, a pronounced priestly/kingly character. In Ezekiel 28:11–19, the king of Tyre is represented as an Adam figure, made clear by the location of the garden, the use of the Hebrew *bara'*, the presence of the cherub, and the idea of sin leading to expulsion. Carol Newsom (1984) argues cogently that the king of Tyre is also presented as a priest in Yahweh's temple. The king's actions in the political realm are seen as a defilement of what is holy. The oracle in Ezekiel 28 asserts the correct relationship between the king and Yahweh. The king is created by and subservient to Yahweh. If Genesis 1 emphasizes humankind's kingship, Genesis 2 presents humanity as functioning in a priestly role in the divine presence. Continuing the idea of sanctuary that we have associated with the garden, the Jerusalem temple is a later source of life-giving streams for the world (Ezek. 47:1–12; cf. Joel 3:18). Adam's king/priest combination anticipates Israel's later role (Exod. 19:5–6) and refers to a dual function that awaits believers in Revelation 1:5–6; 5:10; 20:4–6, and that is realized in the New Jerusalem in Revelation 22:4–5.

Adam's role in Eden raises the question of Israel's relationship to Adam. The analogies between Adam and Israel are significant for subsequent biblical eschatology and mission. Israel, like Adam—in Genesis 2:8, the force of the Hebrew tense is that of an English pluperfect (cf. "had planted" NIV)—is created outside the space to be occupied by the divine. Adam, like Israel, is put into sacred space to exercise a kingly/priestly role (cf. Exod. 19:4–6). Israel, like Adam, is given law by which the divine space is to be retained; Israel, like Adam, transgresses the law; and Israel, like Adam, is expelled from the divine space (Lohfink 1969, 59–60). The placement of Adam and Israel in divine space was conditional. Both parties had to obey the divine mandate to retain the sacred space. Adam possessed an immortality that was limited, and Israel possessed a covenant that could be revoked for national disobedience. The creation account further indicates to Israel the nature and purpose of her special status, of exercising dominion in her world that Adam had once occupied. It will not seem strange, therefore, that Exodus 19:5–6 presents the nation Israel in a corporate, royal priestly role.

The Nature of Dominion

Such interpretation provides some understanding of man's dominion over nature as king/priest. Humankind, authorized to exercise dominion over the world (Gen. 1:28), paradoxically exercises that dominion by worship and service in the divine presence. Service in the garden is denoted by the Hebrew verb *'abad,* the basic meaning of which is "work" or "serve." In Genesis 2:15, the meaning is "till" or "cultivate." Gordon Wenham, however, points out (1987, 67) that the verbs "cultivate" (*'abad*) and "guard" (*shamar*) are translated elsewhere in the OT as "serving" and "guarding," and can be referred to as priestly service and guarding in the tabernacle (Num. 3:7–8; 8:25–26; 18:5–6; 1 Chron. 23:32; Ezek. 44:14; cf. also Isa. 56:6). The only other time the OT uses both verbs together is in connection with the Levitical service and guarding of the sanctuary (Num. 3:7–8; 8:25–26). *Targum Neofiti* on Genesis 3:15 underscores the cultic notion by saying that Adam was placed in the garden to serve according to the law and to keep its commandments, language strikingly similar to the passages cited from Numbers and the Targum on priestly supervision.

Divine service (cf. Jesus in Mark 10:45) is thus humanity's role, first in submission to the Creator and then to the world, paralleling again the way in which the nation Israel will later be presented. Paradoxically, the world outside the garden will be best served by humankind's service at the center of the world in the presence of God.

The Doctrine of Grace in the Garden

Humankind was created outside of the garden and placed within it (Gen. 2:8b). In reporting this fact, the narrative makes the point that humankind was not native to the garden. It is Yahweh, who is also Elohim, who puts humanity in the garden, and it is upon a relationship with Yahweh Elohim that humanity's tenure in the garden depends. In biblical terms, we may describe this as a movement of grace. Occupation of an analogous Eden, as a symbol for full salvation, will likewise depend on God's grace.

Genesis 2 presupposes that Adam's role, transferred to Israel and then to Christ, was to extend the contours of the garden to the world, since this is the transition that finally occurs in Revelation 22. At the same time, Genesis 2 indicates what dominion is and how it is to be exercised. Dominion is the service that takes its motivation from the ultimate relationship with the Lord God, on behalf of whom dominion is exercised. But the possibility existed, even within the garden, for man to exercise his God-given authority independently (Gen. 2:16–17). We know this will happen in Genesis 3 and that it will have disastrous results for man's mandate and role. The seventh-day experience is presented as still possible in a fallen world. Faith in God's purposes can still, the account implies, bring us into an Eden-type human experience in this extended creation Sabbath, in which we experience the personal presence of God.

We may summarize Genesis 1–2 by saying that humankind as the image of God is placed in the "divine temple" that is the "image" of the world (a personal communication from Rikki E. Watts, who argues that creation in Gen. 1 is depicted in temple terms).

The Fall (Gen. 3)

The fall narrative of Genesis 3 reverses the order carefully established in chapter 2 (Walsh 1977, 174–77). God assigns appropriate punishments that strike the serpent, woman, and man, affecting their roles within creation. This reversal suggests that sin attacks the harmony of the created order and is not merely a moral lapse.

We turn to the two trees in the garden singled out for special mention. The prohibition on eating the fruit of the tree of the knowledge of good and evil (2:17) assumes human freedom to choose and thus an inherent moral capacity.

In the center of the garden, and thus in some sense controlling it, is the tree of life—the tree which enhances life (cf. Prov. 11:30; 13:12; 15:4). No prohibition against eating from this tree is placed on the man and woman before the fall. Only after the fall is access forbidden (Gen. 3:22), and then apparently in the interests of Adam and Eve themselves, lest they live forever in a fallen state. Chapter 2 concludes by indicating that fellowship between man and woman is supremely met and experienced within the marriage relationship (vv. 24–25).

What did it mean to eat the fruit of the tree of the knowledge of good and evil? Many suggestions have been offered, including acquiring total knowledge ("good and evil" taken as expressing totality), moral knowledge, and sexual experience. But all of these suggestions founder either on the serpent's claim and God's acknowledgment that eating would make the person "like God" (3:5, 22) or on the facts of human experience. It is therefore better to take the term "knowledge of good and evil" as expressing moral discernment, moral autonomy, and the ability to be self-legislating (Clark 1969, 277). Only God ultimately possesses such knowledge. Humankind is thus presented as usurping the divine prerogatives and snatching at divinity, a situation the second Adam was to reverse (see Phil. 2:6). The results of the fall find the man and woman possessed of this knowledge, that is, self-legislating and morally autonomous. They are able to make the necessary choices but will always remain uncertain whether their choices are wise or right, or whether the means they devise to reach correct goals are valid.

The loss of the garden habitation puts the human pair in the outside world. It is clear, however, that as a result of the fall and the loss of the garden center, the human ministry of dominion over nature can no longer be exercised (cf. Gen. 3:17–20). Humanity is no longer objective about the problems of the outside world but is immersed in them and will contribute freely to them. The ground is now cursed because of humankind (3:17). Verse 17 is not to be taken to mean that, as a result of the human fall, the world of nature is now in a fallen state. Sin and the fall have depended on a human choice and a potentially sinful will. While we can speak of the fall of humanity, we cannot speak, and the Bible does not, of the fall of nature. But nature is fatally affected by the fall. In the outside world, humanity, like God, can make decisions independently of God to shape the future of the world. Unlike God, humanity can never estimate the correctness of its decisions, nor the consequences that flow from them. Care of the world will depend on the mind of God, which humanity does not possess. The ecological disasters to which the world has and will be subject have and will depend on the fallen character of human decisions in world management. Creation thus longs for release (Rom. 8:18–23) from this humanly imposed bondage. Release will not come through human reformation or technology, but only from final divine intervention that will produce a new universe (Rev. 21).

The Effects of the Fall (Gen. 4–9)

Chapter 4 contains an expanded genealogy of Adam. The expansions are Cain's relationship with Abel in verses 3–16, then Cain's descendants in verses

17–24, and, in verses 25–26, Seth's family. The parallel formulas (4:1, 17, 25) show that the Cain genealogy is a continuation of 4:1–2. The genealogy contains seven generations and frames the Cain-and-Abel narrative. Verse 1 indicates the presence of the Lord, and verse 16 indicates the loss of that presence. There are two units in the narrative: verses 3–7 and 9–16, connected by the simple narrative in verse 8. Verses 3–7 describe the exchange between the brothers, and verses 9–16 gradually resolve the tension. The account then moves to judgment in verses 11–12, which employ the same curse pattern as 3:14–17; again, the ground is involved. Cain responds in verses 13–14 with a lament. The mark on Cain of verse 15 will serve as a constant reminder of the opposition to be faced.

There are obvious similarities between Genesis 3 and 4. (1) The personages of both narratives are introduced in terms of their functions. (2) The harmony between two persons is broken by sin. (3) The actors are warned of the consequence before the deed. (4) The principal characters are confronted by God after the deed. (5) When the deed is exposed, God pronounces sentence. (6) The principal characters are driven away from their original context. (7) Separation from the presence of God is the result of sin. (8) At the close of both accounts, the characters dwell east of Eden. Genesis 3 constitutes the paradigm for human transgression, and Genesis 4 supplies the detail.

The purpose of the Adam genealogy is not only to document the spread of the Cain family but also to point to the introduction into the world of human aggression through technology. According to a Mesopotamian tradition, seven wise men, who lived before the flood, were regarded as the originators of the arts and skills of civilization. But the Cain genealogy has been given a negative context, and so his descendants inherit his curse. Possibly, the genealogy of Seth that follows is meant to provide a contrast and thus to speak for hope. The Seth genealogy concludes with the birth of Noah's three sons, and these births link with the following narrative. The expected information on the life of Noah occurs in 9:28–29, after the flood. The effect of this arrangement is to present the flood narrative as an expansion of the biographical narrative and thus as an expansion of the Seth genealogy. The similarities in the genealogies of chapters 4 and 5 have led to conclusions that the two are alternate forms of one genealogy. But there is no evidence of direct borrowing, since four of the six similar names have different spellings, and only one of the six appears at the same point in the genealogy. The genealogies have often been compared with the Sumerian flood story's list of nine antediluvian kings, who reigned up to sixty-four thousand years. The names in the genealogies, however, are different and the length of the Sumerian reigns are far longer. The Sumerian names are also used to justify a city's claim to leadership. No convincing answer has been found to the question of longevity in the Genesis lists.

The effects of the fall are traced in the subsequent narratives, ending with Genesis 11:1–9. The fall, the account of Cain and Abel, and the genealogies of Cain (4:17–24), Seth (vv. 25–26), and Adam (5:1–32) describe the expansion of the human race through time. The episodes of the angelic sons of God

(6:1–4), who intermarry with mortal women, and the flood, as well as the Babel narrative, all have common elements. Each deals with sin, divine confrontation announcing an appropriate punishment, some amelioration of that punishment, and then the imposition of the punishment. Unlike the other narratives, Babel does not seem to include divine grace toward the offenders. It would thus seem that Babel offers a point of transition in the narratives, and so it proves to be. After Babel, the Bible strikes out in an entirely new direction.

Genesis 6:1–8 intimates total destruction to come. Three interpretations are offered of the intermarriages of 6:1–4: (1) The sons of God were nonhuman. (2) They were superior men such as kings or other rulers. (3) They were godly men, descendants of Seth as opposed to the daughters, who were descendants of the godless Cain. The "nonhuman" view is widely held, and provides a climax to the acts of human transgression.

The midpoint of Genesis 1–11 is the narrative concerning the flood, which all but destroys creation (7:11–24). After the flood, the mandate to human beings regarding the relationship to creation is renewed (cf. 1:28 with 9:1–7). It is sometimes suggested that a new beginning occurs with the divine commitment to refrain from direct action in the future and not to curse the ground again (8:21–22). But these verses merely establish the bounds within which the lot of human beings will continue in a disordered world. Nothing is said about the removal of curses resulting from the fall.

After the flood, the effects of sin continue in Noah's family, until we reach the most blatant assertion so far of human authority, in Genesis 11:1–9. Before we take up that account, we must mention the covenant to which God refers in dialogue with Noah in 6:18.

God declared to Noah that, notwithstanding the flood, God would "establish" his covenant. This is the first mention of a covenant that, in fact, receives no detailed treatment until chapter 9. It is therefore customary to suggest that 6:18 is an anticipation of 9:8–17. The verb translated "establish" in 6:18 means, however, in its sustained use in the covenant contexts of the OT, "to confirm what already exists." Second, when used in the divine and secular covenant contexts of the OT, the word "covenant" gives quasi-legal backing to an already existing relationship. It is never used in the sense of initiating a relationship. Third, when a covenant is initiated to confirm an already existing relationship, the terminology invariably used is the phrase "cut a covenant." It is sometimes suggested that the peculiar language of 6:18 reflects a particular literary source, namely the P, or Priestly, document. (P, a strand of supposedly priestly interests, is one of the three sources thought to underlie the present Genesis narrative. The other two proposed sources are the Yahwist [J] and Elohist [E] sources, so labeled because of their respective preference for using the divine names Yahweh or Elohim.) The use of the expression "establish a covenant," however, is too widely distributed in the OT to argue this way.

The emphasis on "my" covenant and the use of "establish" suggest that the reference in Genesis 6:18 is to something which already exists unilaterally. God is declaring a willingness to continue what had already been set up by action in

Genesis 1, and by intention in Genesis 2. In spite of human failure and independent of human participation, the commitment of God to the created order remains.

The details of this arrangement are given in Genesis 9:8–17. The covenant was to be established with Noah, but it includes Noah's descendants (v. 9), every living creature (v. 10; i.e., all animate beings), and, indeed, the whole earth (v. 13). God promises never again to bring a threat like the flood, but to sustain creation. We may suggest, then, that the covenant referred to in 6:18 came into existence in Genesis 1–2. The details of the relationship supposed by the covenant seem to provide the content of Genesis 2:1–17. Such an act established an enduring relationship between God and the world. God's pledge at 6:18 was directed toward the part of creation threatened by the flood and reassured humankind of the providential continuance of the created order. The sign of the rainbow in 9:14–16 is a reminder to God of God's promise to continue the general conditions of the universe, whereby human beings may exercise their role in the created order. The creation covenant is probably further alluded to at Hosea 6:7: "Like Adam, they transgressed the covenant." Jeremiah also refers to it: "Thus says the Lord: if you can break my covenant with the day and my covenant with the night, so that the day and the night will not come at their appointed time . . ." (Jer. 33:20). And compare Jeremiah 33:25: "If I have not established my covenant with the day and the night and the ordinances of heaven and earth . . ." Niehaus (1995, 143–47) sees the formal pattern of a suzerainty covenant in Genesis 1–2.

The strange account of Noah's drunkenness (9:20–27) completes the genealogy of Noah, providing information for the detailed racial genealogy of Genesis 10. Ham, who uncovered his father's nakedness, and his descendants are to be subordinated to Shem and Japhet, and this subordination is indicated by the details of Genesis 10. Divisions within humanity thus arise, and the underlying problem is sin.

Genesis 10

In the genealogy of Genesis 10, written from the perspective of Shem and detailing the expansion of racial groupings, the descendants of Ham are Mitzraim (Egypt), Cush (Ethiopia), Punt (north Africa), and Canaan. Japhet's descendants are Gomer, that is, the Cimmerians and Indo-European people in Turkey. Shem is the forefather of all the sons of Eber, evidently the most important of his descendants. Shem's descendants live in the east from Mesha, east of the Jordan, to the frontier territory (Sephar) in Iran. The Shemites are not the original occupants of Canaan but people who came from the east.

Eber of Shem is mentioned twice and is thus significant. Eber comes from the Hebrew *'abar* 'journey', and thus the name means "passerby," "migrant," "traveler," "nomad." The word "Hebrew" comes from the same root. Israel is described elsewhere as a wandering Aramean, having come from Aram, Syria, or Mesopotamia. Later, the *(h)abiru*, the lowest social class, are the travelers, the nomads, and the outsiders. Driven out of Egypt, the Hebrews with whom the

(h)abiru probably overlap are then the travelers and nomads who formed a social group distinct from the settled population.

Genesis 11:1–9 continues the narratives of the spread of sin with semanti-
cally and structurally related verses. The phrase "whole earth" occurs five times.
The first and last verse describe the situation of the whole earth, the text's frame
of reference. Humankind, which possesses a broad set of unities—a common
language, common ethnic framework, and, if we take Genesis 10 logically to follow chapter 11, a common social basis—congregates at Babel to preserve these
unities. They propose to build a city and a tower, the top of which is to be "in
the heavens." The detail in verse 4 about the tower, despite much speculation,
refers simply to its impressive size. The divine reaction to this human initiative
is to scatter the people and to confuse their language—that is, to frustrate their
ability to communicate. Thus begin the social, linguistic, ethnic, and cultural
distinctions that have frustrated all efforts at human cooperation since Babel.
The implication is that God attacks the problem of the misplaced center.
Human beings regarded themselves as the measure of all things, able to control
their world, able to build a better world. Such human attempts, then and since,
that leave God out of consideration are sin in its baldest and most blatant form.
Note that, unlike the age of Noah, there is no godly remnant at Babel. The im-
mediacy and nature of the divine reaction are therefore understandable.

The Call of Abraham (Gen. 12:1–3)

Though the divine writer offers no interpretation for the Babel episode, the
ensuing narratives provide clues. The genealogy of Shem, which follows in
11:10–32, leads us to Abram, for whom God will provide what the boastful
builders at Babel had sought: a great name (12:2; cf. 11:4). Unlike the narratives
of Genesis 4–11, which record the spread of sin, no movement of divine grace
appears in 11:1–9. The call of Abram, however, displays God's grace, for with
him God will begin again. Chapters 1–11 are critical for the development of a
biblical worldview and thus a biblical theology. Genesis 3–11 perceptively ana-
lyzes the human predicament. God's response to this situation unfolds in the patriarchal narratives, preeminently in the call of Abram from Ur of the
Chaldeans.

In substance, 12:1–3 details what will become known as the Abrahamic
covenant. Although the term "covenant" is not used of the arrangement with
Abram until 15:18, the detail of chapter 15 clearly confirms an already existing
relationship. Progeny and land, the promises offered in 12:1–3, are guaranteed
by the divine oath of chapter 15. Genesis 12:1–3 thus appears to be basic for the
later narratives.

After the introductory verse 1, verses 2–3 present five subordinate clauses,
followed by the final principal clause that ends verse 3, on which the weight of
12:1–3 rests: "in you shall all the families of the earth win for themselves a blessing" (my translation).

Verse 2 has the future of the Abrahamic descendants in view, while the next
verse concerns the wider world's relationship to Abram. Abram's descendants are

to become "a great nation" (v. 2), foreshadowing immediately the political future of Israel. The word "nation," when used of Israel in the OT, is normally used derogatively, in condemnation (Deut. 32:28; Isa. 1:4; Jer. 5:9; etc.). The word normally used of Israel in relationship to Yahweh is "people," a family term which expresses the closeness of the election relationship. "Nation" is a political term, normally applied to an ethnic unity that is geographically delineated and bound by society, land, and culture. Perhaps the political term is used here in contrast to "families" (v. 3), which characterizes the remainder of the world. Perhaps the point is that only in connection with Abram can a true governmental relationship be established. All other possible associations are dismissed in 12:3 as "families" (or "clans"). We bear in mind that 12:1–3 recovers the ultimate divine purpose, namely, a kingdom of God to establish God's rule and to unite human beings with their world.

The choice of the word "nation" here for Abram's descendants may thus have been studied and deliberate. It may initially have had Israel in view, but Israel as representative of the wider saved community to stem from her witness. The centrality of purpose that the Babel builders had vainly sought may therefore be supplied by this call of Genesis 12:1–3. No final political structure will prevail outside of the framework established here. Perhaps the "great nation" of this passage is to be taken eschatologically, to mean the company of the redeemed who will fulfill the call to Abram (cf. Rev. 5:11). We may therefore look to the New Testament to fulfill the concept of Israel, which failed to be realized in the OT.

In Genesis 12:1–3, we need also to note the five occurrences of the word "bless(ing)" and its decided emphasis. Some have contrasted the use of "bless(ing)" in this section with the fivefold occurrence of the word "curse" (Heb. 'arar) in chapters 3–11 (3:14, 17; 4:11; 5:29; 9:25). In short, the call of Abram redresses the curse incurred by the fall. Human alienation, the flight from God, and the bondage to slavery that the curse of chapters 3–11 envisages are all potentially reversed in 12:1–3.

The detail of Genesis 12:3b allows a further word about Israel and its mission in the OT. Much depends on translation of the verb "bless." The rendering "win for themselves a blessing," which also imparts the reflexive sense of the Hebrew verb, seems preferable. This translation echoes the struggle for identification with Abram's God and the blessing to which the world is called. Additionally, the prepositional phrase of verse 3b seems best rendered "in you." The somewhat parallel context of 21:12 supports this translation, as does Galatians 3:28–29. The presumption is that the nations will come to Israel, which the later OT presents as a world light. She is to be the rallying point for other nations, and Jerusalem is to be the divine center.

The Patriarchal Narratives (Gen. 12:4–36:43)

The Abrahamic promises concerned land and progeny, and these two concerns are taken up in reverse order in the patriarchal narratives, where the emphasis is on progeny. The Abrahamic narratives maintain the promises, although they virtually end with the emphasis on Abraham as a stranger and pilgrim in the land (Genesis 23).

Within the Abrahamic narratives is a constant tension between the promises of God and the lack of an heir. There are eight crises in 11:27–25:11 brought on by human initiatives; these crises, interspersed with a sevenfold affirmation of the promise of an heir, threaten to nullify the promise. A famine in Canaan necessitates a sojourn in Egypt, where Abram, fearful, passes off Sarai as his sister. In chapter 13, Lot, probably Abram's heir by adoption, virtually eliminates himself from contention. Yet just after this event (13:14), Yahweh reaffirms the promise of land to Abram's offspring (13:15). Abram is to demonstrate his ownership of Canaan symbolically by traversing its bounds. Chapter 14 finds Abram caught up in a Middle Eastern war involving Lot. Perhaps the fear of retaliation and further involvement in Middle Eastern politics is the reason for the divine oracle of 15:1. Abram falls back on a further human initiative and chooses one of his slaves, Eliezer, as heir by adoption. But this arrangement is divinely set aside (Gen. 15:14). A son related by blood will be the heir, and the promise is expanded to include innumerable descendants and confirmed in a most unusual, though deeply symbolic, covenant ceremony (15:8–23). Yahweh pledges himself unconditionally to fulfill the covenantal promise

In 16:1a, Sarai is still barren. In another human initiative, Sarai, resorting to the legally accepted procedure of concubinage, attempts to achieve issue through her handmaid. Once again Yahweh affirms the divine promise (17:2), now for the fifth time. A name change appropriate to the covenant promise— not a new circumcision covenant, as is sometimes argued (cf. Williamson 2000)—takes place, Abram becoming Abraham. Williamson argues that the Hebrew *natan berit* 'set a covenant' in Genesis 17:2 indicates the inauguration of a new covenant of circumcision, basing his view on the use of *natan berit* in Numbers 25:12, where Phinehas is granted a "covenant of peace" by the same formula. Williamson and Roger T. Beckwith (1987, 100) suggest that this covenant of Numbers 25:12 should be differentiated from the Sinai covenant. The context, however, makes it more probable that the high priestly succession, which devolved from Aaron to Eleazar at Numbers 20:24–29, was not yet automatic. The priestly legislation of Leviticus was clearly part of the Sinai covenant, and the covenant with Phinehas is more likely to have been the regulation of priestly succession within the Sinai covenant, now being limited to a designated priestly family (cf. Ashley 1997, 523). Circumcision in Genesis 17 is a sign of the covenant with Abraham, not a further covenant in itself. The Hebrew *natan berit* in Genesis 17:2 thus means "set in motion" or "give further expression to." Likewise, the Hebrew *natan* in Genesis 9:12–13, a reference not examined by Williamson, refers to setting in the heavens a covenant sign, the rainbow, thus giving further expression to the covenant promise of the early chapters of Genesis (cf. Gen. 6:18).

Circumcision is introduced as a sign of the covenant relationship (17:9–14). Sarah bears an heir, and Ishmael is rejected. Chapters 18 and 19 describe the origin of Israel's two inveterate enemies, Ammon and Moab. In chapter 20, shortly after the announcement of Isaac's impending birth, Sarah is taken into Abimelech's harem. Once again the relationship between God and humanity moves into crisis mode, but Yahweh intervenes. At the beginning of chapter 21, the tension appears to be resolved, for Sarah bears the promised son (21:1–2). The conflict between Ishmael and Isaac becomes an issue, and the sixth crisis is solved by Abraham's sorrowful disinheriting of Ishmael. With God's request for the sacrifice of Abraham's only son, the seventh crisis intervenes. But faith (Gen. 22) triumphs over the greatest obstacle, death, and God provides a ram as a substitute for Isaac. Sarah's death in chapter 23 underscores that the promise of the land has not been fulfilled, inasmuch as Abraham must purchase a burial plot— the only portion of Canaan for which he can produce a deed. The eighth crisis, with which the Abrahamic cycle culminates, is the securing of a wife for Isaac; the crisis is resolved by Rebekah's ready acquiescence to come to Canaan. The Abraham cycle that began with a barren Sarai concludes with God blessing Isaac after the death of Abraham (25:11). The Abraham cycle makes us aware that Israel will only exist through divine interventions. Isaac, to judge from the attention he receives, is somewhat of a lesser figure, though his neighbors notice that God's blessing is with him (Gen. 26:28).

The Jacob narratives (25:19–35:29) take up the questions of progeny and land much more thoroughly. Much attention is paid to progeny, stemming primarily from Rebekah and Rachel, and then from Leah. Rebekah and Rachel, like Sarah before them, are both barren, and blessing comes only, as it always must, by divine intervention. God alone will bring the people of the promise into being. The conflict narratives between Ishmael and Isaac, Esau and Jacob, and Jacob and Laban arise from birth narratives, and thus the ground is laid for the later OT hostility between Israel and the Transjordanian peoples.

Of particular importance is occupancy of the Promised Land. It is significant that this question is raised in the Bethel narrative (Gen. 28:10–22) immediately before Jacob leaves Canaan, and again in chapter 32 immediately before he returns to the Promised Land, blessed with a large family acquired in Haran and with considerable wealth. Jacob is changed by struggle at the Jabbok and, in the rite of passage, receives the new name Israel (which probably means "God strives"). As one with whom God has striven, Jacob can now be said to have prevailed over himself; as a changed man, he is now able to meet and to be reconciled with his brother Esau (Fokkelman 1975, 197–222).

These details foreshadow the later history of Israel. They point to the difficulty that the twelve tribes will have in occupying the land and suggest that the land will come to Israel only when she, too, has learned the meaning of full submission. The Jacob cycle pivots on Genesis 30 (Fishbane 1975a, 20), in which, in Haran, the barren Rachel becomes fertile and Jacob's wealth is established. Up to this point the narratives present themes of family alienation, strife, infertility, and bitterness. From this point onward, the tone becomes one of return, reconciliation, abounding fertility, and blessing. In sum, the Jacob cycle underscores blessing for Israel as national fertility and abundance within the Promised Land, acquired only by discipline outside of the land and by due recognition of the source from which the gift of the land must come.

The Joseph Narratives (Gen. 37–50)

The long and distinct Joseph narratives close the Book of Genesis. As the theme in the Jacob cycle was the establishment of the twelve tribes of Israel, the theme of the Joseph narratives is Israel's remarkable preservation outside the Promised Land. As such, the Joseph account functions as a bridge between the patriarchal narratives and the Book of Exodus, tying the promises to the fathers with the pending occupation of the land. Joseph is presented as the preserver not only of Israel's traditions, but of Israel herself. For Israel, life at this stage moves to Egypt (Gen. 42:2), and Joseph is there at the source of life, having been placed providentially by God after being callously abandoned by his brothers. He is there as a pledge of Israel's future (Brueggemann 1972, 100).

The concern of Genesis to bring Israel into human history concludes with one aspect of the Abrahamic promise having been actualized. Israel is a great nation, and is about to emerge on the political horizon. This people, now so numerous as to pose a threat to the Egyptians, needs a land to occupy. The Book of Exodus will show how this already existent people will gain its territory. The land does not result from the mere fact of historical occupancy, but God gives it as the great redemption of the exodus. The rest of the Pentateuch focuses on a theology of prospect for the people of God, showing how the paradise of Eden might be realized in and through Israel.

2

Exodus

The book, in continuity with Genesis, begins by mentioning the Jacob and Joseph narratives (1:1–6). Abraham's descendants fill the land. Then comes the remarkable statement that, in the oppression of Egypt, God's mandate for humanity's dominion over the world is furthered (see the reference to Gen. 1:28 in Exod. 1:7). Israel's great need begins the book, which concludes with the nation about to embark on the march to the Promised Land, led by the manifested presence of God. The book ends with a discussion of the community at worship. More than one-third of Exodus (chaps. 25–31; 35–40) is devoted to the establishment of Israel's cultic framework, in particular to the erection of, and the regulations for the use of, Israel's tabernacle. This is no meaningless cultic digression, but emphasizes the goal of the exodus and the importance of a worshipful response in Israel's continuing covenantal relationship.

The general contours of the Book of Exodus are erected around this movement from slavery to the concluding picture of worship. The transition from slavery to worship is accomplished through a very great redemption, which is at the center of the book. Basic to all of Israel's later theology is the redemption of the exodus.

The Birth and Call of Moses (Exod. 1–4)

The narrative of the birth and call of Moses occupies Exodus 1–4. Since Moses' experience virtually anticipates Israel's, many episodes in these four chapters point forward to parallel events in chapters 5–14, as Israel seeks to extract herself from Egypt. The background to Moses' birth is described in Exodus 1. After the reference in verses 1–7 to the multiplying numbers of tribal Israel, the account details the rigor with which Egypt dealt with her (vv. 8–14; note the similar pattern of hard labor imposed on a populous Israel in 5:5–19). Attempts to curb the Israelite population by drowning Israelite children (1:15–22) are somewhat parallel to the drowning of the Egyptians that in chapter 14 concludes the Israelite flight from Egypt (Fishbane 1979, 73–76).

Exodus 2 presents Moses' birth, flight, and sojourn in Midian. But God has heard Israel's cries (2:23–25), beginning the process that leads to Pharaoh's defeat, Israel's rescue, and to a formal covenant that brings Israel as a political unit into being. Exodus 3, with its account of Moses and the burning "bush" (Heb. *seneh;* note the similarity to *sînay,* or Sinai) on Horeb, "the mountain of God," where the character of Yahweh is revealed, strikingly anticipates Israel's experience at Sinai, "the mountain of God" (24:13), where the law is revealed. Moses' own experience at Horeb is thus a mirror image of Israel's.

Whether the new divine name ("Yahweh") that God reveals to Moses at the burning bush is new in the absolute sense is a question that need not detain us. Some of the Israelite personal names (e.g., Jochebed, Moses' mother; and Joshua) suggest that the name Yahweh is older than the event. It is probable, therefore, that Moses asks at 3:13–15, not for the name itself, but for the significance of the name (cf. 6:3). To the mind of the ancient Near Eastern person, the name of the deity opened the possibility of a relationship. Once given the name, the worshiper could "call upon the name" in prayer. The revelation of the name assured the deity's commitment; within the name, the deity's character was disclosed. Although the exact meaning of the name Yahweh is still uncertain, it includes some component of the verb "to be." Two translations are possible: (1) he causes to be or will cause to be (i.e., creates), and (2) he is or he will be. The majority opinion and the context of chapter 3 favor the latter possibility; the meaning of the somewhat enigmatic verse 14 ("I am who I am") may thus be "I am he who is"!

Whatever the precise nuances of the name may be—and they are finally unimportant, since no real play is made on its meaning—the general intent of the episode in Exodus 3 is to assure Moses and Israel of Yahweh's presence in the nation's developing history. God would be known by future acts, by the unfolding of God's character in both deed and word, although the name itself preserves the mystery and transcendence surrounding the divine person. We should note also that verses 13–15 link this new revelation to the patriarchal period. Moses is to tell the Israelites that the God who has sent him is "the God of your fathers" (v. 15). This type of expression, which in the singular form (God of your [my, our] father) is prominent in Genesis, appears in the early chapters of Exodus, but is absent thereafter. This peculiar usage is amplified by particular appellations (Shield of Abraham, Fear/Kinsman of Isaac, Mighty One of Jacob) in the patriarchal narratives. On the other hand, Genesis contains more precise descriptions, such as El Roi, El Olam, El Bethel, and El Elohe Israel (Gen. 16:13; 21:33; 31:13; 33:20). In these expressions, El, the common Semitic term for deity, is found in compound with descriptive elements derived from the place or the circumstances concerned. This has led to the suggestion that two strands of religious thought are present in the patriarchal narratives. The older, "God of your father" type of terminology (e.g., Shield of Abraham) was brought into Palestine by immigrants who encountered the El names from Canaanite contact. Certainly the occurrence of these two sets of names in Genesis and, in particular, the occurrence of the "God of your father" type, calls for explanation. El names, however, are hardly Canaanite borrowings, since (1) the term El is generally Semitic; (2) the lofty monotheistic tone of Genesis, which is almost unparalleled in the OT, tells against this hypothesis; and (3) the patriarchs largely avoided direct contact with the urban culture of the period. Finally, a neat separation between these two types of names is to be avoided, since mixing of types occurs in Genesis and Exodus (see Gen. 46:3; Exod. 3:6). Nevertheless, it is clear that the revelation of the name Yahweh in Exodus 3 is in some way a distinct advance associated with Israel's salvation history.

While Moses' origins are priestly (of the tribe of Levi; see Exod. 2:1), his call in Exodus 3 is clearly prophetic, consisting of divine confrontation (vv. 1–4a), introductory divine word (vv. 4b–9), commission (v. 10), typical objections (v. 11), divine reassurance (v. 12a), and the promise of a sign (v. 12b). Having heard Israel's cry (2:23–25), God responds (3:7–8). Covenant continuance is stressed in 3:13–15, for prophet and covenant are interrelated OT figures (for the modeling of the OT prophetic office on Moses, see Deut. 18:15–22). The subsequent narratives typically present Moses as the protector or deliverer of Israel, in the manner of the heroic figures of the Book of Judges. But as the divine messenger whose function was to proclaim God's will to Israel and to keep them within the covenant, Moses' ministry was undoubtedly prophetic. And as the initiator of Israel's cultic institutions, the ministry of Moses was also priestly.

To reassure Moses and to authenticate his ministry, God gives him three signs (4:1–9), culminating in a fourth (vv. 24–26), in which blood is the dominant factor and to which the death of Pharaoh's firstborn (v. 23) stands in relationship. There follows in 4:10–17 a further call of Moses, this time in specific terms. Aaron's role as spokesman is a role to which later chapters also refer (cf. 6:12, 30; 7:1–6).

Moses before Pharaoh (Exod. 5:1–7:7)

Chapters 5–15 narrate the liberation of Israel from Egypt. Exodus 5:1–6:1 sets the scene for what is essentially a conflict between Pharaoh, presented as a threat reminiscent of primeval chaos (cf. Ezek. 32:2), and Yahweh. Exodus 6:2–9 places a revelation of the divine name in this context of Israel's persecution and supplication. Note the revelation in 3:1–15, which had been associated with Israel's oppression in Egypt. Yahweh will now respond to Israel's situation in fulfillment of the promise to Israel's forefathers (6:8). Yahweh is acting in the exodus liberation in response to his covenant with the patriarchs (6:2), the covenant he now confirms (note the use of the Hebrew *heqim berit* in v. 4). I have argued (1984, 25–26) that the Hebrew verb *qum,* when used with the Hebrew *berit* (Gen. 6:18; 9:9, 11, 17; 17:7, 19, 21; Exod. 6:4; Lev. 26:9; Deut. 8:18; 2 Kings 23:3), means "cause to stand" in the *hiph'il* conjugation (*heqim*). It always means to give further expression to (i.e., "to establish") a covenant previously granted by God, in this case in Genesis 15:18. Beckwith (1987, 99 n. 23), followed by Williamson, argues that Exodus 6:4 recalls the inauguration of the covenant, not its continuance. In this case, it is strange that the language of Genesis 15:18 (*karat berit*) is not recalled. The issue seems to be put beyond doubt in verse 5, when, in taking action against Egypt, God is "remembering" God's covenant, that is, remembering the previously given pledge of Genesis 15:18.

Exodus 6:10–7:7 brings Moses and Aaron into close relationship before the onset of the plagues (cf. 4:10–17, 27–31, where the relationship had begun).

The Plagues (Exod. 7:8–11:10)

Exodus 7:8–11:10 presents the narratives of the plagues, which occur in triplets of three, to which is added a final plague that stands outside the total sequence (Greenberg 1972, 606–7). In each triplet, Moses is first required to present himself, in the morning by the Nile, before Pharaoh, to warn him of what will come (7:15; 8:20; 9:13). He is then sent to Pharaoh's palace (8:1; 9:1; 10:1). In the third plague in each sequence, God commands Moses (and Aaron) to commence the plague without warning (8:16; 9:8; 10:21).

The initial plague of each triplet suggests the distinct motif of each sequence. In the first triplet (blood, frogs, lice), the note is the superiority of God and God's agents over the magicians of the court (7:12). In the second sequence (insects, pestilence, boils), God's presence in Egypt and thus God's control are signaled by the separation made between Israel and Egypt (8:18–24; 9:4–7). The third triplet (hail, locusts, darkness) emphasizes the incomparability of Yahweh (see 9:14 and the unique character of the plagues, noted in 9:18, 24; 10:6, 14). Pharaoh's unreasonableness must give way before Yahweh's manifested power.

The tenth plague is set off from the rest of the series. It is announced before Passover but takes place during the celebration. The final two verses of chapter 11 present a theological justification of the plagues, a justification that counterbalances the justification that occurs at the beginning (7:1–5). The continuing and culminating purpose of the episodes is to compel Pharaoh to recognize Yahweh's power. Judgment after Yahweh's merciful long-suffering is a concurrent theme. The plagues have proclaimed God's power to the nations.

Passover and Exodus (Exod. 12:1–15:21)

By the tenth plague we are prepared for the Passover (12:1–13:16), which is both a supreme judgment and a great deliverance. We leave aside the details of this section and the physical deliverance recorded in chapter 14 to dwell on the theological interpretation of the exodus and its prospects, offered in the Song of Miriam (15:1–18); this psalm of praise concludes the account of the exodus. The poem is divided into an introduction (vv. 1–6), an initial strophe (vv. 7–10), a refrain or chorus (v. 11), a second strophe or verse (vv. 12–16a), another refrain (v. 16b), and a conclusion (vv. 17–18).

The introduction describes Yahweh's victory over Egypt in the military coloring of the Late Bronze Age. The picture of Yahweh as a warrior who fights for Israel introduces one of the most impressive presentations of deity in the OT. This imagery of Yahweh engaged in holy war begins at this point and continues through the early conquest narratives, through prophecy and apocalyptic, into the New Testament.

In the poem's second strophe, the conflict imagery of the first half disappears. Yahweh is now the Divine Shepherd (v. 13), a graceful and peaceful image of leadership from the ancient Near East. He leads the people whom he has redeemed by his divine mercy (Heb. *hesed,* which, though not the Hebrew word for "grace," has the note of "unmerited favor"). The imagery of the passage through the waters is reconstituted as a passage through petrified peoples (Philistia, Edom, Moab, Canaan—heralding the exodus route), who stand amazed as the Israelites progress, almost liturgically, into the Promised Land (Lohfink 1969, 79). All this is the language of theological reflection, but the emphasis is on the facility with which God accomplishes God's declared purposes. As the Divine Shepherd, Yahweh leads Israel to the Promised Land, presented with images of sacred mountain and sanctuary (see Ps. 78:54, which refers to the whole of Palestine in this imagery). The Promised Land is thus viewed as the world center, from which divine light and truth will emanate.

Another facet of this poem needs consideration. Careful reading betrays contacts with the creation mythologies prevalent during the Mosaic period. These contacts are the pattern of Egypt's threat to Israel, combat in which the sea is involved—albeit as a passive instrument, which underscores the claim within the poem for Yahweh's incomparability—the victory of the Divine Warrior, the establishment of his sanctuary, and his potential rule over all creation. In *Enuma Elish* and the Baal epics, the creation accounts of Babylon and Canaan, similar sequences are present. The creation motifs of the Baal epics are sometimes questioned, but unreasonably so (Day 1985, 179–89). In Miriam's song, the redemption of the exodus is being advanced poetically as a new creative act, whereby Israel is brought into being as a political entity. Thus the developing theology of redemption is set positively within the more general purposes for humans and the world, as presented in Genesis 1–2.

The exodus age provided Israel with most of its theological language of redemption. Thus, for example, the note of Israel's sonship is present in Exodus 4:22. The significance of the Hebrew *hesed* at Exodus 15:13 has been noted. Important is the introduction of the term "redeem" (Heb. *go'el;* 6:6; 15:13), which becomes prominent theologically in Isaiah 40–55, where the deliverance from exile is described in terms of a second exodus. The term refers to the recovery of something that once belonged to an individual or family but that became alienated, and thus beyond the power of the owner to reclaim. Its use suggests the return of persons or things to their normal position. As next of kin, God intervenes as Redeemer to secure the return of Israel to her rightful relationship. From Pharaoh, God demands God's son, who has become enslaved. In the social regime of the OT, the beneficiary of such an action becomes indebted to the redeemer and relates to the redeemer in a special way. Israel was thus accustomed to describing herself as a bond-slave of Yahweh, as she had once been a bond-slave in Egypt. Thus the OT metaphors for worship often tend to be drawn from the sphere of service. By redemption, Israel passed into the service of the one whose service is perfect freedom. Thus there is an easy transition from the concept of master and servant, to king and subject, to father and son. To *hesed* and *go'el* may be added the term "holy" (15:13), betokening separation to Yahweh as an indication of what is divine or of what is separated for divine service.

Covenant and Tabernacle Building (Exod. 15:22–40:38)

Exodus 15:22–19:2 presents the wilderness itinerary and the details of the journey to Sinai. Israel receives divine sustenance during the wilderness trek to Sinai, learns that it may depend on Yahweh, and experiences divine protection from the nations represented by Amalek (Exod. 17; Leder 1999). Exodus 19:3–6 describes Israel's vocation, 19:7–8 Israel's acceptance of the divine word, and 19:9–25 the preparations for Yahweh's Sinai appearance. Within this unit, verses 3–4 detail what Yahweh has done for Israel, and verses 5b–6 reply by indicating Israel's vocation. The introductory phrase in verse 5 is important: "if you will obey my voice and keep my covenant . . ." The covenant in mind may be prospective and have Exodus 20 in view. In the OT, however, references to keeping a divine covenant are consistently to a covenant already in existence (Gen. 17:9–10; 1 Kings 11:11; Ps. 78:10; 103:18; 132:12; Ezek. 17:14). It is possible that Exodus 19:5 points back to 6:5 and 3:13–15 and that continuity with the patriarchal covenant is involved, especially in light of the patriarchal style of address with which Yahweh begins in verse 3. Involved in the Sinai arrangement that follows is continuity within the Abrahamic covenant, but, for Israel, a specialized responsibility within the covenant. Certainly 19:3–6 forms a unit (note the similar opening and closing phrases at vv. 3b and 6b).

Exodus 19:5–6 turns to a discussion of Israel's vocation. The key term is the noun translated "own possession" (or "special possession"), meaning something of special personal worth. Most OT uses of the noun depend on Exodus 19:5b–6 (see Deut. 7:6; 14:2; 26:18; Ps. 135:4; Mal. 3:17), but two independent references occur at 1 Chronicles 29:3 and Ecclesiastes 2:8. In both cases the word refers to a private fortune, as distinguished from the resources of a realm under general control of the monarch. In Exodus 19:5, this choice of Israel expressed as Yahweh's "own possession" is a choice made from among "all peoples." This latter term expresses the family character, and thus the politically undefined nature, of the remaining world. This choice is then justified by the comment "for all the earth is mine." ("For" here probably both summarizes as well as expresses a causal role.) Israel is separated from all other families, to be presented as the ideal political unit. But the aim of her call is that she may be a world influence, a "light for revelation to the Gentiles" (Luke 2:32). There are remarkable overtones of the Abrahamic covenant in Israel's calling to serve her world by her separateness.

Exodus 19:6 reinforces this calling. Much difficulty has surrounded the phrases "kingdom of priests" and "holy nation." They are best taken as parallels, though there are other possibilities. The word "kingdom" most naturally refers to royal domain. If we take the possessive phrase "of priests" as adjectival, we arrive at the pair "priestly royalty" and "holy nation." These phrases emphasize function and signify not Israel's later priesthood, but the typical priestly role in an ancient society. These two parallel phrases elaborate the notion of Israel as God's "own possession." Israel's relationship to the world is likened to that of a priest in an ancient society, who was called to serve the society by differentiating himself from it. Is Israel's priestly role here conceived to be as a mediator? To the degree that Israel is designated a servant people in the latter part of the OT, the answer is yes. But Israel's primary role in this connection consisted in attracting the world to her form of government (i.e., the kingdom of God) by her embodied holiness. The notions of royalty and kingdom in verse 6 point to the ultimate authority of Israel's suzerain, who stands behind Israel's constitution and calls Israel, as a political entity, into being.

The remainder of Exodus 19 is given over to detailed preparations for the divine appearance, by which the ten "words" (20:1–17) will be introduced. These Ten Commandments, together with the social legislation that follows from them, appear in chapters 20–23. The text distinguishes the two codes; Exodus 20 is denominated "words" and delivered to all Israel, and chapters 21–23 are styled "ordinances" and delivered derivatively through Moses. The Ten Commandments spell out the boundaries of the relationship established by grace and are heard by all Israel. In keeping with this understanding, we note that the later, general word for "law" (*torah*) carries the sense of instruction or guidance. In these terms the Ten Commandments offer a mirror image of how Israel's national life in the land should look, reflecting the relationship of grace. The Ten Words objectified on Sinai seem merely to have codified the divine will for humankind. Most of their content is contained directly or by implication in the preceding material of Genesis and Exodus. From time to time attempts have been made to identify the form and content of the Ten Words in parallel codes from the ancient Near East (or in curse materials, state treaties, etc.), but no analogy for such a collection can be provided.

In Exodus 24:1–11, the covenant is ratified by a blood rite, the meaning of which is difficult to assess. The sacrifices offered (24:5) in connection with covenant conclusion, particularly in the burnt offering, may represent Israel's drawing the curses of the covenant down upon herself. In this connection, Paul's assertion in Galatians 3:13 that Christ had become a curse for us, meaning Jews, recognizes Jesus' removal of the covenant curse, through his death, as the divine affirmation of the new covenant. The closest parallel to the associated blood rite (Exod. 24:8) is the consecration of Aaron in Leviticus 8, which may also be imprecatory, since the blood of the ram is sprinkled on the person of the priest. If we may press such parallels, notes of imprecation and consecration appear in Exodus 24:1–11. In verses 9–11, a covenant meal takes place in which the leaders of Israel and seventy representative elders eat and drink in the presence of the deity. This is important incidental information, since it sets the goal to which the Bible looks in fellowship relationships. This meal on the mountain becomes the focus of later OT projection (cf. Isa. 25:6–8; Rev. 19:7–9), indicating final fellowship in the kingdom of God.

Exodus 25–31 follows up the covenant ratification but primarily concerns plans to erect the tabernacle and its associated institutions. The blueprint for the tabernacle is offered to Moses on the mountain (25:9, 40), thus establishing the tabernacle's heavenly character. Like the later temple, the tabernacle was thought of in Israel as the earthly dwelling or palace of Yahweh (the Hebrew word for "temple" also means "palace"). After the building of the tabernacle, Yahweh is pictured enthroned in the midst of the tribes, which surround the tabernacle. By linking heaven and earth and by its design as the earthly palace of the heavenly king, the tabernacle becomes in its typology a microcosm of the cosmos, linking creation and redemption. With worship inside the tabernacle and Israel outside, Israel is to be kept at a distance as her nature demands, although the tabernacle symbolizes God's immanence in Israel's midst. But God's grace has designed a worship form in which distance from deity is minimized and nearness is stressed.

The account of the preparation for building the tabernacle proceeds in six addresses, with the seventh address, 31:12–17, an exhortation to keep the Sabbath itself, a recognition of Yahweh's ownership of the world. This series of six addresses plus one has often been connected to the creation account (cf. Leder 1999), since the creation accounts of the ancient Near East end with a reference to temple building (cf. Gen. 2 and the temple motif there). God wishes to dwell in Israel's midst. Nevertheless, by the design of the tabernacle, distance is maintained between God and Israel. These chapters are not, as commonly supposed, a digression, but explain the significance of the covenant. Thus they immediately follow the covenant's ratification, a step that involves the acceptance of Yahweh's lordship and kingship. The design of the tabernacle, with its threefold division, reinforces the notion of distance between Yahweh and his people. This in itself enjoins the reverence to be displayed in tabernacle/temple worship. Exodus 25–31 concludes with instructions regarding the Sabbath, while chapters 35–40, in which the tabernacle is actually built, commence with similar instructions regarding Sabbath observance. The point is thus made that tabernacle and Sabbath are closely related. The observance of the Sabbath and the building of the tabernacle are two sides of the same coin, both relating to the manifestation of the kingdom of God, extending over humanity from creation itself.

The connection between the Sabbath and creation has been established by Exodus 20:11. The Hebrew root *shabat* can mean "stop" or "rest," but the underlying meaning points to that which gives completeness, usually by bringing a series to an end (see Gen. 2:1–4), and thus to that which provides a culminating point or purpose (Robinson 1980, 38). As an end to the exodus, then, reflection on the Sabbath suggests building the tabernacle; similar concerns call for building a temple after the conquest of Canaan.

In Exodus 20:11, the Sabbath has also been brought into theological connection with the important idea of "rest." The concept of rest becomes increasingly significant, since the biblical goal of redemption is seen as rest in God's presence. The idea underlying the Hebrew concept is ease or refreshment, the development of an atmosphere that has removed tensions of every kind. Sabbath and rest thus relate to each other as aim and result: Sabbath expresses the divine intention for creation (see Gen. 2:1–4a) and thus directs attention to what will be realized in the future. Rest refers to the nature of the activity once the goal has been realized. Rest from labor, referred to in Exodus 20:8–11 and 34:21, derives from and relates to the pragmatic nature of the then-current form of Israelite society. The primary implication of the word, however, is the presence of God in the Promised Land, presented through the concept of tabernacle/temple, which will make the land the Eden, the sanctuary, that it was meant to be (see Exod. 15:17). God's presence will ensure Israel's permanent occupation. Sabbath and rest coalesce as factors expressing the purpose and result of the exodus.

The actual building of the tabernacle is covered in Exodus 35–40 and concludes the book. The position and the amount of space devoted to this topic show that it attracts the author's paramount concern. In the tabernacle's erection, we have the response of an Israel that has been invited to worship as the proper response to redemption. We need to remember that the tabernacle within the camp was a visible reminder of Israel's form of government. As the earthly palace of the heavenly king, the tabernacle pointed to the locus of final political authority in Israel. The worship response for which the tabernacle called was therefore recognition of divine kingship exercised over Israel and, in this sense, was also a political act. Worship is therefore the protocol by which access to the divine king may be obtained. The Book of Exodus thus presents Israel as a worshiping community regulated by its divine king.

The Book of Exodus also addresses, however, the problem of Israel's inadequacy at Sinai and, thereafter in the OT, in regard to its vocation. This basic unfitness is seen in Exodus 32, in the narrative of the golden calf, which follows immediately after the tabernacle account of chapters 25–31. This narrative alerts us that Israel will probably always fail to respond to the ideals set for her in 19:3–6. This probability is confirmed by the progress of Israel's history. Moses' fracture of the two tables (32:19) is his fracture of the covenant, an action understandable from later Babylonian terms. It turns out that God will be willing to continue with Israel, but only as a result of the extraordinary intercession of Moses reported in chapter 33. Yahweh, who now will not accompany Israel to the Promised Land (33:3–5), plans to gather a people with Moses alone, as he had done with Abraham (note Moses' appeal to the basic patriarchal promises in 32:13–14). Moses alone will bear God's favor—the Hebrew possessive suffix of 33:14, "I will give you rest," is singular, thus virtually transferring the promises of 3:13–15 to Moses.

Attention then shifts to Moses' role as mediator, which for the first time in the book is assumed. The "covenant code," Exodus 21–23, was given "through Moses," but that statement says more about the derivative character of that law than it does about mediation. The tent of meeting (Exod. 33:7–11) is not identified with the tabernacle, which has not yet been built. Most modern scholars follow the rabbinic tradition of two tents of meeting, one inside the camp as the tabernacle, the other outside the camp for oracular purposes, where Moses will meet with Yahweh. In 33:12–17, Moses identifies himself completely with his people. He then pleads that God make a special appearance to him (vv. 18–23), as God had made a special appearance to Israel in chapter 19. The glory for which Moses asks (33:18)—the manifestation of the hidden nature of the essence of God, which in the OT cannot be revealed—is not shared with him. In 33:19, however, the name "The Lord" (the name is a synonym for all God's goodness, God's covenant faithfulness) is proclaimed to Moses as an expression of the continuity of the promises (McConville 1979, 153–54).

In Exodus 34, a second and now-operative covenant—not a renewed covenant, but a "fresh" covenant (cf. *koret berit*, the language of initiation at Exod. 34:10)—is initiated with Israel. The covenant of Exodus 19–24 had been broken by Israel's worship of the golden calf. This further initiative with Israel, through Moses, stems from Yahweh's character alone. Moses' role as mediator, referred to in 20:18–20 but not brought into being, is now dominant. Covenant reinauguration comes through Moses, and the words of the covenant are this time delivered to him alone, not to Israel (cf. 34:27–28).

Exodus 34:29–35 concludes the covenant cycle of chapters 19–34 and comments on Israel's position under the covenant. Israel, openly addressed in Exodus 20, is now unable to confront Yahweh. The glory which suffuses Moses' face as a result of divine contact and which indicates his unbroken personal relationship with God can no longer be shared with Israel. Moses remains unveiled only in the divine presence or when addressing Israel as mediator. When not delivering the covenant word, Moses wears the veil, indicating, as Paul explains in 2 Corinthians 3:7–18, the distance between himself and unbelieving, disobedient, and hardened Israel (see especially 2 Cor. 3:14). Revelation in the remainder of the OT will come to Israel through mediators, prophets, priests, kings, judges, and wise men. Never again in the OT will the situation of Exodus 19–20 occur, when all Israel stood before the divine presence and heard the divine word individually.

Exodus closes with the erection of the tabernacle, which is then filled with the divine presence, Yahweh's glory cloud that will lead Israel to Canaan (40:34–38). Attention has been drawn frequently to parallels between the tabernacle account and the account in Genesis 2:1–3 of the completion of creation (cf. Exod. 39:43 with Gen. 1:31; Gen. 2:1 with Exod. 39:32; Gen. 2:2 with Exod. 40:33; Gen. 2:2 with Exod. 39:43). This concludes a book that has recounted a transition in Israel's fortunes wrought by the exodus redemption. Though Israel will prove unworthy as a nation, it will come as no surprise, given the nature of Israel's God, that the ideals of the Sinai covenant will not be jettisoned, but will find new expression in the New Testament new covenant.

3

Leviticus

The Book of Leviticus is set at Sinai, where Israel remains until Numbers 10:10. Two dominant threads run through Leviticus, which begins and ends with Sinai (Lev. 27:34): the goal of holiness for Israel and the need for forgiveness. However, if the covenant relationship is to apply to Israel's national and personal experience, forgiveness, extended through the sacrificial system, is crucial. So all of Leviticus is to be understood as guidance for how the Sinai covenant was to be preserved. The concept of holiness is dominant (the word appears 152 times). The notion of holiness is best understood as indicating separateness and consecration to Yahweh. The Book of Leviticus explains what is demanded of Israel as a holy people.

Under the Sinai covenant, Israel was called to become a kingdom of priests and a holy nation. Leviticus 1–17 focuses almost entirely on the responsibilities of Israel's priestly representatives. By preserving its purity through these laws, Israel was enabled to remain in contact with God and to witness to God's presence in the world. The closing chapters of the book focus on the demand for national holiness. Chapters 18–26 emphasize that Israel was redeemed to be God's holy people.

The Sacrificial System (Lev. 1–7)

The divine institution of sacrifice (chaps. 1–7) is clearly given within the covenant relationships with which the Book of Exodus leaves us. The system did not operate as a means whereby God could be approached, but rather as a means whereby covenant relationships could be maintained or repaired. To take the common view of the OT sacrifices as being merely typical or symbolic, but hardly efficacious, is to read into the OT the later conclusions of the Epistle to the Hebrews, drawn in light of the finality of Jesus' sacrifice. The clear understanding of Leviticus is that sacrifice did effect atonement (Lev. 4:35), and by sacrifice the worshiper was cleansed and purified from sin. When the worshiper drew near to the sanctuary, killed his own beast, and laid his hand on its head as an indication of its substitution for him, he underscored the personal recognition that a breach in relationships had occurred. Note Leviticus 1:4, in which the imposition of the hand expresses the idea of substitution, "to make atonement for him." To suggest that the forgiveness offered through the system was only symbolic or typical reduces sacrifice in the OT to a vague and meaningless ritual. This was never intended.

The Book of Leviticus and analogous legislation classify sin under two major headings: unpremeditated (or "unwitting"—Lev. 5:15; Num. 15:29) and premeditated (or "with a high hand"—Lev. 6:1–2; Num. 15:30). Leviticus makes clear that both of these types could be forgiven (see Lev. 4 for unpremeditated and 6:1–7 for premeditated). Confession was required for all premeditated sinful acts as a precondition for the *hatt'at* (sin-offering, though better understood as a purification offering). The inadvertent offender was not required to confess, but the repentance of the intentional sinner through his remorse (Heb. *'asham*) and confession (Heb. *hitwaddah*) reduced the intentional sin to inadvertence, thus rendering sacrificial propitiation possible.

However, as in the New Testament, access to forgiveness was denied to the unrepentant. While unpremeditated sins did not need to be confessed, confession made it possible for premeditated sins to fall within the system (see Lev. 5:1–6; 16:21; 26:40; Num. 5:6–8; Milgrom 1975, 195). Forgiveness depended ultimately on divine grace, a fact the OT underscores by reporting occasions in which God forgave without the operation of the system (e.g., 2 Sam. 12). Such instances reminded Israel that sacrifice was the customary means of approach, but that God's forgiveness was not distributed mechanically in a context in which there was a constant disposition to misunderstand the system.

We are not told in the OT how the system operated, but conclusions may be drawn from the threefold presentation of the order of sacrifice in Leviticus 1–9 (Rainey 1970). In 1:1–6:7, the order is burnt-, cereal-, peace-, and then sin- and guilt-offerings, in what seems a grouping by association. There follows in 6:8–7:38 the order of burnt-, cereal-, sin-, guilt-, and then peace-offerings. The content of this passage is described as *torah,* or instruction. The passage seems concerned with administrative procedures relating to the manner of offering. But in Leviticus 9, the system is seen in operation. This third order of sin-, burnt-, and peace-offerings is affirmed by other sections of the OT in which the system is presented in actual performance (cf. Exod. 29:10–34; Num. 6:14–17; Ezek. 45:13–17; 2 Chron. 29:31–36). The conclusion is that the first priority of the sacrificial system is the need for sin to be forgiven. Personal consecration (burnt-offering) follows as a symbol of commitment, and, finally, the celebration of reconciliation takes place through the peace-offerings. While this reasoning may well offer helpful insight into the operation of the sacrificial system, it must be remembered that, throughout the OT, the respective components of the system (burnt, cereal, sin, peace) are usually presented separately. It is clear that the burnt-offering by itself effects atonement (Lev. 1:4; cf. Gen. 8:21), although perhaps in a more general sense than the sin- and guilt-, or propitiatory, offerings. The burnt-offering also witnesses to the worshiper's faith and commitment (cf. Gen. 22 and Exod. 18:11–12). The cereal-offering normally accompanied the burnt-offerings, but could be offered alone. Since the term used to describe the cereal-offering is "tribute," it has been suggested that this offering exemplifies the master/servant relationship in which the covenant had placed Israel (Wenham 1979, 69–70).

The peace-offering, unlike the burnt-offering (which was consumed on the altar), was shared between worshipers and priests. Since there is no agreement concerning the meaning of the Hebrew *shelamim* (e.g., in Lev. 3:1), the purpose of this offering remains in doubt. Neither the peace-offering nor the cereal-offering by itself is said to effect atonement. Both depend on prior atoning sacrifices.

The propitiatory or purification offerings are dealt with in Leviticus 4:1–6:7. The procedures for these two offerings (purification and reparation) differed sharply from the other three; these differences were observed whether the person making the offering was a layperson or a priest. The worshiper did not eat this sacrifice, but it was given over to the priesthood. In cases where a priest was involved, after the mandatory portions had been burnt on the altar, the remainder of the carcass was burnt outside the camp. The purpose of these propitiatory offerings was decontamination and cleansing, since sin is an offense against God's holiness. Though the sin-offering (purification) and guilt-offering (reparation) were related, they involved different rituals and different animals. The purification or sin-offering (Heb. *hatt'at*) dealt with conscious actions that were either premeditated or were realized later to be sinful. The *hatt'at* offering, as in Leviticus 4:1–5:13, dealt with uncleanness as well as with guilt. The shed blood of sacrifice contained the life essence and symbolized a substitutionary death, so that the death caused by sin and uncleanness was annulled. Priestly eating of the *hatt'at* was a duty and privilege with no bearing on the atoning process.

The guilt-offering (Heb. *'asham*) seems to have atoned for trespasses against sacred things or the divine name, with the underlying idea of compensation for losses incurred (Wenham 1979, 111). The *'asham* was thus a reparation offering, an atonement for an offense for which restitution was possible or for violation of anything sacred. It is the most difficult of the sacrifices to understand.

Israel's Priesthood (Lev. 8–10)

The consecration of Aaron and the priesthood occurs in chapters 8–10. The consecration narratives tacitly ascribe to Aaron the dignity and authority of a royal figure (Lev. 8). He embodies for Israel the vocation offered in Exodus 19:3–6. Priestly clothing is of the character that befits an audience with the monarch. In his dress, therefore, the priest, particularly the high priest as king/priest, set forth the prospect of Eden restored (Davies 2000, 186). The anointing of Israel's priests and kings indicated their special relationship to Yahweh. The basic function of Israel's priesthood under the leadership of the high priest was to keep Israel holy, to decide what was clean and unclean, to keep Israel from everything that could defile, and to atone for Israel when defilement had occurred. Aaron's sons were also consecrated to priestly service. Following the elaboration of the sacrificial system, the consecration of Aaron and the priesthood occurs in chapters 8–10.

It is often argued that Levitical specialization in the priesthood developed gradually in the OT. In the pre-Levitical period, it is said that the head of the house exercised the priestly role. Certainly this was true of Israel before the exodus, but it may be a misconception to imagine that such a situation continued. In the period up to the later monarchy, individuals offered sacrifices (Judg. 6:20–28; 13:15–23; 1 Sam. 6:14–15; 1 Kings 1:9; 18:30–39). But one must differentiate between sacrifice at the central sanctuary and at the local altars. The Levitical priesthood was bound up with the official cult, but there was no prohibition of local sacrifice, at least up to the early period of the monarchy (Haran 1978, 64). As the centrality of Jerusalem became ascendant, this practice may have died out, though the evidence either way is somewhat tenuous.

The role of the priesthood and the progressive approach to the divine presence that the structure of the tabernacle and its furnishings demanded pointed to the distinction that Israel was to maintain between the sacred and the profane. The distinction between priests and Levites was probably an original and basic distinction, bound up with the more general distinctions of access to the sanctuary.

Holiness and Laws of Purity (Lev. 11–15)

Leviticus 11–15 contains laws of purity, distinguishing sharply between what was considered to be clean and unclean, thus implementing the priestly vocation specified in 10:10. Holiness, we might note, defines God as wholly other. The word for holiness is used broadly in Semitic languages to refer to a quality of the deity or to divine names, while objects, animals, and persons may be considered holy by virtue of their relationship to Yahweh and his service. Of the 842 references to holiness in the Bible, at least 830 refer to Yahweh, his cult, and his people (Houser 1978, 43). In Leviticus, the term is used with reference to God some fourteen times, describing God's nature, power, majesty, and person. Yahweh as holy is completely separated from human beings, and yet persons and objects may be made holy when dedicated for Yahweh's service by some form of consecration. God as holy is the model for God's people and priests, who are also to be holy and who are to evidence separateness from their world, a separateness that stamps them as people of God.

Things or persons that are not holy are classed as common or profane. Anything belonging to the profane sphere is always available for common use, provided it is ceremonially clean, while a holy thing, although always clean, is never available for common use. Any holy thing may be profaned by improper use. Taking God's name in vain, for example, profanes it. Profane or common things are further subdivided into clean and unclean. The holiness of objects is permanent; they are permanently withdrawn from the profane sphere. The tabernacle required periodical purification, but the presence of associated impurity did not compromise the tabernacle's holiness. In order to minister in the sanctuary, priests had to be holy and thus were consecrated at Sinai (Lev. 8–10). Holiness—separation to and for Yahweh—should characterize Israel in its distinctiveness from other nations, with regard to purity laws (Lev. 11:44–45) or moral behavior (Lev. 19). Uncleanness was transmissible, while cleanness was not, and priests were to avoid contact with what was inherently or ritually unclean. No area of life was exempt from the demand to be holy, for Israel was separated as a holy people to Yahweh. Thus the term "holy" is moral as well as ceremonial. In the final analysis, holiness for Israel and her priests involves obedience to the divine commandments.

Recent anthropological studies have suggested that "cleanness" is a broad term, encompassing what we would label normal or acceptable. The distinction between clean and unclean foods seems to have been based on what was acceptable to the society and what was not. Fish without scales, for example, were viewed as serpentlike and abnormal and, therefore, as unacceptable for eating. Bodily discharges seen as deviations from the usual were also said to make a person unclean. Some unclean items were unclean only temporarily, for, in other circumstances, cultic action could be taken to cleanse them. The regulations relating to clean and unclean in chapters 11–15 reinforce the underlying thesis of Leviticus that holiness, which belongs to God by nature (11:44–45), must be reflected in the life of the elect people.

Day of Atonement (Lev. 16)

The Day of Atonement (chap. 16), perhaps the most significant day in the national calendar, was the day on which the previous year's sins were symbolically atoned for by cleansing the sanctuary. The high priest was specially clad and entered the inner sanctum, or Holy of Holies, for the only time during the year. Dominant in the chapter is the notion of atonement. The meaning of this term, however, is still in dispute. Perhaps in ritual texts such as Leviticus 16 the meaning is "cleansing." Certainly, however, in the more personal sacrificial texts (e.g., 12:7; 14:18; 15:15) a meaning like "ransom" seems more appropriate. The notions of both ransom and cleansing are required to account for the New Testament understanding of the death of Christ. In any case, the Day of Atonement legislation, with its elaborate procedures for cleansing the tabernacle, complements and concludes the extended section on clean and unclean (chaps. 11–15). The central problem of the Day of Atonement ritual lies in the relationship between the *hatt'at,* which purifies the sanctuary, and the Azazel goat, which carries the guilt of all the Israelites into the wilderness. The meaning of the Hebrew verb *kipper* ("atone") includes both purification and bearing guilt. It is likely that in purifying the sanctuary Aaron bore the guilt associated with uncleanness, and that he laid it on the head of the Azazel goat when he confessed the sins of all the Israelites. In this interpretation, the Azazel goat ritual can be seen to meet the demand in Leviticus 10:16–20 that the guilt Aaron bears as the head of the house and for Israel must be removed. The Azazel goat as an integral part of the Day of Atonement ceremony was itself the *hatt'at* and constituted its climax. The ritual was a special form of the burning of the *hatt'at*, designed to eliminate the guilt that Aaron bore (Kiuchi 1987, 152–58). Israel may thus have been able to begin a new year as a cleansed and forgiven people.

Holiness Code (Lev. [17] 18–26)

The Holiness Code of chapters (17) 18–26 emphasizes the more positive aspects of biblical holiness. The code constitutes not merely withdrawal from what is tainted, but exhibits the wholeness and completeness that characterizes God and that must therefore be the property of God's people (see, e.g., 19:2; 20:7, 26; 21:6–7). When Yahweh manifests himself, his holiness is visible as glory, the radiant power of his being. Glory is not identical with holiness, but it stresses a power included in holiness. Glory is often the exterior manifestation of the power and holiness of Yahweh himself, while holiness denotes Yahweh's intimate nature and often has a moral aspect that is not necessarily included in the concept of glory. So holiness refers to Yahweh's inner nature and glory to his outward manifestation. Because Yahweh's holiness implies his absolute power over the world, mighty upheavals in nature attend God's appearing (Mic. 1:3–4; cf. Judg. 5:4–5).

The call to be holy meant that the people were to develop in themselves characteristics similar to Yahweh's. This process is called sanctification. The process is reciprocal. Yahweh sanctifies (20:8; 21:8, 15, 23; 22:9, 16, 32), and the people are to sanctify themselves (11:44; 20:7). By keeping the law and by worship the people sanctified themselves and revered Yahweh as the holy God in their congregation (22:32). Yahweh also sanctified them by his holy power working in their lives, affirming the noble and purging the corrupt. Yahweh's holiness sought to penetrate the whole person and not merely the soul.

Yahweh had revealed the character of his holiness in his laws—note the frequent formula of self-introduction, "I am Yahweh" or "I am Yahweh your God." The laws describe for Israel the behavior congruent with Yahweh's holy nature. Two qualities undergirded the national holy life: justice and love. Justice means equity, stated fundamentally in the principle of *lex talionis*—an eye for an eye, a tooth for a tooth, a life for a life (24:20). This principle did not imply that punishment was carried out in kind, but that it must be commensurate, not greater as revenge dictates or less as indulgence desires. This principle was a great advance in the law codes, for it raised personal injury from a civil tort to a criminal law, increasing the citizen's social worth. For Israel, justice meant deciding matters by Yahweh's law. But the law calls for doing justice in love, for both concepts, ideally exhibited, are interdependent. So the great commandment of 19:18 was "love your neighbor as yourself." The love here is to be expressed primarily in deeds of kindness and caring. The emphasis falls on helping and caring for one another, not on people's feelings toward one another. Israel was also to rise above the natural tendency to take advantage of foreigners. Some of the fields were to be left for gleaners. Finally, Israel was often exhorted to fear God, which addressed an inner attitude to God somewhat similar to the faith of the New Testament.

Because only Yahweh is intrinsically holy, any person or thing is holy only as it stands in relationship to him. Thus there are degrees of holiness, depending on the proximity of an item or person to Yahweh. The description of the tabernacle and the pattern of OT worship witnesses to the degrees of holiness. The closer a person or thing gets to God, the holier it becomes and the holier it must be, lest it be consumed by the nearness of God's holiness.

Chapters 18–20 form the core of the holiness corpus. Laws calling for separation (chap. 18) are complemented by material dealing with moral (and ceremonial) requirements (chaps. 19–22). Surrounding chapters 18–22 are instructions on worship. Chapter 17 legislates that all sacrifices were to be made at the official altar and that no blood was to be consumed. Chapters 23–25 regulate times for worship. Chapter 23 opens with rules for the Sabbath and then regulates the three annual pilgrim festivals, the Feast of Passover and Unleavened Bread, the Feast of Weeks, and the Feast of the Booths. Chapter 23 makes the first day of the seventh month a day of rest and sets a date for the Day of Atonement. Chapter 24 has two distinct sections: verses 1–4 regulate the quality of oil for the holy place and verses 5–9 the bread of the presence for the table. These matters deal with periodic rituals and have some connection with chapters 23 and 25. The second section of chapter 24 reports a case of blasphemy (vv. 10–12), to which laws treating blasphemy and injury to persons and animals have been appended (vv. 13–23). Chapter 25 regulates multiple-year cycles, the seven-year sabbatical cycle and the fifty-year cycle of the year of Jubilee. Integrated into Jubilee are laws on the redemption of patrimony and a debtor slave. These high, festive, and special years are to be observed in order to exalt the worship of Yahweh over material concerns. Because Yahweh is a holy God, he demands that sacred times be proclaimed for community worship and celebration.

The holiness section concludes in chapter 26 with blessings and curses, a fitting end to this section and the Holiness Code. The section places the material on cultic purity and ethical integrity within the context of the covenant. Restoration of Israel, should an exile occur, is also possible (vv. 40–45). These verses stand as an enduring word of hope to Israel.

Chapter 27 discusses vows and dedicatory gifts. It may be seen as the proper human response to chapter 26, describing the divine announcement as it bears on Israel's future (Wenham 1979, 336). In any case, its concern is with what is to be dedicated and thus with what belongs to God—the subject matter of the whole book.

Leviticus is a book operating within a context of grace. God has redeemed Israel, separated the people from their world (18:24), and given them laws by which they are to live (18:5) and by which the land to which God is bringing them is to be protected (chap. 26). In the final sense, Leviticus is a political document describing Israel as a theocracy, an entity ruled by God. God is to be obeyed because of God's holiness, demonstrated in the saving history of Israel.

Underlying the demands for ritual and personal purity in Leviticus is the theology of redemption (11:45; 22:32–33; 25:38, 55; 26:13, 45). Yahweh is thus to be served exclusively and completely. The book is concerned not with antiquarian or peripheral issues, but with the practical issue of how life within the covenant is to be maintained. Obedience within this framework is the final requirement. As Israel and the Israelite people reflected the law that was the product of their covenant connection, they were impelled by the divine injunction, "You shall therefore keep my statutes and my ordinances, by doing which a man shall live; I am the Lord" (18:5).

4

Numbers

The Book of Numbers concentrates on the aftermath of the Sinai revelation and on the preparations for entering the land. Six stages had moved Israel from Egypt to Rephidim, the stage before Sinai (Exod. 12:37; 13:20; 14:1–2; 15:22; 16:1; 17:1), and six stages moved Israel from Sinai to the steps of Moab (Exod. 19:2; Num. 10:12; 20:1, 22; 21:10–11; 22:1). The forty years serve as a transition, allowing a new generation to arise (26:65). The book opens with Israel still at Sinai, one month after the erection of the tabernacle and thirteen months after the completion of the exodus. It describes the journey of the Israelites from Mount Sinai to the border of Canaan.

Numbers relates the account of two generations: a generation that perishes in the wilderness through unbelief, and a generation placed in Moab with the advantage of having seen firsthand the disastrous results of disobedience. This second generation, however, repeats the curious and continual paradox of the OT. Once it enters the land, Israel shows the same tendencies and behavior patterns as the first generation, raising the prospect of another wilderness situation, which finally led to exile. The Book of Numbers is, in essence, two-sided. The somber side is the side of judgment. After the wonderful experience of exodus and Sinai, the book records many lost opportunities. Positively, however, Numbers is concerned, like Leviticus, with establishing for Israel the sharp contrast between the sacred and the profane. The message of the book is that if Israel wishes to enjoy the blessings of the Land of Promise, it must follow God's unfailing guidance and keep itself unspotted.

These years in the wilderness established the character of later Israel. Testing produced occasional faithfulness, but mainly it led to repeated displays of apostasy. This massive army of Israel, with which the book began, moved irresolutely from place to place, organized for battle, meeting no enemy except the righteous God. The people continually offended God and consequently were brought into judgment for their rebellion. When the army did engage in rare skirmishes in the wilderness, it was the power of God, not the army's prowess, that provided the victory. Despite the faithlessness of Israel, Numbers reports Yahweh as holding true to his promise. Thus, though one Israel dies in the wilderness, an Israel of comparable size replaces it (Num. 26). Eleazar, Aaron's son, replaces Aaron (20:28), as Moses is replaced by Joshua (27:12–23).

There is little consensus on the structure of Numbers. Some have used chronology to create a structure, and the book does contain chronological indicators. Using the month of the first Passover in Egypt as its starting point (cf. Exod. 12:2), the book at various points lists the year, the month, and usually the time elapsed since the first Passover (1:1; 9:1, 5; 10:11; 20:1; 33:3, 38). The book begins on the first day, in the second month, in the second year after Israel had come out of Egypt (1:1). Numbers 9:1 and 9:5 indicate the date on which Israel had celebrated the second Passover, in commemoration of the first Passover a year before. Numbers 10:11 gives the date for the inauguration of Israel's march, after its constitution as the holy people of God.

Numbers is basically divided into two halves (chaps. 1–25; 26–36) with three geographical movements: 1:1–10:10 at Sinai; 10:11–21:35 in the wilderness; 22:1–36:13 in the plains of Moab. The first half begins with the census and organization of the holy people of God in their preparation and ritual organization, before the people's march.

The Two Censuses of Numbers

The census lists of Numbers 1 and 26 provide the major edifice on which the organization of the book stands. The census lists make a theological claim for continuity of the covenantal promises given to the patriarchs. They also make a claim for the inclusiveness of the covenant and its laws for all Israel. The expanded segments of the genealogies in Numbers 26 suggest a partial fulfillment of the promise of abundant descendants.

The first census list marks a new beginning of life after Sinai. It is linked with the people's organization into a holy camp, with the tent of meeting in the middle and the priests, Levites, and people encircling it in concentric circles of holiness. The census of Numbers 1, taken only months apart from the tabernacle census (cf. Exod. 30:12–16; 38:26; Num. 1:46), yielded the same results and perhaps was the same. The only previous census comes at the end of Genesis, listing the sons of Jacob and their immediate offspring. This list, from the descent into Egypt, includes seventy persons, while recognizing the great expansion of the tribes in Egypt (Exod. 1:1–6). The Israelite people were making their first step as they put their commission as a holy people before the Lord into practice.

At Sinai (Num. 1:1–10:10)

Chapters 1 and 2 report a census and camp arrangement predicated on military criteria. Numbers 1 tells us that the multitudinous descendants of Jacob have now become a great people. Though primarily concerned to display the people's fitness for battle (1:2–3, 20, etc.), the census also indicates how each Israelite clan contributes to the whole and stresses the family links, and thus the unity, among the tribes.

The first census (chaps. 1–2) raises the problem of how one clan of seventy persons could increase by such an extent in a few hundred years (Num. 1 = 603,550; Num. 26 = 601,730). The figure of six hundred thousand presupposes a population of more than two million. Many ingenious proposals have been made to reduce the figure (cf. Davies 1995, 14–18). But the present text clearly assumes that the disputed Hebrew *'elef* means one thousand. That the lists represent an actual census cannot be denied. It seems that the figure of six hundred thousand is legitimate, and we may compare the large numbers in Chronicles. The Levites are mustered separately (1:49–50). They are to retire at fifty (4:47; 8:25).

In chapter 2, the tribes are arranged in battle order around the tabernacle, the symbol of Israel's leadership. The book thus begins on a high note of national discipline. Israel is equipped for conquest, with the symbols of her charter and authority in her camp. In a sense, the message of the book appears here, for it is by discipline, self-control, and divine national regulation in obedience to its sovereign king that the Promised Land will be attained.

Chapters 3–4 and (7)–8 deal with the Levites. The Levites do not appear in Leviticus but predominate in Numbers. They serve most importantly as guardians of the tabernacle (31:30, 47), and the Levitical cordon was empowered to strike down an encroacher. For this duty they were rewarded with the tithe (18:1–6, 21–24). In chapters 3–4, the census of the Levites is taken and a poll tax provided. The Levites receive carts from the tribal chieftains for tabernacle transport (7:1–9), are purified prior to their entry into tabernacle service (8:1–22), and are informed of their retirement regulations (8:23–26).

The laws in chapters 5–6, concerned with the prevention and elimination of defilement in Israel's camp, are inserted into these preparations. The Aaronic priestly blessing ends the section (6:22–27), in which God's intention for Israel is repeated.

Numbers 7–9 details events such as tribal offerings for the tabernacle, the dedication of the Levites, and the institution of the second Passover (chap. 9), all of which happened within the period covered by chapters 1–6. God's fire-cloud descended on the ark whenever God wished to address Moses (7:89). Moses alone is admitted into the divine presence, although the language of God speaking with Moses face-to-face is presence language and must not be taken literally. To receive the Ten Commandments, Moses had entered the cloud as it rested on Mount Sinai. Moses only enters the outer room of the tabernacle after the *kabod* fire has descended, and he hears the deity's voice emanating from inside the veil. But he did not enter the tabernacle's Holy of Holies. Chapters 7–9 ostensibly revert to the first month of the second year (cf. 7:1 and 9:1), but the phrase "on the day" at 7:1 and 9:15 should be rendered "when," and the verbs in 7:1 and 9:15 should be taken as pluperfects (cf. 9:11).

The text describes the manner in which the glory-cloud provided guidance (9:15–23). The text states, moreover, that the presence of Yahweh in the midst of the camp is the sole guarantee of victory (cf. 14:44). A dark, heavy cloud by day and a fire by night, which covers the tabernacle, symbolize the presence of Yahweh as king (9:15–16). This cloud precedes Israel on her march, not only providing her with direction, but also regulating the journey's stages (see 9:15–23; 12:5–10). The glory-cloud is God's manifested presence, serving both to save and to judge Israel during this wilderness period. Its starts and stops determine Israel's stages and stations. Its constant visibility is a sign to Israel and the nations of God's presence. The divine presence will enter the Promised Land with Israel. The divine presence demands the purity of the camp (5:1–4; 31:19, 24), and demands that Israel not pollute the land (35:33–34).

Finally, in this first geographical division, instructions appear to help coordinate the assembly's movement (10:1–10). This first section of Numbers has constructed a picture of an ideal Israel and of God dwelling in its midst. It has also provided the institutions to serve Israel's vocation and the priesthood to provide a model for Israel's behavior.

Through the Wilderness (Num. 10:11–25:18)

The first part of the middle block, 10:12–14:45, occurs at the beginning of the period, to judge from 14:34 and the last part 20:1–21:10, at the end of the wilderness period. Events of the final chapters (21:10–36:13) occur within five months of the fortieth year (cf. 20:28–33:38). This would leave the events of the Korahite rebellion (chaps. 16–17) and several laws (chaps. 15, 18–19) as all that can be attributed to the forty years in the wilderness.

Numbers 11:1–25:18 may be divided into two sections: 11:1–20:29 and 21:1–25:18, marked by a geographical indicator at 20:22. Chapters 11–20 deal with a time of transition. This section is marked by profound promise, mingled with failure. As proof that the Israelites are the people of God, God feeds them in the wilderness with manna and quails and provides water from the rock (11:7, 31–32; 20:11). The rebellion of chapters 11–12 climaxes in the spy episode in chapters 13–14, which brings death for the first generation. The exodus generation does not survive the wilderness because, when it arrived at Kadesh-barnea (13:26), a highly suitable point of entry into the Promised Land from the south, it refused to heed Caleb and Joshua's promising report. This refusal took place within two years of the exodus. There is some glimmer of hope in regulations for when the people enter the Promised Land (chap. 15). But much of the rest of the section, up to Numbers 25, recounts further rebellions, plagues, and deaths (chaps. 16, 17, 20, 21, 25). Chapters 16–17 show Israel demoralized by the majority report of the scouts and condemned to die in the wilderness. The people, at this point, are psychologically receptive to demagogic appeal to overthrow their leadership and to return to Egypt. The aftermath of Korah's priestly rebellion (16:1–11, 16–19 [20–24], 32–35) and of Dathan and Abiram's civil rebellion (16:12–15, [20–24] 25–31) vindicates Aaron (16:36–50) when his censer-offering brings life and stays the plague (41–50), and when his rod blossoms miraculously (17:1–12). As a result of their hazardous responsibility guarding the tabernacle, the priests and the Levites are granted specified endowments (chap. 18). Further instruction aimed at cultic regulation (chaps. 18–19) again emphasizes the national need for purity and separation. God's purposes for Israel have not lapsed, rebellion notwithstanding. Numbers 10:11–20:29 is designed to show the disastrous results of Israel's contact with the profane in the wilderness and of her incessant murmurings, in spite of the continued divine providence and presence (Exod. 15:22–16:36).

From Kadesh to the Plains of Moab (Num. 20:1–22:1)

Material concerning the final stage of the march from Kadesh to the steppes of Moab appears in chapters 20–21. Chapter 20 reports the sin of Moses at the waters of Meribah (vv. 1–13). Moses in Numbers is presented, in almost royal terms, as the supreme commander. He makes the final decisions, regulates the cult, and, above all, is the community's true prophet and intercessor (11:24–25; 12:6–8). But even he exceeds his authority and, rather than merely addressing a word to the rock in Yahweh's name, strikes it. Moses, the greatest of the Israelite prophets (Exod. 33:11; Num. 12:8; Deut. 34:10), committed the ultimate heresy of attributing the miracle at 20:10 to himself. Edom's refusal to grant passage is reported in 20:14–21, and the death of Aaron in verses 22–29. A positive tone is struck for the first time with Israel's victory over the Canaanites at Hormah (21:3). A previous defeat at Hormah (14:45), following the previous generation's abortive attempt to enter the land, had signaled its role from that time on as aimless pilgrims. Yet there is no indication that this new generation will fare better than its fathers. So failure to trust, buoyed by battle success over Arad (21:1–3), produces murmuring. The murmuring resurfaces immediately after the victory at Hormah, and the judgment that comes on Israel is assuaged by the salvation symbol of the brazen serpent (21:4–9). Chapters 21:10–25:18 deal with the fortunes of Israel after this heartening victory. The new itinerary list (21:12–20) contains two ancient poems (21:14–15 and 17–18). Numbers 21:21–36:13 locates Israel east of the Jordan Valley. The subsequent defeat of Sihon the Ammonite (21:21–26) gives rise to the Song of Heshbon (21:27–30), which introduces Israel's victory over Og of Bashan and the conquest of the remaining Transjordan (21:21–25, 31–35).

In the Plains of Moab (Num. 22:2–36:13)

The Balaam Oracles

The function of the Balaam oracles is to reaffirm the faithfulness of God's promises to Israel in the face of all opposition. God is able to control even those who would curse God's people. Yet the faith of Israel is fickle and shallow (cf. Num. 25). While Israel encamps on the plains of Moab, God holds spiritual opposition, in the form of Balaam the Mesopotamian seer, in check (chaps. 22–24). Balaam must bless, though called by Balak of Moab to curse. The Balaam oracles describe the glorious future of Israel as it stands on the brink of the Promised Land. Characteristically, this further documentation of the divine intention for Israel is followed by the dire apostasy at Baal-Peor (25:1–15), provoked by contact with the Midianites. Balaam himself is killed for causing the apostasy at Shittim (25:1). God had done everything to prevent the curse falling on Israel but, in the end, the nation drew the curse upon itself. Even an ass can recognize an angel of God, and a pagan seer can do God's will, but not Israel.

The apostasy at Numbers 25, which follows the Balaam oracles, and the spy story (chaps. 13–14) are mirror images. In both cases, the people stand on the brink of the Promised Land. Likewise, this apostasy at Baal-Peor (25:1–18), which removes the remainder of the exodus generation, resembles the golden-calf narrative of Exodus 32. Both involve illicit worship, the slaughter of the guilty, and the choice of the Levitical line. Both describe the fall of Israel after having obtained the Lord's promise, in the Sinai covenant and in Balaam's blessing, of future greatness. Virtually none of the Israelites of the exodus period survives the testing in the wilderness. Of the adult males, Caleb and Joshua, who returned with a favorable report from the Promised Land (Num. 14:6), are the exceptions.

The unifying theme in the wilderness trek is God's provision for Israel. God provides water and all of Israel's other needs.

Second Generation (Num. 26:1–36:13)

A new census called for in Numbers 26 indicates that the forty years of wandering are over. It heralds a new beginning. The second census, following the plague of chapter 25—that is, after the death of the first generation—lists a new generation. The new generation offers a model for future Israel, and its future is open-ended. The expanded genealogies in Numbers 26 suggest partial fulfillment of the promise of abundant descendants. All the OT tribal lists that include Levi ultimately derive from Genesis 49. The OT lists that do not include Levi derive from Numbers 1:5–15 or 26:5–51. Numbers 1 divides the Joseph tribes into Ephraim-Manasseh, while Numbers 26 has Manasseh-Ephraim. Genesis 49 seems to be the earliest tribal list since it contains Levi as a secular tribe.

The final section (Num. 27–36) is bracketed by an *inclusio*. Chapters 27 and 36 both deal with the daughters of Zelophehad and the inheritance of property. The resolution of the issue in both cases strikes a positive note for the second half of the book, in which no Israelite dies. The final ten chapters of Numbers are motivated by a single theme: the immediate occupation of the Promised Land. Chapters 27–30 concern laws relating to its possession and retention, including, in chapters 28–29, brief repetition of the sacrificial code, particularly in regard to public sacrifices. The section also includes material relating to inheritance (27:1–11) and succession in Israel's leadership (vv. 12–23). Numbers 31–32 paves the way for entry by recounting the defeat of the Midianite confederation and the settlement of the Transjordanian tribes (Reuben, Gad, and part of Manasseh). Chapter 32, with the allotment of Transjordan, warns the Transjordanian tribes of possible extinction unless they see the conquest through.

Numbers summarizes the wilderness stations (33:1–49), reminding Israelites of the first generation's wanderings. That account is followed by a narrative addressing eviction of the land's inhabitants and extirpation of their cult (33:50–56). The text discusses the land's boundaries (34:1–15), supervisors for the process of division (34:16–29), Levitical holdings (35:1–8), and the establishment of cities of refuge for the prevention of pollution by homicide (35:9–34). The boundaries of the Promised Land concur with the boundaries of Egypt's Asian empire from the fifteenth to thirteenth centuries b.c. The book ends with Israel in the plains of Moab some forty years after Sinai, poised to enter the Promised Land after repeated national failures. Numbers is thus the narrative of a spiritual pilgrimage. Israel's continuance as a people, with the possibility of inheriting the promise of land, is due entirely to the superintendence of her affairs by God, who never ceases to address her infidelity. The wanderings through the wilderness—the Hebrew title of the book means simply "In the Wilderness"—are calculated to teach Israel the essence of obedience. These lessons are designed to offer Israel, once again, the possibility of being the true people of God. The nation never recovered from the failures of this wilderness period, and the remainder of the OT presents the history of an Israel provided with countless unrealized opportunities to become what it was meant to be—a separated people of God.

5

Deuteronomy

The book is a collection of words of command and instruction, words of preaching and exhortation contained in a series of speeches by Moses just prior to entering the Promised Land. The speeches underline the redemptive grace of God, to whom obedience is to be expected. Deuteronomy is thus a book of Torah, a book of preached law. Torah is the instruction and teaching that, grounded in the exodus redemption, will retain the Promised Land.

With good reason, scholars in recent years have seen definite parallels between the structure of the Book of Deuteronomy and the form of the ancient Near Eastern state treaty, an instrument by which diplomatic relationships between powers were regulated. Such treaties are best known from Hittite archives (ca. 1400–1200 B.C.) and in their ideal but extrapolated form consist of (1) preamble, (2) historical prologue, (3) stipulations, (4) covenant sanctions, (5) ratification, and (6) blessings and curses. Requirements for periodic readings were sometimes included. While this form does not match exactly the material of Deuteronomy, the fit is close enough to justify the comparison. Such modifications as exist would have been undertaken by Deuteronomy's author to provide the necessary theological adjustments. The most serious difference is that Deuteronomy has to do with covenant renewal, and not with initiation.

Deuteronomy 1–4

Most of the book's primary themes appear in chapters 1–4, which introduce the concerns raised by Israel's wilderness wanderings. This first speech recounts the beginning of the history of the covenant people. Chapters 1–3 recapitulate what transpired in the earlier book of Numbers, illustrating Israel's general failure to trust Yahweh, whose redemption had accounted for their nationhood. These chapters position Israel on the border of the Promised Land. The historical retrospect reaches back to Horeb (chap. 1), and Israel under Moses' leadership progresses through Edom, Moab, and Ammon, as well as through the lands of Sihon and Og that it captures. But the failure of Israel to obey, as in the surveillance of the land from Kadesh-barnea, which meant the first generation's exclusion from the land, bodes ill for the future. The review ends with the land east of the Jordan under Israel's possession, with Moses' exhortation in chapter 4, and with the Promised Land still ahead (3:23–29; 4:44–49). To secure the future and to receive the promises to Abraham that the Promised Land would be retained will be to hear and implement Moses' final charge. These chapters report a journey led by God, designed to put Israel in the new Eden from which, in response to continued obedience, blessing upon blessing may be expected. Everything on this journey, even what appears aimless wandering, is under the direction of God (2:1–3).

Call to Obedience (Deut. 4:1–49)

Deuteronomy 4 begins with an injunction to keep the commandments (vv. 1–8), with emphasis on keeping the second commandment (vv. 9–31). The emphasis on avoiding idols was necessitated by Israel's placement in Moab before entering the Promised Land (4:44–49), where the Canaanite religion would entice. The identification of the covenant with the Ten Words in 4:13 indicates that the retention of the covenant—that is, the retention of the land—depends on Israel's fidelity, expressed through conduct. Life in the land or the alternative, national death through its loss, is made to depend on keeping the second commandment, thus on the reality of Israel's worship of Yahweh, by means of which his *mysterium* is encountered (v. 15). Israel needs to remember that even Moses was excluded from the land for disobedience (vv. 16–24). So chapter 4 deals with the essence of the Sinai covenant, which requires obedience, in opposition to what the heady attractions of Canaan will present. Verses 25–31 are a sermon on the second commandment. Verses 32–40 return to the thought of 4:1–8 in a recollection of Israel's Sinai experience. At the same time they reinforce verses 25–31, pointing to the aniconic nature of the Sinai revelation. Deuteronomy 4:41–43 sets up three cities of refuge in Transjordan. Failure to obey the covenant will certainly bring exile (4:26–28).

The Essence of the Book (Deut. 5–28)

The introduction to Moses' second address appears in 4:44–49, in which "testimonies" probably refers to the Ten Commandments expounded in chapters 5–11. "Statutes" and "ordinances" refer to the legislation in chapters 12–26.

Deuteronomy 5–11 provides the central thrust of the book, and its content is decisive for those who would cross into the Promised Land. In these chapters, the community receives the Ten Commandments—the basic summary of community life (5:6–21)—and the Shema, which embodies all the commands of God (6:4–5); indeed, it provides the sum of all that matters in the relationship between God and people. Dean McBride (1987) has suggested that the purpose of Israel's law expounded in this section was to provide a constitutional center for her life and administration.

Moses bases what he will teach in chapters 12–26 on the covenant and its stipulations; chapters 12–26 must be secured on what appears in chapters 5–11. Deuteronomy 5:3 insists that the covenant continues to be made with succeeding generations of Israelites. So Moses insists that the covenant at Horeb was made with "us," not with the fathers, that is, the Sinai generation, and thus was made with subsequent generations as well.

The Ten Commandments, as direct revelation, are separated from other laws as the basis for the community codes derived from them. The Ten Words are unchangeable constitutional law laying out basic guidelines for living. The first two commandments are strictures against polytheism and images. The third commandment deals with misuse of the divine "name." For Israel, responsibility to God comes first, followed by responsibility to the neighbor. The Sabbath commandment is the bridge to one's neighbor in that it deals with relations to God and responsibilities in the human sphere. The fifth commandment, concerning the family, is also transitional, dealing with persons who, like God, are authority figures. The remaining commandments also move in order, from the taking of life to spouse to property, from an act against to a word against (false witness) to internal attitudes against a neighbor (covetousness). These attitudes may come out in actions such as killing, adultery, and stealing. The commandments are prohibitions, forbidding without stating the penalty. Though the Ten Commandments are community polity, given to all, each address is singular. This concern for Israel's moral government is basic to Deuteronomy as a whole, reflected in the provision for levels of leadership and governance and then in instructions about the responsibilities of leaders, all of which contribute to a theology of leadership.

In the Shema, 6:4–6, and its elucidation, the community receives theological structure that should continue throughout life. Such a structure operates on two axes: the relation between faith and love (or obedience) as set forth in the Shema, and the relationship to God and others as embodied in the Ten Commandments. The Shema, the great commandment that sums up the Ten Commandments, but more precisely the first and the second, calls on Israel to hear (v. 4) and love God (v. 5). In doing so, it forms a bridge between the commandments and the other laws (chaps. 12–26). Each Israelite was to recite the Shema every morning and evening; thus, the Shema was to shape daily conduct. Israel's loyalty is to the one, the only, God; to love is to be loyal to God. Deuteronomy 6:6–19 indicates how the Shema is to be kept, and these verses elaborate 6:5–6. But Israel's future lies in successive generations coming to this faith. Israel, therefore, must teach the faith to children in subsequent generations (6:20–25).

Deuteronomy 7:1–26 concerns the doctrine of Israel's election, whereby Israel is to have nothing to do with the present occupants of the land and their customs (vv. 1–5), because Israel is set apart (v. 6) and elect (vv. 7–11). If Israel responds, the opportunities for life are abundant (7:12–16). God will keep his promises, and Canaan will belong to Israel (7:17–26). But the Israelites are to destroy the Canaanite images of deity, lest these images corrupt them.

In Deuteronomy 8:1–20, Israel's obligations under the commandments devolve upon her daily. In the time of her prosperity she is to live by the great commandment. The command to remember—the key charge in this chapter—is reinforced by lessons from the past (vv. 2–6). Remembering, plus continued obedience, will produce thankfulness for blessing from the land (8:7–17). Remembering will bring blessing, but forgetting will bring destruction (8:18–20). Chapter 9 exhorts Israel not to misconstrue the conquests that Yahweh will give (vv. 1–6). As humans, the Israelites will forget. As their behavior from Horeb onward (vv. 7–21), continuing through the wilderness (vv. 22–24), evinces, the Israelites are basically stiff-necked. Only Moses' intercession (9:25–29) had brought them to Moab. Deuteronomy 10:1–4 relates the making of the second covenant at Sinai, verses 6–9 the death of Aaron and the setting apart of the tribe of Levi. Deuteronomy 10:12–22 mandates the reaction that should come from review of God's fidelity to promises made to the patriarchs. Deuteronomy 11 continues to range over the past, reviewing God's graciousness (11:1–5) and Israel's customary reaction—rebellion (11:6–7). But grateful remembrance of what has been done, together with obedience, will bring gifts from the rich and abundant land they are entering (11:8–17). Love of God, issuing into obedience, holds the key to the future of Israel (11:18–25). Israel must choose its future—blessing or curse (11:26–28)—alternatives to be dramatized on Mount Gerizim and Mount Ebal in this Promised Land (11:29–32).

Deuteronomy 12–28 constitutes Moses' third speech. For the most part (including chaps. 12–25), the speech applies the constitutional laws of chapters 5–11 to Israel's circumstances and social situation. Various proposals have been made about the interrelationship of the laws in chapters 12–25. Duane Christensen (2001, 223–24) has surveyed the material, concluding that:

> Deut. 12:1–14:21 = first to third commandments
> Deut. 14:22–16:17 = fourth commandment (Sabbath)
> Deut. 16:18–21:9 = fifth and sixth commandments
> Deut. 21:10–22:9 = seventh to tenth commandments

Deuteronomy 12:2–28 forms the interpretive crux of the book and the first section of chapters 12–28. This section has usually been associated with Josiah's reforms of the late seventh century, particularly because of the key prescriptions in 12:4–12 concerning the centralization of the sanctuary. But there is nothing in Deuteronomy that cannot go back to the pre-conquest period. Deuteronomy 12:1–12 provides a rationale and definition for correct worship of God, the first section (vv. 1–7) dealing with Canaanite practices and the second section (vv. 8–12) with how Israel is to worship in the land. The contrast is made with present worship (vv. 13–19), with an explication of right sacrifice (vv. 20–28). Deuteronomy 12:29–32 returns to the message of 12:1–3, the danger of worship to Canaanite gods.

Chapter 13 opens with legislation dealing with sedition and enticements to apostasy. Deuteronomy 14:1–21 moves from the demand for distinctiveness for Israel as the people of God to emphasis, through the laws concerning clean and unclean, on Israel's separateness from her political environment.

Deuteronomy 14:22–29 discusses the tithe and sacral dues to support sanctuary personnel. Deuteronomy 15:1–18 deals with sabbatical release for slaves and debtors, and 15:19–23 with the consecration of firstling males of the flock. Deuteronomy 16:1–8 enacts provisions for the celebration of Passover. Verses 9–17 prescribe the celebration of other yearly festivals (vv. 9–17).

Deuteronomy 16:18–19 prescribes the appointment of leaders, while verses 21–22 condemn Asherah worship. Deuteronomy 17:1 prohibits offering blemished animals; 17:2–7 refers to further apostasies and provides, by example, how a case is to be handled in fairness and with responsibility. Deuteronomy 17:8–13 refers to a central court of appeal staffed by priests.

Significant constitutional matters are dealt with in the third part (17:14–18:22). Kingship (17:14–20) is to result from divine choice, and the king is to rule as an obedient Israelite. Dynastic rule is assumed (see the mention of descendants in v. 20). A copy of the law is to be with the king at all times, since his reign is to reflect its precepts. Likewise, the Israelite priesthood is regulated (18:1–8), and the section concludes with identification of the true prophet (18:9–22) over against persons who might claim divine authority (magicians, diviners, and false prophets). The true prophet will act on divine initiative, not by use of the human devices mentioned in verses 10–11. True revelation will come through the divine word (v. 18). Two kinds of false prophet are differentiated (v. 20): one who speaks falsely and one who speaks in the name of other gods. Truth and consistency are the criteria of true prophecy (cf. 13:1–5).

Matters treated in 19:1–25:19 bring into relief the social policies that the covenant community is sworn to protect. Egalitarian justice is demanded. The issues range from the safeguard for property of the deceased, to protection of heirs, to help extended to the neighbor and animals, to the proper care of fruit trees, to codes concerning building safety. These statutes appear more wide-ranging, formally diverse, and discretely focused than legislation in the preceding textual divisions. This indicates clearly that humanitarianism must have a concrete application (McBride 1987, 242–43). Most of the statutes in this division deal with conflicts in which individual life, livelihoods, and personal liberties are at stake. Each member of the community, whether male or female, child or adult, native-born or sojourner, culprit or law-abiding citizen, landowner or laborer, refugee or slave, must be treated with dignity. The precise detail of the legal requirements show just how the covenant community was to affirm the worth of the individual. Such affirmation was remarkable in its age, an attitude that in itself set Israel apart as Yahweh's special people, manifesting Yahweh's holy will. This section of text shows in sensitive detail what it means to be a member of the covenant society.

Provision is made for cities of refuge, providing sanctuary so that revenge would not take place (19:1–13). Deuteronomy 19:14–21 deals with fraternal disputes within the community. Rules of war are discussed in chapter 20. Deuteronomy 20:1–9 deals with preparations for battle, verses 10–20 with behavior during a siege. Deuteronomy 21:1–9 shows concern for the purity of the land and for people threatened by an unsolved murder.

Deuteronomy 21:10–14 legislates for the rights of female prisoners of war. Relationships between parents and children are featured in 21:15–17, and the rights of a firstborn son are made precise. Deuteronomy 21:18–21 deals with the case of a stubborn and rebellious son and 21:22–23 with the burial of a hanged criminal. Deuteronomy 22:1–9 offers guidance on relationships with neighbors and prohibits men and women from wearing one another's garments. Verses 6–7 mandate care for bird life, and verses 8–9 contain building and agricultural regulations.

Deuteronomy 22:10–21 relates to a bridegroom's expectations in marriage and the penalty when these expectations are not met. Verses 22–30 contain prescriptions covering adultery, rape, sexual intercourse before marriage, and sexual perversion. Chapter 23 concerns purity in public worship (vv. 1–8), camp hygiene (vv. 9–14), and treatment of an escaped servant (vv. 15–16). Verses 17–18 prohibit prostitution and sodomy; verses 19–24 contain regulations covering usury, the necessary observance of vows, and respect for the ownership of agricultural produce.

The application of the seventh commandment (24:1–4) restricts remarriage after divorce. The exception to this (25:5–10) is Levirate marriage (Latin *Lever* = husband's brother), which is a safeguard for property of the deceased. Protection is provided against economic oppression (24:6, 10–15, 17–22). Loans in Israel were not commercial, but were designed to help the poor. Wages were to be paid promptly, while gleaning laws are to exhibit society's compassionate face. Deuteronomy 25 covers limits on corporal punishment (vv. 1–3), the protection of a working animal (v. 4), immodesty (vv. 11–12), just weights (vv. 13–16), and vengeance to be exacted on Amalek (vv. 17–19).

Deuteronomy 12–26 concludes with a liturgy at 26:1–15. Deuteronomy 26:1–4 focuses on liturgical expressions of gratitude for the gift of the land. Israel's story is told in 26:5–11 to indicate to future generations how God had dealt with Israel. The first-fruit offering in 26:1–11 and three-year tithe offering (26:12–15) prescribe liturgical acts of gratitude to follow possession of the Promised Land (26:1–15), bringing us back to the sanctuary as the institutional center of Israel (chap. 12). The covenant is reaffirmed in 26:16–19 with obligations taken on by the Lord and Israel.

Deuteronomy 27:1–10 requires recording and confirming the law at Ebal and Gerizim, and this is done later in Joshua 8:30–35. Encouragements and sanctions, blessings and curses occupy 27:11–28:68. The curse ritual does not promulgate new demands, for the deeds cursed were liable to the wrath of God. The curse brings into the legal sphere prohibitions whose violation in secret would escape the ordinary legal process, involving, through these covenant formularies, the inescapable vengeance of God. The blessings in chapter 28 have to do with three areas: land and people (vv. 3–5, 8, 11–12), victory over enemies (v. 7), and Israel's exalted place as God's people (vv. 1, 9, 10, 13). The blessings, as we might expect, are much longer than the list of curses, and traditional formulations are expressed.

The third address (chaps. 29–30) details the covenant affirmed following the instruction of chapters 12–25. The text divides into covenant superscription (29:1), historical prologue (29:2–9), parties to the covenant (29:10–15), and basic stipulations (29:16–19). Curses occur in 29:20–28 and preaching of repentance and restoration in 29:29–30:14, when the land has been lost. Finally, Moses closes with a call for Israel to choose fullness of life in the land, which would be the realization of the Abrahamic relationship (30:15–20). The choice between life or death is offered (vv. 15–18), witnesses are invoked (v. 19a), and a call for a decision is made (vv. 19b–20). So, in the plains of Moab, Israel's vocation is again set before her. The implications of the choice appeared in chapters 27–28. The differing ways of life that will result from obedience to or rejection of the divine will, and the blessings or curses that will flow from acceptance or rejection of the covenant, are laid out. The Israelite assembly must accept full accountability for its common life (29:2–30:20).

Since the language of inauguration (*karat berit*) is used, this covenant in the plains of Moab is generally seen as a new covenant, added to the Sinai covenant. This view is correct. Deuteronomy 29:11–13 deals with a covenant by which Israel binds itself to live together in the Promised Land; this agreement is based on the new regulations in Deuteronomy 12–26, added to and not previously included in the Sinai legislation (cf. Miller 1990, 200–201). Paul Williamson (2000, 200) errs in suggesting that the Hebrew *'br* in this section (Deut. 29:11) is a replacement for *karat*. Williamson proposes that *'br* is one of the many verbs that, in his opinion, could attest to covenant inauguration. However, careful examination of the contexts in which alternatives to the precise formula *karat berit* are suggested argues against Williamson's proposal. Here, God makes the covenant (29:11). Israel is to "enter" (Heb. *'br*) into it, now that it has been made. In verse 14, the covenant is again referred to by the traditional terminology (*karat berit*).

The emphasis in this section falls on Moses' departure and on how Israel will survive without his leadership. There are many allusions in the book to Moses' death and thus a strong interest in it. Moses will not accompany the Israelites across the Jordan River. But he will not leave them leaderless (31:1–6), for Joshua will oversee the conquest (31:7–8, 14–15, 23). Moses' guidance will be with them forever in the constitutional Torah (31:9–13, 24–26), together with its prophetic witness to its efficacy (31:16–22, 27–30), taken further in the prayer of Moses (32:1–47). Israel is to live by the Torah that Moses taught. The death of Moses is reported in chapter 34, after his blessing of the tribes in chapter 33.

Themes of Deuteronomy

The Promised Land

The land is not only the context in which blessing and life and prosperity take place. It is also the sphere in which Israel does what Yahweh desires and in which obedience will be visible (4:5, 14; 5:31; 6:12; 12:1). In 12:1, the law that is to follow is set in relation to the land. Disobedience leads to war, loss of land, and death (4:26). But law is also the norm for life in the land (4:5–49; 12:1; 17:14; 19:1; 21:1; 25:19; 26:1). Many laws are specifically associated with the land: the year of release (15:1–6); judicial procedure (16:18–20); law of kingship (17:14–20); law against abominable practices (18:9–14); cities of refuge (19:1–3); law against removing a neighbor's landmark (19:14); expiation for an unknown murder (21:1–9); law against leaving a hanged man's body on the tree (21:22–23); divorce law (24:1–4); and law requiring just weights and measures (25:13–16). An introductory or motive clause relating to the land appears in all these laws. Virtually all the blessings in Deuteronomy have to do with the land. Each member of the community must have access to the benefits of the land. Land and life depend on firm adherence to justice and righteousness.

While Exodus deals with Israel's redemption, Deuteronomy from the start sets the boundaries of Israel's Land of Promise (Deut. 1:7–8, where the boundaries detailed by Moses are substantially those of Gen. 15:18–21). Deuteronomy 1:10–11 continues the Abrahamic note with reference to the multitudinous character of Israel, leaving us in no doubt as to the theological bent of this last book of the Pentateuch.

The land is, on the one hand, God's bounty to Israel, hers by right. On the other hand, she must take it by conquest (Miller 1969, 455). The notion of a deity owning national territory was generally accepted in the ancient Near East. For Israel, this was a potentially dangerous notion, since she was entering territory whose owner was also considered to be Baal, the god of fertility, storms, and war. The capriciousness that characterized the blessings of the fertility deities in the ancient world is rejected in Deuteronomy 27–28 in favor of a system of blessings and curses, which followed respectively from covenant response or rejection. The book makes clear that Yahweh's ownership of Palestine arises from his sovereignty over all things, from his lordship of creation (Deut. 32:8–9 LXX). Since the land was Yahweh's, it could not be sold, and thus the rights of particular Israelite subgroupings were preserved by complicated rules of land tenure, namely, by the laws of the Sabbath and Jubilee years. To some extent these laws may always have been idealistic—they are detailed in Leviticus 25, but seem never to have been implemented—but they did preserve an understanding of Israel's right relationship to the land.

Promised Land as Sanctuary

The view of Canaan as God's Promised Land, in which Israel is to live as an ideal political unit in service to Yahweh, is developed further by a depiction of the land in Eden-like terms as a highly desirable and fruitful place (Deut. 8:7–9; 11:10–12) and as a sanctuary (cf. Exod. 15:17).

In these circumstances, as we might expect, the boundaries of the Promised Land are always carefully defined. This demarcation is always in terms of possessions west of Jordan. Such weight is placed on crossing the Jordan that the verb "to cross" can be used to express the actual conquest of the land (Deut. 6:1).

Since the land is viewed as a sanctuary, it is appropriate that a central shrine should have been designated, where the twelve tribes in regular festival pilgrimages were to recognize the nature of Yahweh's rule. It is often suggested that this law of the sole altar in chapter 12 indicates that Deuteronomy was the book discovered in Josiah's time (2 Kings 22:10–20). But it is clear that the material of Deuteronomy basically reflects an earlier period and that the law of the one sanctuary is a fundamental provision of the book.

Deuteronomy and the Altar Law

This law dominates chapters 12–26, appearing not only in law in which worship is a major theme (Deut. 12; 14:22–29; 15:19–23; 16:1–16, 21; 18:1–8; 26:1–15) but also in a law about the administration of justice (17:8–13) and in one worship context outside chapters 12–26 (31:11). The idea of the Lord's choice is always there, and this idea is often expressed by using the Lord's name to suggest the special association. Deuteronomy's altar law is commonly seen as having been put into effect in the Josianic reforms, representing the Jerusalem priesthood's victory over rivals from local sanctuaries. But Jerusalem is not named in the book. The language about Yahweh's name in Deuteronomy 12 and similar texts is, as has long been pointed out, an ownership formula, not a solution to the problem of transcendence versus immanence. That Yahweh's name—all that he is known to be—should be associated with the central sanctuary indicates that Israel's worship there is an acknowledgment of Yahweh's sovereignty. That the chosen place refers to one sanctuary is unlikely, although the intent is surely that, at any one time, Yahweh would have chosen one place for worship. Yahweh's remarks in 2 Samuel 7:6 suggest the continued mobility of the tabernacle prior to erection of the temple. It is probable that the position of the sanctuary was regulated by the association of traditional sanctuaries with certain festivals. The movement of the ark, if not the tabernacle to house it, was associated with festival celebration.

Perhaps the formula "the place which the Lord your God shall choose" (Deut. 12:5) establishes the principle of the sole altar but, for the time being, leaves the particular site undecided. In any case, the emphasis is on Yahweh's choice (McConville 1984, 31–32) and not on the place. It is noteworthy, in connection with the sanctuary, that the key chapter of Deuteronomy 12 opens (vv. 1–4) and closes (vv. 29–31) with a polemic directed against Canaanite gods. In Deuteronomy we probably have to distinguish between a central sanctuary and a sole sanctuary. Josiah's reform gives the impression of the desire to create Jerusalem as a sole sanctuary and not merely as the central sanctuary.

Idea of Rest

Bound up with the land is the important question of "rest." Rest signifies the firm possession of the Promised Land, free from all threats (Dumbrell 1994, 54). This concept of rest finds frequent expression (3:20; 12:9; 25:19) and is bound up with the notion of a pleasant life (15:4; 23:20; 28:8; 30:16). Israel is to enjoy without threat the blessings of creation in her Eden-like situation. Like

Adam in the garden, Israel is meant to enjoy the blessings of creation and to worship before God in ever-increasing awareness of the significance of the divine presence. Deuteronomy insists that only a correct view of Yahweh and a proper response to his gift can secure this rest. We are therefore not surprised to find that the important chapter 12, which deals with the centralization of the sanctuary, treats rest and sanctuary as interdependent notions (vv. 10–11). When Yahweh has given Israel "rest," he then "will make his name dwell" at the central sanctuary, guaranteeing Israel's presence in the land.

Holy War

Since the land, although a gift, had to be taken, the Book of Deuteronomy develops the important theology of holy war (i.e., of Yahweh). To express this truth, Deuteronomy commences with the awareness that the land can be Israel's only if Yahweh gives it to her. A theology of conquest arises, stemming, to be sure, from Israel's history, but more from the nature of Israel's deity. In this way, the tensions between the land as a gift and as an object to be conquered and possessed are resolved.

The spoil taken in holy war belonged to Yahweh; Israel was not to benefit materially from holy war. Spoil was thus put under the "ban," or devoted to Yahweh (Heb. *herem*), and thus was slaughtered or passed (in the case of metals, etc.) through the fire. On occasion, the enemy's men, women, children, cattle, and valuables are mentioned (Josh. 6:17). The ban appears to have been conceived as an acknowledgment of Yahweh's help.

Torah

The concept of *torah* is critical for Deuteronomy. Usually the term is understood as "teaching, instruction," but its meaning in Deuteronomy is stronger. Torah is covenantal law, the divinely authorized social order of Israel that attests its election. Deuteronomy is entirely about this law and the blessings that obedience to the law will bring. Thus 1:2–5 introduces the Mosaic memoirs of 1:6–4:40 and 4:41–43, and an editorial supplement follows, all leading toward promulgation of the Torah. The Decalogue is presented in Deuteronomy 5, summarized in 6:4–5, and expounded in the remainder of Deuteronomy 6–11. The remaining constitutional matters are set forth in 12:1–26:15 and then sealed and ratified (Deut. 26:16–19, 26–29). A two-part conclusion of blessings (Deut. 27) and curses (Deut. 28) follows. The Sinai covenant is amplified by an additional covenant in the plains of Moab (29:1–32:52), and the remainder of the book is epilogue.

Law and Love

Complementing law in Deuteronomy is the command to love God, which, in turn, is set against the background of God's love and choice of Israel. The totality of the law is thus comprehended in one demand (Deut. 6:4–5). Love, however, is more than mere affection or devotion. Love always appears in association with some activity: walking in the Lord's ways (10:12), keeping the

Lord's commandments (5:10), obeying the Lord's voice (13:4). Love thus demands that the person engage in practices that demonstrate covenant fidelity. We need to understand that Deuteronomy sets the context for love and the demands that flow from love. Israel is constantly reminded of her previous servitude in Egypt. Redemption has now made her a bond-slave to Yahweh. Deuteronomy also attends to fear as the appropriate inner response to Yahweh. Fear and love are sometimes set side by side, and thus seem to be used interchangeably (10:12–22), although, in NT terms, fear is closer to faith and love is closer to works. Trustful behavior (love) stemming from a changed heart (fear) is what Deuteronomy seeks.

Deuteronomic Humanitarianism

In essence, Deuteronomy is never interested merely in providing civil or social legislation by which the community may be regulated. From beginning to end, we are confronted with a preached ethic. Torah is expounded and explained in pronouncedly sermonic and exhortatory terms. Laws providing for civil regulation, settlement of civil suits, or property matters, which are dominant in Exodus 21–23, barely rate a mention (Weinfeld 1972, 282–97). The author centers his attention on human welfare, underscoring the laws that relate to human life and personal happiness. But humanitarianism in Deuteronomy stems from Israel's relationship to Yahweh. In keeping with this focus, the major statement concerning Yahweh—"The Lord our God is one Lord" (6:4)—is not a statement regarding God's essential nature, God's ontological indivisibility; rather, it concerns the exclusive demand that Israel's life and worship be directed to God. If Israel is centered on love for Yahweh, the humanitarian ideals with which the book abounds will readily fall into place.

Deuteronomy: A Summary

Primarily, Deuteronomy offers Israel life in the Promised Land, with such a life depicted as a return to Eden. But it is also a book about how the future for Israel may be secured and, as such, offers a central statement of OT theology. Its basic message is that when Israel breaks the covenant she will suffer sanctions for falling away from Yahweh. But even in exile (cf. Deut. 30), Israel's hope for the future concentrated itself in a national conversion or return to Yahweh, in a renewed hearing of his voice. Could the Sinai covenant be reconstituted by repentance if revoked by Yahweh in exile? As early as Deuteronomy 4:29–31, the book supposes a background of defection, perhaps exile. When, in exile, Israel searches for Yahweh with all her heart, she will find him and, in these latter days, Yahweh will let himself be found. Repentance will not be Israel's means of finding grace, but, in her extremity, if Yahweh's words find Israel, then Israel will be granted repentance.

An Overview of the Pentateuch

We see reflected in the Pentateuch's history of Israel both the possibilities provided for in Genesis 1–2 and the disappointments encountered in Genesis

3–11. In this sense, the remainder of the Pentateuch comments on Genesis 1–11. By the time that the covenantal theology of Israel is fully developed in Deuteronomy, a program to which the rest of the OT remains committed, the national failure of Israel has been anticipated. The Pentateuch makes clear, however, that this failure in no way vitiates the eschatology already developed in these books. A people of God will be constructed and will enjoy the ideal of rest in a Promised Land. God will be their God and will indwell them forever.

Part **2**

The Books of the Prophets:
The Former Prophets

6

Joshua

The book deals with the acquisition and maintenance of the land. It has a close theological relationship with the Book of Deuteronomy (Wenham 1971, 148); however, the emphasis within the Book of Joshua is on Yahweh—his fidelity to the covenant promises and his willingness to put them into practical effect. Joshua is an optimistic book: with the burials of Joshua and Eleazar, it closes on a note of an era successfully ended, inviting future generations to build on that success. In leading the conquest, Joshua is portrayed throughout as Moses' successor and as his virtual extension.

Conquest (Josh. 1–12)

Joshua 1

Joshua 1 sets the tone for the book by introducing the dominant themes, the gift of the land being the major item, although law and land (Mitchell 1993, 30) are constantly bound as the obedience required to respond to the gift. Verses 1–5 summarize the book (Hess 1996, 68). The crossing of the Jordan River in Joshua 1–5:12 is referred to, and the conquest is outlined (v. 3; cf. 5:13–12:24). Verse 4 implies the distribution of the land (13:1–22:3), and Joshua's death is anticipated. God gives the land because God owns the land (Lev. 25:23; Ps. 24:1), and God has granted it to Israel, God's tenants, to use for God's purposes. This is the meaning of verse 3. The tenants must fulfill certain conditions before they can have full use of the land (v. 2). They must take the land, but above all they must display full covenant obedience by keeping the Torah; they must, in effect, reduplicate the exodus/Red Sea crossing by crossing the Jordan, and they must be prepared for a dire struggle with the Canaanites. It was Joshua's role to see that the Israelites fulfilled these conditions. Israel must agree to a fair distribution of land among the tribes (v. 6), which looks forward to chapters 13–19. They must found a covenant society (v. 7, anticipating 8:30–35). It is clear that Israel will receive the land, because Yahweh will take it (v. 5).

Three times in Joshua 1, Joshua, in words similar to Deuteronomy 3:28; 31:7, 23, is told to approach the task with courage. Encouragements are given to face the Canaanites, to work with the people, and for Joshua to be a witness to Torah obedience (v. 9). God's promise to go with Joshua implies Joshua's readiness to go where God wanted him to go.

Joshua's task was to help the people possess the land (1:10–11). The people must cross the Jordan, which was, as it were, to recross the Red Sea. For the three-day period before the crossing, they must make provision for the journey as the exodus departure from Egypt had required (1:11; 3:2). The three days for purification and preparation and consecration are a reenactment of the waiting time before Sinai (Exod. 19:10–11).

The east Jordan tribes (1:12–15) were forbidden to settle in their numerous allotments until the land was conquered, for no group could occupy land without the others. Joshua reminds Israel that she was promised rest in the land (1:13), that is, secure possession of the Promised Land as the goal of the conquest. But this promise will always depend on the ready type of obedience that Israel had given Joshua at 1:16–18. The undertones of the book's holy-war theology emerge in chapter 1. Joshua has only to adhere to the relationship through trustful obedience to Torah precepts. The summary first chapter ends on this note. The end of Joshua 11 transfers the prospects held out in Joshua 1 into initial achievement. The theological summary of 11:23 reports that the conquest of which Yahweh is the architect has been completed, in response to the promises given to Moses.

Joshua 2–5

Chapters 2–5 deal with the extension of God's mercy to Rahab, who may also find a place in Israel through the mission of the spies (chap. 2). The crossing of the Jordan is presented in liturgical terms (chaps. 3–4). Rahab's confession, the focal point of the unit (2:9–13), focuses on the gift of the land and provides divine assurance of the certainty of the conquest in holy war.

The crossing of the Jordan, the barrier to the Promised Land, occurs in Joshua 3 and is given a cosmic dimension by mention of the ark of the Lord (3:13), the symbol of the Lord's presence. The crossing is seen as a divine progress, whereby a Sabbath day's journey was to be maintained between Israel and her priests, God's representatives. Israel's twelvefold number is mentioned seven times in chapters 3–4 (3:12; 4:2, 3, 4, 8, 9, 20). Memorials of the crossing are struck. Details of the order for crossing the river appear in Joshua 4. The circumcision in chapter 5 of the new generation born in the wilderness presents circumcision, not emphasized since Genesis 17, as a restoration to life—like a death and resurrection (5:8). This circumcision separates the new Israel from the disobedient, wilderness Israel. Not only does it mark Israel off from the inhabitants of the land, but it also ritually prepares Israel for conquest. The reproach of Egypt's slavery had been taken away. The term "nation" (5:8) is now used of Israel, since the territorial requirements for that title are about to be accomplished. The Gilgal Passover formally brings the wilderness wanderings to a conclusion, and thus the wilderness food, the manna, ceases (Josh. 5:10–12). The six Passovers in the OT each occur at turning points in history, constructing a bridge between the past and the future (Hamlin 1983, 36–37). Yahweh, coming as the conquering Divine Warrior to this newly constituted people (5:13–15), makes clear that this new land is holy. The conquest for a purified Israel is to begin. Yahweh's coming also makes clear that the conquest of Jericho to follow will be his and not Israel's.

The Conquest of Jericho (Josh. 6)

The conquest of Jericho, which calls for precise obedience to the divine commands, serves as a paradigm for the manner in which Yahweh will dispossess Canaan and make it sacred space. Jericho (chap. 6) is dedicated to Yahweh in an elaborate act of worship headed by the ark, again as the symbol of the Lord's presence. Jericho will be given as a divine gift to Israel, indicating the way in which the Promised Land will be occupied. The blowing of trumpets announces Yahweh's presence and, after the last circumambulation of the city, signifies its capture. The seven-day march around Jericho completes the seven-day celebration of the Gilgal Passover that had anticipated Jericho's conquest. Israel embarks on a holy war, not a war of conquest from which material benefits may be derived. This distinction is emphasized by detailing the requirements of the ban on taking possessions, mentioned six times (as a verb in 6:18, 21, and as a noun in 6:1, 17, 18 [three times]), whereby the spoils of conquest are to be dedicated to Yahweh. The institution of the *herem* ("ban") is designed not to counter a military threat but to counter a religious threat. The enemy cult and everything likely to contaminate Israel religiously are to be destroyed (cf. Deut. 7:1–5).

Joshua 7–12

The story of Achan and Ai (Josh. 7) serves as a quick reminder of what Israel will do if left to herself. The reading of covenant teaching at Mount Ebal (8:30–35), fulfilling Moses' instructions of Deuteronomy 27:4–8 exactly, appears to be the centerpiece of the narrative. It formally reestablishes Israel's covenant relationship in her new locality. From Mount Ebal, the narrative looks forward to the establishment of the Torah centers in the land (chap. 21), to the final summaries (23:6–11; 24:14, 23), and to the covenant ceremony at Shechem, after which a rededication ceremony is held, again reminding Israel of the centrality of Torah for success (8:30–35).

The ill-advised compact with the Gibeonites in Joshua 9 prefigures the type of unthinking political compromise in which Israel later indulged. The south and its city-states are then miraculously delivered to Israel. Yahweh, with the ban on material acquisition, this time completely observed (chap. 10), gives Israel success. The conquest of the north is recorded in chapter 11, and chapter 12 provides a list of defeated kings. The summary of the conquest in chapter 12 is presented in two sections, each introduced by "now these are the kings of the land." The first section refers to the territory in Transjordan—Moses' conquests—which includes the kingdoms of Sihon and Og (12:1–6), while the second section refers to Joshua's conquests, the territory in cis-Jordan (12:7–24).

Division of the Land (Josh. 13–21)

Chapters 13–21 detail the division of the land, defining precisely the relationship between God and Israel in regard to Israel's inheritance. Historical background can be provided by boundary descriptions that occurred in the ancient Near Eastern suzerainty treaties (Hess 1996, 47). In Joshua, the land is apportioned to tribes and families, but not to individuals. This apportionment phase likewise proceeds under divine direction. Chapter 13 emphasizes the generality of reporting in chapter 12, whereby much territory remained for Israel to possess in cis-Jordan. Joshua 13:2–6 is contrasted by an account of the complete conquest of Transjordan (13:18–23).

Chapters 13–14 report the use of the lot and thus express dependence on divine initiative. Various dating proposals—including the time of David's census (2 Sam. 24), of Solomon's administrative reforms (1 Kings 5), or of Josiah's reformation—have been advanced for these city and boundary lists, but Richard Hess has pointed out (1996, 248–49) that only during the Amarna age were regions demarcated in a way so closely resembling the tribal allotments of Joshua. Hess states that the argument for later dates for the lists points to continuity of use but not to origin (1996, 249). The borders of Joshua 13–19 appear to reflect traditions extending back to the Bronze Age city-states of Canaan.

In the stele of Merneptah (ca. 1230 B.C.), Israel is described not as a city-state, but as a separate ethnic group. No single population center gave Israel an identity, since the people were scattered across the hill country and beyond, inhabiting numerous small villages. The Song of Deborah describes Israel still as a collection of tribes. Joshua 13–19 does not know of developed cities that were administrative centers. Natural landmarks and villages described the boundaries. Joshua 13–19 records divine allotment of land, and the detail suggests that the territorial division was critical. The division defined the area of tribal responsibility, with Israel perhaps taking over Canaanite divisions.

Towns to which the inadvertent manslayer may flee for refuge are set aside (Josh. 20:1–9; cf. Exod. 21:12–14). Three are appointed within the Promised Land and three in Transjordan. The provision for Levitical cities at the end of the distribution (21:1–42) again focuses attention on the centrality of Torah teaching for Israel's tenure. The final conquest summary (21:43–45) is clearly related to chapter 1 and ties the whole story together. Joshua ends with the proclamation of Yahweh's rule over Israel.

The unity of Israel is the aim, despite the division that the Jordan has imposed (see chap. 22, which notes the Transjordanian tribes' ill-advised attempt to build an altar on the river's western bank).

Covenant Renewal (Josh. 23–24)

The farewell address in 23:1–16 shows that possession, inheritance, and security can only be complete and enduring with a personal and corporate commitment to love and serve God. A decisive point in the possession of Canaan had been reached, but the struggle would continue (23:13).

In this closing address, Joshua reviews the divine achievement (23:1–5), challenges Israel to absolute covenant obedience (23:6–11) that will bring blessing, and gives timely warnings (23:12–16) about disobedience that will bring national curse. Rest, in the sense of general occupation of the Promised Land, has been achieved (23:1). Although "very much land" (13:1) remains to be possessed, at least in broad terms Israel has been established in the land and is instructed how to keep it. Joshua addresses adherence to the Mosaic Law, the sole worship of Yahweh (23:6–8), the recognition of the land as Yahweh's gift (vv. 9–11), the maintenance of Israel's special character by avoiding intermarriage with other nations (vv. 12–13), and, above all, complete fidelity to the demands of the covenant (vv. 15–16). The book closes with covenant renewal and national rededication at Shechem. God's gracious work of redemption in Israel's history is rehearsed (24:2–13), and the covenant is concluded by ratification (24:14–27). Settlement in the land and the death of Joshua (24:28–33) conclude the account. The text also indicates that, with the deaths of Joshua and Eleazar, the leaders of the wilderness period, Israel faces another period of transition (vv. 29–33).

The Book of Joshua is a paradigm of the kingdom struggle that continues in every generation and is a sign pointing to God's ultimate victory over the powers that distort, subvert, and destroy life. Although written much later, the story is set in a period of social breakdown at the end of the Bronze Age and at the beginning of the Iron Age.

7

Judges

The Book of Judges recounts the results of Israel's failure to complete the mandate for conquest issued in Deuteronomy and Joshua. Judges 1 surveys the later geographical placement of the tribes (from Judah to Dan, south to north) and points to the pattern of irresolution, absorption of foreign elements, and gradual tribal disintegration that foreshadows the remainder of the book. At the close of the book (chapters 19–21), however, comes a movement toward recovering the unity that characterized the earlier conquest period.

Judges 1–2

In the main body of Judges (3:7–16:31), Israel lurches from crisis to crisis because of the apostasy inevitably produced by failure to separate from the land's inhabitants. Furthermore, Judges 1, resuming where the Book of Joshua left off, arranges tribal episodes in a south-to-north orientation to foreshadow the geographic orientation of the Judges cycle in 3:7–16:31. The Israelites in these clashes usually did not drive out the Canaanites, and only in one case is this attributed to inferior armament (1:19; cf. vv. 21, 27, 29, 30, 31, 33). We are meant to understand that these defeats usually were intentional failures. This was a deliberate violation of the older injunction that commanded the removal of the nations of Canaan. The climax was the failure of the Danites; not only did the Danites fail, but they themselves became oppressed.

Note the use of the verb "live" in Judges 1:1–3:6. Beginning with the tribe of Judah, there is an absence of any statement concerning Canaanites living in Judah. Canaanites are next said to be living among the tribes of Benjamin, Manasseh, Ephraim, and Zebulun (although Zebulun subjected them to forced labor). The tribes of Asher and Naphtali then are stated to have been living among the Canaanites, and finally Dan is oppressed by the Amorites. The narrator of Judges 1 has presented the narrative so as to emphasize this moral decline. In 1:1–2:5, success and failure are mixed, but the outlook is increasingly negative, a pattern mirrored in the book of Judges as a whole. Whereas 1:1–2:5 deals with Israel's military failure, 2:6–3:6 deals with her religious failure, providing a cyclical account to reinforce 1:1–2:5. The book's double introduction (1:1–2:5; 2:6–3:6) is balanced by a double conclusion (chaps. 17–18, 20–21).

The angelic messenger of 2:1–5 simply reinforces the message previously delivered through Joshua: covenant infidelity will inevitably bring judgment, for which the tribes must now prepare themselves. The superficiality of Israel's response to inspired leadership is pointed out in 2:6–10.

The sorry history of this period is summarized in 2:11–23. (1) Israel identifies herself with Canaanite society, indulging in apostasy. (2) As punishment, she suffers attacks from one foreign invader after another. (3) Yahweh exhibits his graciousness and fidelity to the covenant by raising up inspired leadership, or judges, by whom Israel is delivered. (4) After each judge's death, there is the inevitable spiritual lapse, with the resultant repetition of the cycle. This is the basic pattern of Judges 1–16. Chapters 17–18 deal with the migration of the tribe of Dan from the south to the far north and the tribal corruption of the period. A certain unity resurfaces as the tribes join in holy war against the offending tribe of Benjamin (chaps. 19–20). Judges concludes with the twelve tribes united, Benjamin reintegrated, and the cult at a central shrine. This shrine is Shiloh (chap. 21), which will be rejected in the early chapters of Samuel. Since the shrine's dubious character seems underscored by the tribal activities conducted there in Judges 21, the book's conclusion does not give the reader confidence in the future of Israel or in her capacity to overcome difficulties.

Israel's Judges (Judg. 3–16)

The core of the book contains the exploits of the heroic figures of the times, who are raised up by Yahweh to "save" Israel and who "judge" Israel thereafter, for the remainder of their lifetimes. The verb "judge" generally bears the wider meaning of the Semitic root for "administer," "govern," and "rule." Thus the heroes of the period (of whom the noun "judge" is rarely used) are authority figures and must be seen as governing Israel representatively on behalf of Yahweh, who is the true Judge (11:27). Such a conclusion is supported by the fact that the Spirit of Yahweh rushes upon many of the heroic figures (3:10; 6:34; 11:29; 14:6). I have argued in more detail elsewhere for associating the Spirit with divine rule (Dumbrell 1974). Divine kingship seems to have been exercised in this surrogate manner by these heroic figures.

In keeping with this emphasis on divine rule is the background of the judges themselves. Rarely do the judges come from influential families. Gideon was the youngest in his somewhat obscure family, and his clan the smallest in his tribe. Deborah was a woman, and thus a person to whom leadership would not normally have been entrusted. Jephthah was of very dubious descent and a bandit by profession. Only in the case of Ehud (3:15) is something resembling a genealogy presented. Again, none of these heroic figures seems to have been associated with a significant power base such as Gilgal, Shechem, Bethel, or Shiloh (Malamat 1976, 161–63). Deborah does not seem to have been considered one of the heroic judges. She is the only major personality in the book to be engaged in the service of Yahweh—a member of the institution—before her call. Yahweh does not, as in the case of the other judges, raise her up. She is not spiritually empowered as are Othniel (3:10), Gideon (6:34), Jephthah (11:29), and Samson (14:19; 15:14). She is not said to "save" Israel. Deborah goes on campaign with Barak, but she does not head the force, and she is not associated with the battle.

Indeed, Israel during this period was also judged by a number of men about whom no heroic narratives have been written. It is customary to point to two lists of what are called minor judges (10:1–5; 12:8–15), limited personal details about whom are presented in a stereotyped fashion. It is unwise, however, to conclude that these men are lesser figures or that they exercised a different function during the period. Generally speaking, the same terminology is used of them as is used of the so-called major judges. In 10:1–2, for example, Tola "arose to deliver Israel" and "judged Israel." Probably a principle of selectivity has operated in the presentation of this epoch's materials, as seems clear from the fact that we encounter twelve judges in the book. Commencing with Othniel (chap. 3) and concluding with Samson (chaps. 14–16), the order of judges is geographic by tribe of origin, ranging from Judah in the deep south to Dan in the far north (the final position of this tribe after migration). No tribe contributed more than one major judge, and in each case the foreign aggressor differs.

Israel in the Judges Period

It is also customarily suggested that the Book of Judges describes merely local incidents involving isolated tribes. However, no OT book uses the term "Israel" or the phrase "all Israel" more frequently in relation to its length. From beginning to end, we are concerned with what will happen representatively to "all Israel." Since each local event in a small territory like Palestine inevitably influences the whole, each event assumes an "all-Israelite" dimension in the writer's mind.

In the book, the authority of the judge always transcends both his or her tribe and locality. In any case, as noted, local incidents in such a small area would have quickly assumed national significance. The case for a confederacy of twelve tribes—united in entry into and exit from Egypt, recipients of the Sinai covenant, and involved together in conquest—is made first in the detail of the early Historical Books, including Judges. A confederacy is also required, moreover, to account for the Israel that we see united in Samuel's period, in a request for kingship.

Of particular importance is the last deliverer-judge, Samson. Barry Webb (1987) has argued that the point of Judges is embedded and culminates in the paradigmatic Samson narrative. There is complete affirmation in the narrative of the theophany controlling Israel's affairs. Israel does not cry for deliverance, although the enemy dominates Judah (15:11). Samson, the judge-deliverer, compromises his Nazirite vows (14:1–2), as Israel has continually put the Sinai covenant at risk. Philistine technical superiority could destroy Israel, but when it looks as if Israel is finished, Yahweh intervenes in the culminating Samson narrative. Samson is the blind captive and looks impotent, but at the darkest moment God engineers a great victory through him. Samson's amazing victory stresses God's universal sovereignty.

Samson also foreshadows Israel's history. Called to be a Nazirite in utter separation to God (cf. details in Num. 6), he is committed by a lifelong vow. Since Judges has been shaped by a final redactor to foreshadow Israel's history (see Judg.18:30–31, which points to an exilic date for the final edition), we are reminded that Israel's calling was for an unspecified period. But Israel, like Samson with Philistine women, harlotry, and apostasy, had continually flirted with the world. This leads for Israel, as it must for Samson, to captivity; Israel is held captive by her enemies. The last king of Israel, Zedekiah, like Samson, had his eyes gouged out (2 Kings 25:7; Judg. 16:21). By so shaping the narrative, the author has been able to warn Israel of the reason for the exile, namely, unfaithfulness to the covenant. But he also could give the exiles reason for hope. Samson's hair grew in captivity (Judg. 16:22), that is, he looked like a Nazirite at the end. The deterioration in the period of the judges may be seen in the stark contrast between the last judge, Samson, and the first, Othniel, whose marriage to Acsah was exemplary (1:11–15; 3:7–11). Samson, like Israel's leadership, needed both strength and moral firmness if covenant ideals were to be preserved. The two triumphs for Samson occurred when the Lord helped him (15:9–20; 16:23–31), but faith, which triumphed in the end, was achieved through brokenness and prayer. Samson's victorious death lays the foundation for future deliverance.

Judges concludes with two stark accounts that emphasize the sordid character of the period. The blatant apostasy of Micah (chaps. 17–18) is no worse than the picture of institutional religion in chapters 19–21. The depraved Shiloh sanctuary of chapter 21 provides the setting for the early sanctuary narratives of 1 Samuel 1–4.

Above all, Judges affirms theocracy as the only model of government. Yahweh is Israel's king, and he can be counted on to raise up human deliverers to preserve the nation's future. Even flaws in human deliverers do not defeat Yahweh. Israel's destiny is not in human hands, but in the hands of Yahweh the living God. Thus there is no need for Israel to rely on human kingship.

The Purpose of Judges

The book's final verse—"In those days there was no king in Israel; every man did what was right in his own eyes!" (21:25)—appears at first sight to affirm that the unity of Israel, a significant issue for the writer, can be preserved only by the type of political movement to be undertaken, that is, the move from a tribal society to an urbanized society under dynastic kingship. The difficulty about such a view of 21:25 is that kingship as an office is roundly condemned within the book itself. Gideon, the great hero of Israel, pointedly refuses kingship, dynastic kingship in particular (8:23). In doing so, he draws attention to the reality of Yahweh's kingship, which must always be recognized by Israel and from which the earthly office that Israel wished to bestow on Gideon presumably would have detracted. Kingship is ridiculed in the fable of Jotham (9:7–15) as an ambition at which only charlatans and adventurers aim. The only "king" in the Book of Judges is Abimelech, the half-Canaanite son of Gideon. Abimelech brutally seizes power after the death of his father and exercises an abortive reign in Shechem. That reign is the antithesis of judgeship. What in Abimelech's story receives emphasis—family background, establishment of institutional government, mercenary backing, and power base—receives no mention in the cases of the other heroic figures who are the book's successes.

Perhaps the concluding comment of Judges 21:25 is to be taken another way. The Book of Judges is inextricably bound up with the view of history propounded by the Former Prophets (Joshua through 2 Kings), who were critical of the kingship exercised within Israel (and later Judah) up to the exile, even though the prophetic movement endorsed the theological aims of the Davidic covenant. Thus it is likely that the general antimonarchical stance of the Former Prophets is reflected in Judges, since the Former Prophets' view of Israel and its infidelity is clearly evident. What Judges 21:25 may be reflecting is the remarkable persistence of Israel, notwithstanding her sustained apostasy and her continued attempts to undo herself. It is remarkable that, after such a chaotic period, when the people did what was right in their own eyes and when social abuses were glaring, Yahweh was still not prepared to give up on Israel. But just as during the preceding period, it would be Yahweh—and he alone—who would account for Israel's continuance.

The Book of Judges emphasizes the character of Israel as a theocracy. Everything in these bizarre accounts commends God's direct leadership of God's people as the sole guarantee that Israel will have a future. The real judge behind the scenes is Yahweh (11:27). It always had been and always will be the kingship of God that sustains the nation. The sad truth is that, because of Israel's neglect of Yahweh's rule, prompted largely by the inopportune and inadvisable behavior of her kings, Yahweh will finally give up on Israel and give her over to exile. But as the Book of Judges concludes, Israel still has a future. The closing verse foreshadows human kingship. It is another matter, however, whether it commends it. It merely sees Israel approaching a new phase in its political future. For the character of that future we turn to the Books of Samuel.

8

Samuel

The Books of Samuel provide a natural continuation for the Book of Judges. We begin the two books with action located at the corrupt shrine of Shiloh, staffed by a degenerate priesthood. The quiet piety of Hannah (1 Sam. 1) provides a fitting contrast to the censured conduct of Eli and his two sons, Phinehas and Hophni. We conclude 2 Samuel with David's purchase of the temple site from Araunah the Jebusite (2 Sam. 24) and are thus on the threshold of the shrine's permanent movement to Jerusalem. This movement from Shiloh to Jerusalem reverses the prevailing worship situation in 1 Samuel 1–3. Since worship, as already noted, is the official response in the cult to Yahweh's kingship, such a movement involves a progressive renewal of divine authority. The Books of Samuel thus operate as a theological endorsement of the kingship of Yahweh, rejected so frequently by Israel during the period of the judges. In these books, the offices of Israelite prophecy and kingship also emerge, making plain that the function of these two offices is to contribute to a correct understanding of Yahweh's relationship to Israel.

Samuel's Roles (1 Sam. 1–3)

In 1 Samuel 1–3, the later ministry of Samuel as prophet, priest (a term never specifically applied to Samuel), and judge of Israel is anticipated. As priest, Samuel is apprenticed to Eli at Shiloh. As the replacement for Eli, he is Israel's judge (see 4:18). As the last of the judges (note Samuel's role in chap. 7), he ushers in the monarchy and draws the era of the judges to a close. But it is upon the note of prophecy that the first three chapters, which introduce Samuel, end. This note is in itself clear evidence of a reversal of a situation in which there has been "no frequent vision" (3:1). The pointed comment on Eli's failing eyesight (3:2) may suggest his responsibility for the absence of frequent vision. The author had indicated that there was still hope for renewal within Israel when, in 1 Samuel 3:3, he reports that the lamp of God in the tabernacle had not gone out. First Samuel 3:1–3 sets the scene for Samuel's call (3:4–10). These first three chapters move from despair to hope, with this movement reflected by the parallels between Hannah's barrenness in chapter 1 and the opening of the prophetic word through Samuel (Janzen 1983, 91). We can conclude that this reversal is to be effected by the word of Yahweh in prophetic pronouncement. It is noteworthy that the Song of Hannah focuses on the theme of reversal (2:1–10). The narrative prepares us for Hannah's full speech of 2:1–10, which presents the basic theology of the book. She recalls Israel's history in terms of Yahweh's interventions, and she voices Israel's long-term royal hope. As Walter Brueggemann has pointed out (1990, 41), the transformation of Hannah from affliction to speech anticipates and prefigures the transformation of Israel from historical marginality to international possibility.

The Song of Hannah constitutes the interpretive key for all that follows. This is the song about powerful inversions caused by Yahweh, and such inversions become the perspective from which the rise of David can be understood. Childs (1979, 274) has suggested that 22:1–51 forms the counterpart to 2:1–10, as poetry that gives voice to Yahweh's role in the life of Israel. In this way, the details of the song provide a theological introduction to the two books of Samuel, just as the poetry at the end of 2 Samuel (22:1–23:7) sums up. In these poems, the pious assert that the real power in Israel's life and history belongs only to Yahweh and not to the king or to any other human agent. First Samuel 1–2 introduces a larger narrative, as Luke 1–2, the narrative of Jesus' birth, introduces Luke's Gospel and Acts.

Since the books have much to do with the establishment of messianic kingship as representative of divine rule, it is appropriate that 1 Samuel 2:1–10 should end on that note. This theme is not unexpected, in view of Deuteronomy 17:14–20; consider also the promise given to the barren Sarah (Gen. 17:16) in a situation somewhat analogous to that of Hannah.

The Ark of the Covenant (1 Sam. 4–6)

Chapters 4–6, from which Samuel and, thus, his corrective leadership are absent, consider another facet of divine leadership in the fortunes of the ark. It is clear that the hand of Yahweh, experienced formerly in the exodus and now turned against Israel (see 1 Sam. 4:3, 8; 5:4; 6:11), had brought about the Philistines' successive victories over Israel. Yahweh's intervention results in the prophesied death of Eli and his house (2:34) and in the "exile" of the ark. Yahweh thus virtually withdraws from the Promised Land, in what the writer interprets as a reverse exodus. Yahweh has gone into exile, leaving Israel in the Promised Land. Again we are left wondering whether the people of God have a future (A. F. Campbell 1975, 83).

Our doubts are temporarily removed by the return of the ark at the conclusion of 1 Samuel 6. But the penalty inflicted on the inhabitants of Beth-Shemesh, who gaze into the ark, indicates that there is mystery about Yahweh that will always rebuke Israelite presumption or attempts at manipulation (6:19–20). The ark remains at Kiriath-jearim for the next twenty years, on what at that time was virtually the border of Israelite-occupied territory within Canaan. The ark resides within the household of Abinadab, who, ominously, is the father of the ill-fated Uzzah of 2 Samuel 6:3. Its return under David (2 Sam. 6) will inaugurate a new theological era, just as the voluntary exile of Yahweh concludes the period of the judges.

Kingship (1 Sam. 7–12)

Chapters 7–12 introduce the Israelite monarchy. In 7:6, we see Samuel operating as the last judge of Israel, as the architect of victory who saves Israel from external aggression and then protects her internally by wise administration (vv. 14–15). In view of these details, the request for a king in chapter 8 is baffling, although kingship is expected and has been sanctioned. Paradoxically, however, Samuel's family has gone the way of the house of Eli (8:1–3). The elders of Israel put the request for a king in terms that provoke the tensions of the next few chapters. "Appoint for us a king to govern [Heb. 'judge'] us like all the nations," they say (v. 5, repeated in vv. 19–20). That this request echoes the anticipation of Deuteronomy 17:14 does not lessen the difficulties that the request provokes.

Yahweh grants the request (1 Sam. 8:22), but the request has an inherent incompatibility that events and dialogues of the next few chapters are given to resolving. The basic difficulty is the nature of the kingship that the elders have in view. Kingship like that of the other nations would be dynastic, bureaucratic, tightly regulated, and thus antithetical to the concept of judgeship with which the request was linked (cf. v. 5). Dynastic kingship would eliminate from Israel Yahweh's spontaneity and direction, which judgeship had provided, thus cutting the cord of such spiritual guidance by providing for an ordered succession. Moreover, the demand to be "like the other nations" carries with it a virtual unilateral withdrawal from the Sinai covenant, which mandated Israel's difference from the world. Israel in the future will be tempted to look for deliverance from its king, ignoring leadership from the kingdom of God, and this would be its covenantal undoing. As noted, the phrase "like the other nations" is used in Deuteronomy 17:14, but there only Israel's demand is presented and responded to correctively by Moses (vv. 14–20). Samuel presents the issue of Israel's requested kingship before the people. Kingship of this character, says Samuel, will mean a continuous "take" by autocratic kings from Israel (1 Sam. 8:11, 13, 14, 15, 17). Nevertheless, after Samuel's speech, the demand of verse 5 is again presented (v. 20).

The Sinai covenant (Exod. 19:3–6) had foreshadowed a separated Israel, who would witness to her world through her distinctiveness. Clearly the demand for kingship as other nations have identifies Israel with the world and must be adjusted to become compatible with covenant. The statement "make us a king to judge us" illustrates Israel's failure to recall the theocratic nature of the judge's appointment and her inability to see that such a request was incompatible with kingship, which would, in the manner of Israel's world, be dynastic. We shall see that this adjustment is achieved by the time we reach 1 Samuel 12. The matter is resolved in two ways within these chapters, after Samuel first outlines the implications of Israel's request (chap. 8). First, in chapter 9, the office of prophet as an ongoing institution is brought into being. The call of Samuel to exercise this function—verse 9 seems to refer to the change in status and designation of Samuel from that point onward—is a direct rejoinder to the request for kingship. The call seems designed to ward off any threat to Israel's covenant base, a threat that kingship may present. Samuel's prophetic role in relation to the emerging kingship of Saul is clearly designed to provide checks and balances whereby kingship, with all its dangers of independent action, would not put the covenant at risk. The struggle of prophecy and kingship, of spiritual goals versus political aims, characterizes the subsequent history of Israel until the exile of north (722/721 B.C.) and south (587/586 B.C.).

The second movement in 1 Samuel 9–12 comes by the gradual integration of kingship itself into a covenant office. This movement happens in two ways. First is the development of a theology of kingship that separates kingship from the surrounding models that had so heavily influenced the elders of Israel. While there is nothing inherently wrong with the office itself (cf. Deut. 17:14–20), the model chosen by Israel from the surrounding world would always put the covenant at risk. The sequences in both the choices of Saul and David need to be noted carefully (Knierim 1968, 30–32). Since what happens to Saul and David is not repeated elsewhere in the OT, an ideal framework of kingship is being erected in their calls. Saul is divinely selected (9:16), brought to the prophet by whom he will be anointed (10:1), and is endowed for his office with the Spirit (vv. 6–13). Finally, Saul is publicly affirmed by his victory over the Ammonites (chap. 11). Similarly, David is selected (16:1), anointed by Samuel in the midst of his brothers (v. 13), and receives the Spirit for rule (v. 13). The Spirit then leaves Saul (v. 14), indicating the transfer of authority and thereby making clear that, in Israel, the gift of the Spirit is bound up with the office of leadership. Finally, like Saul, David is affirmed before all Israel (chap. 17).

In both cases, the anointing constructs a relationship between the king and Yahweh, not between the king and people (Mettinger 1976, 191), whereby the Israelite king is then called Yahweh's messiah. While the term "messiah" merely means "anointed," in the OT the word becomes specialized to refer to Davidic kingship in Israel; thus, it forms a set of expectations that finally leads to Jesus of Nazareth, king of Israel (John 1:49). Performed by Yahweh's representative, anointing here seems to be, as in the rest of the ancient Near East, authorization for office (cf. Exod. 29:6–7; Lev. 8:9–12, for somewhat similar analogies). Though anointing is occasionally referred to until the exile—especially where succession is contested (Malamat 1968, 140; see 2 Kings 23:30)—and thus seems to have been practiced, no northern king after Saul is ever called messiah to indicate the king's precise relationship to Yahweh. Establishing the close personal relationship that it does, anointing may have involved a contractual obligation. It seems, in any case, to have provided authorization to act. Following the anointing, the king is Yahweh's representative, his messiah. David's continued use of "messiah" in referring to Saul (1 Sam. 24:6, etc.) indicates that only Yahweh could abrogate the relationship, just as he had begun it.

With the erection of the office of kingship, then, an undergirding theology of ideal kingship has been supplied. We have come to expect office and theology to develop together as OT institutions are formed (cf. the priesthood). The office of messiah is thus not one that grows out of disappointment with the empirical monarchy, a psychological improbability in any case, but arises with the advent of kingship itself. The four elements—choice, anointing, gift of the Spirit as empowerment for office, and mighty acts publicly recognized as fitness for office—are not again associated with kingship beyond Saul and David, until we arrive at the ideal kingship demonstrated in the ministry of Jesus of Nazareth (Knierim 1968, 43–44).

The second way in which emerging kingship is integrated into the covenant is seen in the narrative structure of 1 Samuel 11–12. After Saul's victory over the Ammonites, Israel assembles at Gilgal (11:14–15) to "renew the kingdom" ("kingship," NIV). Saul's kingship is not being referred to, since it has so far not suffered a threat, and the verb "renew," where used this way elsewhere, means to repair something already in a state of deterioration (cf. Isa. 61:4; 2 Chron. 15:8; 24:4, 12; Ps. 51:12; 104:30; Job 10:17; Lam. 5:21). The context suggests that it is in fact Yahweh's endangered kingship over Israel that stands in need of renewal. Since this assembly is called together at Gilgal, the first point of entry into Canaan and the place where the "new Israel" was then convened (Josh. 5:2–9), the appropriateness of the site for the occasion is obvious. Saul is indeed made king in this context (11:15), but only after Yahweh's kingship over Israel has been renewed in verse 14 (Vannoy 1978, 81).

First Samuel 12 also seems to occur at Gilgal (no change in site is indicated) and focuses on renewal of the covenant. Though the monarchy is now a matter of fact and its existence cannot be undone—for God, after all, had approved of it—Samuel aims to reduce its importance in the eyes of the people and to reassert their dependence on Yahweh and on his own good auspices. The narrator wished to make clear that the monarchy did not come by public initiative, from dazzling personalities or because of socioeconomic or military power, but because of the will of Yahweh. Far from being his farewell speech, chapter 12 outlines Samuel's continued role as Israel's intercessor (vv. 23–25) and thus as the ultimate guide of the new order. With 1 Samuel 12, kingship of a modified character has been grafted into the Sinai arrangement.

It is clear from chapters 13–15, however, that the experiment with Saul has proved a failure. While the breach with Samuel appears to be minor, Saul defies the order to wait until Samuel comes to Mizpah (chap. 13). In chapter 14, Saul is overly circumspect religiously, thereby alienating Israel in the matter of his food taboo and the proposed death of Jonathan. In chapter 15, the Lord's instruction to destroy the Amalekites brings Saul and Samuel into sharp conflict, with Saul initiating a clear breach of the holy-war code in the matter of objects and persons spared. The issue, however, that clearly divides the two personalities is that of relative authority. Kingship must submit to prophecy; the contemplated office of kingship requires divine guidance for success. We understand, therefore, the necessity of a further theological movement of the type embodied in 2 Samuel 7. Saul had been the people's desire, but the people's desire for this type of kingship had been ill-founded. God disapproved of the nation's desire, necessitating a new model for kingship. But in a fallen world, human kingship is inevitably flawed (8:10–18).

David's Rise to Power and the Davidic Covenant (1 Sam. 16–2 Sam. 7)

David's rise to power (1 Sam. 16–2 Sam. 5) may be passed over quickly. These chapters deal with the patient manner in which David waits for power and the gradual dissolution of Saul as a personality, until his death in 1 Samuel 31. The chapters also lay the groundwork for the essential network of personal relationships that David exploits once he comes to power. These chapters are also concerned to distance David from any complicity in the fall of the house of Saul and from the passage of Saul's kingdom to David (McCarter 1980, 499).

After the capture of Jerusalem in 2 Samuel 5, most of Palestine falls into David's hands. This territorial expansion follows David's anointing by Israel to be its unifying king (v. 3). The Philistines, Canaanites, and others are incorporated into his growing empire. Fortified by this success, David attempts in chapter 6 to bring the ark back from its exile in Kiriath-jearim and thus to centralize all of Israel's sacral traditions in his new capital. He draws rebuke, however, for this move is blatantly political. Later, escorted by the necessary Levites, the ark returns to the center of Israel's religious life—but only with Yahweh's sanction. This return spells the rejection of the house of Saul, a step made clear at the close of chapter 6 by the dismissal of Michal, Saul's daughter.

Chapters 6 and 7 are fundamental. The former treats divine rule from Jerusalem by return of the ark, while the latter treats an enduring dynasty for David. Thus we have divine kingship in view under the guise of concern for the proper lodging of the ark, in a temple that will betoken Yahweh's kingship. We also have as an issue the Davidic dynasty and, thus, of royal stewardship toward the temple. This pattern, of temple (and thus divine kingship) in 2 Samuel 6 and of dynastic kingship in chapter 7, conforms to the ancient Near Eastern order, whereby provision of a residence for the deity must precede provision for the city-state ruler, who is a servant of the deity.

David, who is given "rest" from enemies as a precondition of building the temple, indicates a desire to build a house in which Yahweh may dwell. "Rest," "house," and "dwell" (2 Sam. 7:1) form the keywords of the chapter, and great play is made on these terms. David is first refused permission to build the temple, with the reasons advanced in 2 Samuel 7:5–7. The refusal is not absolute, however, and thus not a prophetic victory over the more centralizing priestly forces, for Solomon later receives permission to build (v. 13). Second Samuel 7 concerns the basic role of David as the giver of the political rest that stems from the completed conquest (Carlson 1964, 119). As the chapter progresses, it is clear that the rest from enemies "round about" of which verse 1 speaks is inconclusive, since the real blessings from occupancy of the Promised Land have not yet been produced. Under David and the conquests that lead to empire (chaps. 8–10), control over Palestine is finally realized politically. Thus the conquest begun by Joshua but left incomplete by the judges (7:11) will be completed. Second Samuel 7:8–9a reviews David's career to that point, leaving no doubt of the exalted station to which he has been elevated (note the language of vv. 5–7: David as Yahweh's "servant" is Israel's shepherd).

In 2 Samuel 7:9b–11, David's prospects are considered. (1) Yahweh will make "a great name" for David (v. 9b, clearly reminiscent of Gen. 12:2 and the Abrahamic promises). (2) Yahweh will appoint a "place" for Israel—"place" is the distinct term in Deuteronomy for the Promised Land, particularly as outlined in the promise to Abraham (cf. Deut. 11:24 with Gen. 15:18). (3) Yahweh will then give David rest from all his enemies (v. 11; Carlson 1964, 116–17). In short, David's greatness must be established, Israel's living space determined, and the conquest completed before Yahweh will erect his sanctuary. The Jerusalem temple will then testify to the sanctity and the divine ownership of the Promised Land. But Yahweh himself will build the temple, since he will provide the circumstances on which construction will depend: the riches of empire previously conquered by David and the accession of Solomon the builder. The refusal of 2 Samuel 7:5 thus defers temple building until Yahweh has acted further. It also operates as a mild rebuke, for this temple is not a static dwelling that Yahweh will inhabit (note "dwell" in v. 5). Yahweh will not be confined in houses built with hands, for the heaven of heavens cannot contain him (1 Kings 8:27). Nor can a person build such a house. Note Yahweh's question in 2 Samuel 7:5: "Would you build me a house?"

The eternal character of Davidic kingship is established in absolute terms (2 Sam. 7:13b). Thus the necessary steps beyond Saul's interim kingship have been taken. The remainder of 2 Samuel, which is largely given to more somber presentations of David, who is involved in court intrigue, family difficulties, and so forth, reminds us that the promise of continuity establishes the office and not David the man and his physical line. The OT thus oscillates between describing the Davidic covenant as eternal (the word "covenant" is not mentioned in 2 Sam. 7, but appears in 2 Sam. 23:5; Ps. 89:33–37) and as conditional (1 Kings 2:4; 8:25; 9:4–5; Ps. 89:29–32; 132:12). Such oscillation is designed to draw a distinction between, on the one hand, the promises and blessings to David that would not fail and, on the other hand, the punishment and fate of specific individuals within the line of promise. In physical terms, the line of David foundered in 587/586 B.C. with the fall of Jerusalem, but, in spiritual terms, a promise such as 2 Samuel 7:13 directs us to look to New Testament Christology for ultimate fulfillment.

The tenor of David's prayer in 2 Samuel 7:18–29 indicates the degree to which he has understood the nature of the divine commitment made in the first half of the chapter. Particularly puzzling, however, is David's summation of what has preceded: "this is the law for man" (v. 19 rsv, marginal note). In view of the extrabiblical parallels for this phrase, the meaning is best taken as "this [i.e., the detail of the first half of the chapter] is the manner in which human destiny is to unfold" (Kaiser 1974, 314). The thrust of the Abrahamic promises operative through Israel has been revealed as, henceforth, bound up with Davidic kingship.

Empire and Division (2 Sam. 8–20)

In 2 Samuel 8–10, the Davidic empire is extended. David is presented as the architect of conquest; thus preoccupied, he could not be the temple builder (1 Kings 5:3; cf. 1 Chron. 22:8; 28:3). Solomon, as the man of rest (1 Kings 5:4), will be the temple builder. His prosperity is an index of the conquest sanctified and the Abrahamic promises fulfilled, at least in Israel's political history (note the Abrahamic tenor of 1 Kings 4:20 and 5:4, where the Solomon era is seen as the great age of fulfillment). David never secured the ideal borders of the Promised Land (Tyre and Sidon were never included in the Davidic empire). This might suggest that the scheme of 2 Samuel 7, according to which temple building is to follow conquest, is an idealization never translated into biblical reality.

Indeed, we recognize that 2 Samuel 11–20 is given to the depiction of David's fall from grace and to his essential human weakness. Through David's actions, discord is sown among members of David's family and between north and south. The thrust of these chapters is to deflate the character of David, just as 1 Samuel 16–2 Samuel 5 was to idealize it. The final chapters of 2 Samuel indicate that the Davidic promises would not be fulfilled by sound political management, but only by the intervention of Yahweh in the history of salvation. Second Samuel 9–20 and 1 Kings 1–2 have commonly been termed the succession narrative and have been viewed as dealing with the problems of dynasty. But this view overlooks that David is at the center of 2 Samuel 9–20 and that the Books of Samuel are more concerned with temple and divine kingship than with David's own reign.

The Temple Site (2 Sam. 24)

The final four chapters of 2 Samuel are carefully structured. They begin and conclude with narratives that emphasize the fragility of the Israelite monarchy (Saul's in 21:1–14, David's in chap. 24). Second Samuel 21:15–22 and 23:8–39, heroic narratives related to the Philistine wars and military lists, bracket a central poetical section (22:1–23:7) offering a theological summary of the two books. Chapter 22 follows David's rise to power and implicitly offers reasons for the rise, while 23:1–7 presents the Israelite king as the ideal Israelite, ruling by the fear of God and thus bringing blessings and life. Chapter 24, which includes David's ill-advised census of Israel, followed by the purchase of the temple site, concludes the books. The mention of Uriah the Hittite at the close of chapter 23 prepares us for the outburst of divine anger that the census provokes against David. Political realities had seduced David to number an Israel that could not be numbered (perhaps he had a standing army and taxation in view). David, Israel's shepherd, is then smitten through his flock. As shepherd he must make sevenfold restitution (cf. 24:15 with 18:3; see Carlson 1964, 204). When the plague visited on Israel and David has been stayed, the temple site is chosen and purchased under Yahweh's direction. The books close by underscoring the sovereignty of Yahweh in Israel's affairs and in the unfolding of her history.

In summary, 1 and 2 Samuel concern Yahweh's sovereign conduct of Israel's affairs and inform us how difficult and indeed impossible it was for Israel to recognize Yahweh's sovereignty. The movement between the two books is from sovereignty ignored (1 Sam. 1–3) to sovereignty expressed (2 Sam. 24), from an indifferent response to divine kingship (1 Sam. 1–3) to the required response to divine kingship (2 Sam. 24). First and Second Samuel place before Israel a future as the people of God. The Books of Kings will comment on how the opportunities afforded to Israel were transferred into historical reality.

9

Kings

The Books of Kings chronicle the growth and development of the Davidic empire from the economic greatness and political influence under Solomon, to the decline and fall of kingship in Israel as a result of two exiles. The details of the book have been carefully selected (cf. 1 Kings 11:41; 14:29) and theologically exploited since reference is made to the historical sources (Book of the Acts of Solomon, Book of the Annals of the Kings of Israel, etc.) from which they are drawn. God's will for Israel in the decline and fall of kingship is traced from Solomon's great potential to the final caricature of kingship, illustrated by the elevation of Jehoiachin at the Babylonian court in 2 Kings 25:27–30. Solomon's reign (1 Kings 1–11) witnesses the transition to dynastic kingship, accompanied by all the difficulties foreshadowed by Samuel. Within the two books, the building of the Jerusalem temple (1 Kings 6–8) provides a sound theological basis for the continuance of Davidic monarchy, just as the political factors of Solomon's reign threaten to destroy it. Solomon's autocratic apostasy presages the demise of empire in 2 Kings 25. First Kings 1–2 and 11:14–43 frame the account of the Solomon monarchy. First Kings 1:1 supposes continuity with what has preceded. Chapters 1–8 present Solomon favorably. There is, in 1 Kings 1–8, a progression of accession and consolidation, efficient administration and skillful diplomacy, palace and temple construction, international commendation, and unrelieved prosperity. First Kings 9:1–11:13, however, underscores his faults, which lead to the division of the kingdom. First and Second Kings will make it clear that no human king can lead God's people, not even the second David, Josiah. During the building of the temple, at the height of the monarchy, we are made aware of the fallibility of the human players. How can the dynasty succeed if there is no man who does not sin (8:46)? Yet at the conclusion of the reign (1 Kings 11:36), the permanent validity of the Davidic promise (2 Sam. 7) is reasserted.

First Kings 1–2 narrates Solomon's ascent to the throne legitimized by prophecy (cf. 1 Kings 2:24 and Nathan's role in 1 Kings 1:22–27). His consolidation of power as the summit of monarchical achievement follows and concludes with the summary statement that the kingdom was secure in Solomon's hands, indicating the potential that Solomon's reign could express. This statement of 1 Kings 2:46, however, is followed by an ominous anticovenantal political notice concerning Solomon's marriage to Pharaoh's daughter (3:1a), who lived in the city of David (1bα), a statement that Solomon had not yet completed his secular and religious building projects (1bβ), and a notice concerning the people's sacrificing at the high places because the temple had not yet been built. First Kings 3:1–2 reports building projects, although it notes the building of Solomon's own house before the temple, which raises questions of Solomon's priorities. The report in 3:2 of the continued worship at high places and the continued lack of a central sanctuary, raises further initial questions about the significance of Solomon's reign, and his reign proves to be a violation of the Deuteronomic kingship ideals. First Kings 1–2 and 3:1–2 provide the necessary background to the inevitable decline into which Solomon's reign sinks.

The dreams of 3:1–15 and 9:1–9 are the main structuring devices of 1 Kings 3–11. The divine promises accorded to Solomon (3:10–15) anticipate the writer's presentation of Solomon's reign. First Kings 3:16–5:18 presents a nation and its king flourishing together. This judicial and diplomatic prowess follows on from Yahweh's Gibeon revelation to Solomon. First Kings 4:1–5:18 champions not only Solomon's judicial talent but also his administrative abilities, notably, in the interests of absolute monarchy. Solomon breaks up the older tribal structure of Israel (1 Kings 4—the only tribal names recorded are Ephraim, Benjamin, Naphtali, Issachar, and Asher), dividing the realm into twelve economic districts, significantly excluding Judah (4:19, though the LXX includes Judah) from any financial contribution. The appointments include two of Solomon's sons-in-law (4:11, 15), pointing to the nepotism of the times whereby friends and family were favored in clear covenant breach. This favoring of the south and the gradual depletion and surrender of territory in the north makes Solomon the architect of the later divided kingdom. But the narrator makes it clear that Solomon is now ruling over a political Israel (Judah and Israel, 4:20), which, in fulfillment of the Abrahamic promises, is as many as the sand by the sea and is enjoying a tremendous surge of economic prosperity. Israel, in reaching the summit of its national political success, now begins the inevitable slide down to the nadir of the exile.

As Solomon's realm takes on international dimensions, his capabilities keep pace. His knowledge is as vast as the sand upon the seashore (1 Kings 4:29), his renown extends far beyond the borders of his land (1 Kings 4:31), and his wisdom is greater than all the people of the East and greater than Egypt (4:30). Solomon becomes, as a prodigious sage, the inaugurator and patron of Israel's wisdom movement (4:32–33). His trading alliance with Hiram of Tyre (5:1–12) and his coordination of Israelite labor resources, specifically in the interest of the building of the temple, demonstrate Solomon's wisdom.

The Temple

The construction of the temple took seven years (Solomon's palace, thirteen years). In the temple the Sinai and Zion traditions would coalesce. The temple, by its building, would register the completion of the conquest and end the exodus. The placement of the ark in the temple sanctuary brings the divine response of the exodus-cloud filling the temple. This movement of the ark brings the period of the exodus to a formal close, with all political goals having been achieved. The Sinai and Davidic covenants are now formally linked together. The temple would provide the Promised Land with a national shrine (cf. Deut. 12), thereby securing the elusive promise of "rest" and the firm possession of the land. The building of the temple is presented as the culmination of Solomon's wisdom, providing the basis for the development of the relationship between Yahweh and the people, which Israelite kingship was obligated to foster.

First Kings 6:1 dates the building of the temple to 480 years (LXX 440) after the exodus, more or less the halfway mark between the exodus and exile and thus the high-water mark of Israel's Old Testament history. But at the beginning of the project (1 Kings 6:11–14) the fulfillment of the Davidic promises and the divine presence within Israel is made to depend on Solomon's obedience, not on the existence of the temple.

The temple inaugurates a new era in Israel's cult (1 Kings 8). Its dedication is the high point of Israel's cultic history. The dedication commences with the transfer of the ark into the temple (8:1), and ends with Solomon extolling the promises to Moses (v. 56) and leading all Israel in the celebration of the Festival of Booths. First Kings 8:1–13 initiates proceedings, Solomon offers preliminary remarks (8:14–21), prays (8:22–53), and concludes the ceremony (8:54–61). The temple was completed in the eighth month (Bel, 6:38), but its dedication was held over until the seventh month (of the next year), indicating the carefully planned character of the occasion. The Feast of the Tabernacles, the occasion of the temple dedication, was biblically associated with covenant renewal (Deut. 31:9–13). Solomon plays a priestly role, convoking the elders of Israel, supervising the elevation of the ark, blessing the people, interceding for the people, twice offering sacrifice, consecrating the middle court before the temple, and leading Israel in the observation of the "festival" (1 Kings 8:65). The role of the king is thus to sustain, defend, and protect the Jerusalem cult. The installation of the ark, the repository of the covenant statutes, as Israel's central cult item in the holiest of holy places (Yahweh's throne room), legitimates the temple. The somewhat strange mention of the "poles" for transportation protruding from the ark (8:8) may indicate that such poles provided a visible object lesson of the portability of the ark, and were a warning against presumption in the matter of the divine presence (Seow 1999, 70). The temple thus becomes a tangible witness to the fact of God's kingship and a permanent symbol of Israel's kingdom of God government. A magisterial theophany confirms the sanctity of the new institution. Just as God appeared to Solomon at Gibeon, setting the stage for Solomon's initiatives, so God appears to Solomon following the temple's dedication confirming Solomon's work. The temple becomes the new point of divine revelation. Timing the temple's dedication to coincide with Israel's major festival of the Feast of Tabernacles lent an aura of respectability and tradition to Solomon's new sanctuary. The temple, however, is not the place where God is, but rather the place where God's presence may be known (Seow 1999, 72). God is enthroned in heaven, not in the temple, and even the heaven of heavens cannot contain him (8:27).

The temple is also a public validation of the Davidic dynasty (1 Kings 8:14–21). Solomon explicates Yahweh's promises to David (vv. 15–21), commending his father's intentions. Jerusalem and David are the clear subjects of divine choice. As a further covenant initiative, all Israel participated in the dedication so that the temple becomes central to the history of the Israelite people. Monarchical obedience, in the Books of Kings, is measured in terms of deference to the temple. The Torah, however, is not dismissed or devalued. Indeed, the penalties for national disobedience are rehearsed in 8:31–53. Solomon prays that the temple would function as an inducement toward fidelity (1 Kings 8:57–58). God's presence in the temple is neither a mechanical association nor guaranteed. The Hebrew verb used (*shakan*) speaks for a temporary and occasional location, not a permanent enthronement, which would demand the Hebrew *yashab*. In the closure (8:54–61), the blessing for all Israel, which proper attitudes toward the temple will convey, is asserted.

Post-temple Activities (1 Kings 9–10)

Following the narration of God's second appearance to Solomon (1 Kings 9:1–3), the potential for blessing, which has come about through the building of the temple, is qualified—first for Solomon in the second dream of 9:1–9 by the demand for integrity and uprightness (9:4–5), and, second, by the demand of obedience from Israel (9:6–9). Otherwise the temple will be cut off, the land given to Israel surrendered, and the nation scattered for neglect of its covenant with God (9:9).

First Kings 9–10 does not begin to depict Solomon's decline, but evaluates his heightened success and building projects. Early in Solomon's reign, nations had brought tribute (4:21). First Kings 9 codifies Solomon's international successes. Hiram dispatches 120 talents of gold as his payment for ceded northern Israelite territory (1 Kings 9:14), and Gezer is given to Solomon by Egypt (9:16) as a marriage dowry. Illegitimate forced labor (1 Kings 9:15, 20–21) enabled massive building projects (9:15–23). Solomon's bureaucracy created jobs for Israelites as warriors, attendants, officers, and leaders of his chariotry (1 Kings 9:22). Hiram and Solomon's joint expedition nets Solomon the enormous sum of 420 talents from Ophir (probably East Africa; 1 Kings 9:28). The fortification of cities governing trade routes ushered in a new era of increased wealth and tribute from other states, so that Solomon also received 666 talents of gold annually, enabling prodigious expenditures and a lavish court style (1 Kings 10:14–22). In addition, all the kings of the earth sought Solomon, each bringing yearly tribute (1 Kings 10:24–25). Additional building projects proceeded. Rounding off 1 Kings 10, verses 26–29 deal with Solomon's horses. Verse 27, in the middle of the account, signifies that this new stable establishment was a further example of Solomon's extraordinary wealth.

The visit of the Queen of Sheba was undoubtedly the premier example of the international adulation of Solomon's splendid kingdom. This was seminal for the later Israelite eschatology of a universal pilgrimage of the world to Jerusalem. The queen becomes the paradigm for the later nations, by blessing Yahweh for placing the Davidic representative on the throne of Israel to render justice and righteousness (10:9). In coming to Solomon and acknowledging the source of his wealth, influence, and wisdom (10:9), the Sabean queen, the ruler of probably the largest trading empire of its day, brought her world with her (10:24). Her visit and her acclamation of Israel's God were a confirmation of the promises to Abraham (Gen. 12:3). This provided inspiration for the later prophetic vision that saw Gentile kingdoms coming into Jerusalem to receive wisdom and Torah from Yahweh's shrine. The summary of Solomon's accomplishments in 1 Kings 10:23–24 confirms his peerless status. Solomon was greater than all the other kings of the earth in riches and wisdom. First Kings 10:23–24 comprises an *inclusio* marking the end of Solomon's initiatives, as the dream revelation at Gibeon had begun them.

The Fall of Solomon

First Kings 11 marks a new and negative stage in Solomon's rule. A stunning set of reversals in 1 Kings 11 contrasts with the tone, mood, and content of the earlier chapters, most noticeably 1 Kings 3. First Kings 11 details the results stemming from the divided state of Solomon's heart (v. 4). Solomon goes from experiencing triumph over his enemies (1 Kings 1–2) and enjoying the absence of adversaries (1 Kings 5:4) to experiencing the covenant curses in the shape of his adversaries (1 Kings 11:14–25). Finally, Solomon suffers prophetic opposition (11:29–38) and not prophetic legitimization (1:11–14, 23–27, 38–40). First Kings 11 points to the legacy of the Solomon reign as providing a decisive turning point in the history of Israel. The charges leveled against Solomon plainly associate him with Israel and Judah's worst kings. The divine wrath manifested in 1 Kings 11:9–10 is followed by the judgment: division of the kingdom (11:11–13) as a punishment for covenant breach. First Kings 9–11 refers to frequent and blatant violation of the Deuteronomic warning (Deut. 17:16–17) against economic and political temptations in the form of horses, wives, and wealth. Significant loss of territory occurs (Edom, potentially, 1 Kings 11:14–22; Aram, 11:23–25; and, to come, the north, 11:26–40). Such revolts are presented as divine retribution in 1 Kings 11, but it is clear that they characterized much of the reign (11:25). Solomon's punishment is ameliorated, however, because of the oath to David. The dynasty will survive, and Solomon will not live to see the division of the kingdom (1 Kings 11:34).

Evaluation

Solomon's reign was the great age of the fulfillment of promises. The nation, in Abrahamic promise terms, had become a great nation, now too numerous to be counted (3:8; 4:20). Israel now occupied the covenantal boundaries from the Euphrates to the border of Egypt (1 Kings 4:21), save for Phoenicia, which in itself nullified David's achievements, and had achieved rest from her enemies all around (cf. 4:21). The building of the temple fulfilled the structure of national institutional covenant obedience. Nevertheless, these gifts were not to be compared with the incomparable national loss of faith under Solomon, concurrently with the erection of Israel's greatest kingdom of God symbol.

Now the older tribal democracy gives way to new royal nobility. The new array of foreign alliances flies in the face of the older holy-war theology, which demanded faith in Yahweh's person for Israel's protection. The north is eventually sundered from the south by the ill-advised concentration upon the south and by the location of resources there due to an emerging Egyptian threat. The north was virtually abandoned, and valuable trade routes surrendered to the emerging Aramean states. Solomon's policy of forced labor (5:13; cf. 9:20–21) strikes at older concepts of egalitarianism. Extravagant building projects and the taxation measures associated with them, as well as the sale of Israelite territory (9:10–14), alienated the north (Halpern 1974, 522). However, in all the human failures that documented Solomon's monarchy, God's will was being inexorably worked out.

A Divided Israel (1 Kings 12–13)

The kingdom, rife with potential divisions, is torn from Solomon by the prophetic movement based in Shiloh (11:26–40). After Solomon's death, only two tribes remain in the south—Judah and (probably) Benjamin. The division occurs in chapter 12, where Jeroboam, the one-time forced-labor supervisor in the north, capitalizes on the ineptness of Solomon's son, Rehoboam (ca. 922–915 B.C.), and leads the northern ten tribes into secession as the kingdom of Israel. Under Rehoboam, the first successor to Solomon, the people did what was evil in the sight of the Lord (1 Kings 14:22), a contrast with the Davidic ideal. Rehoboam, who could not tell what was good advice, suffered the forfeit of ten tribes to the new north and the retention of only one in addition to Judah (either Benjamin or Simeon).

The religious moves of Jeroboam (ca. 922–901 B.C.) in chapter 12 seem to have been artful gestures to draw support from the older sacral traditions familiar to the average Israelite and traceable to the exodus and conquest period. Jeroboam, in setting up alternative cultic institutions to Jerusalem in the north, identified the two calves (12:28) with the God of the exodus. Two shrines are set up, at Dan in the far north and Bethel in the extreme south of the new kingdom of Israel to discourage pilgrimages to Jerusalem, a non-Levitical priesthood is established in the north, and probably the festival calendar dates were changed. However, the prophetic editor is not impressed with this attempt to return to a pre-Jerusalem tradition of multiple sanctuaries and sees Jeroboam's moves as tantamount to a repetition of Exodus 32 (cf. 1 Kings 12:28 and Exod. 32:4). This rejection of Jerusalem by the north comes as the great apostasy of the period, and keeps south and north apart thereafter. So Jeroboam's "gods" are polytheistic and idolatrous. For the prophets, Jeroboam's cult revives and perpetuates Aaron's Exodus 32 apostasy.

The prophetic rebuke and dismissal come for Jeroboam in 1 Kings 13, and exile for Israel is to result (1 Kings 14:15). The sin of Jeroboam would determine the future of Israel. The house of David and Jerusalem is reaffirmed in the strange but symbolic chapter of the disobedient prophet (13:1–10); then the theme of obedience to the voice of true prophecy is highlighted (vv. 11–34). It is clear that Josiah is to be the second David, the restorer of the kingdom and the reviver of the fortunes of empire, bringing north and south together again, as his ancestor had done (13:2).

The prophetic movement continues to be active in the affairs of the apostate north. The prophetic word brings down successive northern dynasties—Jeroboam's (Jeroboam ca. 922–901 B.C., his son Nadab 901–900 B.C.); Baasha's (Baasha ca. 900–877 B.C., his son Elah ca. 877–876 B.C.); and Omri's, commencing after the brief interlude of Zimri (2 Kings 16:8–16, Omri, ca. 876–869 B.C., Ahab ca. 869–850 B.C., Ahaziah ca. 850–849 B.C., and Jehoram ca. 849–843/2 B.C.). The house of Omri was brought to an end in about 842 B.C. by Elijah's word pronounced through Elisha (19:16; 2 Kings 9:1–2). Jehu's dynasty of four (Jehu ca. 843/2–815 B.C., Jehoahaz ca. 815–802 B.C., Joash ca. 802–786 B.C., and Jeroboam II ca. 786–746 B.C.) is also brought to an end by prophetic assault (cf. Amos 7:9), while Hosea and Amos announce the fall of the north itself. The duration of the northern reigns are synchronized with the contemporary southern kings. At the end of each northern reign, there is a reference to archival material drawn upon and an evaluation.

The southern monarchies receive little credit from the author. Of the next kings after Rehoboam, Ahijah's reign (ca. 915–913 B.C.) of three years is undistinguished other than by a divided heart (1 Kings 15:3), but the Davidic promises continued and were nevertheless maintained (1 Kings 15:4). In spite of infidelity, the perpetuation of the Davidic promises becomes the story of the southern monarchy during most of the years of the division. Asa (ca. 913–873 B.C.) began the movement of reform in Judah. Both Asa and Jehoshaphat (ca. 873–849 B.C.), his son, were reforming kings, generally judged righteous, that is, covenant keeping. The assessment of Asa (1 Kings 15: 9–15) is qualified because of a failure to remove the high places (v. 14a). Jehoshaphat is also, basically, covenant keeping (1 Kings 22:41–44) but suffers the negative judgment that he made peace with the king of Israel (i.e., Ahab's Israel), also concluding a marriage alliance with the north. The influence of Ahab on Judah long survives his death. Jehoram (ca. 849–843 B.C.—the same name as Ahab's son) and Ahaziah (ca. 843/2 B.C.), his successor, were related to Ahab via Athaliah, the usurper queen (ca. 843–837 B.C.) and a granddaughter of Omri (2 Kings 8:16–18, 25–27). Her son, King Ahaziah, in alliance with Jehoram of Israel, was slain by Jehu (ca. 843/2–815 B.C.; 2 Kings 9:27). So Ahab's influence lived on in

Judah particularly in the interregnum of the queen mother Athaliah. Her grandson Joash's (ca. 837–800 B.C.) purification of the cult indicated a break with the house of Ahab, and thus with the north. But the reform was always short-lived. For Joash (2 Kings 12:17–19) also buys off Aramean Hazael with temple gold and subsequently suffers assassination. Amaziah (ca. 800–783 B.C.), basically a good king, made overtures to the northern Jehoash, but the move leads to a war and a defeat for Judah that seems to be the fruit of the king's misguided policy. Amaziah himself was assassinated. Azariah (Uzziah), his son, reigned for forty-two years (783–ca. 742 B.C.) in a politically successful reign but a reign that led to the corruption with Judah that Isaiah faces at the beginning of his prophetic mission (cf. Isa. 1:11–20). Jotham, his son (ca. 742–735 B.C.), succeeded him. The intrigue-ridden reign of Ahaz (735–715 B.C.) follows, in which Judah becomes an Assyrian puppet, a situation later to be redeemed by the reforming Hezekiah.

Elijah and the House of Omri (1 Kings 16–2 Kings 1)

Omri, a significant early king of Israel, founded a dynasty of four. The biblical writer barely devotes six verses to Omri, though a century later in Assyrian records the kingdom of Israel was still called by his name. We must not interpret this lack of detail regarding Omri, however, as indicating a lack of interest in history on the part of the writer. The Books of Kings are prophetic works, a theological interpretation that displays a sense of what was ultimately important for the history of the people of God. Omri's foreign policy called for the restoration of good relationships with Judah, close ties with the Phoenicians, and a strong hand against the east and north. Omri consolidated his position with a marriage pact uniting Jezebel, the daughter of the king of Tyre, with his son Ahab. A further alliance between Israel and Judah involved the marriage of Ahab's sister (or daughter) to Jehoram (ca. 849–843 B.C.; 2 Kings 8:26), son of Jehoshaphat, king of Judah. Omri defeated Moab. The times seem to have been a period of great economic prosperity and expansion for both north and south (1 Kings 22:44–50), but with an inevitable religious decline, especially in the north (arrested, to some extent, in the south by the reforming Jehoshaphat).

During the reigns of Omri and Ahab, great surrenders were made to foreign religious influences, particularly to the worship of Baal of Tyre. Ahab built a temple for Baal in Samaria as part of a chain of concessions made to Canaanite interests (1 Kings 16:32). He married Jezebel, an ardent Baal worshiper and the daughter of the king of Sidon. Such compromises provoked a religious crisis in Israel. In chapter 17, in response to the growing syncretism, Elijah suddenly appears on the scene from the Transjordan region. Elijah throws down the gauntlet, and the issue of Yahweh or Baal (a choice which may well have puzzled the average Israelite, who seemed to have identified Yahweh with Baal) is settled on Mount Carmel (chap. 18). The call by Elijah for undivided allegiance to Yahweh is virtually a recall to the Sinai relationship (note the tenor of 18:21), and thus to covenant renewal for the north. Elijah's challenge is met by silence on the part of the spectators. Then Yahweh himself asserts his sole sovereignty, as he had done on Sinai, by fire in a spectacular theophany (v. 38). Like Moses at Sinai, Elijah turns the sword on the apostates (v. 40), having made clear the indivisibility of the people of God (vv. 30–32) by his selection of the twelve stones to repair the older altar.

The national question having been settled, 1 Kings 19 directs us to the inner life of Elijah himself. His life now sought by Jezebel, he turns back for strength to the source of Israel's original experience, to Sinai itself. Sustained by an angelic presence, he finally reaches what seems to have been the scene of the original theophany to Moses, at an analogous phase in that great man's ministry (note "the cave" in 1 Kings 19:9 [Heb.]; cf. Exod. 33:22, seemingly the cave of Exod. 33:22). We note the obvious Mosaic posture in which Elijah is cast throughout the narratives.

The new theophany that Elijah receives assumes a different form. It entails a divine question as to the reason for Elijah's journey to Sinai and Elijah's response that he is the sole believer amongst an otherwise apostate Israel (1 Kings 19:10). Accompanying (but not constituting) the theophany are the traditional elements of earthquake, wind, and fire, in which there is no direct divine manifestation. Heralded by the spectacular elements, the divine appearance comes, as expected, after them in what the Hebrew text designates "the voice of drawn-out silence" (v. 12). But the repetition two verses later of the same question by God and answer by the prophet (cf. 1 Kings 19:9–10, 13–14) indicates that Elijah has heard nothing. We should not interpret this incident, as some have supposed, as the replacement of strident Baalism by the still, small voice of prophecy, since the effect of the theophany is unperceived by Elijah and the prophetic voice is neither still nor small. Nor does it signal the end of the drama in Israel's experience of Yahweh, since the theophany tradition continues throughout the OT. However we may interpret this passage, the eerie phenomena drew Elijah out of the cave to be questioned a second time as to the reason for his return (v. 13).

We may draw two conclusions. First, since nothing is heard from the encounter related in 1 Kings 19:11–13, we may assume that Yahweh has nothing further to add to what was delivered upon Sinai in Exodus 19–34. Second, by implication, Elijah would have been better employed by being about the kingdom's business elsewhere (1 Kings 19:15–16). In any case, he does not carry the spiritual burden alone. The notion of a godly remnant, a unit within the nation, is now brought into prominence for the first time in the OT. There are seven thousand who have not bowed their knee to Baal (v. 18).

With this incident, the place of the Israelite prophet as an international figure begins to emerge. Elijah is commissioned to anoint Hazael king of Syria and Jehu king of Israel. Elijah is also to anoint his successor (the only attested case of prophetic anointing in the OT). Clearly the purpose is to present Elisha as an extension of Elijah, authorized by Elijah through this extraordinary anointing for office. The remainder of the narratives in 1 Kings largely concern the conduct of Israel and Judah in concert in the Aramean wars. We note, though, Elijah's firm adherence to Pentateuch law in the matter of the sale of Naboth's vineyard (1 Kings 21), the unsavory episode that brought about the demise of both Ahab and Jezebel. First Kings 22:19–23 reports the religiously significant heavenly council vision of Micaiah ben Imlah, where the prophet is both spectator and auditor (cf. Isa 6:1–13). Yahweh is imaged in the manner of an earthly monarch surrounded by his counselors and retinue. Such heavenly visions become a feature of prophetic affirmation of commission.

2 Kings

By the extensive space devoted to the ministry of Elijah and Elisha at the center of the two books, the importance of prophecy to the welfare of Israel is stressed. After the ministry of Elijah had been extensively covered, virtually the first third of 2 Kings represents an extended description of the ministry of Elisha. The activity of prophecy in the monarchical period is underscored by reports in the early chapters of 2 Kings of "the sons of the prophets" (2:3, 5, 15, etc.)—the term used in the OT to denote prophetic activity in different periods, without any necessary relationship between the groups being referred to. The centrality in these two books accorded to the work of prophecy during the monarchical period emphasizes its key role. In 2 Kings 1, Ahaziah, who challenges prophetic authority, dies without progeny. The climax of the first two chapters of 2 Kings is the ascent of Elijah in 2:11, witnessed by Elisha (2:10, 12), whose rightful succession as Elijah's heir (cf. his request for a double portion of Elijah's spirit, 2 Kings 2:9) is confirmed by this witnessing of Elijah's rapture. He assumes the mantle of the departed prophet (2:13) as his successor. Elijah's departure would signal a great crisis for the people of God, very much like that of the departure of Moses (Josh. 1:1), for Israel and Joshua. Elisha is very much a second Elijah, and his crossing of the Jordan in 2:14 back into the Promised Land implies that he is now in charge of Israel. Indeed, an expression of contempt for Elisha (2 Kings 2:23–25) elicits a covenant curse, uttered by Elisha, in the light of proclaimed covenant intention (cf. Lev. 26:22) of the judgment of God for profanation of Israel's covenant leadership. All the Elisha miracles stamp him as Elijah's successor by their parallel with the Elijah miracles of 1 Kings (cf. the analogies of Moses to Joshua and Christ to the disciples). The long arm of Elijah reaches to the revolt initiated by Elisha, in which the usurper Jehu brings down the house of Omri and the last vestiges of Baalism in the north (chaps. 9–10).

During the reign of Omri, the Moabite stone tells us that Israel had strengthened its hold on Moab. But for the last quarter of the ninth century, Syria assumes a major role in the west, eventually to be replaced by Assyria and Babylon. The death of Shalmaneser III (824 B.C.), whose interests lay outside of the west, and who had conducted his last and abortive campaign in the west against Damascus, introduced a period of comparative quiet in the west. The years between 838 and 806 (the advent of Assyrian Adad-Nirari) marked the period of Assyrian absence in the west in which the kings of Syria, Hazael and his son Ben-Hadad II, were free to engage Israel, Jehu, and Jehoahaz. Syria thus took substantial territory from Israel, reducing Israel to insignificance (2 Kings

13:7). But Adad-Nirari's campaign in the west in 806 relieved Syrian pressure on Israel, making him Israel's "savior" (2 Kings 13:5) during the last days of Jehoahaz. Assyria's western expeditions continued until 802. The entire west became tributary to Assyria. After the death of Adad-Nirari in 803, Israel, under Joash, son of Jehoahaz, was able to inflict defeat on Syria. Jeroboam II was later to reverse the earlier loss of Transjordania to Hazael of Syria (2 Kings 10:32–33).

Jeroboam (ca. 786–746 B.C.), son of Joash, is depicted in seven verses in 2 Kings 14:23–29, which narrate the military victories that brought tremendous territorial expansion in an empire for the north, paralleling the expansion of David and Solomon in the same area. The Assyrian Empire in the first half of the ninth century was in trouble on its eastern and northern boundaries. Under Tiglath-pileser III (745–727 B.C.), Assyrian fortunes revived and from 743, renewed western campaigns were conducted. The reign of Zechariah, the son of Jeroboam, lasted one month, when he met his death at the hands of Menahem (2 Kings 15:13–14). Kings does not report Uzziah of Judah's battles in northern Syria against Assyria, but they appear in Assyrian inscriptions. Tiglath-pileser waged war (ca. 743–742 during Menahem's reign) against a coalition led by Azariah of Judah (i.e., Uzziah). Two Assyrian references record the military clash and the subsequent administrative arrangements under which Syrian regions were annexed and deportations began.

The history of the northern kingdom of Israel was brought to an end with the fall of Samaria (722 B.C.). Second Kings 17:1–6 narrates the historical events leading to the Assyrian conquest of the north. Hoshea, the last king of the north, was established as king by Tiglath-pileser in 732 in the place of Pekah (ca. 734–732; 2 Kings 15:30). At first, Hoshea became vassal and then rebelled and appealed to Egypt. He was arrested and imprisoned by Assyria. Sargon II of Assyria (722–705) claimed the capture of Samaria. This suggests that Sargon's brother, Shalmaneser (727–722 B.C.), died during the siege, though the Babylonian Chronicle credits the capture to Shalmaneser. A prophetic commentary upon the reason for the fall of the north, given as the failure to heed the prophetic word, appears in 2 Kings 17. Not only Israel, however, but Judah also does not keep the commandments; but the time of her punishment is not yet. In 2 Kings 17, the people have been reminded that they have squandered their heritage of exodus, covenant, wilderness, and conquest. In spite of Yahweh's deliverances, they have ignored his law. The message is for Judah, for the north had gone. But will Judah heed?

Kingship in the South

Our attention switches to the south. It is generally assumed that Ahaz became king in Jerusalem in 735/4, and thus his twelfth year would be 722. With the reforming reign of his son Hezekiah, its reversal under his son Manasseh, and then the advent of Josiah (2 Kings 22–23), the hopes projected by the prophetic movement in 1 Kings 13 are fulfilled. The judgment on Hezekiah (18:1–8) is entirely positive for his comprehensive religious reforms. He was without a peer among the Judean kings surveyed after David (2 Kings 18:5).

However, Sennacherib's invasion in 701 B.C., following western revolts with the death of Sargon II in 705 B.C., was the opposite of what might have been expected for Judah under the pious king. Hezekiah bought off the Assyrians in their first campaign against Jerusalem (2 Kings 18:14) with the temple gold. It is only after Hezekiah pays tribute (18:14b) that an oracle of deliverance for Judah comes (20:6). But in his preoccupation with his own health (2 Kings 20:1–11) and his reception of the Babylonian embassy (2 Kings 20:12–21), the promise of deliverance is transmuted into a prediction of downfall at the hands of Babylon. Hezekiah seems a paradigm for Judah, suffering a sickness that should have led to death (20:1–7). He was restored (20:8–11) only to resort in the future to foreign assistance for salvation (Seow 1999, 271). Manasseh is depicted as undoing Hezekiah's good. He seals Judah's fate. The Davidic promise is now compromised by the threat of exile (2 Kings 21:7–9, 13).

Under Josiah, the son of Amon (642–640 B.C.), the reform movement has its greatest hour. It is the fulfillment of the prophecy made to Jeroboam against Bethel (2 Kings 23:15; 1 Kings 13:2), and it involves reclamation, at least symbolically, of the entire Promised Land in defiance of the imperial power Assyria, submission to whom had bedeviled previous reforms. The reform culminates in a magnificent Passover (2 Kings 23:21–23).

Josiah (2 Kings 22:2) fulfilled the royal mandate of doing what was right in the eyes of the Lord (cf. Deut. 17:20). Fulfilling the duty of a pious ancient Near Eastern king, Josiah began temple renovations (22:3–10) before the finding of the book of the law was reported. Josiah's commission, in response to the finding of the law (22:8–10), for his messengers to inquire of Yahweh for him, at the hands of Huldah, showed covenant sensitivity for prophetic direction. K. Baltzer (1971, 13–18) has noted that in Hittite treaties, two offenses constituted violation: disobedience and loss of the treaty document. Second Kings 22 presupposed the latter and mentions the former as the source of Josiah's agitation (2 Kings 22:11–13). Josiah's ancestors had not been totally disobedient but selectively disobedient. The finding of the scroll justifies Josiah's unprecedented intervention into the religious affairs of Judah with his radical reforms. Huldah's two oracles announce punishment for "this place" (i.e., land and temple), and then postpone it until after Josiah's time (22:15–20).

Second Kings' report is governed entirely by the finding of the law book, but the three-stage reform movement of Chronicles, related to Josiah's eighth, twelfth, and eighteenth years, seems to reflect the opportunities for national assertion presented by the decline of Assyria from 632 on. A comparison with the account of Josiah's reforms in 2 Chronicles 34 indicates that the report of the reforms has been condensed in 2 Kings to throw major emphasis upon the finding of the book of the law in 621 B.C. (Josiah's eighteenth year). Thus the major part of the reforms (which involved the extirpation of Canaanite, not Assyrian, practices) was conducted before the book of the law, on which they seemed to depend, was actually found (cf. 2 Chron. 34:1–13 with v. 14). In Kings, Josiah heads every major initiative in the reforms (2 Kings 22:3, 11; 23:1, 4, 21). Such were the discovery of the Torah (22:11–20), the consultation with Huldah

(22:15–20) and the conclusion of a national Passover (23:21–23). The discovery and recitation of the Torah scroll had exposed Judah's plight as that of national crisis. Josiah's response was to convoke a national assembly. A covenant renewing the Sinai compact was ratified among deity, king, and people, providing support for Josiah's further interventions.

This was not a new covenant but a renewal of the Sinai covenant. Josiah acts as covenant mediator ensuring a united front behind his reforms (23:4–20). Josiah's role in generating public interest, defining the terms of the covenant, and supervising its conformation is highlighted. Josiah's southern reforms (23:4–14) are then set in motion. He begins with reforms which are chronologically and geographically more immediate (2 Kings 23:5–6) and then moves on to reforms which are chronologically and geographically more distant (Knoppers 1994, 2:181). He begins at the house of God, the Jerusalem temple, and then moves progressively through southern to northern centers (vv. 15–20).

Hezekiah was praised for obeying the commandments that Yahweh gave to Moses (2 Kings 18:6), but the reforms in detail were unreported in Kings (cf. extensively 2 Chron. 29–31, in which Hezekiah assumes the proportions of a second Solomon). But Hezekiah's reforms were apparently short-lived. Reforms before Josiah were sporadic and limited, and they failed to address the root of the problem. Moreover, it was Kings' intention to climax the narrative with Josiah's reforms, since Josiah is the author's second David and is in mind from 1 Kings 13 onward.

Josiah's Northern Reforms

The reform movement reached to the old north. The celebration of the national Passover, the only one attested in the Former Prophets, climaxed the reforms (2 Kings 23:21–23). Yet not even Josiah's good work could roll back the approaching accumulated wrath shortly to descend on Judah (23:26–28).

In view of the tenor of 2 Kings 22–23, in which phrases reminiscent of Deuteronomy occur ("walk after the Lord"; "keep his commandments and his testimonies and his statutes"; "with all his heart and all his soul"; "words of this covenant" [23:3]), the identification of the book of the law with the Book of Deuteronomy seems very plausible. This is the more so as the book of the law contains a clear threat of judgment upon national evils (22:13) and an emphasis upon covenant (23:2). However, it is difficult to explain the finding of Deuteronomy in 621 B.C. Both Josiah's reforms and those of Hezekiah (reported in 2 Chronicles and substantially identical with Josiah's) show familiarity with the demands of a book such as Deuteronomy. The nineteenth-century theories that the finding was a pious fiction to give ancient authority to Deuteronomy, which allegedly was composed at this time, are not only intrinsically improbable (in view of the undoubted antiquity of the contents of Deuteronomy) but also are at variance with the detail of Chronicles and Kings previously referred to. What was found in the temple at this time was perhaps a document on the duties of the king in Deuteronomic terms, prepared for the royal court and incorporating the obligations and covenant responsibilities of the Jerusalem kings. The nature of any conclusions in this area, however, must remain tentative.

For his piety, Josiah went down to his grave with his kingdom intact (the apparent meaning of "in peace" in 2 Kings 22:20). But the accumulated sins of the southern kingdom, particularly the apostasy of Manasseh, required the end of the Jewish state. Even Josiah's more thorough reforms (the high places defiled to prevent their subsequent use, etc.) did not last, though the focus of both reforming kings was the temple, the symbol of divine authority. It is thus a somewhat fitting commentary upon the failure of the monarchical period that the Books of Kings end with the temple in ruins and thus divine authority withdrawn from the Promised Land.

The Last Days of Judah

When Josiah was killed in battle at Megiddo (609 B.C.) opposing Egypt's movement north, his eldest son Jehoiakim was passed over for his pro-Babylonian brother Jehoahaz, installed by the influential people of the land (2 Kings 23:30). Jehoahaz reigned for only three months and was removed by Pharaoh Necho returning from the north. Necho now installed the pro-Egyptian Jehoiakim, whose resolute apostasy is clear from the Book of Jeremiah. Egypt was soundly defeated by Babylon in the decisive battle of Carchemish on the Euphrates in 605 B.C., and hegemony of the Fertile Crescent and its perimeters fell to Nebuchadnezzar. Circa 602 B.C., Jehoiakim rebelled against Babylon, following Babylon's defeat on the Egyptian border. Nebuchadnezzar put Jerusalem under siege and prepared Jehoiakim for exile (2 Chron. 36:6). Jehoiakim continued to rule until his strange death (Jer. 22:18–23), when Jerusalem was again under siege for revolt (December 598). His son, the boy-king Jehoiachin, succeeded him and reigned from 598 to March 597 B.C., when Jerusalem fell and Jehoiachin, with the cream of the upper echelon of Judah, was taken into exile in Babylon. Zedekiah, the uncle of Jehoiachin, succeeded him, and the indecision of this vacillating monarch and his inability to relate to the deteriorating political situation are clear from the Book of Jeremiah. Eventually, Zedekiah appealed to Egypt and revolted against Babylon (ca. 589 B.C.). After a long siege, Jerusalem fell (587/6 B.C., July). Zedekiah at Riblah witnessed the death of his sons (2 Kings 25:6–7), and was then blinded and taken captive. Gedaliah was appointed governor of Judah, but he was killed in a conspiracy in about 582/1 B.C., headed by Ishmael of the seed royal. Fearing the implications, the leading Judahites then fled to Egypt, taking Jeremiah with them.

Purpose of Kings

The Books of Kings deal with the decline and fall of the Davidic empire. The history of this period is cast into the familiar pattern of rebellion and punishment, unrelieved except by the personalities of the reforming southern kings—Josiah, Hezekiah, and, to a much lesser degree, Asa, Jehoshaphat, and Joash. With the reforming kings, however, there was an intensifying insistence that even reform (imposed from above by the king) would not bring the desired results. Reform under Hezekiah had led to wicked Manasseh and under Josiah to Jehoiakim. So the failure of Josiah to usher in a period of salvation for Judah was no surprise. The author wrote to confirm the justice of God's acts in the destruction and exile and to convince his readers of that fact. The judgment of the exile had been foreshadowed in Deuteronomy 29:1–30:10, in the prophetic poetry of Deuteronomy 32, and again in the last words of Joshua 23 and 24. The author underscored his theme in his assessment of each king's performance, his interpolations into the words of the prophets, and his selection and arrangement of incidents. The reader cannot escape the conclusion that Yahweh was justified in his judgment, that his people were amply prepared for it, and that they should accept the blame. The author of Kings understood Yahweh to be presiding over history and recompensing the deeds of his covenant people. Israel had persistently violated the covenant and therefore undermined its hold on the land.

While the issue dealt with in Kings is clear, there has been a division of opinion as to whether the books offer any message of hope for the future to the exiles. Has the history of Israel come to an end with the exile, now that all the externals (temple, cult, priesthood, kingship, even land) have gone? Some have seen in the message of Jehoiachin's elevation from prison in Babylon a note of hope being offered to Israel as the period closes (2 Kings 25:27–30). Perhaps this indirect reference to the promises given to the Davidic line (2 Sam. 7) is a glimmer that in the midst of despair and uncertainty, Yahweh is still at work, but Jehoiachin, the Davidic king in exile, is now dead. He indeed had been released, but the portrayal of the Davidic monarch, eating defiled food puppetlike at a pagan king's table, contrasts markedly with that of the faithful Jew, Daniel, whose uncompromising conduct indicates a faith that would survive the exile. We are thus left with the distinct impression that, once again, a question mark has been raised over the future of Israel. The monarchical period began with the recognition of the need for a more ordered institutional life under Yahweh's leadership (Judg. 21:25). The period witnessed the growth of Israel's institutional life but also the progressive denial of the authority of Yahweh by gross acts of apostasy.

The collapse of the Israelite state saw the failure of a national experiment. This failure seemed to make it clear that neither a national state nor a system of institutionalized religious practices would henceforth be the carrier of the promises to Abraham. With the fall of the Israelite state, the dawn of the New Testament age had virtually begun. For, after the exile, though many attempts to revive the past would be made, it would eventually become clear that the visible carrier of the promises would not finally be physical Israel as such, but a community of faith. In retrospect this had always been so. The exile would underline this biblical truth.

Part 3

The Books of the Prophets:
The Latter Prophets

10

Isaiah

Old Testament prophecy, as instituted, continued the Mosaic office and was therefore covenant-centered (Deut. 18:15–22). Like Moses, the prophets offered what was given on Sinai and reapplied it to current social, religious, and economic questions. They were therefore not innovators. They dealt with a faith, once delivered, which needed to be possessed by the communities of their day. Since the Israelite prophet was primarily a covenant mediator, his appearance and intervention meant that covenant breach in some shape had occurred. Thus the prophetic ministry was most normally associated, up to the exile at least, with impending judgment. But their message was actually a saving message. For unless the sin of Israel was so deeply ingrained that it could not be eradicated, the threat of judgment was an implicit invitation to repentance.

Israel's prophets spoke with the authority of the sender. For warrant for their message, they appealed to participation in the deliberations of the heavenly council (see Isa. 6; Jer. 23:18), where the message had been heard and from whence commissioning proceeded. As opposed to the more formally appointed kingship, Israelite prophecy was a Spirit-filled office that continued the charismatic type of ministry of the Judges period. We now turn to consider the implications and effects of the prophetic message to Israel. Here we shall move away from chronological order, taking the Major Prophets first and then considering briefly the message of the remaining twelve so-called Minor Prophets.

Literary and Theological Unity of Isaiah

Since the epoch-making commentary of Bernhard Duhm (1892), the division of the book into three segments (chaps. 1–39, 40–55, 56–66), each with its own historical or thematic interest, has been widely accepted in biblical scholarship. Recent discussion has tended to look more for inner theological connections that bind the book together. Factors such as divine kingship, the notion of holiness, the Davidic and Zionistic emphasis of much of the book (Davidic only in chaps. 1–39, however), as well as the very high ethical tone of the whole, have been cited as general tendencies giving a common theological direction. At the same time, B. S. Childs (1979, 325–34) has suggested that Isaiah 40–55 functions as prophetic interpretation and elaboration of the traditions of Isaiah 1–39. Childs and others have seen Isaiah 56–66 as elaborating and applying the message of Isaiah 40–55.

If the book is read as a unit, one overarching theme may be seen to effectively unite the whole: Yahweh's interest in and devotion to the city of Jerusalem. This concern provides for the theological cohesion of Isaiah and gives it its unitary stamp. The thesis of Jerusalem as the integrating factor in the book finds support in the initial emphasis placed on Jerusalem in Isaiah 1, and again in conclusion, in Isaiah 66. This idea is also supported in the internal structuring of the various subsections of the book (chaps. 1–12, 13–23, 24–27, 28–33, 34–35, 36–39, 40–55, and 56–66). In each subsection, the interest in Jerusalem is dominant and often ties somewhat disparate topics together.

Isaiah 1 presents a decadent Jerusalem, whose sacrifices can no longer be accepted and whose prayers must be turned aside. This chapter functions as an introduction, not only to Isaiah 1–12, but also to the whole book. Appropriately, therefore, the prophecy concludes (66:20–24) with the emergence of a New Jerusalem as God's holy mountain to which the world will go up in a pilgrimage of worship. From the final chapters it becomes clear that the notion of the New Jerusalem is intimately linked with the prophecy of a new creation (65:17–18). This New Jerusalem, in fact, functions as a symbol of the new age and is presented in the conclusion as an obvious offset to the city with which the book begins.

We should note that the emphasis on Jerusalem is not found merely at the beginning and the end of the book. The first half of Isaiah ends in Isaiah 39 with a threat of exile pronounced on King Hezekiah and his city, Jerusalem. Isaiah 36–39 bridges the two major parts of the book, the Assyrian section in chapters 1–35 and the Babylonian/Persian section in chapters 40–66. The Assyrian section anticipates a judgment by Assyria, followed by a restoration, and the Babylonian/Persian section presupposes a judgment by Babylon and anticipates a restoration about to take place. The second half of the book begins with an announcement of a prospective return from exile (40:1). Immediately, the prophet translates the "comfort" to be extended to "my people" into a tender speaking to Jerusalem (v. 2). Indeed, the focus of the introduction to this section of the book (vv. 1–11) is on Jerusalem (cf. the correlation between vv. 1–2 and 9–11). Once the general tenor of the return has been discussed in Isaiah 40–48, Jerusalem/Zion becomes the point of direct focus in 49–55. The Zion theme also begins and ends the final section (chaps. 56–66).

Promise and Threat (Isa. 1–12)

Isaiah 1 is undoubtedly the key to the book. It is a very thorough indictment of the failure of Israel to be the people of God and a rejection of Jerusalem, the political and cult center. Isaiah 1:2–3 discusses the focal point, covenant breach, the accusation which Isaiah 1:4–17 then makes; Isaiah1:4–9 discusses Israel's refusal to be God's people; and Isaiah 1:10–17 discusses the problem of the perverted cult. Isaiah 1:18–20 presents an offer of forgiveness. Isaiah 1:21–23 resumes the indictment of Isaiah 1:2–3; Isaiah 1:24–26 then deals with the threat of punishment; and Isaiah 1:27–31 issues a verdict that reveals for the first time in the OT an emergence of two groups within the nation—the wicked who will be punished and the righteous remnant who will be redeemed.

What accounts for the savage nature of this divine assault on Jerusalem in Isaiah 1? Here it may be helpful to turn to Isaiah 6:1–9:7, an apparently intrusive element into the structure of threat and promise that prevails in Isaiah 1–12. Isaiah 6 contains the call of the prophet and directs our attention toward his vocation and the difficulties that he will have to confront. It is significant that Isaiah's call is narrated in connection with Isaiah 7–9, which deals with the fate of the house of David, and thus continues the idea of prophecy as the supervisor of kingship. Given the pattern of threat and promise that we have found in the surrounding chapters, we expect it also in Isaiah 6:1–9:7. Isaiah 6–8 deals with judgment directed against the Davidic house in Jerusalem and the resulting desolation that is to come upon the city. Isaiah 9:1–7 returns us to an idealized picture of Davidic leadership, to be brought about by divine intervention at a later period.

Isaiah 6 begins with an account of the prophet's call in the year of Uzziah's death. Uzziah's long reign of forty-two years had marked for the south a return to Davidic and Solomonic greatness. However, in the year of the death of this king, Isaiah is encouraged by his vision of the Lord (Isa. 6:1), the King (Isa. 6:5), to put politics into their proper perspective. He sees that Judah's security and continuance depend on Yahweh's guidance within history, not on the deft political kingship or the foreign alliances that have served to hold the southern kingdom together. The scene that Isaiah beholds seems to be the heavenly council in session, Yahweh surrounded by his royal court. The question under discussion, as the later context indicates, is the coming judgment upon Jerusalem and the exile that results (vv. 11–12), leaving only a token remnant (Isa. 6:13) as heirs to the promises. Isaiah sees Yahweh sitting ominously upon his throne, a normal judgment posture (cf. the judgment vision of Micaiah in 1 Kings 22:19). The message of dire judgment that the chapter foreshadows is the message to be taken to Israel (Isa. 6:8–10). The nation and its leadership, incorrigible in both ministries, are being rejected; nothing is said about the status of individuals within the nation.

Important for the understanding of what is being conveyed to Isaiah are the actions of the seraphim, which are offering a doxology in response to the heavenly judgment (Isa. 6:3). In the light of what they do in heaven, Isaiah realizes that he is a man of unclean lips and dwells in the midst of a people of unclean lips (Isa. 6:5). This is not merely the language of prophetic diffidence, since verse 5 presupposes that what characterizes Isaiah also characterizes Judah. This language points to the proper response from pure lips to Yahweh's kingship, namely, the seraphim's worship, which acknowledges his sovereignty. At once Isaiah realizes that his own and Judah's failure to reflect Yahweh's kingship at the center of Israel's covenant life, the cult, accounts for the tremendous decline from prosperity to desolation that this chapter projects. We see clearly the reasons underlying the sweeping condemnation of worship and sanctuary in Isaiah 1:10–20.

The eschatology of the Book of Isaiah aims at reversing the situation described in Isaiah 1, made specific by the detail of Isaiah 6. That is perhaps the reason for what seems a new introduction in Isaiah 2:1; certainly, it is the reason for the presentation of the prospect for Jerusalem that we find in 2:2–4. I have argued elsewhere (1977, 39–41) that the Zion imagery in Isaiah 2:2–4 received its impetus from the choice of Jerusalem in 2 Samuel 6. The particular form that the hope concerning Jerusalem developed was influenced by the contours of the Solomon empire, particularly as acknowledged by the visit of the queen of Sheba (1 Kings 10) as a representative of her world. This incident anticipated the picture developed in Isaiah 2:2–4, in which the chosen city Jerusalem becomes the redemptive center of the world and a towering mountain, the place of divine revelation. Nations that had previously assailed Jerusalem will come in pilgrimage for the divine will. The nations will come to Yahweh as Judge (i.e., world king) for law. Since "law" is paralleled by the general expression "word of the Lord" (Isa. 2:3), we are not dealing with a prescriptive code but with divine instruction understood in the broadest terms—divine regulation of the affairs of the world in the new age. Nothing concerning the Davidic traditions is stated here or in the extensive expansion that this passage undergoes in Isaiah 60–62. This eschatology of 2:2–4 becomes basic in Isaiah 40–66. But throughout Isaiah 1–12 (indeed, chaps. 1–39), the vulnerability of Jerusalem is made plain (1:21; 10:24–32; cf. 18:7; 24:10; 29:1–8; 32:13–14), while at the same time it is emphasized that the Zion ideal would survive (7:1–9; 10:24–34; cf. 14:28–32; 17:12–14; 29:1–8; 30:27–33; chap. 31). Isaiah 2:5–22 reveals the religious condition of sinful Jerusalem. The Day of Yahweh will come.

In 3:1–4:6 are two blocks of material that deal with the cleansing of Jerusalem needed to fit it for its end-time role. Isaiah 3:1–4:1 discusses the punishment of Jerusalem's leaders and the women respectively. Isaiah 4:2–6 speaks of Yahweh's protection of Jerusalem after he has cleansed the city. Isaiah 5–12 deals with a preliminary judgment on Judah and Israel to be effected by Assyria. In 5:1–30, the subject is judgment against Judah and Israel (Isa. 5:7). Isaiah 5:1–7's vineyard parable is directed to the totality of Israel (O'Connell 1994, 188), with a description of past benefits (v. 2a) and a series of accusations (vv. 2b–4) for lack of expected performance. Isaiah 5:5–6 presents an ultimatum with the threat of destruction. Isaiah 5:7a discloses that the judged (5:2b–4) are in fact the accused. Isaiah 5:7b instances specific violations. If 5:1–7 deals generally with the accusations to be leveled at north and south, 5:8–24 begins to render it specific by a series of woe speeches. These speeches spell out the shortcomings of the leaders, whose corrupt behaviors led to the people's downfall. Isaiah

5:25–30 announces Yahweh's anger against the people and the punishment to come: the Assyrian army.

Within the oscillation between threat and promise directed at Judah and Jerusalem in Isaiah 1–12, I have noted the intrusion of 6:1–9:7 regarding the Davidic monarchy in which hope was to be reposed. In this section the same pattern of threat and promise emerges. Isaiah 6:1–8:15 is largely autobiographical, reporting Isaiah's experiences in relation to the Syro-Ephraimite War, but also Judah's rejection of Yahweh, which will bring the resulting judgment by means of Assyria. While these chapters deal mainly with the rejection of Davidic kingship and the eventual substitution of ideal kingship, the notion of a remnant—a community within a community—receives prominent attention. Within Isaiah 7–9, the house of David (currently represented by Ahaz) is rejected, while the future is tied to the motif of a faithful remnant that will emerge from the coming disaster. It is probable that the name of the prophet's son, Shear Jashub ("a remnant shall return" [7:3]), foreshadows the remnant community, which will turn in repentance and faith to Yahweh. This faith community provides the positive side of the double-edged sign of Immanuel ("God with us," in judgment or salvation) that is to confront the world (7:14; 8:8). Consider that the latter half of 7:15 may be translated as a purpose clause ("in order that he may know how to refuse the evil and choose the good"), as Joseph Jensen (1979, 228) argues, and not as a temporal clause. Then the announced birth of a child to a young woman (7:14) could involve a reversal of Israel's fortunes in the far-distant future (i.e., far beyond the immediate Assyrian crisis), and be a promise that concerns the house of David, finally (cf. 7:13), more than it does Ahaz, the current ruler. This point is reiterated in 8:1–15, but with regard to the people. Yahweh instructs Isaiah (8:1–4) concerning a sign to announce the defeat of Syria and Israel. The defeat of the Syro-Ephraimite coalition will not bring deliverance to Judah as expected, but even greater danger (8:5–10). This threat is not from the nations, but from Yahweh himself (Sweeney 1996, 165–74).

Isaiah 8:16–12:6 is composed of two major sections, divided at 9:7. The first of these sections (8:16–9:6) announces Isaiah's withdrawal from prophetic activity to await Yahweh's announced actions in relation to his people. These actions involve a period of distress and hunger, followed by a period of restoration ushered in by the birth of a new king. The very highly developed pictures of a God-given ruler in 9:1–7 and 11:1–10 refer, in the first instance, to contrary contemporary leadership, but see future welfare as bound up with divine kingship. The second section (9:7–12:6) expects, in greater detail, a period of distress (9:7–10:4, united by the "outstretched hand" formula), and a period of restoration. Isaiah 10:5–11:16 describes the process and the period of restoration. Assyria, for her arrogance as the agent of punishment, will be punished by Yahweh in turn (10:5–23). The reestablishment of Judah and Israel under a Davidic king who begins the Davidic dynasty again, is described in 10:24–11:16. The Assyrian suzerainty is soon to end, and the Davidic monarchy is to be reestablished. A hymn of thanksgiving in 12:1–6 ends the book's first section by noting that prophetic expectation calls for the presence of the Holy One of Israel in the midst of Zion and her inhabitants.

Oracles against Foreign Nations (Isa. 13–23)

Isaiah 13–23 contains prophecies against foreign nations. The origin of this genre of prophecy is difficult to establish. There is much to be said for the view that the judgment oracles against foreign nations are offshoots of the Zion traditions. We should consider, however, the manner in which such oracles are employed. The individual oracles in Isaiah 13–23 stem from different occasions and reflect a complex history, but in their present context they reveal one overarching goal: the impending disasters intended to humble the proud and to destroy the wicked, so that Yahweh alone will be exalted and honored (cf. Isa. 2:9–22; 25:2–3). The link that joins chapters 13–23 is their concern with nations that have encountered or will encounter Assyrian rule or threats and who will take part in useless coalitions against Assyria (Erlandsson 1970, 102). Thus, there seems to be implied condemnation in these chapters for these four nations: (1) *Judea* (Isa. 13–14), for its attempts to establish diplomatic contacts with Babylon. (2) *Philistia* (14:29–32); the foreign policy of Israel/Judah is rejected out of hand, since Yahweh has founded Zion and he will protect it. (3) *Ethiopia* (18:1–5); it is noted that Yahweh himself will intervene for his people before the final harvest, that is, before complete destruction by Assyria. Perhaps verses 6–7 refer to the subsequent fate of the Assyrians and their submission to Yahweh in Zion. (4) *Egypt,* whose lack of dependability is stressed in Isaiah 19. Yahweh will punish Egypt by internal division (19:1–10). Isaiah 19:11–15 levels a taunt against Pharaoh and his official, and 19:16–25 specifies future consequences for Egypt. Isaiah 20:1–6 features symbolic action that sets the scene for a prophecy on Egypt, and seems to relate to Sargon's campaigns in 713–711 B.C.

Isaiah 15–16 is directed against Moab, and may refer to the abortive stand by that state against Tiglath-pileser III in 734 B.C. The threat against Damascus (17:1–11) seems to fall into the same category and time. Isaiah 21:1–10 links the names of Elam, Media, and Babylon and could thus point to a time around 700 B.C. The message of verses 1–10 is clear: no nation is to repose its hope in the doomed Babylon. Verses 11–17 appear to be related to Assyrian campaigns against the Arab peoples. Isaiah 22 refers to political measures taken when Jerusalem was threatened during the reign of Hezekiah. Finally, Tyre and Sidon, which were involved in the western coalition against Assyria (ca. 734 B.C.) and which had strong commercial links with Judah, are the subjects of Isaiah 23.

The recurring theme of Isaiah 13–23 is that faith in Yahweh's purposes, and not foreign policies, will protect Jerusalem. Yahweh will crush Assyria, and he alone is the guarantor of Zion's security (14:27–32). Perhaps 17:12–14 refers to an attack upon Zion thwarted by Yahweh, with the attackers being described in the typical chaos imagery of "many waters." Isaiah 13–23 thus carries forward the dominant Jerusalem theme struck in Isaiah 1–12.

The City of God (Isa. 24–27)

It is clear that Isaiah 24–27 consistently follows chapters 13–23 in shifting its concern from individual nations to the entire earth. In these chapters, judgment has been pronounced upon the earth, with the focus on one city (Isa. 24:1–13, 17–23). The perspective is universal, for the focus is on the punishment of the world, followed by its restoration, including a banquet for all nations held by Yahweh on Mount Zion (25:6–8). Features prominent in later apocalyptic appear, such as Yahweh's judgment on the earth—the end of the nations. With Yahweh's rule on Zion established, mythological motifs of the defeat of Leviathan—the conquest of death—the banquet on Zion, and the interpretation of earlier prophecy are all featured. Yahweh will not stop with the fall of the city of chaos but intends to overthrow all the kings of the earth in preparation for his rule on Mount Zion.

The Certainty of Divine Defense (Isa. 28–33)

In the absence of detail, Isaiah 28–33 is difficult to date precisely. There is nothing, however, in this section to disprove the position that it deals mainly with Assyrian activity directed against Judah and Jerusalem later in the reign of Hezekiah (715–687 B.C.). Isaiah 28–33 identifies Yahweh as the cause of the threat and presents Yahweh's plans for emergence of a royal savior in Jerusalem as well as the downfall of the Assyrian empire. Editorially, the chapters are unified by the introductory formula "woe to . . ." (28:1; 29:1, 15; 30:1; 31:1; 33:1). The details of these chapters confirm their Zion bent and call on that city and her people to rely on her cornerstone, the temple in Jerusalem. The themes of the importance of avoiding foreign alliances and the certainty of Yahweh's defense of Jerusalem are characteristic of these chapters.

Isaiah 28:1–4 judges Samaria regarding the coming Assyrian invasion; verses 5–22 concern the implementation of the means, Yahweh's assumption of leadership, by which the purpose of verses 1–4 will be realized. Isaiah 28:7–13 dismisses Ephraim's leadership, and verses 14–22 dismiss Judah's. Verses 23–29 demonstrate the purpose of the prophetic instruction, illustrated by the example of the farmer. With the removal of Judean and Ephraimite leadership and its replacement by Assyrian leadership, the prophetic word has been pronounced. Assyrian leadership will not deliver a thoroughly crushing blow (Isa. 28:23–29), but a limited, positive outcome may be expected from the political changes. The condemnation of Ephraim in verses 1–13, fulfilled in the fall of Samaria (722/21 B.C.), provides the background for the fate of Jerusalem announced in verses 14–22. The mention of a covenant with death (Isa. 28:18) appears to refer to activity of Hezekiah with Merodach-Baladan and warns Hezekiah against it.

In the Ariel paragraph (Isa. 29:1–14), Yahweh first occasions the siege of Jerusalem and then relieves it. Ariel, as the temple altar, is a metonymy for the temple itself, which Yahweh himself is to assault, reversing the expected outcome of the Zion tradition. The second half of the chapter (vv. 15–24) provides prophetic instruction regarding Yahweh's future deliverance of Jacob. Isaiah

29:1–14 can be assigned to 705–701 B.C. as a warning to Hezekiah not to revolt against Sennacherib.

Isaiah 30:1–11 expresses Yahweh's dissatisfaction with the people's embassy to Egypt. Isaiah 30:12–26 indicates the consequences to flow from Yahweh's dissatisfaction. The people will suffer punishment, and Yahweh will delay their deliverance. The three major units of this passage (vv. 12–14, 15–17, 18–26) detail the punishment to come and the self-assertion that characterizes Judah. Deliverance will come, but it will be delayed and come through judgment (v. 20). Isaiah 30:27–33 celebrates Yahweh's victory over Assyria in the presumed setting of 705–701 B.C.

The contrast between the search for support (from Egypt, vv. 1–5) within the same chronological setting and the true source of Zion's protection (Yahweh, vv. 6–9) continues in Isaiah 31. The overall intention of Isaiah 31 is to dissuade resort to an Egyptian alliance during the Assyrian threat. The hymn of Isaiah 32 appears to draw out the consequences of the new era of deliverance granted to Zion, and seems to have in mind the Assyrian reversal of 701 B.C. The announcement of a royal savior, who will bring salvation out of disaster, is made in verses 1–8. Verses 9–19 are a prophetic announcement arising from Isaiah 32:1–8 of salvation out of disaster. The chapter concludes (v. 20) with a beatitude to confirm the happiness of the righteous.

The interaction of the communal complaint song (33:1–4) is followed by an exhibition of Yahweh's characteristics and deeds (vv. 5–6, 10–13, 14–16) that fit him to act as the royal savior (vv. 17–24). The chapter presumably relates to the period of Yahweh's deliverance of Jerusalem in 701 B.C. W. A. M. Beuken has argued that Isaiah 33, which reflects the themes and motifs and vocabulary of Isaiah 1–32 and 34–66 and links the two major halves, is the chapter on which the prophecy pivots (cf. Sweeney 1996, 430).

Destruction and Deliverance (Isa. 34–35)

In the next section, the Zion motif provides a clear contrast between Isaiah 34 and 35. Aggression in the shape of the old enemy, Edom, is ranged against Zion, but Edom will be destroyed (Isa. 34:1–15). The nations are instructed (vv. 16–17) to read the account (Isaiah's book?) of Edom's punishment as a manifestation of Yahweh's power. Isaiah 35 focuses on Yahweh's power as redeemer and creator by emphasizing the renewal of creation (vv. 1–2) and the return of the redeemed (vv. 3–7) to Zion; this return occurs in a new exodus, along a highway through the transformed desert (vv. 8–10). Commentators often link these two eschatological chapters with Isaiah 40–55.

The Siege of Jerusalem (Isa. 36–39)

Isaiah 36:1–39:8 concerns Hezekiah and the Assyrian campaign of 701 B.C. (2 Kings 18:13–19:37). P. R. Ackroyd (1987, 181–82, 187–88) draws attention to the parallels between Ahaz and Hezekiah. Both texts open with historical notes (7:1; 36:1). The location is the same for both events—by the water conduit near the highway of the Fuller's Field (Isa. 7:3; 36:2). Prophetic signs (Heb.

'ot) are involved in both events (7:11, 14; 38:7, 22); Ahaz rejects the signs, but Hezekiah accepts them. The clause "the zeal of Yahweh Sabaoth will accomplish this" is used at climactic points in both narratives (9:6/9:7 and 37:32). The reference to the steps of Ahaz (Heb. *ma'alot Ahaz*) in 38:8 links Isaiah 36–38 with the Ahaz narrative.

Hezekiah's exemplary faith and piety contrast with Ahaz's groundless fear and faithlessness in a similar crisis. Hezekiah's reign may well provide historical fulfillment of Isaiah's words in the first part of the book. He is thus seen, in contrast to Ahaz, as the first fulfillment of the expected ideal monarch (9:1–6), although Hezekiah does not express all that the author has in mind in regard to the role of the Messiah in the salvation of Israel and in the new creation.

The three major units (chaps. 36–37, 38, 39) are each introduced by time references. Chapter 38, with its addition of fifteen years to Hezekiah's life, must have preceded chapters 36–37 chronologically. Isaiah 39 then narrates Isaiah's condemnation of Hezekiah on the Babylonian delegation's visit from Merodach-Baladan. Merodach-Baladan's embassy presupposed Hezekiah's previous illness, and it could not have been later than 703 B.C. when Sennacherib finally drove him from his throne. Isaiah 36 presents Sennacherib's surrender demand on Hezekiah, which is unanswered. Isaiah 37:1–7 reports Hezekiah's reaction and his request to Isaiah for Yahweh's help. Isaiah 37:8–13 reports Sennacherib's second message to Isaiah, challenging Yahweh. Isaiah 37:14–20 records Hezekiah's prayer to Yahweh for deliverance.

Isaiah 37:21–35 reports Yahweh's response of judgment against Sennacherib. Finally, Isaiah 37:36–38 reports the judgment on the besieging Assyrian army and reports Sennacherib's assassination. Isaiah 38 narrates Hezekiah's sickness, recovery, and his letter of thanksgiving.

Isaiah 36–39 provides a literary bridge between the Assyrian period depicted in chapters 1–33 and the Babylonian and Persian periods (chaps. 34–66). Hezekiah presents a distinct contrast to Ahaz in 7:1–9:6, showing the exemplary piety and faith that Ahaz lacked. His desire to praise Yahweh in the temple is highlighted. Isaiah 39 closes the first half of this great prophecy with an announcement of exile, but refers primarily to the deportation of the Jerusalem leadership (vv. 5–8). Thus, the first half of the book has ended with a prophecy of virtual destruction and the cessation of the Davidic house. At the same time, Isaiah 1–39 has maintained emphasis on the role appointed for the eschatological Zion of 2:2–4.

The Ministry of the Servant (Isa. 40–55)

Isaiah 40:1–11

As Isaiah 1–39 had ended with the prospect of exile before Jerusalem, so Isaiah 40 commences the second half of the prophecy on the comfort to be extended to Jerusalem and the exiles in Babylon. The emphatic tone of hope at the beginning of Isaiah 40 is maintained throughout chapters 40–55. The communication from what seems to be a divine council is that punishment is now over for Jerusalem, and she is now acknowledged, in tender language, as "my people" and is extended comfort from "her God." In this way, the relationships of the Sinai covenant are vividly recalled ("my people . . . your God"; cf. Lev. 26:12) and are now to be reinaugurated. The prophet presents Jerusalem as the substitute for everything that had resulted from the Sinai covenant. The speaker in verses 1–2 is Yahweh, and the directive appears to be issued to the heavenly council, of whom the prophet is apparently a member. The proclamation is to be addressed to Jerusalem, which is now a synonym for "my people" as the parallelism of the two lines in verse 1 suggests. The comfort to be extended to Jerusalem is not consolation in the midst of sorrow, but rather the message that sorrow has been removed (2 Sam. 12:24), foreshadowing an imminent change of fortunes. God has neither forgotten nor forsaken God's people. Verse 2, again containing two imperatives, is closely related to verse 1. Where a double imperative occurs in Isaiah 40–55, it is continued with further imperatives and linked carefully to the following context (51:9, 17; 57:14; 62:10).

"Double for all her sins" (v. 2 RV) does not contemplate a strict doctrine of the equivalence of punishment, but simply that Jerusalem's sufferings have now gone beyond the limits of endurance. There are three causal clauses in verse 2 that offer reasons for the main statement of verse 1 (which sets the tone for Isa. 40–55), and these are balanced by three "behold" clauses in verses 9–11. Somewhat like verses 1–2, verses 9–11 begin with an imperative and continue with a double imperative (v. 9b).

Verses 3–5 refer to a divine herald's summons to prepare a divine way through the wilderness, and thus to the beginnings of comfort. In view of this prophecy's specific references to the return from exile as a new exodus (42:16; 43:16, 19; 49:9, 11; 51:10; etc.), we are to see the way through the wilderness as the call to the people of God to come out in a second exodus, this time from Babylon. The face of nature is to be changed before the final coming of Israel's God in glory, that is, in God's manifested sovereignty. All flesh—corporately, not individually—will join in public recognition of the impending great change. It is possible, as many suggest, that in the image of the way, the language of divine enthronement parallels the Babylonian enthronement of the state deity Marduk at the annual New Year's festival. There is no incompatibility in seeing both the ingredients of enthronement and exodus, since the kingship of Yahweh is recognized by the physical salvation of his people.

A further herald cry is raised by verses 6–8, which the prophet understands as an address to himself. He no longer believes in the possibility of a new beginning because of the frailty of human personality. The herald voice in verse 8 replies to the prophet, conceding that all flesh is grass, but that the supreme power of the divine word confronts this hopelessness. God's word will shape history and will change history.

Isaiah 40:9–11 concludes the introduction. Though the text is ambiguous, the general context demands that Jerusalem be evangelized and that she not be the evangelist (with NIV). The message is disarmingly simple: God comes as Jerusalem's king. This message is stated clearly in Isaiah 52:7. The shepherd imagery of verses 9–11, frequently used imagery for royal kingship in the ancient world, implies the kingship of Yahweh. The arm of Yahweh, the saving instrument of the first exodus (Isa. 40:10; 52:10), will achieve this kingship. Through a new exodus revealing his royal power, Yahweh will reestablish his covenant with Israel, who are to be gathered to the divine center, Jerusalem. The despair of the exiles is recognized (v. 11), and God is now willing to meet their needs. The closing verses (vv. 9–11) of this introduction to Isaiah 40–55 also carry the Jerusalem theme further. The concern of Isaiah 40–55 will be with the return of the exiles to Jerusalem and the significance of this return. The three themes of 40:1–11—consolation for Jerusalem (vv. 1–2, 9–11), the return as a new exodus (vv. 3–5), and the power of the divine word to effect the change (vv. 6–8)— are developed in 40:12–48:22 (the return from Babylon in a new exodus), in 49:1–52: 12 (consolation for Jerusalem), and in 52:13–55:13 (the powerful efficacy of the divine word).

Isaiah 40:12–31

The exiles in Babylon are in view. Isaiah now seeks to persuade them that Yahweh is aware of their complaint, that their cause has not been overlooked, and that Yahweh is aware of their exhaustion from captivity (v. 27). Yahweh will intervene and is able to give the exiles strength. The exiles assume that fate favors the Babylonians, who defeated and now rule them, and the other nations, who moved in to occupy Judah. Isaiah declares that nations are only a fraction of the earth's raw material, malleable in the hands of Yahweh, Israel's God.

Isaiah 40:12–31 leads directly to the argument of Isaiah 41, and then to the first Servant passage of 42:1–4. Isaiah 40:12–31 begins a dispute between Yahweh and the exiles on the exiles' adoption of paganism. The questions are rhetorical though the answers are, in fact, to be forthcoming from the people addressed, who would know the answers from their faith. The argument moves from the known to the unknown—or, rather, from common knowledge to specific knowledge—through this series of questions (Gitay 1981, 83). What kind of a God is the God of Israel? The required answer —that he is a Creator God— is given in verse 12, and the language turns at once to the sovereignty of God over God's creation and God's initial control over the cosmic waters, the heavens, and the earth. In verses 13–14, the infinite wisdom of Yahweh is referred to. Yahweh, unlike his ancient (mythical) contemporaries of the heavenly council, created alone (Clifford 1984, 80). The argument then passes to Yahweh's rule over the world. The nations who seem to have triumphed and who now occupy the Promised Land are not powerful (vv. 15–16) when their power is compared to Yahweh's power (v. 12). They would be swept away like a puff of wind (v. 17). Yahweh is incomparable (v. 18), certainly in comparison with any visible likeness that comes from human ingenuity (vv. 19–20). Yahweh's unassailability (vv. 21–22) is pitted against the contemptuous princes, who are represented in traditional language as "shoots" or "plantings" (v. 24; Clifford 1984, 81–82). The astral deities worshiped by Babylon (vv. 25–26) cannot be compared to Yahweh, for Yahweh created the heavens. It follows (vv. 27–31) that God has not forsaken

God's people. So, far from Yahweh growing faint, he gives strength to the weak (vv. 28–29). In verse 27, the real content of Israel's complaint emerges—that God has ignored her fate within history, her present exile. But the rejoinder is that Yahweh's changelessness and his inexhaustible resources guarantee Yahweh's ability to protect his people (vv. 28–31).

Isaiah 41 progresses by means of vivid dramatizations of a cosmic trial. There is the summons to trial (41:1, 5–7, 21–22b), the legal questioning of nations and their gods (41:2–4, 22c–29), and a verdict on the nations and Israel (41:8–20; 42:1–9). Each of the parallel sections (41:1–20 and 41:21–42:9) presents a complete scene. Summoned by Yahweh, the nations bring statues of their patron gods and repair to the place of judgment. When questioned, they are unable to produce oracles predicting Cyrus's victories, and are declared to be without power. Yahweh announces that he had predicted Cyrus's victories; hence, he is the power behind the nations' power (41:1–7). He then announces a verdict on Israel and the nations (41:8–20) and addresses Israel in endearing terms (vv. 8–16) before finally arraigning the nations' gods (41:21–29). Isaiah 41 indicates that servant Israel will be triumphant and secure in the midst of the nations' general devastation. In Isaiah 40–66, the trial narratives aimed at the nations state Yahweh's universalism and exist primarily for Israel's benefit, to provide confidence and faith in Yahweh. The polemics against idolatry were meant to universalize what had been an article of faith for Israel only, namely, the sole deity of Yahweh.

The Servant

It is now generally conceded that the four Servant passages (Isa. 42:1–4; 49:1–6; 50:4–9; 52:13–53:12) fit their contexts and contribute to the message of Isaiah 40–55. It is clear that the Servant is Israel in some form, since the Servant is juxtaposed with Israel in 41:1–42:17 and placed opposite Jerusalem in 49:1–26 (A. Wilson 1986, 253). The issue to be discussed before the identity of the Servant is taken further, however, is the role of the Servant. The Servant figure in Isaiah 40–55 is instrumentally and integrally bound with the redemption of Jerusalem. Indeed, the Servant's ministry is to effect Israel's return to Jerusalem.

The role of the Servant is fully anticipated in the call narrative of Isaiah 42:1–4 and is commented on by Isaiah 42:5–9. We turn to the Servant's role in 42:1–4 and in 49:1–26, before we pass to a brief review of his role in Isaiah 52:13–53:12. We then examine the consequences stemming from his ministry, which are assessed in theological and practical terms in Isaiah 54–55. The Servant's work is to institute the new covenant, whereby Jerusalem becomes the world center; from Jerusalem, the blessings of salvation flow. All of this identifies Isaiah 40–55 with the exilic theology of Jeremiah and Ezekiel, though, for the author of Second Isaiah, the renewal of Israel always has the incoming Gentiles in view.

Isaiah 42:1–4 seems to continue the address to the divine council (cf. 40:1), although Israel is indirectly in view. Thus, in verse 1 the LXX supplies the name Jacob before *'ebed* 'Servant' and Israel before the verbal form of *bahar* 'choose'.

Isaiah 42:1 seems clearly to operate as a formula of introduction. Yahweh presents the Servant. The parallels between the appointment of the Servant and the royal Messiah are striking. In fact, there is close correspondence between the designation of the Servant and the choice of David in 1 Samuel 16:1–13; in addition, the titles "Servant" and "chosen one" are applied in the same way as they are to David in Psalm 89:3. The gift of the enabling Spirit, and the close parallels of 42:1–2 to the call of David in 1 Samuel 16:1–13, have often been noted, adding weight to the supposition that the Servant is a royal (as the Targum supposes at v. 1) and prophetic figure. This contention has further support from the fact that "to take by the hand" (42:1), that is, to uphold, may be a coronation formula. The mission of the Servant, by which his divine empowerment is demonstrated, is summarized by verse 1b, where the Servant is to bring justice (*mishpat*) to the nations.

The key term in 42:1–4 is the Hebrew *mishpat* 'justice'. Isaiah 40:12–14 had associated *mishpat* directly with Yahweh's work of creation. Through such a divine act it seems that the divine principles of harmony that sustain the universe were provided. In Isaiah 40:27, *mishpat* and *derek* 'way' were associated, as Israel complained how history had swung against her. This complaint was apparently aimed at Yahweh's control of history. In the first trial narrative of Isaiah 41:1–7, *mishpat* establishes Yahweh's case against the nation. This *mishpat* is Yahweh's supremacy over history, shown particularly by the present elevation of Cyrus, whose exploits will liberate Jerusalem (cf. 41:27–29). Isaiah 41 thus makes plain what is implicit in Isaiah 40:12–31, that *mishpat* involves nothing less than Yahweh's superintendence of the created order. This point is also conveyed in Isaiah 42:1–4.

Above all, however, *mishpat* concerns Israel and Yahweh's covenant with Israel, since the justice that the Servant will bring to the nations will vindicate Israel's special position. So the question of *mishpat,* the subject of Israel's complaint, has widened in Isaiah 40:12–31, and *mishpat* has been associated with Yahweh's immeasurability, incomparability, and uniqueness. God's unassailed mastery over the universe has been on view in *mishpat*—not merely God's dealing with men or nations.

Verses 2–3 then indicate the method of the Servant's ministry. The Servant's office is described negatively, and only at the end of the verses do we have positive reference to his role, taking us back to verse 1b. The tirelessness of the Servant is referred to in verse 4a, which perhaps summarizes verses 2–3. The figure of the bruised reed and smoldering wick in verse 3a is not Palestinian but Mesopotamian (Jeremias 1972, 36–37). If the Babylonian background from which the image stems is pressed, the image refers to the release of a condemned man near death (cf. Isa. 43:17; 2 Sam. 14:7). The reference is then to the grace that the Servant's ministry extends to Israel, who will then be raised from the near-death of exile.

The Hebrew *'emeth* 'truth' (v. 3b) has God's faithfulness and steadfastness in mind. The expression *le'emeth,* which does not occur elsewhere in the OT, is to be taken directionally, meaning "with truth in mind," or to establish truth, to display steadfastness (cf. Beuken 1972, 3). It is thus covenant steadfastness that the Servant will display, and this will result, as we shall see, in the consummation of Israel's covenant history. The action that verse 4 reports then follows naturally.

In regard to "the Isles" who "put their hope in his law" (v. 4; cf. 42:4 and 51:5) and in similar contexts, the *torah* 'law' for which the people wait is a general concept, meaning something like "shows the way." The word's occurrence in this context seems to take us back to the similar eschatology of Isaiah 2:2–4. Isaiah 2:3 indicates that, in the future, Yahweh himself will dispense Torah from Jerusalem as he teaches Gentile pilgrims his "ways." In Isaiah 42:1–4, the Servant will establish Yahweh's *mishpat,* which will lead to the Torah's proclamation from Jerusalem (cf. 41:27–29). In light of Isaiah 2:2–4, the Servant's ministry will implement Yahweh's designs for divine rule from Jerusalem. The Servant's work will result not merely in the restoration to Jerusalem contemplated by Isaiah 40:1–11, but in the elevation of that center to world prominence as the city of God, with the Torah's rule over the wider world.

Commentary on the First Servant Song (Isa. 42:5–9)

Isaiah 42:5–9 comments on 42:1–4 and is Yahweh's address to the Servant. The context is now broadened to include Yahweh's lordship over creation, thus providing the broader purposes against which the Servant's call is to be measured. In verses 6–7, Yahweh states his intentions for the Servant, and in verses 8–9 he reveals himself. Verses 1–4 had thus identified the Servant and indicated how he will accomplish his mission, and verses 5–9 provide evidence of what he will do. Yahweh has called the Servant in righteousness, that is, in fidelity to his creative purposes (Isa. 41:9–10). The Servant will now effect a new covenant for Israel (Isa. 42:6), with worldwide ramifications.

In 42:6, the phrase "covenant to the people, a light to the nations," by which the servant's vocation is summed up, is difficult and has been variously interpreted. The translation "covenant people" defies the Hebrew word order. However, "covenant of the people," with the Servant carrying the traditions of redeemed Israel—traditions that once belonged to the nation as a whole—is possible and plausible. What the Servant will do will relate to Israel initially, but will affect the world through her. Redeemed Israel, when released, will call other nations to her, and they will run to her (55:3–5). Kings and queens will attend her (49:23), nations will bow down (49:23; cf. 45:15), while nations who oppose Israel will be consumed (cf. 49:26). It is clear that the salvation of all nations is contemplated after their submission first to Israel. This attitude to the nations in Isaiah 40–55 makes clear that ideal Israel is conceived of as a saved remnant only.

Cyrus Song

Vitally important in Isaiah 40–55 is the material relating to Cyrus, king of Persia beginning in 559 B.C. This material is contained in the "Cyrus Song" (44:24–45:13). Cyrus acts on behalf of the divine warrior to establish Yahweh's world sovereignty from Jerusalem. Three identifiable units occur within the song (44:24–28; 45:1–7; 45:9–13). The opening unit is clearly introductory, since the call of Cyrus does not specifically occur until 45:1–7. An *inclusio* on the function of Yahweh as Creator and Lord of history is formed by 44:24 and 45:12. Cyrus will build the temple (44:28) and return the exiles (45:13). Isaiah 44:24–28 is a single lengthy sentence built around the initial noun clause, "I am Yahweh," a formula that dominates the song (45:3, 5, 6, 7) and that appears in contexts within Isaiah that emphasize Yahweh's creative and redemptive power (41:4; 42:6; 43:25). The clause is used in exilic and postexilic contexts in association with impending judgment (cf. Ezekiel). Isaiah 44:24–28 is composed of three strophes concerning Yahweh's sovereignty in creation, over idols, and in history.

Isaiah 45:1–8 is made up of five strophes, and is concerned with the commissioning of Cyrus, but the stress is on what Yahweh will do for the exiles. Verse 1, the first strophe, emphasizes Yahweh's action in directing Cyrus's progress; verses 2–3 describe the aid given to Cyrus on the march, so that Cyrus, unlike the boastful Assyrian of Isaiah 10, might know Yahweh's power. The third strophe (vv. 4–6a) describes the irony of Yahweh calling the unwitting Cyrus and notes the progression in Yahweh's purpose for Israel extending to the world. The fourth strophe (vv. 6b–7), through merism ("I form light and create darkness, I make weak and create woe"), describes Yahweh's creation of all things. The fifth and final strophe (v. 8) is a short hymnic passage. As Yahweh has created all things, so righteousness and salvation spring from heaven and earth. The Divine Warrior will first fructify the desert and then take his place in the Jerusalem temple in the rebuilt Zion. Isaiah 45:9–13 has three strophes (vv. 9–10, 11–12, 13). This is not a woe oracle (as the introductory woe might suggest) but a disputation with Israel, which refuses to believe that Cyrus is Yahweh's agent. Verses 9–13 answer Israel's rebellious questioning.

The use of *go'el* 'redeemer' at 44:24 puts us in touch with a key theme of Isaiah 40–55, a theme that bears on the new exodus redemption. There is a deeper purpose at work in Cyrus (cf. the intention expressed in three purpose clauses in 45:3, 6) that Cyrus might know Yahweh, that Israel might see the connection and that the world might see Yahweh as God alone (45:6). So the commissioning of Cyrus is not for the narrow interest of Israel only. Yahweh's choice of Cyrus expresses Cyrus's righteousness (41:1–4; 45:13). Yahweh had raised Cyrus up from the beginning (41:1–7; 45:1) to destroy Babylon (45:1–3) and to rebuild Jerusalem (44:26–28). Cyrus is Yahweh's shepherd (44:28) and his anointed, the man of Yahweh's purpose (46:11). Yahweh loves him, has chosen him (48:14), and Cyrus will carry out Yahweh's good pleasure in Babylon. The emphasis is on Yahweh having raised Cyrus up (44:28; 45:13; 46:11; etc.). However, Israel refuses to accept Yahweh's wise plan. Therefore, the chapters stress the immutability of Yahweh's word and his wisdom (see 40:12–14, 28; 44:25–28; 55:5–9). In rejecting God's plan for its redemption via Cyrus (Isa. 45:9–13), Israel shows itself as obdurate and rebellious as ever. The presentation of Yahweh as Creator and Lord of history serves as an apologia. The increasingly hostile tone of the prophecy reflects the feeling that the exile has changed nothing in Israel.

The remainder of the material through Isaiah 48 cannot be dealt with in detail, but the emphasis is on the impending return of the exiles, the overthrow of idolatrous Babylon, and the role of Cyrus. The root issue in these chapters is the conflict between the prophet's revelation of Yahweh's plan and the conventional idolatrous wisdom epitomized in Babylon. Nothing has changed, the old national sins persist, and the nation is Israel in name only.

Isaiah 49–55 discusses Zion's future and exhibits remarkable contrast in both tone and theme. The enigmatic Servant figure appears at center stage; disputation with and strident criticism of Israel is absent. Whereas Isaiah 40–48 has been concerned with Cyrus's exaltation and Babylon's humiliation, Isaiah 49–55 deals with the Servant's humiliation and the deliverance of Jerusalem-Zion.

The Servant and the Restoration of Zion (Isa. 49:1–26)

The vocation of the Servant is further delineated in 49:1–6, as the nations are addressed (v. 1), in the manner of a typical prophetic call. A. Wilson (1986, 275) points out that most of the chapter's subsections (vv. 1–6, 7, 8–13, 14–16, 17–18, 19–21, 22–23, 24–26) all end by demarcating the attitude of the nations. These nations are successively called to recognize the Servant, to render homage to Yahweh, and to bring the exiles to Zion as they come in submissive pilgrimage (vv. 7, 12–13, 18, 22–23). The Servant thus will regather Israel from afar, reestablish the nations in all their lands (v. 8), and effect Zion's restoration. The Servant's exaltation is thus inextricably bound up with Zion's glorification (A. Wilson 1986, 286).

The Procession of the Nations

Isaiah 49 raises the question of the eschatological pilgrimage of the nations to Jerusalem, a vital theme for Isaiah 40–66. The delegated victories of Cyrus will result in the restoration of Jerusalem, the rebuilding of the temple as the focus of Yahweh's rule (44:28; 45:13)—a necessary consequence after Yahweh's victories (cf. Exod. 15:17)—and the return of a renewed Israel. All this will vindicate Yahweh in the sight of all the nations and will glorify the Servant (49:7; 52:13; 53:12), who is looking increasingly messianic, like a "son of David" (cf. Isa. 55:3–5), as the prophecy continues. God's sovereignty will be established in Zion, a shrine to be honored by all nations, and Zion will thus fulfill the expectations of the Psalms and the Prophets (Ps. 47; 68:29–33; 96, 97, 98; Isa. 2:2–4; see A. Wilson 1986, 232). The procession to Zion will be accompanied by signs of a new creation, the desert in bloom with all nature transformed and rejoicing (Isa. 35; 41:17–20; 49:9–11; 55:12–13). The nations will recognize the sovereignty of Yahweh (Isa. 45:4–5), and the eschatological reign of God will begin. Submissive nations will be blessed, the idolatrous purged (A. Wilson 1986, 248).

Isaiah 50–51

The point is made in 50:1–3 that the exile is for discipline, not divorce. Isaiah 50:4–9 tells the Servant to persevere and to call on the exiles to respond to his voice. Isaiah 51:1–8 addresses a faithful Israel, who will inherit the promises, while verses 9–11 spell out the return to Jerusalem in terms of a new creation. Verses 12–16 console Jerusalem, for Yahweh stands behind her, and the covenant is thus to be restored. Jerusalem is then called upon to rouse herself (vv. 17–20), since her cup of wrath will be passed on to Babylon (vv. 21–23).

Evaluating the Servant's Ministry (Isa. 52–55)

With Isaiah 52:13–53:12 we are able to evaluate the effectiveness of the Servant's ministry. In Isaiah 52:1–5, Zion is challenged to prepare for the return of the captives. The messenger then comes to Zion, announcing the return of God to Jerusalem; thus, the messenger comes as the comfort of his people. Jerusalem has been redeemed (vv. 6–10). There is then the call for the captives to move out in a new exodus (vv. 11–12). The evaluation of the Servant's ministry follows before further assessments of its results in Isaiah 54–55.

Rikki E. Watts (1990, 56–59) points out that the identification of the Servant with Jacob-Israel material is absent from Isaiah 49–55, in which the mission of the anonymous Servant is center stage. As the general prophecy has proceeded, Israel is looking less and less like the Servant figure. She is criticized for her spiritual obtuseness (40:27; 42:18–20). She is blind and deaf, a frequent theme throughout the prophecy of chapters 1–66 (cf. 43:8; 48:8; etc.), often linked in context with critiques of idolatry. Watts notes that the great bulk of the salvation promises in chapters 49–55 are future-oriented proclamations of salvation oracles. Their future emphasis suggests that there has been a postponement of the full hopes for the new exodus, since Jacob-Israel's response to the divine initiatives in Cyrus have made it clear that she is incapable of fulfilling the servant role delineated in 42:1–9.

In Isaiah 49–55, the prophet looks forward to the future, when the servant role will be fulfilled by a personality as yet unknown. The pronounced notes in the Servant presentation, especially in Isaiah 52:13–53:12, indicate that the remnant community, meant to be the idealized servant community in Isaiah 40–48, upon whom Israel's hopes reposed, has been reduced to one. At some time in the future, this Servant figure will redeem Israel and extend the revelation of God to the world at large. Watts thus very plausibly suggests that Isaiah 40–55 explains the non-materialization of the glorious promises associated with the prospective return of Israel from exile, and, in particular, the failure of the new exodus to eventuate. Such a scenario is confirmed by the detail of Isaiah 56–66. However, the divine intention still stands. The Day of the Lord will finally mature, the new exodus will occur, and remnant Israel will function as a light to the Gentiles (Isa. 56–66).

Isaiah 52:13–53:12. In Isaiah 52:13, our attention is drawn to the Servant's active obedience and, thus, blessedness. The Servant's action has been wise and well-thought-out. However, if the Servant is acting in the way of obedience and living rightly in covenant relationship with Yahweh, the question arises, why does he suffer? The answer lies in Isaiah 53, for the way in which the Servant suffers gives *shalom* to the speakers of 53:1–11 and heals them. On the face of it, this *shalom* does not seem to apply to the nation. Israel had remained unperceptive throughout the experience. Understanding for Israel could only come after the exile (cf. Isa. 41:20). In the determination of the speakers at Isaiah 53:11, much depends on the identity of the Servant figure. The term "servant" is applied to Jacob-Israel in the body of the prophecy at 41:8, 9; 44:1; and 45:4, although passively. Jacob-Israel, however, is blind, deaf, and without understanding, in contradistinction to the unknown Servant of the Servant songs, who exhibits the obedience that stems from complete trust. The punishment incurred by Jacob-Israel is merited, while the anonymous Servant is guiltless and suffers vicariously, spurned and rejected by his own people (Watts 1990, 53).

From the vocabulary of Isaiah 52:13, it appears that something like the elevation of a victorious king is contemplated where the face of the Servant has been disfigured either by violence or by putrefaction. The Servant is perceived as judged, inconsequential, and thus ignored. Even Gentile kings (Isa. 52:13–15), who are notoriously hardened, will be appalled.

In Isaiah 53:1–9, Israel seems to be speaking and stands astonished at the Servant's ministry and at the realization of its atoning significance. The elevation of the Servant will mean the elevation of Israel, and the nations will discover that their future blessing depends on Israel and her God (cf. Isa. 45:14). Without the redemption of Israel, there could be no world redemption (Isaiah 45:20–25), and thus no return to Eden. Such a world redemption as this would in its turn mean the universal acknowledgement of Yahweh's *torah* and *mishpat*. It would be through the mediation of the Torah that Israel would fulfill her vocation (Exod. 19:3b–6) and become a light to the nations. It would be Torah, however— demonstrating Yahweh's will for the world through Israel—that would be the light, and not Israel herself. The explanation of how such world redemption will come is contained in the closing chapters of Isaiah 40–55. As a result of the ministry of the Servant (Isa. 53), the nations will gather around a new Israel (Isa. 54) and a new David (Isa. 55:5). The Servant is thus a mysterious figure of the future.

Israel's acknowledgement in Isaiah 53 of the significance of the Servant's atonement will lead finally to the ministry of Israel to the world, since the Servant appears to be an incarnation of faithful Israel. Israel herself confesses (Isa. 53:1–9) that she had misunderstood the Servant's relationship to God as well as her own, but that now she sees these relationships in a different light. A changed perception of this character means a religious and moral conversion, leading to a restored Israel. This conversion provides the essential ground for the Servant's exaltation, for he has seen light from his travail, the success of his ministry, and from his teaching and his intercession for the transgressors (v. 12). This was the spoil that the Servant was destined to receive. This theology had been formed in Isaiah's time, but the major application would come in the future.

The poem is not clear as to what triggered the Servant's reversal, although, in part, it must have been the Servant's willingness to die for the sake of his message and his vocation. In the end, the text tells us (v. 11) that the reversal came from the Servant's knowledge, that is, from his understanding of the revelation of God in history, in the light of which he was prepared to suffer (Ward 1978, 129). A prophetic critique (53:10–11) and a divine assessment (53:12) of the ministry follow Israel's confession (53:1–9).

The Aramaic translation, the Targum of Isaiah 53, defines the Servant as the Messiah. There is in the Targum an intermixing of the roles in Isaiah 53 of the Servant and Israel. The Messiah prospers and Israel suffers, but the Messiah does not suffer for Israel beyond being despised by the nations (Isa. 53:3). The Messiah's role is intercessory only and not substitutionary. The tension that the Targum obviously felt about the prospect of a suffering Messiah is thus resolved by identifying Israel as suffering and the Messiah as triumphant. But this paradox, which was clearly there, was to be resolved finally and remarkably by identifying Jesus of Nazareth as at once the expected Messiah, but also as the fulfiller of Israel's destiny to suffer for the world. The exile had clouded the patriarchal promises, and there was now a need for a new covenant, a new Moses, a new David, and, most important for a new Israel, a need for a people willing to abandon idolatry in favor of faithfulness to Yahweh. In addition, the mystery of Isaiah 40–55, which the New Testament finally makes clear, was that the Servant Israel must "bear sin" (v. 12) for the many, uniting in herself priestly (Num. 18:1, 23; Lev. 10:17) atonement for others and prophetic intercession (A. Wilson 1986, 301–6).

Consequences of the Servant's death (Isa. 54–55). In Isaiah 54–55, the consequences of the Servant's death in terms of a new covenant based on Zion and her world position are spelled out. Isaiah 54 is replete with covenant imagery, Abrahamic (vv. 1–3) and Sinaitic (vv. 4–6). Zion (vv. 4–6) is set forth as a woman who, in her youth, has been espoused and cast off again because of her sins, but who then had been recalled to the status of a wife. In this Sinai covenantal marriage metaphor (cf. Jeremiah and Hosea), the Sinai relationship is looked on as the time when Israel was called into political nationhood. Sinaitic theology is also to be perceived in the terminology of *hesed* (Exod. 15:13; 34:6), "Holy One of Israel," and "Redeemer" (*go'el*).

The Noah comparison of verse 9 adds to the bewildering complex of covenant motifs applied in this chapter to complete the picture of Zion. The covenant of peace (v. 10) has in mind the implementation, at some future period, of Yahweh's world renewal. The figurative language of verses 11–17 attempts to describe the beauty and splendor of the new Zion, anticipating the magnificent description we find of the new city of God in Revelation 21. This outward glory of Zion is reflected in the inward glory of her children, who, in terms of the new covenant framework (Jer. 31:33), are all taught about the Lord (v. 13). The new city is one whose maker and builder is God and whose foundations have been divinely laid (v. 11), and thus is unshakable in the terms used in verse 10. The consequences of this new arrangement are drawn out in verses 14–17, and the note of righteousness encloses these verses (Beuken 1974, 61). This righteousness is not, however, Israel's own response to this new arrangement—the parading of established conduct by the redeemed people of God—but rather a display of divine righteousness, divine fidelity to the covenant arrangements of righteousness that alone will guarantee access to the new age. The old Promised Land terminology in *nahalah* 'inheritance' in verse 17 foreshadows the goal of perfect occupancy of the land and thus the enjoyment of that rest, the presence of God in the land.

Building on Isaiah 54, in 55:1–2 the faithful are then summoned to participate in the messianic banquet on Mount Zion (A. Wilson 1986, 222), in the new life that will flow forth from Jerusalem as the waters of life from this new Eden. This invitation to the restored Israel is made on the basis of the covenant with David (vv. 3–5), for the redeemed must now assume Israel's position of a kingdom of priests (Exod. 19:5–6). Israel is now empowered because of Yahweh's cosmic victories, as David had been empowered of old (A. Wilson 1986, 226), to summon the nations, who come running to serve and glorify her. The sure mercies of David are not David's faithful acts but Yahweh's fidelity to the Davidic covenant. The life offered is proximity to the deity's shrine and, thus, participation in the presence of the deity.

The invitation to the redeemed goes forth. Isaiah 55:6 is a summons to participate in the new exodus to the sanctuary, which verse 7 completes; verses 8–11, to elaborate the sanctuary's holiness, call for putting aside all human devices and conduct that would prevent the assumption of the divine will (Clifford 1983, 31). The democratization of these promises does not extend to all, but only to those who come in obedience to Mount Zion to respond to the divine call. The light for the nations is the heavenly glory that has been imparted to the holy city (Isa. 60:1) and to the new pilgrims (60:5). The word of God finally must prevail (55:11). Verses 12–13 describe the new exodus procession to Zion and the temple by the miraculously transformed way—the sign itself of the new exodus and conquest, of fertility's victory over sterility, and of the new creation that will be the Lord's memorial (Clifford 1983, 34).

The logic of the placement of Isaiah 54 and 55 suggests that all has been achieved by the suffering and death of Yahweh's Servant (Isa. 53). He will do nothing less than usher in the new era, the new creation. The restoration of Jerusalem, prominent in the prophecy of Isaiah 40–55 and with which the ministry of the Servant has been so closely bound up, triggers the advent of the new age, the everlasting rule of God.

The Inheritance of the Remnant (Isa. 56–66)

Isaiah 56–66 expands the material of chapters 40–55, with more reference to the divisions within the community. Isaiah 54:17 had forecast the future for the servants of Yahweh, and chapters 56–66 describe this future in further detail. At the same time, however, Isaiah 56–66 deals with persistent community problems of the return that prevent Yahweh's promise of democratized servanthood in a New Jerusalem from becoming reality (Beuken 1990). It turns out that the reason for the delay of salvation and restoration is the necessity of a future judgment for the community that must precede restoration and the restriction of salvation to a particular group. Within Isaiah 56–66, much seems given over to the difficulties of the Israelite community, arising from the return from exile. Yet within these chapters, although the presentation is more muted, the same worldview prevails, with Israel taking her place at the center of her world. The prophecy concludes with a magnificent description of the restored age, whereby the saints come back to Zion to live in peace, when the new creation prevails and nature once more experiences harmony.

Isaiah 56:1–8, the prologue to Isaiah 56–66, presupposes the role of "the servants" and gives the concept programmatic place. Isaiah 56:1–8 contains a high estimate of the temple and states who is to be admitted as Yahweh gathers his servants in his house (56:6–8). The temple is Yahweh's holy house built on Yahweh's holy mountain, a house of prayer and house of sacrifice. Yahweh announces "righteousness" as the goal of his acting and unfolds his intention to his servants (vv. 1–2, 6–8). His servants are depicted as people who honor the Sabbath—the preeminent marker of Israel in the postexilic period—and who hold onto the covenant, who will therefore be gathered by God on his holy mountain and in his house of prayer. On the other hand, this category of belief expands, because it appears that foreigners can join themselves to Yahweh in order to serve him (v. 3). Therefore, the connotation of servants is elaborated over that of chapters 40–55. An international pilgrimage to a sacred mountain, presumably Jerusalem (56:1–8), begins these chapters, just as the note of a similar pilgrimage ends them (66:18–24).

Isaiah 56:9–57:13 constitutes an attack on the elders of the restoration community and a diatribe against various cultic acts. In 56:9–57:3, three groups are singled out for condemnation: watchmen, seers (cf. 56:10; Schramm 1995, 125–26), and shepherds. The "you" (57:3) attacked are the leaders of the previous chapter. Accusations multiply in 57:4–13; worship among trees is said to be a foreign intrusion. Such worship was possibly an Asherah cult (Asherah meaning the goddess Asherah of Canaan, *asherah* the stylized wooden tree that represented the goddess). Idolaters had set up alternative worship sites (vv. 7–10, to Asherah?) and offered child sacrifice to Moloch (v. 7). Isaiah 57:11–13 pronounces judgment on those who have taken part in the practices of 57:4–10. Verse 13c announces salvation to a group that has not participated in such practices. Isaiah 57:14–21 is a salvation oracle reminiscent of chapters 40–55. The recipients of the proclamation are "my people," set in contrast with the wicked who participated in the practices in 57:3–10.

Isaiah 58:1–4 is addressed to "my people . . . the house of Jacob." The passage is a sermon or speech of admonition, not an oracle of judgment. It is a call to the community to change its behavior. The subject of the passage is the relationship between ritual fasting and the arrival of Yahweh's promised salvation. In 58:5–7, the prophet declares that legitimate fasting and social action go together. Isaiah 58:8–12 answers the question of 58:3a as to the reason for fasting.

Both the prophet and the people agree that the realization of Yahweh's promises depends on behavior. The Sabbath must be exalted, and its observation is also necessary (58:13–14).

Isaiah 59

Isaiah 59:1 links with the addressees of Isaiah 58, people of the house of Jacob (58:14) who, in 59:1–8, are now charged with numerous abuses. While in chapter 58 the question is how one obtains salvation, in chapter 59 the question is why one has not obtained it. The people have claimed that Yahweh is not able to carry out the earlier promises (of Isa. 40–55). Yahweh has not acted on his earlier promises, but the behavior of people is the problem. This antisocial behavior has resulted in a society lacking in justice and righteousness, as is evident in the two verses about the abuses (59:4, 8). A new act of judgment must now precede restoration. The announcement of this new act distinguishes the proclamation of chapters 56–66 from that of chapters 40–55. In 59:9–15a, the oppressed acknowledge, reluctantly, in a confession of sin that is in agreement with 59:1–8, that righteousness does not exist in the community (59:9, 14). The purpose of these verses is to contrast the present situation with what was announced in 56:1. Isaiah 59 thus shows that confession leads to salvation, but this salvation comes only after a new act of judgment on Yahweh's part that will separate the righteous from the wicked, dividing an inner Israel from Israel. What the community says about itself is now matched by what the Lord has said about it.

Isaiah 59:15b–20 is the climax, in which the theophany is announced and Yahweh is pictured as a warrior going to battle. Those marked for defeat are named in 59:18 (adversaries, enemies, islands), while the beneficiaries of his action are named in 59:20 (Zion and those in Jacob who turn from transgression). All the terms in 59:18 appear to refer to those who do not turn to Yahweh. Then, when God's righteousness comes to help (vv. 16–19), the holdouts are converted (v. 20). Having become righteous themselves, they are commissioned to carry forward the voice of prophecy (v. 21). They are also promised offspring (seed) so that, until the third generation, they will testify to God's covenant (v. 21). In these generations the promise is realized that the Servant "shall see offspring [seed], he shall prolong his days" (53:10).

The Righteous Progeny in Zion (Isa. 60–62)

In these chapters, the prophet speaks of a righteous generation in which the promise to the Servant will come true. Isaiah 60:1–3 transfers the task of the Servant—to be a light to the nations (42:6; 49:6)—to Zion. As the nations come in pilgrimage (vv. 4–9), they bring Zion's scattered children with them. Thus the promise of world influence, by which Zion is to be the legatee of the Davidic promises, is still to be achieved and soon will be. The dignitaries of the foreigners and kings who will rebuild Zion's walls (vv. 10–11) represent the subjugation of the nations. The wealth of nations will stream into Zion (vv. 12–20) as fulfillment of the Abrahamic covenant and as an illustration of Israel's righteousness (v. 21), resulting in the Abrahamic expansion of Israel's numbers (v. 22). The inhabitants of the new Zion will be Yahweh's redeemed people, who will now fulfill the Servant role. This is the initiative of Yahweh, who has appointed "righteousness" to rule the new order (v. 17).

In Isaiah 61, the shape of Israel's future is further reassessed. The question of the righteous seed and the erection of the new servant community is continued. In Isaiah 61:1–3, a figure like the Servant of 42:1–4 is commissioned by Yahweh's Spirit to bring a message of hope, cast in terms of the messianic expectations associated with the new age (cf. Isa. 11:1–16). The Servant figure of 61:1 addresses the oppressed, those who mourn in Zion, presumably for Zion's inability to demonstrate her destined role, and transforms them by his Spirit-filled ministry into those who assume the mantle of praise. Through the ministry of the Servant, they also become ministering servants and receive a new name betokening (v. 3) a transformed existence. Those who exhibit this transformation (v. 3) have become oaks of righteousness, bastions of the covenant.

Israel (vv. 4–9) will enjoy the blessings of her inheritance and exercise her mandate, acclaimed by the world, as a kingdom of priests (v. 6; cf. Exod. 19:5–6). The covenant promises of Isaiah 40:1–2 have now become manifested in the New Jerusalem. They are never to be annulled (v. 8). The world will acknowledge that the people of the new Zion are the offspring (i.e., the regenerated servant community; cf. v. 9) whom God has blessed, and this exercises the compulsive drawing power of verses 5–6. The Israel of the new age is not destined for political importance but to be the servant of Yahweh, maintaining world peace presumably by the distribution of *mishpat* and *torah*.

Isaiah 61:10–11 returns to the theme that Yahweh will make "righteousness and praise . . . spring up before all the nations." Israel is now restored to a transformed, Eden-like land. The world offers homage to the bride, Zion. This figurative language announces that the new order of righteousness will be visible in the offspring/converts of the prophet, who look like the Servant and who are already clothed, as a pledge, with righteousness. An important element is the phrase "praise . . . before all the nations," the final phrase of verse 11, which fulfills the expectation of verse 9 that this generation will secure worldwide fame because of the blessing Israel has received. This new righteousness is a cosmic happening (v. 11), coming forth from the earth itself as the new principle of the world. In the ideal community of return, the redeemed are the offspring of the Servant and continue his ministry. The final goal of God's actions is not the Servant but the Servant's descendants (Beuken 1990, 68).

The peculiar election of Zion to privilege is the subject of Isaiah 62. Zion is vindicated and restored (vv. 1–2a) as the light to the world, and a new name is given to her community (vv. 2b–4a). Her future is delineated in the covenant imagery of marriage (vv. 4b–5). God's faithful intention to fulfill the promises made to Zion is the tenor of verses 6–9, while the call to the people of God to enter Jerusalem completes the chapter (vv. 10–12). We already know that righteousness is necessary for admission to the sanctuary (cf. Ps. 15; 24; Isaiah 33:14–16). The decision on entrance must be made at the gates because, behind the gates, the recovered covenant is celebrated to the praise of Yahweh (v. 9). Therefore, the summons of verse 10 implies the righteousness of those addressed and their acceptance by Yahweh. These are now "the people of the holy place" (v. 11). The dispersed of Israel are assembled in the house of Yahweh, together with the foreigners. Altogether, they are the servants of Yahweh (cf. 56:6–8). All this results from the prior act of Yahweh, who established the primacy of Mount Zion.

Isaiah 63:1–6, the Divine Warrior hymn, is mythico-apocalyptic in character. The gospel now unfolds further. Israel's enemies are symbolized by "Edom" (63:1), who is the archenemy (63:2); red is the traditional image of divine judgment. From this judgment, salvation will come. The Lord has come to carry out final victory in the plan to subdue all the peoples of the earth. In the second question and answer (vv. 2–3), the Lord is pictured covered with the blood of a war that he has fought alone, taking vengeance on his adversaries (v. 4). His own arm wrought the needed salvation (v. 5). To this portrait of the Lord, the implied audience responds in 63:7–64:12. In the moving communal lament (63:7–64:11), there is initially a recollection (63:7–9) of Yahweh's merciful acts toward people in the ancient past (Schramm 1995, 150). The response from Yahweh's rescued people then, however, was rebellion (v. 10). Now the plea of the community is for Yahweh again to intervene to bring about the new exodus redemption (63:11–14).

The account (63:15–64:12) moves into lament proper as it takes up the addressees' present plight (Schramm 1995, 152). Days of the past to which the community has appealed are also the days of the patriarchs, but neither Abraham nor Israel (v. 16) would acknowledge this community that, by its conduct (v. 17), is cut off from its past. For this, the community recognizes, it had been cast into the hands of its enemies, who are still dominant (vv. 18–19). The fervent pleas of 64:1–3 for God's intervention climax in the recognition of God's incomparability (v. 4). The intimacy of the new relationship the implied audience feels is exemplified in the address to Yahweh as "our Father" (v. 8), even though the community recognizes that it is the Lord who has burdened their hearts and caused them to err from the Lord's ways (63:17). In 64:9–11, the speaker calls attention to the desolation of the temple and the holy city; the purpose of this recitation seems to be to challenge God's honor and thus to provoke intervention. The lament concludes with an anguished question in 64:12 as to whether God will remain silent and continue the affliction.

God replies to the community in chapters 65–66. Isaiah 65:1–25 makes clear that Yahweh's failure to restore Jerusalem is due to misplaced worship. The translation of promises into reality must wait until a community of true servants has been produced. The salvation-judgment oracle of Isaiah 65 reads as the answer to the lament of 63:7–64:11. The primary function of 65:1–16 is to attack a fundamental presupposition of the lament that "we are all your people." Yahweh replies negatively in criticism of this presupposition. The traditional terms "Yahweh's people," "servants," and "chosen" are redefined. Yahweh's servant is not the nation but the pious that seek him (65:1–7). The people who, in the lament, called themselves God's people are now a "nation that does not call on my name," a stubborn people (65:1–2). In rapid succession, a series of accusations about cultic abuses strikingly reminiscent of 57:3–13 follows (vv. 3–6). Israel's old infidelities of the preexilic period have resurfaced (v. 7). Yahweh then reveals his intention (65:8–16a). For the sake of the remnant the nation will not perish (v. 8). The servant remnant is identified in verses 9–10 as "my servants, my chosen, the people who seek me." Salvation is no longer conceived of in national terms. One's membership in the covenant is not, and never was, a matter of birthright. This division within the community becomes clear in 65:11–16, in which the twin proclamation of salvation and judgment is directed to the one community. The glorious promises given by Isaiah 40–55 have been narrowed, as within Isaiah 40–55, to a small remnant in Israel.

Isaiah 65:17–25 proclaims salvation for the servants, drawing on elements from chapters 1–55. A new heaven and new earth are announced in 65:17a, and, in 65:18, are identified with the New Jerusalem, whose glory is announced in verses 19–25. The new community of the saved again will be in right relationship with Yahweh, living long and prosperous lives at peace with each other and with the natural world (vv. 19–25). They will enjoy the blessings of the new covenant emanating from Yahweh's temple (Isa. 65:25b). The temple will be the microcosm of the new creation, and the creation of a new heaven and a new earth will mean the enthronement of Yahweh.

Chapter 66 both summarizes the message of chapters 56–66 and concludes the book. Isaiah 66:1–17 is a single salvation judgment oracle. Since Yahweh fills heaven and earth, what sort of a temple could be built to contain him (Isa. 64:1)? In short, the community's problems will not be solved by temple rebuilding itself. What God seeks in response (v. 2) is the submission of a humble and contrite spirit. Isaiah 66:3–4 evaluates the worth of what is going on in the temple, namely, sacrifice. Sacrifice is irrelevant without a commitment, from which it proceeds (vv. 3–4). Judgment will be visited on the temple itself for abominable activities (vv. 5–6). Verses 7–14a return to the theme of the glorification of Zion. When the new age comes, Zion will bring forth the new community—incredibly, without labor pains. It will be as if the nation were born on one day (vv. 7–8). The prosperity of the New Jerusalem will be prodigious for Yahweh's servants, but the enemies of Yahweh will be destroyed (v. 14b). The theme of judgment against enemies is elaborated in verses 15–17. This judgment is not for foreign nations but for those within the community who indulge in apostate worship (66:17).

Isaiah 66:18–24 turns attention to the world outside the Promised Land. Survivors (v. 19) from the nations will come, streaming to Jerusalem (v. 18). This Jewish remnant shall then be sent to the nations, that the world may see what Yahweh has done for Israel (v. 19). They will bring dispersed Israel back to Jerusalem as their temple offering (v. 20). Verse 21 is a crux, but the "of them" of verse 21 seems to refer to some of the dispersed Israelites who are coming to the temple and who will thus break the monopoly of the Jerusalem priesthood (Schramm 1995, 172). Isaiah 66:22–24 combines elements of everlasting worship and everlasting judgment, with the latter idea occurring for the first time in the OT. Finally, the new age is described as a new creation, an age of universal worship (vv. 22–23), while verse 24 carries us back in thought to the first oracle (Isa. 1:2) and forms an *inclusio* of judgment that surrounds the promises of this great book.

This emphasis in Isaiah on the restoration of Jerusalem makes us aware that Jerusalem has become a symbol that unites that worship center and those that inhabit it, combining sacred space and sanctified people. Isaiah has made clear that there could be no thought of a restored Israel without the prior restoration of Zion. Throughout, however, it is clearly maintained that Yahweh's presence alone makes Israel the saved people of God, the new Israel. The Davidic king and the temple have had little space devoted to them in the latter half of the book, since Isaiah has been talking about the ultimate end—the reign of Yahweh himself, from Jerusalem. This was Isaiah's Zion ideal, the perfected community of the righteous people of God, the banner to which the world would rally. In God's good time the enigmatic Servant figure, by his death, would usher in the new age.

11

Jeremiah

The Book of Jeremiah is the most political of all the OT prophecies. It covers the period from 627 B.C., which was either the year of Jeremiah's birth or of the beginning of his ministry, to 582/1, a few years beyond the fall of the Judean state. The question of whether the date 627 B.C. refers to his birth or to the beginning of his ministry is disputed—it depends on the interpretation given to Jeremiah 1:1—but the evidence favors 609 B.C. as the beginning. We find no oracles which can be assigned with any confidence to Josiah's time. There is also no oracle in Jeremiah about the death of Josiah.

In a broad sense, the book reviews the period of Judah's history that included the reforms of Josiah (639–609 B.C.), the reigns of three of his sons—Jehoahaz (609 B.C.), Jehoiakim (609–598 B.C.), and Zedekiah (597–587/586 B.C.)—and of one grandson, Jehoiachin (598–597 B.C.). That is, the thought moves from the reforms of Josiah to the fall of Jerusalem, which revealed the reforms' superficiality. During the period of Jeremiah, Assyria fell to Babylon. The Book of Jeremiah defies precise dissection, since it seems to have been organized topically rather than chronologically. It needs to be noted that, in the Septuagint, the oracles against foreign nations (chaps. 46–51) follow 25:13.

The Compilation of Jeremiah

A brief analysis of the literary complexity of Jeremiah must be offered, since the book is a diffuse collection of oracles, not necessarily arranged chronologically, and often following no discernible order. Difficulties of this character led earlier commentators to divide the book into three groups: poetry, first-person prose, and third-person prose. It was suggested that the poetic sections of the book were the oldest, offering insights into the career of Jeremiah and his preaching ministry. These parts were then complemented by a first-person prose account written by Baruch, Jeremiah's secretary. Baruch was responsible for reading Jeremiah's scroll before King Jehoiakim (Jer. 36) in 605 B.C. Though analogous to Shaphan's reading of the law before Josiah (2 Kings 22), Baruch's reading had startlingly different results.

I do not propose to discuss recent refinements of the literary analysis of the Book of Jeremiah. They have tended to take two directions, namely, to label the Baruch materials as a Deuteronomic editorial device, thus reducing three components to two, or to suppose that the third-person prose accounts are homiletical expansions from the hands of those responsible for the other stylized biographical accounts.

Jeremiah's Earliest Oracles (Jer. 1:5–20:18)

Chapters 1–20, which have been identified as a major section of the book, are framed by references to Jeremiah's birth (Lundbom 1975, 28). They end on a note of somber gloom, driving us back to 1:5. In the first half of Jeremiah, the emphasis falls on imminent judgment. We are then left with the success of Jeremiah's message of terrible judgment but also with the tensions it has provoked within his character. A break certainly comes after chapter 20, for Jeremiah 21 begins the first datable biographical prose in the book. It has been proposed that chapters 1–20 constitute the scroll read by Baruch before Jehoiakim (chap. 36). However that may be, most scholars do believe that these chapters represent the earliest material of Jeremiah's ministry, although not many of the book's poetic oracles can be dated with accuracy, and the final arrangement of the book is due to the work of the redactor/editor (Baruch?). It is possible that chapters 2–6 are to be related to Josiah's time and thus give evidence of the inconsistency of the Josianic reforms, while chapters 7–20 may relate to the reign of Jehoiakim.

Chapter 1 deals with Jeremiah's call (1:5–10), vision, and interpretation, with the coming invasion (1:11–16), and with Jeremiah's painful ministry (1:17–19). Generally speaking, chapters 2–3 contain poems lamenting the covenant disloyalty of Judah. In chapter 2, however, the name "Israel" is used as well as "Judah" (vv. 3–4, 14, 26), so that the reversal of salvation history contemplated for Judah but already actualized for Israel is in terms of the historic Israel. The appearance of the term "Israel" to recall Israel's historical exodus predominates in the chapter (2:6, 21, 28; cf. Exod. 32), so that Judah is being addressed as the embodiment of the historical people (McConville 1993, 29). Israel as the northern kingdom seems indicated in verses 26–28, which begin with Israel (v. 26) and end with Judah (v. 28). The oscillation between Israel and Judah may convey the purpose of comparing Judah with the former northern kingdom and with the northern pattern of apostasy.

The overarching theme of the seven poems in chapter 2 is that the people have departed from their original loyalty to Yahweh and have rebelled against him. In the first poem (2:2–3), the metaphors of the bride and the first fruits emphasize that Israel is Yahweh's special possession, and while the picture of Israelites' devotion during the wilderness wanderings is idealistic, it is appropriate in the context, providing a contrast with current apostasy. According to the second poem (2:4–13), the people's apostasy is without excuse. Yahweh states his charge (vv. 5–8), makes clear his intention to take legal action (v. 9), and calls the heavens as witness (v. 12), repeating and underlining his accusation (vv. 10–11, 13).

The third poem (2:14–19) deals with the implications of Israel's apostasy on the international scene. Alliances with Assyria and Egypt will be of no avail. In the fourth poem (2:20–25), Jeremiah turns to the results of his people's apostasy in their everyday life. Now that a crisis threatens, the people cry to Yahweh in desperation, remembering their traditions of how he had saved their forefathers at the time of the exodus and in the days of the judges. But as the fifth poem (2:26–28) makes clear, Yahweh will not help them, and their false gods cannot. The sixth poem (2:29–32) builds on the theme of the fifth. The people complain against Yahweh (v. 29a), and the reason is undoubtedly that he does nothing to help them in their crisis. But the reply in verses 29b–32 shows that this complaint is groundless. In the seventh poem (2:33–37), Jeremiah speaks of the judgment to come. The people are apostate, and their social life is marred by injustice (vv. 33–34). They still protest that they are innocent and believe that Yahweh will save them from their crisis, but they are blind to their guilt (v. 35). They think that their religious disloyalty is of little consequence, and want Egypt to help them. But Egypt will let them down, and they will be put to shame (vv. 36–37).

Alliances with nations have proved a vain hope, so that the foolishness of the present intention to appeal to Egypt (vv. 18, 36) is met by the negative examples of previous dealings with Assyria. Verse 36 in particular is a warning to Judah not to trust in political alliances with Egypt, due to Judah's experience. Yahweh's wrath against disloyalty will break out like fire. Such is the theme in 3:1–5 and 3:19–4:4, which form the second stage of Jeremiah's argument.

Repentance and Hope (Jer. 3:1–4:4)

In 3:1–5, Israel had broken the covenant by its apostasy, and Judah has done likewise. The impossibility of reconciliation between Yahweh and Judah is declared in 3:6–10. This question of 3:1–5 is answered (vv. 11–12) and gains fuller development in verses 13–18. Verse 11 levels a retrospective accusation of faithlessness against Israel, but Israel is less guilty than Judah. The stylized address to the north becomes a way of setting before the readers—in particular, exiled Judah—that there lies a way back beyond the exile that Judah in turn must endure. A new note of Yahweh's redemption of his people beyond exile is sounded. Verses 13–14 then appeal to faithless Judah. The ability of Judah to repent will be brought about by Yahweh's intervention (v. 14b). Yahweh's prevenient grace will stimulate Judah to repent (vv. 15–18, 22–24). A return to Yahweh would bring days of such fervent inner faith under right leadership that the older reliance upon externals (temple, land, cult, etc.)—even upon the ark of the covenant (3:16)—would be abandoned. Jerusalem would once again be Yahweh's throne (3:17), and the world would gather in prophetic pilgrimage to Zion (3:19–20). Verses 19–20, taking up the term "faithless" from verses 12 and

14, address the central problem of verses 1–5, the tendency of Israel to turn away from Yahweh. Yahweh's intention for them (3:19–20) is disclosed; there cannot be a simple reunion with him.

Jeremiah in 3:21–4:4 describes the way of true repentance and the conditions for a renewed relationship with Yahweh (McConville 1993, 33–41). If Israelites are firm in their desire to return to Yahweh, they will again fulfill his purpose for them and become a source of blessing for all nations (4:1–6). If not, the divine wrath will burn against them with none to quench it (4:4).

The Enemy Advances, Judgment Is Inevitable (Jer. 4:5–6:30)

The third stage of Jeremiah's argument is introduced (4:5–31), but the advancing enemy brings Yahweh's judgment. Repentance is not a present possibility (cf. 3:10), since repentance must be preceded by punishment. The inevitability of the coming judgment dominates 4:5–6:30. The atmosphere is one of panic. Jeremiah jumps from one thought to another, and the text jumps from one speaker to another. Jeremiah is filled with agony and distress, and in 4:19–21 he expresses not only his own feelings, but also those of his compatriots to the question "how long?" (v. 21). Jeremiah, in the image of the de-creation in 4:23–27, sees that, not only is the covenant with Israel at stake, but the covenant with the world. The as yet unnamed terrible foe from the north (later identified with Babylon) will execute bitter retribution, the scope of which requires this graphic reversal of creation to depict its horror (vv. 23–28). The vision becomes a picture of the land of Israel after the enemy comes (vv. 27–28).

The description of the enemy's advance reaches its climax in 4:30–31. Jerusalem as a harlot in her hour of crisis acts true to her character and, with all the more enthusiasm and energy, seeks security from political alliances. Chapters 2–4 thus gradually close down any hope for averting the exile and replace it with a different kind of hope, which takes place after judgment has come. Jeremiah himself is a model of hope for surviving judgment.

Now Jerusalem is about to be destroyed, and Yahweh offers to pardon her on even more merciful terms, that is, if one person who does justice and seeks truth can be found (5:1; cf. Gen. 18:22–33). No such person exists, for although the people take oaths in Yahweh's name and thus claim him as their God, they are insincere (5:1–2). Measures in the past to make the people repent have had no effect (5:3–6). How can Yahweh then pardon Jerusalem (5:7–9)? The theme of Israel's idolatry and complacency, which is judged by means of an incursion from the numinous "north," advances in Jeremiah 5:10–17. The attack by the as yet unnamed enemy (5:14–17) is about to come. But there will still be a witness to Yahweh's justice in Israel (vv. 18–19). The poems of 5:20–31 charge the people with perversity (vv. 20–25) and injustice (vv. 26–29) and indict the leaders (vv. 30–33).

The impending attack is in fact mounted in 6:1–8. Judah's corruption is total (6:9–21); its citizens have rejected the ancient paths. In 6:1–8, the enemy besieges the city, and in 6:22–26, they ride upon horses for battle against the daughter of Zion. Thus, while some of the poems can be interpreted as referring more generally to the people of Judah, the focus in chapters 5–6 is chiefly on Jerusalem. Jeremiah clinches his argument by emphasizing that, in the destruction to come, Jerusalem will not be spared. The reported advance of the dreaded foe (vv. 22–26) demands obedience, not sacrifice (vv. 16–21). In the final brief poem of 6:27–30, Yahweh addresses the prophet, for Jeremiah is to sift Judah for what may be saved (vv. 27–30). In summary, the poems in 2:1–6:30 have been carefully arranged for a definite situation. The people of Judah have been disloyal to Yahweh, but, in their desperation, they call on him to save them. They are warned that superficial, temporary repentance is not enough, and if they do not truly repent, they will experience the full fury of the divine judgment, in which Jerusalem will not be spared.

Such a collection would be most appropriate to 605–604 B.C., when the Babylonian army defeated the Egyptians and Assyrians at Carchemish. After a brief interruption, while Nebuchadnezzar returned to Babylon to ascend the throne, he began to advance into Syria and Philistia and Israel. The poems may likely be identified with the scroll dictated by Jeremiah to Baruch in 605 B.C. and read by Baruch in the temple in December of the following year, as recounted in chapter 36. The thematic arrangement of the poems strongly suggests that Jeremiah on occasion collected his prophecies to speak to a definite situation.

Religion without Reality (Jer. 7–10)

Chapters 7–10 are integrated by the major theme of institutional religion that has become apostate and the punishment that necessarily follows (Thompson 1980, 271–339). Jeremiah's renowned temple sermon is delivered in chapter 7 and is appropriately assigned to the first year of Jehoiakim (i.e., 609 B.C.; cf. Jer. 26:1). There is yet hope, Jeremiah states, for if the people cease from their wicked ways, they will be permitted to dwell in the land (7:5–7). Clearly the people have failed to recognize the temple as the focus of Yahweh's kingdom rule and as the final point of authority. Reliance on the externals of worship is leading Judah to ruin (vv. 8–11). The outstanding feature of this sermon is the use of the word "place" in the twin sense of temple (7:3) and Promised Land (v. 7), the latter a customary use of the word in Deuteronomy. Replying to Judah's presumption, Jeremiah states that Jerusalem and the temple will be destroyed like Shiloh, which presumably had been destroyed without trace by Philistine aggression (7:12–15).

The message is very clear—a right attitude to the temple would have secured the Promised Land. Jeremiah does not resort, as the false prophets do, to the traditional theme of inviolability. The divine intention for Judah is further indicated in the thrice-issued command to Jeremiah not to pray for the people (implying that he might otherwise have done so in the hope that they would repent; 7:16; 11:14; 15:1). Jeremiah soundly condemned the temple, sacrifices, priesthood, and Judah's theology of the Promised Land, and foreshadowed the institutional end of Judah/Israel (vv. 21–26). He apparently rejects not sacrifice itself, but only the misplaced emphasis that has been put on the system. The people had treated the divine word through the prophets with contempt (cf. 7:25–26). Judah is a people that cannot repent, that is given over to falsehood, and that will not accept Yahweh's word (7:27–28), yet that places unthinking trust in his temple. Punishment is impending, and the use of the term "nation" (Heb. *goy*, v. 28) for Judah underscores this fact. Judah is simply a *goy* that deserves punishment (5:9, 29; 9:9). Yahweh's mind is now fixed on a course of action from which he cannot turn. The chapter also indicates that the Josianic reforms have now been jettisoned. For example, idolatrous practices flourish again at Topheth (7:29–8:3), practices which Josiah had purged (2 Kings 23:10).

The theme of "the foe from the north" is taken further from 8:4 to 10:25. This second group of poems climaxes in the instruction to prepare for exile, and so 597 B.C. is a highly likely date for its collection. The first poem (8:4–7) in fact emphasizes that the people have been persistently disobedient in a way that is contrary to nature. Receiving Yahweh's revealed will cannot help them because they have distorted it (8:8–12). The enemy is upon them, and their hopes for peace are frustrated (8:13–17). Jeremiah expresses his grief and abhorrence at both their corruption and their sufferings (8:18–9:9). The theme of falsehood (*sheqer*), one of the special characteristics of Judah's apostasy as presented in Jeremiah, is developed particularly in 8:22–9:8. Jeremiah calls the people to lament (9:17–22). This theme of impending attack (8:14–17; 9:17–22; 10:17–25) is interspersed with laments from Jeremiah over the prospect (8:18–9:1; 9:2–9; 9:10–16), and the chapter features a wisdom piece reflecting on the true grounds for confidence (vv. 23–26). At 9:25–26, Judah is included in a list of nations that, although circumcised, really are uncircumcised. Verse 26 (cf. Rom. 2:29) puts Israel in the even worse state of being uncircumcised in heart. An attack upon idolatry (10:1–16) stresses the incomparability, power, and kingship of Yahweh over all nations (note the remarkable title "king of the nations" in v. 7, a title which underscores the thematic world interest of Jeremiah). The juxtaposition of 10:12–16 with 10:17–18 is dramatic. The hymn anticipates the judgment against Babylon, but verses 17–18 tell of the folly of reliance on election. Judah has no hope of escaping judgment. Yahweh will bring judgment on Judah by the foe (vv. 17–25). So Jeremiah instructs the people to prepare for exile (10:17–22).

Jeremiah's Confessions (Jer. 11:18–20; 12:1–6; 15:10–21; 17:14–18; 18:19–23; 20:7–18)

After the prose warning of a curse to come for covenant breach (11:1–17), the prophecy assumes a particularly personal note until 20:18. Most of the introspective reflections of Jeremiah on his lot and ministry, the so-called confessions, are found here (15:10–21; 17:14–18; 18:19–23; 20:7–18; cf. also 11:18–20; 12:1–6). The confessions in chapters 11–20 have been set off from the previous and subsequent narratives by the framework of curse (11:1–4; 20:14–18). The exilic audience needed to reflect. If Jeremiah had correctly proclaimed Israel's fate, might it not be that his predictions about the future would be equally correct? There is some hope, up to chapter 18, for Judah, but after Jeremiah's visit to the potter (18:1–12), there is none. It is clear from Jeremiah 19 that Yahweh is about to intervene to vindicate the prophet. In chapter 20, the foe from the north becomes the Babylonians.

The confessions constitute a particular form of the individual psalm of lament that, although met elsewhere, is unique in prophecy. They provide (1) a description of the prophet's situation; (2) an expression of trust in Yahweh; and (3) Yahweh's reaction (see 11:18–23; 12:1–6; 18:18–22). They cannot be regarded as private confessions pure and simple because, like the national psalms of lament, they bear some relationship to public national life. It would be wrong to eliminate the personal element from them, for the material betrays the inner life of both Jeremiah and Yahweh. In a sense this material also reflects the nature of Yahweh, who is anguished because he loves Judah (12:7). In the confessions, Yahweh's inner tension arises because of his need to punish the people that he has chosen and loves, a tension resolved by the triumph of love over anger (cf. 31:20). When Jeremiah expresses his own anguish, he is pointing profoundly to a suffering of Yahweh's (cf. 4:19–22; 8:22–9:2). The people do not realize the devastating consequences to come. They do not understand what seeking the presence of Yahweh, when they have failed to honor their covenant responsibilities, will mean. Jeremiah expresses this lack of understanding by conveying his perplexity about the judgment of Yahweh that he himself will endure. Specifically, 15:5–21 resolves the tension in Jeremiah that has reached a climax in 15:1–4, and in verses 19–21 come words of personal reassurance from Yahweh. Jeremiah's representative prophetic role forces him into a relationship with his ministry that issues in the confessions and, indeed, in the word of assurance that comes in their train. Such assurance about the future will come to Judah in chapters 30–33, and the result is to cast Jeremiah in a kind of servant role.

These confessions are not conditioned announcements to Israel, but complaints to God. But these personal words also functioned prophetically, testifying to the severity of the divine anger to be vented against Judah, and this representative note probably helped account for their preservation. The Jeremiah of the confessions is not merely an example of great personal piety, nor is he a detached cultic functionary. But there is an incarnational aspect in that he embodies the experience of the people and also of Yahweh, without ever ceasing to be an individual personality. This portrayal of the prophet has hope as its framework, and in turn helps to create the idea of hope for Judah through and beyond suffering. The distinction between Jeremiah as a private person and as a representative confessor is a false one.

Jeremiah argues in the confessions that he is a true prophet, identified with the will of Yahweh and with Yahweh's people. Jeremiah is presented in the confessions as faithful to his task. Yahweh is likewise presented as the controlling power and originator of the prophet's word who must take responsibility for Jeremiah's predicament. Yahweh deceived him and overpowered him when Jeremiah sought to evade his prophetic duty. By means of these arguments, Jeremiah further separated himself from the false prophets. The point of these confessions seems to be, however, that Jeremiah is in fact speaking for the people who, in their corporate agony, do not understand the reality of the covenant relationship. Jeremiah's message is bound up with his own suffering, while the salvation prophets continually say what is in keeping with covenant expectations. In Jeremiah's confessions, the tensions of his ministry are seen giving rise at times to bitter protest at his calling.

Within the chapters is an arrangement that intensifies the accusation, threat, and warning of chapters 2–10. The first two confessions, however (11:18–12:6 and 15:10–21), do not move the text forward, but contribute evidence of Israel's crimes. Chapters 18–20 pull all the themes together. The major themes not treated in chapters 2–10 find their completion in this portion. The confessions provide evidence of the prophet's rejection and persecution, and the final confession celebrates his vindication. Jeremiah 2–10 presents the warning, and chapters 11–20 the rejection.

In the confessions, Jeremiah has become the bearer of the nation's hopes of salvation. Although he is a model of prayerfulness and obedience, his individuality exists in his desire to throw off his ministry. In the midst of his representative role, he can still be distinguished from the people by what is expressed in his isolation and anger. His frustration is exemplified in 15:10–12 and comes to a head in 20:7–12, where he admits (v. 8) that he has repeatedly tried to refrain from prophesying. For this reason he can be rebuked and recalled to his duty (12:5–6; 15:19–21). But even here Jeremiah's complaints correspond to something in the life of Judah, namely, to her reluctance to shoulder her own vocation as the elect of Yahweh. Jeremiah's very reluctance thus has a positive role: to occasion the words of rebuke that also carry the words of promise.

Between the interspersed confessions of chapters 11–20, the previous chapters' emphasis on impending punishment is reinforced. Jeremiah 11:1–17 deals with problems stemming from the broken covenant—the curse of having lost the land. Jeremiah 12:7–17 reapplies the extreme covenant curse pertaining to the loss of the land. Prophetic strictures against Judah's pride take the form of the analogy of the linen girdle, purchased and then secreted, and then finally recovered as spoiled (13:1–11). A further analogy (13:12–14) is directed against Judah's leadership and against the inhabitants of Jerusalem, threatening destruction. A poetic call to lament (vv. 15–17) precedes a lament over the royal house (vv. 18–19) and over Jerusalem (vv. 20–27), so deeply stained by apostasy that she cannot remove it. Further material bearing on Judah's crimes—crimes to be punished by drought and banishment—follows in 14:1–10. False prophets are condemned in 14:11–16, followed by Jeremiah's laments concerning the impending situation (vv. 17–18) and a communal lament in verses 19–22. Jeremiah 15:1–9 deals with the inevitable exile, which cannot be avoided by superficial, or, indeed, by any type of repentance. Confessional material completes chapter 15.

In chapter 16, Jeremiah is commanded not to marry or mourn or attend feasts. His loneliness in ministry inevitably separates him from an idolatrous nation. Jerusalem's future is too bleak (vv. 2–9). Verses 10–13 present the inquiry of the people and the prophetic answer of impending exile. The way forward for

Judah is through the suffering of exile, but the possibility of a new exodus is raised (vv. 14–15). The foe is on the way, and none will escape the judgment (vv. 16–18). Yet the future of Israel is secure, and the chapter ends on a passage reflecting the eschatology of a Gentile pilgrimage and the conversion of the nations (vv. 19–21). Judah's deeply ingrained corruption is then reflected upon (17:1–4). Trust has been placed in human beings and not Yahweh (17:5–8). This has occurred because the human heart is naturally corrupt (vv. 9–11). Yahweh is Israel's only hope (vv. 12–13). After a personal lament by Jeremiah on his reluctance for ministry (vv. 14–18) and a charge to keep the Sabbath and thereby to protect Davidic kingship, discussion of Jerusalem and the temple (vv. 19–27) completes chapter 17.

Jeremiah receives two commands to visit the potter, indicating the importance of the parallels to be drawn. In 18:1–12, Jeremiah witnesses the potter making, breaking, and then remaking the pot, and Jeremiah draws from the incident an analogy with Israel in the hands of God (18:4–6). Jeremiah makes the application in 18:13–17. The passage is a clear picture of salvation beyond judgment. Everything is contingent on the repentance of Judah. This is the message of hope, but the remainder of the chapter emphasizes the reality of Judah's stubborn intransigence and, thus, the imminence of her judgment. In chapter 19, the message is repeated by another analogy. Jeremiah is to buy a potter's earthen flask (v. 1) and then to break it before the elders and people (v. 10). Now the flask is to be broken so that it can never be mended (v. 11). Whereas chapter 18 had opened up the future to possibility, 19:1–13 shuts it down. Any way forward must come through exile. In response to his further temple preaching (19:14–16), Jeremiah is temporarily arrested and beaten but is defiant in his prediction of exile (20:1–6).

A confessional reflection on his call follows (20:7–13). Jeremiah completes the first major section of the prophecy (chaps. 1–20) by lamenting his birth (vv. 14–18), the passage forming an *inclusio* with 1:5. This finale underscores the reality of the judgment that at the beginning of the prophecy Jeremiah was called upon to pronounce.

Oracles against the House of David and Foreign Nations (Jer. 21–25)

Chapters 21–25 function as an appendix to chapters 1–20, dealing with the fall of Jerusalem as a fait accompli and why it happened (through the failure of monarchy [21:11–23:7] and prophecy [23:9–40]). Then chapter 24 and the appendix in chapter 25 report the prose writer's main themes. No longer are these chapters about Israel converting in order to avert disaster, for the disaster has happened. Chapters 21–25 offer instructions to survive the disaster. The transition from imminent punishment to a doctrine of hope that lies beyond punishment is contained in chapters 21–24 in a sustained way. This section opens and closes with words about King Zedekiah. Zedekiah's introduction at 21:1 and the attention to him in 21:1–10 fix our gaze on the exile and fall of Jerusalem, since chapter 21 is unequivocal about Judah's doom. Jeremiah offers no hope in reply to Zedekiah's embassy. Yahweh will be fighting against Israel and Judah (21:5).

Jeremiah 21:8–10 calls upon Judah to accept the Babylonian yoke. The review of Judean kingship which is then conducted (vv. 11–14) produces the conclusion that Davidic kingship as exercised must lead the nation into exile.

In chapter 22, there is no future for David's line. A model for kingship clearly drawn from Josiah is offered in 22:1–9, and affords the ground to sharpen the criticism and judgment on his successors Jehoahaz (vv. 10–12) and Jehoiakim (vv. 13–19). A general lament over kingship follows in verses 20–23. Then the popular hope in Jehoiachin (vv. 24–30) is dismissed, Zedekiah having been dealt with in chapter 21. The end of human kingship is announced, since Jehoiachin, the last surviving king of Judah, is to be written down as childless in the genealogies (22:30), even though in exile he was the father of at least five children. That Jeremiah indicates no future for Coniah (Jehoiachin) makes it impossible to interpret the end of the book of Kings (2 Kings 25:27–30 or Jer. 52:31–34) as hopeful. It is clear from Jeremiah 36, 34, 37, and 38 that the Davidic dynasty is doomed.

Yet Jeremiah does not repudiate the Davidic covenant, for God in the future will establish shepherds for Judah (23:1–4). The righteous branch who will be raised up for David (vv. 5–8) in the uncertain future bears the name "Yahweh is our righteousness" (v. 6), a direct reversal of Zedekiah's name ("my righteousness is Yahweh"). This is a clear denunciation by Jeremiah of Judah's present ruling house. The prophetic movement, which ought to have displayed leadership, is arraigned in 23:9–40. Each of the three previous kings had gone into exile or been buried in disgrace, and Zedekiah must take warning lest he should so suffer. Thus, by repeating earlier prophecies, Jeremiah was aiming to combat the optimism of the king and people after 597.

Yahweh has plans for Israel beyond the exile (chap. 24). The future of the people of God is seen as lying with the exiled community. Jeremiah contrasted the "good figs," who went into captivity, to the "bad figs," who remained behind after the exile of Jehoiachin. Undoubtedly Jeremiah is supporting a popular conviction, arising after this removal of Jehoiachin, that the exiled community provides the grounds for hope. The exile will prove to be a beneficial factor in Judah's history, because God would produce "good figs" among the exiles by giving them a heart to know God (24:7). Jeremiah 24:7 follows Deuteronomy in that Jeremiah speaks of a heart to know Yahweh, which will be given to "them," and Jeremiah adds the covenant formula "they shall be my people and I will be their God, for they shall return to me with their whole heart" (24:7). Chapter 25 could be read as a conclusion to the first part of Jeremiah or as introduction to the second. Chapters 21–24 set the message by their orientation to the last Judean king, Zedekiah. Chapter 25, by its adumbration of the downfall of Babylon, injects a further strain of hope for a future beyond exile, so the hope sounded in chapters 21–24 develops.

In Jeremiah 25, Judah is placed among the nations of the world, all of whom must submit to Babylon. This matter is taken further in chapters 46–52 and forms the closing insistence of the book. Thus, by the end of chapter 25, nation, land, priesthood, cult, kingship, and even the ark have been disowned.

Jeremiah has thus prepared Judah for the grim reality of the coming days when Israel will cease to exist as a geographical entity, never to be restored to its pre-exilic dimensions.

Israel under the Word (Jer. 26–36)

Though we cannot trace the growth of the book, Jeremiah 26–36 is a collection of oracles and sayings presented for the most part within a narrative framework. The connection between chapters 26 and 36 occurs by the focus of Jeremiah 26 on the prophetic word, a focus echoed at the end of Jeremiah 36.

The introductory chapter 26 again provides the ground of hope for Judah, namely, submission to Yahweh's authority, which the temple symbolizes. The concluding chapter 36 notes the rejection of the word by the Davidic king. The repeat of the temple sermon in 26:1–19 shows that enmity against Yahweh was at the heart of the nation even in the temple, which overtly proclaimed the name of Yahweh. The second feature of chapter 26 is the appeal by the princes and people (v. 12) against the hawkish priests and prophets who were evidently most threatened by Jeremiah's message. The sermon may be read as a reaction to Jeremiah's preaching, missing from chapter 7. It is thus a demonstration of the public hardness of Judah's heart that is characteristic of the second part of the book. Uriah's death at the vicious and frustrated hands of Jehoiakim shows that the king's real enemy is the word of Yahweh and that this enmity will manifest itself against any of its bearers.

Chapters 27–28 show the prophetic conflicts of the time. Immediately after the temple sermon, Jeremiah, by symbolically assuming a yoke of bondage (27:1–11), throws down the gauntlet to the Jerusalem prophets. Jeremiah's political stance provokes his celebrated clash with Hananiah, spokesman for the prophetic group, and ends in Hananiah's death (chap. 28). The problem that faces the audience of Jeremiah at this point is the evaluation of the respective prophetic criteria. Basic tests of true prophecy were proposed in Deuteronomy, namely, consistency (13:1–5), subordination to the Mosaic pattern (18:15), and fulfillment (v. 22). Hananiah comes before the people as an advocate of the Zion traditions and of the inviolability of Jerusalem and its temple—a doctrine unchallenged since Jerusalem's amazing rescue in 701 B.C. Jeremiah had rejected these traditions, however, because they did not correspond to the historical reality of his day; the traditions, in Jeremiah's definition, amount to falsity. His position is made all the clearer by prefacing the temple sermon with the issue of what constitutes true prophecy. It is clear for Jeremiah that the popular appeal to inviolability has served the status quo, which Yahweh has now rejected. We see this clearly in retrospect, but the people at the time had no such advantage.

Chapter 29 transforms Jeremiah into a salvation prophet. Jeremiah is careful to restate in this letter to the exiles that the exile will last seventy years (29:10). The command to seek the welfare of Babylon arises from and supports the teaching that there is no future for Judah apart from exile, and certainly no hope of an early return to a now-forsaken land (vv. 16–19). The seventy years specified may be a round number alluding to the period of Sabbath rest that the land now deserves (cf. Lev. 26:34). But the change of tone is real, for there is no doubt now about Judah's future. If Israel was classified ominously in chapter 27 with the nations at large, Yahweh now speaks reassuringly. He has plans for welfare and not evil, plans for a future and hope (v. 11).

The Book of Consolation (Jer. 30–33), so styled because of its hopeful content, deals with the restoration of Israel's fortunes, land, and institutions. Central to this section is the prophecy of the new covenant (31:31–34) that unveils the real mind of Yahweh. Yet the tension in chapter 30, of salvation through judgment, is evident in 31:15–20 following the salvation poetry of 31:1–14. The grief of Israel is evoked with the image of Rachel weeping for her children. Ephraim bemoans her loss. Yahweh suffers with them, an identification that had been prepared by Jeremiah's confessions. The culmination is Yahweh's heartfelt cry in 31:20 that he is unable to cast off his son Ephraim (cf. Hos. 11:8–9; McConville 1993, 96). Verses 18–19 have Ephraim accepting his past punishment and then turning back to Yahweh. This prophecy posits a new exodus as a prerequisite to the new covenant, and a new entry into the Promised Land as the result.

Because of the impending change in Israel's political situation, a review of the Sinai covenant, which had brought the political constitution of Israel into being (31:31–34), is undertaken. Though there is no mention of the new covenant as exercising influence beyond Israel, nor of a world pilgrimage of the nations, the emphases of 31:35–40 combine to affirm an international context. These verses refer to the certainty of God's new-covenant purposes as grounded within the order of creation itself (vv. 35–37), and to the (muted) note of the New Jerusalem (vv. 38–40), which will function as the world center. By his new-covenant doctrine of one Israel, Jeremiah is building a bridge between Israel's past and her future hope. Note especially the structure of 31:31–34, where future hope is juxtaposed with the negative past.

The announcement of Jeremiah 31:31, "Behold, the days are coming," points to an age in transition. The emphasis on the divine initiative makes clear that the covenant will be divinely imposed, not negotiated. Yahweh will "cut" (i.e., initiate), a word that always refers to the beginning of a covenantal arrangement. Since the Sinai covenant is clearly the model that Jeremiah has chosen for his meditation, some specific redemptive intervention in the manner of the exodus seems to be contemplated to bring this new arrangement into being.

Jeremiah's contemplated covenant is described as "new." There is possible ambiguity here, for the Hebrew word can refer to temporal (Exod. 1:8; Deut. 32:17; 1 Sam. 6:7; Eccles. 1:10) or qualitative (Lam. 3:22–23) newness. Perhaps we are to balance both nuances of the word and suggest a new dimension of faith to be imported into Israel as a result of the exile, yet not so radical a dimension that it constitutes a complete break with the past.

That the new covenant will be continuous with the old and will deal with present historical difficulties is signified by the fact that it will be made with the traditional geographical entities, north and south, referred to in Jeremiah 31:31 as "the house of Israel" and "the house of Judah." Like the notion advanced in

Ezekiel 37:15–28, the recall from exile will involve a divine grafting that makes the two warring brothers one. It is sometimes argued that "the house of Judah" in Jeremiah 31:31 is a scribal addition, since only "the house of Israel" occurs in verse 33. But the thought is rather that the imposition of the new covenant will mean the healing of the long-standing breaches between the two kingdoms. The new covenant will express the prophetic conviction that there can be, and that there has been, only one unified people of God.

We can hardly expect that the new covenant will display greater grace than the redemptive act of the exodus. It would also be a mistake to see the new covenant as grace and the old as "demand." Rather, 31:32 stresses the fallibility of the Sinai covenant. Israel breached the Sinai covenant, and it was continually breached ("my covenant, which they broke"). The divine fidelity to the Sinai arrangement is referred to in 31:32 under the familiar prophetic symbolism of marriage. No divorce was possible under the old arrangement, and, though Israel had been an unfaithful wife, the bond still held. By contrast, it will not be possible to breach the new covenant—and herein lies an element of newness. Both parties will keep the new arrangement.

Newness seems to be on full display in Jeremiah 31:33, in which the law of the heart is taken up. Would not a radical inward change, both personally and nationally, be necessary to create the response to Yahweh for which the new covenant would call? Such change would be required, but it would be wrong to suggest that the Sinai covenant, which is clearly in view, had not entailed some inward change.

Obedience to the law was incumbent on all those within the framework of grace (see Deut. 6:20–25). Moreover, in Deuteronomy it was always presumed that the place of the law was in the national (and personal) heart (6:4–6; 11:18). Perhaps the oscillation between the second-person plural and second-person singular in the exhortations of Deuteronomy was consciously employed to address national Israel through Israelites. The notion of the law in the heart is usually advanced by command in Deuteronomy (e.g., 6:4–5), but such references point to the desired ideal, which presumably was possible. The demand for "circumcision of the heart" is similarly made (e.g., 10:16) and seems a requirement to which Israel must rise. But in Moses' moving final address, Israel is addressed as in exile (chap. 30). The recall of the nation is anticipated, but only after Yahweh, as he must do if the law is to be obeyed, has circumcised the national heart (v. 6).

The salvation of the individual in the OT always presupposed the "law in the heart," as did Deuteronomy of the nation. Thus the demand for purification of the heart, the creation of a clean heart in personal renewal, is frequent in the OT. Contrition always stems from the heart (Ps. 51:10, 17; 73:1; Prov. 22:11; Isa. 57:15). Jeremiah makes clear that a national change of heart would mean a return to Yahweh, and uses the language of circumcision in this connection (Jer. 4:4; cf. 9:25–26). Indeed, the OT always requires the law of the heart for spiritual experience (Ps. 37:31; 40:8). In Isaiah 51:7, which addresses the exiles, the prospect of a return to Jerusalem and a new covenant is advanced to "you who know righteousness, the people in whose heart is my law."

Of course, tensions exist between God's placement of law in the heart and the obedience that stems from it, but such tensions are not confined to the OT. They are also inherent in the struggles between flesh and spirit in the New Testament. It would thus go beyond the evidence to suggest that the newness of the new covenant consists solely in the emphasis on the inwardness of the law. When the OT insists that the law in the heart is essential for spiritual experience, it does not suppose that the individual or nation has put it there. Thus, to suggest that Jeremiah is breaking new ground in 31:33 may go too far. Moreover, this verse closes with the traditional covenant formula, derivable from Sinai, "I will be their God, and they shall be my people!" Jeremiah 31:33 may be plausibly viewed as saying no more than that Yahweh is returning to the idealism of the Sinai period in this new-covenant relationship. The problem that remains is how the perfect expression of this new relationship, implicitly demanded by verse 32, will be manifested in the new age. As the major statement emphasizing the radical discontinuity of the new covenant, verse 34 takes us further.

With Jeremiah 31:34, we seem to have reached the climax of the presentation and to have entered a new phase of human experience. The divine initiative of verse 33 is now seen to issue into something more than had been possible through Sinai. The "no longer" of verse 34 moves us to the radical character of the contemplated change. Because the old system was mediated, it required constant institutional support. No such support will be needed in the new situation. No more exhortation will be required to produce constancy in the relationship. A new set of circumstances is envisaged that takes us beyond human limitation, within which spiritual experience has had to operate in Jeremiah's day and ours.

What makes the new covenant truly new becomes evident at the end of Jeremiah 31:34. In the new age, says Yahweh of the changed nation, "I will forgive their iniquity, and I will remember their sin no more." Forgiveness in the OT was normally extended through the sacrificial system, which was efficacious for sins confessed. But in the new age, sin will be more than forgiven—it will not be remembered. This is a remarkable statement, and its tenor must be appreciated. There is technical use of vocabulary, for "remembering" in the OT is not limited to the power of psychological recall. Particularly when describing Yahweh, "remembering" implies taking action to effect a new condition whose rationale stems from some past event. God thus "remembered" Noah and caused the waters to abate (Gen. 8:1). God also "remembered" Hannah (1 Sam. 1:19), and the promise of a son became an actuality.

In Jeremiah 31:34, for God not to remember means that no action in the new age will need to be taken against sin. The forgiveness of which this verse speaks is so comprehensive that sin has finally been dealt with in the experience of the nation and individual believer. In this verse we are also looking to the effects of the work of Christ in the final experience of the believer. In the eschatological age of which Jeremiah is speaking, sin will not be a factor; it will be foreign to all human experience. The point advanced is not a contrast between the restrictions under which the old covenant labored and the freedom the Spirit gives in the new. In Jeremiah's new age, sin will not need to be confessed nor progressively forgiven. This verse points us beyond present human experience to the perfected, unfettered fellowship of the new creation, to the time when tensions within human experience have finally been overcome.

In short, the new covenant of Jeremiah points to God's final gift to Israel and to the world through Israel's ministry. It does not point to a new measure of forgiveness, since God's forgiveness is freely given within both Testaments. But the new covenant points to a new apprehension of that forgiveness within human experience, an apprehension that will mean perfected human service and response. Jeremiah 31:31–34 thus looks beyond the community of the New Testament age to life within a revealed new creation. In Jeremiah 31, the nationhood of Israel is reaffirmed (v. 36), and the setting for the fulfillment of the promise is seen to be none other than a rebuilt Jerusalem, in which Torah is to be written on people's hearts. Forgiveness is not the new thing in the new covenant. In view is the final transformation of the people of God.

The Book of Consolation concludes with two chapters that promise the restoration of Judah's land (Jer. 32–33). Jeremiah 32:1–5 records Jeremiah in confrontation with Zedekiah, who alone of the kings in the book seeks a word from Yahweh, but who lacks the will to respond. Thus we revert to the inevitability of the coming disaster and the impossibility of resistance to Babylon. Jeremiah had bought a field in Anathoth as a sign that normal life would one day be resumed in the land (32:6–15), and he could now begin to preach salvation. The remainder of the chapter, in two parallel speeches (vv. 16–25 and 27–44), is a meditation on this logic. Jeremiah prays, "Nothing is too hard for you" (v. 17), and Yahweh responds, "Is anything too hard for me?" (v. 27). Jeremiah's prayer (vv. 16–25) appeals to Yahweh's lordship in creation and in Yahweh's dealings with the covenant people. It records salvation from Egypt, the gift of land, and Israel's covenant departure. The city's imminent end is the prayer's logical outcome. Thus the purchase of a field makes no sense to Jeremiah. Yahweh, for his part (vv. 27–44), calls to mind Israel's earlier blessing, laments its present apostasy, and stresses the inevitability of judgment. The change to a new future comes in verses 36–44 with an illogical *laken* 'therefore', which indicates that, in spite of the past, Yahweh will ensure the future of his people.

Jeremiah 33 adds only a little to this picture. The exile is inevitable, but there is hope of Davidic reestablishment beyond the punishment. The chapter closes with the divine assurance that Judahite and the Davidic dynasties will continue (33:26). There is a new fixity of purpose in this chapter, since the created order (with its general background in the unconditional promises to Noah in Gen. 8:21–22; 9:8–17) illustrates the irrefragability of the covenant that will now be made (vv. 23–26). Jeremiah presents the very message that he earlier had criticized. The question arises how a new covenant can have better success than the old. This question may be answered in chapters 34–36. The poems in the Book of Consolation in chapters 30–33 were probably connected to the final siege of Jerusalem in 586 B.C. The one essential message is that the people must now hope for restoration. The judgment had taken place.

Jeremiah 34 records matters relating to the final Babylonian siege of Jerusalem—a word to the vacillating Zedekiah (vv. 1–7). Zedekiah himself will die in peace, with the prospect of a decent funeral (v. 5), as Josiah had been assured (2 Kings 22:20), but the precipitous fall of the once-mighty Davidic dynasty is about to occur. Zedekiah, by releasing the slaves (Jer. 34:8–22), reverts fleetingly to covenant-keeping (cf. Deut. 15:12–18; Exod. 21:2–6), but the people who take their slaves back show Zedekiah's ineffectiveness. Such covenant breach brings its own punishment. There is an implicit analogy here with Josiah's reform (cf. the comparable death prophecy [v. 5]).

Jeremiah 35 switches to Jehoiakim, son of Josiah, and contrasts Jehoiakim's regime with the faithfulness of the Rechabites, who are steadfast to their commitments. Verse 19 points to an analogy between the house of David, fortified by the dynastic promise in Jeremiah 33:17 (cf. 1 Kings 2:4; 8:25), and the Rechabites, who will lack no one to stand before Yahweh. The Rechabites are a paradigm of required fidelity (vv. 1–11). There is a future for them but none, in this address, for Judah and David (vv. 12–19).

Jeremiah 36 ends the sequence, underscoring the nation's rejection of the word. Like Josiah, Jehoiakim is brought a scroll. Jehoiakim's studied impiety is to be contrasted with Josiah's pious response. The one king does what he can to let the words have their full effect; the other does what he can to destroy them. Thus, Jeremiah 34–36 focuses on Judah's inability to repent under the influence of Davidic kings. The narrative discards chronology and proceeds from Zedekiah in chapter 34 to Jehoiakim in chapter 36. Jeremiah 36 brings the flow of thought from 34:1 to a climax. The issue continues to be the failure of the monarchy and the certainty of exile. Jehoiakim will have no heir to sit upon the throne of David (v. 30), in contrast to the Rechabites, whose place in Israel will continue. Jeremiah 34–36 agrees with 2 Kings: there is no hope for the Davidic dynasty, but, unlike Kings, there is a larger hope for Judah.

The Fall of Jerusalem and Its Implications (Jer. 37–52)

Jeremiah 37–44 is a distinct section bounded by the *inclusio* formed by 37:1–10 and chapter 44 on Egypt. The most obvious formal difference with chapters 25–36 is the adherence in chapters 37–44 to a chronological pattern and the focus on the fall of Jerusalem and the aftermath. Jeremiah 37–38 preserves a dimension of the book never far from the surface: the charge of human responsibility for what will happen. The nation has victimized Jeremiah by his final arrest (37:14). Jeremiah 37 revolves around two confrontations between Jeremiah and Zedekiah (vv. 1–15, 16–21). In the first confrontation, the message is repeated curtly and without compromise. The second offers Zedekiah a choice: surrender and be spared or refuse and die (37:17). The logic of the restoration of Israel's fortunes (Deut. 30:3) can be seen in Jeremiah 37. Jeremiah prophesies imminent doom so that ultimate salvation might happen. In spite of proffered grace, judgment for Zedekiah does come. Serving as an analogy of the nation as a whole, he refuses the word of salvation.

There continues to be reflection in chapter 38 on the nature of peace (*shalom*) and falsehood (*sheqer*). The *shalom* motif is taken up in 38:4. Like the salvation prophets who are their spiritual kin, the princes fail to perceive that the way of *shalom* is through Jeremiah's preaching. Zedekiah's delusion is that Jeremiah is at his disposal (v. 24). Chapter 39 finishes with a report on the fall of Judah and the exile of the king, together with anyone of significance in Judah. In Jeremiah 40:1–43:7, the fall of the city has occurred and the Babylonian armies have gone (40:1–6). Jeremiah, committed to his message that the only way for Judah is through the fires of exile, opts to join the Babylonian appointee Gedaliah in submission to the Babylonian yoke, as he has always advocated. He will remain the mouthpiece of Yahweh (40:1–6). The news that Nebuchadnezzar had appointed a governor in Judah brings a flood of exiles back (40:7–12). The murder of Gedaliah (41:1–10), about which he had been forewarned (40:13–16), and its immediate aftermath lead to a popular uprising against the assassins that, though successful, raises the possibility of Babylonian reprisals for Gedaliah's death. The decision is once again between Babylon and Egypt, and the remnant of Judah decides for Egypt (41:11–18).

In chapter 42, Jeremiah again enters the scene. The remnant now asks for Jeremiah's word, which comes after some delay and affirms his view that those left should endure the Babylonian yoke. But again the prophetic word is rejected. Jeremiah is forced with the remnant to go into exile in Egypt (43:1–7). In Jeremiah 43:8–44:30, the final scene is played out in Egypt, framed by prophecies against Egypt (43:8–13; 44:24–30) and of impending Egyptian defeat by Babylon.

The reference (Jer. 45:1) to the words that Jeremiah spoke to Baruch in the fourth year of Jehoiakim links chapter 45 to chapter 36. Jeremiah provides the assurance that he usually receives. In verse 3, Jeremiah adopts the vocabulary of the confessions (15:10) and, at verse 4, that of the call narrative in 1:10. Chapter 45 reaffirms the verdict of chapter 36 and also the sentence pronounced in chapters 37–44. Yahweh's word was rejected even in Egypt. Chapters 37–45, while discussing the divine word and the human response, thus form a unit justifying God's immediate judgment on Judah. Judah under Zedekiah had made a fateful choice.

The Septuagint places Jeremiah 46–51 after 25:13. OT oracles against foreign nations have features in common with ancient Near Eastern curses. Chapters 37–44, which close the narrative account, prepare the way for the oracles and should not be taken as unrelieved doom, for the oracles revive in their own way the great message of consolation. The nations are now condemned. Yet Egypt (chap. 46), Moab (chap. 48), Ammon (49:1–6), and Elam (49:39), who, like Judah, had been involved with Babylon, are all promised salvation. Exile should not have been Judah's fate as a covenant people (cf. 49:12). Jeremiah 50:2–20 details Judah's apostasy (vv. 6–7) and her need of forgiveness (vv. 4, 20). Yahweh will forgive the remnant that he had determined to preserve (vv. 19–20). To do this, he will bring about the fall of Babylon (vv. 2–3, 8–16, 18) and return his people to their homeland (vv. 5, 19). Chapters 50–51 offer a different picture of Babylon from that of chapters 27–29, although, in chapter 29, the seventy-year limit on exile (29:10) had implied judgment in store for Babylon. Babylon was a scourge on the nations, but Judah and the nations deserved punishment.

Summary

The function of the Book of Jeremiah may be to introduce a new moment in Israelite salvation history. The Josianic reforms had revived dreams of Davidic grandeur. But Jeremiah's ministry saw increasing declension from Josianic ideals—a nation given over to apostasy and idolatry and thus deserving of the most severe covenant curse in Deuteronomy 28: the loss of the Promised Land itself. With the fall of Jerusalem, all externals of the faith had gone: temple, Davidic kingship, ark, sacrifice, priesthood, and the land itself. Judah in its structures had failed to live under the authority of Yahweh's word. The Book of Jeremiah raises the obvious questions: How intrinsic were these externals to the true nature of Israel? How would Israel be identified in the absence of the precise geographical and religious markers by which she had become known? How is the true Israel identified?

With the dissolution of nationalism in Jeremiah's time, the way is open for the emergence of the heavily individualistic apocalyptic movement, appropriately in exile (e.g., Daniel). Like his fellow preexilic prophets, Jeremiah looks beyond the disaster to the reconstitution of the people of God. His expectation is cast in the familiar terms of a new exodus, the return to the land, and a new covenant. Jeremiah 31:35–40 hints that a new covenant would necessarily operate within the contours of a new creation, as Isaiah and Ezekiel also make clear. Accordingly, Jeremiah looks for an idealized return to the land. That an actual return from exile, as the exilic prophets hoped, did not materialize did not mean that expectations for such a return were abandoned. They were simply postponed, for we cannot speak of a failure of prophecy merely on account of its nonfulfillment in a particular era.

The ministry of Jeremiah, however, was not a failure. It was a saving ministry, for it provided reasons for what happened in 587/586 B.C. His ministry was designed to prepare Israel for the great changes that would occur in exile. Israel was to become a community of faith, a status that the exile will make clear. The term "Israel" will not be able to be used again to refer solely to the nation. Although the postexilic writings witness disappointing attempts by the returned community to set back the historical clock, the course of the future people of God has been determined. Jeremiah prepares us for Israel's final punishment, then for a new exodus to be accomplished by the death of Christ, followed by the divine imposition of a new covenant. In effect, the proclamation of a new Israel—Jeremiah uses "Israel" predominantly as a theological term—a new covenant, and thus a new age for the people of God is the book's message.

12

Ezekiel

The overall structure of Ezekiel is not difficult to present in broad terms. Chapters 1–24 are given to the denunciation of Jerusalem, to prophecies of exile for Jerusalem's leadership and her people, and to prophecies relating to Jerusalem's destruction. Chapters 25–32 are oracles against the surrounding foreign nations; that is, they are prophetical judgments against Israel's world. Finally, chapters 33–48 deal with prophecies of restoration. The time references range from 593 B.C. (Ezek. 1:1, on the most probable interpretation) to 571 B.C. (29:17). The book thus covers Ezekiel's ministry to the exiles in Babylon prior to the fall of Jerusalem (587/586 B.C.) and the period immediately thereafter. Again, speaking broadly, chapters 1–24 deal with the foreshadowed destruction of the city and temple, while chapters 33–48 culminate in the presentation of the new temple complex, which is virtually identical with the New Jerusalem. Of the fourteen dated references in the book, all but the difficult 1:1, normally taken to be the prophet's age, are directly correlated to King Jehoiachin's reign (exiled in 597 B.C. but still considered by the deportees to be king in exile). This fact may suggest that Ezekiel strikes a pronounced Davidic note. But, in fact, the Davidic line is rarely referred to directly; when it is, the reference is almost always disparaging. The message of the book, indeed, is that the prior political leadership has failed and that the future of the people of God will be guaranteed only by the imposition of divine leadership. Ezekiel's intense interest in priestly matters—sacrifices, cultic regulations, purity, and temple—as well as his precision in description and dating, all point to his priestly background. His attention to the Zadokites (44:15–31) might more narrowly locate him. Ezekiel is a strange prophet, perhaps the strangest, a remote figure hidden almost completely behind his message, and we learn virtually nothing about him personally.

There is no evidence that he ever prophesied outside of Babylon, and he journeyed back to Jerusalem, which fell in July 587/6 B.C., only in a vision. But the deportation in 597 B.C., in which Ezekiel was involved, had raised the question of who was the true Israel. If Judah still occupied its land and worship continued at Jerusalem after 597 B.C., what was the exiles' status? Some reasoned that the boy-king Jehoiachin, exiled in 597, was the true Davidic figure, although equal claims were made for Zedekiah, who remained in the land. How then was Israel to be defined? The answer is by her election, since the visible institutions—land, king, temple, priesthood, and sacrifice—had all been removed. Prophetic conflict arose over the question of the exile. Whom were the exiles to believe? And what would be the fate of Jerusalem? Would Yahweh defend it as he had done in the past, or abandon it to its enemies? Was Yahweh the supreme Lord (cf. Isa. 40–55)? Although the exiles' confidence in Yahweh's supremacy had taken a battering, such questions were burning issues.

Ezekiel's prophecy is coordinated around the three visions (chaps. 1–3, 8–11, 40–48). Only in these visions is the "hand of the Lord" (i.e., visionary possession) reported as being on the prophet; this phrase is associated with the reports of 1:3; 8:1; and 40:1. The first vision returns the prophet to Chaldea (3:12–15) without mentioning that he had left. In the second vision (8:3), the seer is spiritually transported to Jerusalem and returns (11:24). In the third vision, he returns to the restored sanctuary (40:2) but does not return to Chaldea. The visions thus summarize the career of Ezekiel. His first vision was as if he had come to the exiles for the first time. At the end of the book, having traced not only Israel's sin and punishment but also its future restoration, his task is finished. He has come home to the land of Israel in prophecy, if not yet in fact, and there he will stay. A further symmetry binds the three visions. The first vision that emphasizes the glory of the Lord becomes in effect the central element in the chiastic structure of chapters 8–11, that is, chapter 10. There, it depicts the departure of the Lord from the doomed city and temple. Similarly, the pattern of revelation in the form of a sanctuary tour, established in chapters 9–11, forms the core of chapters 40–44 regarding the rebuilt temple. Thus the cult, dismissed in chapters 1–2 and 8–11, is reestablished, and the glory of the Lord once more takes up residence in the temple, indicating the careful interrelationship of the three visions.

The prophecy of Ezekiel may be regarded as the immediate precursor of the apocalyptic movement. There is a strong affinity between Ezekiel and Daniel (cf. Dan. 7); the connection may be confirmed by explicit reference to Daniel in the Book of Ezekiel (14:14, 20). If the animal symbolism in those two books is influenced by the Babylonian context, it represents a bold introduction of symbols and art forms of the pagan world. Both books also make a sharp distinction, familiar from later apocalyptic, between the heavenly and earthly spheres. Both have a pessimistic view of the earthly sphere and see little hope in the historical process. Hope is centered in the heavenly realm, from whence Israel's salvation will come. These perspectives are characteristic of apocalyptic. Ezekiel 38–39, indeed, contains many ingredients of a developing apocalyptic.

The Call of Ezekiel and the First Temple Vision (Ezek. 1:1–3:15)

The first vision of Ezekiel sets the tone for the book. The five paragraphs of Ezekiel 1 (commencing in vv. 4, 7, 16, 22, and 26) are tied together by the use of the same idiom, "like the gleam of" (see vv. 4, 7, 16, 22, and 27). The first and last paragraphs (1:4, 26–28) describe the figure that rides on the chariot, while the intervening paragraphs describe the living creatures (vv. 5–14) and their relationship to the wheels beside them (vv. 15–21) and to the platform or firmament above them (vv. 22–25). Ezekiel 1:4 graphically introduces the vision with a general description of the divine manifestation, expanded in verses 26–28 by a repetition (in reverse order) of the three items seen in 1:4, namely, flashing fire, brightness, and storm (Parunak 1979, 124). These are not incidental details furnished by the prophet, but are the characteristics of the Lord who appears. The description of the platform and what is above it (vv. 25–26) is reminiscent of the description of the enthroned Yahweh seen by the elders of Israel (Exod. 24:10). In this way, continuity with the Sinai traditions is indicated. The last temple vision (chaps. 40–48) also promotes this connection (Parunak 1980, 72).

The servant creatures (Ezek. 1)—the cherubim (10:15, 20)—elsewhere are supporters of the ark throne (see 1 Sam. 4:4; 2 Sam. 6:2; Ps. 18:10). This identification increases the probability that it is Yahweh, as both locally enthroned and yet omnipresent, whom Ezekiel encounters. The attention to the throne, and the similarities to Isaiah 6, suggest not only association with the Zion traditions, but Yahweh's judgment against what is clearly the Jerusalem temple (see Ezek. 10).

That the storm vision emanates from the north, the numinous area from which judgment at the time of the exile was expected to come (cf. the "foe from the north," the chaoslike irruption of judgment in the Book of Jeremiah), confirms this interpretation. Yahweh is depicted in Ezekiel 1 as enthroned and accompanied by ministrant attendants. Unlike the seraphim of Isaiah 6, they are cherubim (identified in chap. 10)—temple guardians or door deities in the ancient Near East. They function only as bearers of the throne. Yahweh is moving from his heavenly palace, in judgment against the Jerusalem temple. The book thus commences with Jerusalem and her temple under imminent judgment. Yet the covenant faithfulness of Yahweh has led us to expect a movement beyond judgment. So the Book of Ezekiel concludes with the magnificent conception of Yahweh enthroned in what must be the New Jerusalem, permanently located among his people in a new city from which, in Eden terms, the waters of life flow.

The vision of chapter 1 reduces Ezekiel to ineffability. What he has seen defies human description verbally or visually. He is addressed (2:1–2), sent to a rebellious people (vv. 3–5), and encouraged by divine assurances in a manner somewhat similar to the call of Jeremiah (2:6–3:3). The continuing vision of chapter 2 indicates that Ezekiel is the true prophet, for he has stood in Yahweh's presence and heard his word (Jer. 23:18, 22). The throne and the living beings indicate that Ezekiel has been admitted to the heavenly court (cf. Isa. 6;

40:1–11; Amos 3:8; Zech. 3). Thus, Ezekiel 1:1–3:5 is an intricately structured adaptation of the classical call narrative, modified to express the heightened transcendence of the deity to which Ezekiel gives expression. Set over against the rebellious people, who are more rebellious than the heathen (3:6–7), with hard foreheads and stubborn hearts (3:7), Ezekiel ("God hardens") is made hard for his task. He is recommissioned (3:4–11) before being returned by the Spirit to his exilic location (3:12–15), conscious of Yahweh's exodus power and of the unique and ecstatic nature of his experience. "The hand of the Lord" had been upon him (3:14). The call vision assured the exiles that God had not rejected them. Ezekiel sees the divine throne coming to rest on Babylonian soil, and the divine presence suggests that the deportees remain part of the true Israel. However, at this point it was not clear what Yahweh's presence among the exiles meant, for the issue had not yet been determined.

Finally, seeing God's presence in Babylon raises the question of God's presence in the Jerusalem temple. Had God rejected the traditional Israelite sanctuary, and, if so, what were the consequences of this rejection? The answers will come in chapters 8–11. God would in fact leave the city to the mercy of the Babylonians. This would mean that the fate of the city had been sealed.

Ezekiel seems devoid of free will when carrying out his tasks. He does not act unless God, through the Spirit, has caused him to act. The prophet only speaks the divine word that has been put in his mouth (3:27), and he does not elaborate the message in any way. In contrast with his contemporary, Jeremiah, Ezekiel does not engage in conversations or arguments with God, and, in fact, rarely responds verbally to divine commands. The effect is to portray Ezekiel as an automaton, an individual with no human personality but who is under God's control. He is simply the conduit through which the unaltered divine word comes, and it is impossible to accuse him of speaking falsely. Whoever hears Ezekiel hears the divine word directly. In 2:8–10, Ezekiel is told to eat the scroll inscribed with words of lamentation, mourning, and woe. He does so and reports that the scroll tasted sweet (cf. Jer. 15:16). This means that eating the scroll has determined the form of the words, a form that cannot be changed. He is then commanded to speak God's word to the house of Israel (2:8–3:4). There can therefore be no doubt of the prophet's authority, since all the words that Ezekiel speaks are the words God puts inside him. By speaking of the divine origin of a completely filled scroll, Ezekiel claims that the entire book was given directly by God. Both the oracles and the context in which they are given are divinely set. Ezekiel delivers to the exile community and to later Israelite communities a prophetic book to which they must respond (cf. Jer. 36). Based on the description of the scroll, it seems that the prophet primarily was to speak words of judgment or threat that might warn the exiles to repent.

At the beginning of the charge to Ezekiel, God states clearly the reason for sending a prophet to Israel. The people are rebels who must be condemned for their crimes. The general context of the call narrative, as well as the specific command at the end of the commissioning to prophesy to the exiles (3:11), indicates that the rebels are Ezekiel's fellow deportees. They may have reacted violently to the message, feeling that they had already been sufficiently punished and that they did not need to repent. So Ezekiel is warned about popular opposition, and God exhorts him to continue to prophesy, although the people ignore him. God promises to strengthen Ezekiel so he can withstand the attacks of the exiles (2:4–8; 3:8–9).

Ezekiel's call ends on a somber note. He is told that the exiles will not listen to him, for they have already rejected the divine message he brings (3:5–7). His attempts to save the exiles by exhorting them to repent will fail, and the judgment will come. Is his work an exercise in futility? Still, Ezekiel's call stands as an eloquent testimony to God's refusal to let Israel be destroyed. Even though it is clear from the beginning that Israel will not respond, God continues to call her.

Ezekiel's Role and Message (Ezek. 3:16–7:27)

In 3:16–21, Ezekiel is appointed as a watchman at the end of the seven days of the vision. He is addressed as Son of Man (cf. Dan. 7), that is, as a frail human with a responsibility toward the backsliding righteous. Ezekiel, on pain of his own life, is to warn those otherwise doomed. The exiles' foe, against whom utmost precautions must be taken is, of course, Israel's deity, Yahweh. The office is to be exercised faithfully toward sinners and the backsliding righteous, no matter what the people say. Even though there is little hope that Israel will repent, God still appoints a watchman to warn the nation of the approaching divine wrath.

Ezekiel 3:22–5:17

The section consists of two unequal parts: 3:22–5:4, a complex series of commands to perform certain actions; and 5:5–17, a prophecy of doom loosely related to those actions. The section opens with Ezekiel being seized by the Spirit and runs without formal introduction to 6:1, where a revelation formula marks a new beginning. Somewhat paradoxically, Ezekiel is then confined to his house and told that he is to be bound and rendered dumb (vv. 24–27), actions that seem to negate the charge he has just received. We are therefore to take the phrase "unable to reprove them" (v. 26), that is, to act as a mediator (the probable meaning in this context; see R. R. Wilson 1972, 98), as an interpretation of what will be meant by Ezekiel's dumbness. Until this dumbness is removed (by the fall of Jerusalem; see 33:22), the prophetic word to Israel is one of undeviating judgment relating to the destruction of city and temple. Any messages of hope in chapters 1–24 beyond this destruction do not weaken the stark character of the prophetic threat directed against Jerusalem and her temple in its historical context.

Ezekiel's message commences with two acts of paradigmatic symbolism, graphically depicting the siege (Ezek. 4) and the fall (Ezek. 5) of Jerusalem. Unlike sympathetic magic, whose purpose was to influence the deity, the OT prophets saw symbolic acts as self-effective proclamations of the divine word pointing to a new divine intervention into Israel's history. While the prophetic act was not identical with prophetic word, they were inseparable. The prophetic act provided the occasion for the prophetic announcement, but the symbolic act required prophetic interpretation.

Verses 4–5 and 7–9 depict Ezekiel lying on his left side for the iniquity of the house of Israel for 390 (LXX 190) days, while prophesying against the besieged city. If this were not sufficiently complicated, verse 6 prescribes lying on the right side to bear the iniquity of the house of Judah for forty days. The nation's sin, calculated apparently from the beginning of Solomon's reign (ca. 970 B.C.), was still going on and would continue for the allotted 390 years, when the city would be destroyed (587/6 B.C.). Ezekiel's first act is best taken as betokening the sin of Israel during the First Temple period; the second act indicates that Judah's exile will last forty years and further symbolizes the paralysis of exile. After enacting the siege of the city (4:1–17), Ezekiel represents the annihilation and dispersion of the population (5:1–5). Verses 9–11 and 16–17 provide for scant food and drink to be consumed during this siege period. Lying on one side (v. 6) and eating unclean food (vv. 12–15) are parallel depictions of the exile.

Ezekiel's ritual shaving (5:1–4) is meant to suggest surrender of power or of personality and vitality. The threefold sifting of hair seems to put emphasis on a remnant's survival. Ezekiel 5:5–10 emphasizes balanced punishment. The second part of the prophecy (vv. 11–17), which refers to defilement of the sanctuary, is the ground of the final punishment, dispersion, and annihilation. God's inexorable anger is signaled by the double repudiation of pity.

Ezekiel 6–7

There is some logical progression in chapters 5–8. The symbolic acts of 4:1–5:4 portray God's judgments on Jerusalem. The specific reason appears in the oracle of 5:15–17: ". . . because you have defiled my sanctuary with all your abominations" (5:11). There follow, in chapters 6–7, two oracles against the "mountains of Israel"—that is, the land of Israel—in which the theme of abominations is developed (cf. 6:11; 7:3, 4, 8, 9). The abominations here are the pagan shrines located throughout the land, but especially on the hills. In chapter 8, the focus narrows to the temple, where the crowning abominations are seen—those that defile Yahweh's sanctuary itself. Chapters 6–7 thus form a logical bridge between chapters 5 and 8.

The apostasy of the land is treated by reference to the "mountains" on which syncretistic acts of covenant disloyalty had occurred (Ezek. 6:1–14). It is usually assumed that Ezekiel's mountain imagery refers to the Zion traditions. In Ezekiel, the mountain where God is worshiped does not mean a singular mountain (cf. 17:23, "on the mountain height of Israel"), but the land itself. At the time of Israel's restoration, offerings will be made on "my holy mountain" (20:40), but this phrase in the next clause refers clearly to the land. The vision in Ezekiel 40–48 concerns a mountain often seen as Zion/Jerusalem, but the passage makes no such identification. In 48:9–16, not only is the temple no part of the city, but the citylike structure is situated on the south side of the mountain (40:2). The temple must be on the summit, since the special status of the temple in 48:9–18 stems from its being the holiest part of the land. The top of the mountain would be the temple site, and the city is on the south side of the temple (Maio 1998, 74, 80). Ezekiel 6:1–14 is spoken entirely to the land, dealing with the land (vv. 1–7), the survivors (vv. 8–10), and the desolation (vv. 11–14). In chapter 7, Ezekiel delivers the announcement of the "end," which is due to the people's social and religious wrongdoing (cf. 7:6, 24). Such behavior results in the land's virtual dismissal as a Promised Land.

Departure of the Divine Glory (Ezek. 8–11)

The cycle of vision followed by prophetic ministry begins again in chapter 8. A response to the implicit inquiry of the elders (cf., similarly, 14:1–3), Ezekiel's vision presents the actuality of judgment about to befall Jerusalem, which the vision of chapter 1 foreshadowed. Unthinkably, Yahweh, resident in the temple since its dedication by Solomon, is about to depart by means of the heavenly chariot of Ezekiel 1.

Ezekiel is transported by the Spirit to Jerusalem and is moved to four different locations in the temple to witness its defilement by Judah's elders (8:5–17a). Judgment is to be visited upon Jerusalem's inhabitants, though a remnant is to be marked off and spared (8:17b–9:11). Chapter 9 describes the first stage of the judgment announced in 8:18. This stage consists of the slaughter of most of Jerusalem's inhabitants, although the godly remnant is marked for protection. The second and final stage of the punishment is recorded in chapter 10, namely, the burning of the city (10:2, 6). Therefore, chapter 9 is linked to what precedes and follows.

Chapter 9 also describes the first stage in the departure of the divine glory from the temple and city (9:3). Further stages of the glory's departure are described in chapters 10 and 11 (cf. 10:18; 11:22). Ezekiel 10:1–22, the center of chapters 8–11, oscillates between the temple and the divine chariot. Ezekiel 10:1 recalls the vision above the firmament in 1:26–28. The glory of Yahweh, which had previously consecrated the temple (Exod. 40; 1 Kings 8), now fills the temple destructively (Ezek. 10:2–7). The order to burn the city (10:2) is linked to chapter 9 by the figure of the man clothed in linen. In chapter 9, his role was preservation, but now it is destruction. The divine chariot is seen, positioned for departure. The creatures of Ezekiel 10, used to transport the *kabod* 'glory' out of the temple, are identified as cherubim, the guardians of sacred space (cf. Gen. 3:24). The theophany cloud fills the inner court. The glory arises from its permanent position above and between the cherubim in the Holy of Holies, moves to the temple threshold (v. 4a), and departs (vv. 18–19). Verses 20–22 reinforce the connection between Ezekiel 1 and 10 (Parunak 1980, 68–69).

Ezekiel 11:1–21 repeats the sequence of judgment on the conspirators. The death of Pelatiah, a principal conspirator (v. 13), brings divine word regarding the future of the exilic congregation (vv. 14–21). Promises previously associated with covenant, Jerusalem, and temple are transferred to a new temple (the "sanctuary" of v. 16), which Yahweh will convene in exile. In Ezekiel 11:19, the people are given one heart and a new spirit. In using the phrase "one heart," that is, a single heart, Ezekiel is undoubtedly influenced by Jeremiah 32:39 and the promise there of a single, national heart devoted to Yahweh. Ezekiel explains that Yahweh will remove the people's heart of stone and replace it with a heart of flesh. The heart in this context, as in the OT generally, is the center of willing and acting, the locus of the moral will. The sense is thus that the people will obey (11:20). The new heart is not an end in itself, but symbolizes a new era of corporate covenant faithfulness to Yahweh, a new beginning for Israel. Verses 22–24 return the prophet to the scene of 8:1. The glory of the Lord departs from the east gate of the temple, to which it will return in the prophecy's closing vision (43:1). Ezekiel shows his priestly background with his emphasis on cultic and ritual, rather than social, abuses. Israel's cardinal sin is the defilement of her sanctuary (5:11). Her cardinal blessing will be to have Yahweh's presence in a perfect temple (chaps. 40–48).

So, in this vision received six years before the fall of Jerusalem, Ezekiel foretold the divine abandonment of Jerusalem. He foresaw that its population would be massacred and its buildings condemned to flames. Twice he cried out on behalf of the doomed (9:8; 11:13), and these are his only attempts to intercede. Otherwise, the message is one of unconditional doom. The Jerusalemites had appropriated the exiles' property on the grounds that God had removed the exiles. God's answer is that God will serve as the exiles' sanctuary, and that they will return to the land (11:14–16) and purge it of the abominations perpetrated by the present doomed occupants. Human agents would wreak the destruction, but the enemy was God. The Babylonian army was only an instrument of God's heavenly executioners.

The Exile Symbolized (Ezek. 12–23)

Clearly unmoved by Ezekiel's further parables (12:1–16, 17–20), the Israelites still in the land disown Ezekiel's prophecy (12:22). This disavowal is embedded in a section running from 12:21 to 13:23, in which Ezekiel attacks false prophecy of various descriptions as an ineffectual and apostate substitute for the real proclamation. Again, the elders assemble and, like their condemned compatriots in Ezekiel 8–11, are identified as idolatrous. There is no word for them unless they repent (14:1–11); it is not sufficient for the present generation to plead the merits of its ancestors. Noah, Daniel, and Job, whose piety was renowned, are cited (14:14), since Ezekiel is emphasizing the responsibility of individual Israelites. Israel is now only fit for burning (chap. 15).

Ezekiel 16 looks at sin from the perspective of the land's inhabitants. (Ezekiel 23, in a similar review, focuses on sin from the land's point of view.) Verses 3–14 focus on Yahweh's saving actions, and Jerusalem's misdeeds do not begin until verse 15. Verses 3–5 focus on Canaanite Jerusalem's depravity (cf. Lev. 18) before it was taken over by Israel. It was only Yahweh's kindness that led him to reverse her fortunes. "Jerusalem" here is not the people but the place God had chosen for God's sanctuary. Jerusalem's transformation under Yahweh is the subject of verses 4–14.

From verse 15 there is a contrasting descent into prostitution. The woman is said in verse 15, and again in verse 25, to offer herself to "every passerby." Verses 15–22 focus on the idolatry of local Canaanite gods. In contrast, verses 23–29 relate to Jerusalem's prostitution with Egypt, Assyria, and Babylon, thus indicating different political alliances. Nothing could exceed Jerusalem's brazenness (vv. 30–34).

Two categories of punishment are presented without break in verses 35–43. Yahweh hands the woman over to her lovers for ravaging (vv. 35–39), while verses 40–41 suggest that an army will undertake its judgment before many women (v. 41). Yahweh has allowed suspension of his covenant protection.

Verses 44–58 and 59–63 pursue one theme, namely, the comparison of Jerusalem and her sisters Samaria and Sodom. These two cities, to the north and south, live with their daughters. Yahweh had destroyed both. Jerusalem's sins are greater and, thus, she must also be destroyed. Both cities have loathed husbands and children, an attitude that suggests unfaithfulness and irresponsibility and that represents the region's low religious standards. Jerusalem throughout her history had proved herself an adulteress (16:1–43), more corrupt in fact than Sodom or Samaria (vv. 44–58). Yet divine fidelity to the covenant may be expected, and Israel will be reestablished (vv. 59–63).

Kingship (chap. 17), which had contributed to covenant breach, will cease, and the reigning king will be removed to Babylon. Hope of messianic kingship, however, is advanced at the end of this chapter (vv. 22–24). Yahweh will pluck a sprig from a tall tree and plant it on the mountain, that is, in the Promised Land. The sprig grows to a vast cedar tree in which many birds nest. Yahweh himself will restore the nation as a kingdom no longer under vassalage (cf. the vine lying low), but as a strong nation in its own right (cf. the tall cedar tree).

The Doctrine of National Responsibility (Ezek. 18)

The sin of the nation is surveyed in Ezekiel 18, in terms of the responsibility of each generation. Each individual is presented as responsible for his or her own sin. This doctrine of responsibility, which is not new with Ezekiel, is exhibited in verses 1–20 by an examination that moves through three generations (cf. the same three-generation span referred to in an examination of Israel's history in chap. 20). It is made clear that past associations do not determine present conduct, but Yahweh desires the nation's life, not its death. Ezekiel is not to be understood as denying corporate responsibility, an old biblical doctrine (see Exod. 20:5–6), but at this critical time in Israel's history is providing a counterpoise or a complement to the older doctrine. Israel's attempt to disclaim responsibility for the exile is thus rejected. On the one hand, the people are to get a new heart (18:31), yet Yahweh will give it (11:19; 36:26). Yahweh commands the people to undergo a transformation, but when they fail to do so, he undertakes this task on their behalf. In 18:31, the command to get a new heart is the challenge to avoid disaster. In verses 21–22, the wicked should turn from their sin so that they will not be punished. Yahweh (v. 23) has no wish to punish. If only the people would get a new heart to control their own will, there would be no need for punishment. Immediately after this challenge and in an indication of the inevitable, Yahweh asks, "Why will you die, O house of Israel?" (18:31).

Review of Judah's Kingship from Josiah to the Exile (Ezek. 19)

A review of kingship since Josiah is conducted in Ezekiel 19. There is no prospect of its continuance, however, for the chapter ends on the note of lament. Only the first king in the chapter can be identified without controversy—Jehoahaz, whom Necho took to Egypt in 609 B.C. (2 Kings 23:30–34). The capture and deportation to Babylon of the second figure suits the situation of Jehoiachim (cf. 2 Kings 24:8–9) or Zedekiah (2 Kings 25:6–7). The royal figures depicted by the figure of the mighty boughs are difficult to identify. The first figure might be Zedekiah while the final figure might be Jehoiachin, transplanted but to remain without issue. The mother figure of the chapter appears to be the Davidic royal house. Chapter 19 wonders about the future of the Davidic dynasty and thus about the messianic hope in the postexilic period. There seems to be no messianic emphasis in the Book of Ezekiel, and the prophet firmly turns his back on Jerusalem and its temple (and, thus, on the associated royal court). The emphasis in the prophecies of restoration in Ezekiel is on the kingship of Yahweh, with a disinclination to use the term *melek* of the Davidic figure. Indeed, Davidic restoration is not emphasized or anticipated in the entire postexilic period.

Salvation History in Review (Ezek. 20)

Ezekiel 20, in its review of the history of Israel, is a key chapter. The fulfillment of the promise of land is the major theme of 20:1–44. The elders (v. 1) inquire concerning a promise of salvation that has to be an imminent return to the land. Yahweh, in response, provides a theological overview of Israel's past and future in relation to this promise. Beginning with the ancestors' desert wanderings (vv. 5–26), Yahweh declares that the period was characterized by the people's consistent rebellion and idolatry, making them (vv. 5–6) undeserving of the land. As a consequence, Yahweh does not fulfill the promise, even though they are brought into the land. The people are therefore to be scattered to the nations (v. 23). In verses 27–29, each generation that dwells in the land is shown to continue its ancestors' idolatry, performing abominations on every high hill or under every leafy tree. Thus the refusal of land is shown to be justified.

From verse 30, the perspective of the oracle changes, with Yahweh shifting from the past to the present. In verses 30–32, he reveals the people's inner desire to become assimilated to the practices of surrounding nations. There can be no prophetic word for such people, but Yahweh will not allow an inclination toward faithlessness. Yahweh's determination to carry out his program is outlined in two stages (vv. 33–38 and 39–44). In the first stage, Yahweh announces that he will again intervene to save his people by an exodus-type act, bringing them into the wilderness of people, thus alluding to the wilderness of Egypt in the first exodus. Monarchy seems to have been the problem, but Yahweh will impose his kingship upon them (v. 33) and bring them out from among the nations. He will bring them again into the wilderness, which turns out to be a metaphor for a time of judgment through which the rebellious will be purged and prevented from entering the Promised Land (vv. 35–39). The others will indeed be brought to the Promised Land. On God's holy mountain, that is, in the Promised Land, Israel will once again serve God (vv. 40–44). The central concern in this section is that Yahweh's holiness be revealed among the nations, just as the sanctity of Yahweh's name was presented as the motivating force for actions in verses 5–26. Thus, Yahweh's reply to the elders confirms his land promise but demonstrates that the salvation will be neither quick nor painless.

The aim of this review of history and its consequences for Israel and her future is that Israel might have knowledge of Yahweh (see 20:26, 38, 44, at the end of each section). The phrase "you will know that I am Yahweh" occurs in Ezekiel freely, chiefly to indicate the goal of a divine action. Such knowledge of Yahweh is not arrived at by speculative insight, but by recognition of divine control over history. This realization comes through the prompting of Yahweh's agents (i.e., prophets), and in the final analysis is a demand for submission to divine sovereignty.

The Fall of Jerusalem (Ezek. 21–23)

The threat of Ezekiel 20:45–49, judgment by fire, is developed in 21:1–27, where Jerusalem, the sanctuaries, and then the land are depicted as falling to Nebuchadnezzar's sword. Not Israel alone, but also those who have afflicted her (Ammon is singled out in vv. 28–32) will suffer.

The people as well as the leaders must bear responsibility. Ezekiel 22 details the abominations of Jerusalem in covenant breach. She must be thoroughly purged from sin (vv. 1–16), with the barest hint offered in verses 17–22 that a cleansed people would result. Judah's leadership has been responsible for her catastrophe (22:23–31). Chapter 23 resumes the adultery allegory of Ezekiel 16. The sins described in Ezekiel 23 can be divided into categories of prostitution and idolatry. Verses 1–35, the main section of the chapter, is an allegorical presentation of a history presenting the prostitution (foreign alliances, etc.) of Oholah (Samaria) followed by her punishment (vv. 9–10). The passage then turns to Oholibah (Jerusalem), whose prostitution exceeded that of her sister (vv. 11–21). Her punishment is inevitable (vv. 22–35). Verses 11–35 detail Jerusalem's sin, as verses 5–10 do Samaria's. The passage is thus primarily concerned with Jerusalem (Oholibah) but uses Samaria (Oholah) as a foil to show how the former's offensive behavior exceeds the latter so that punishment will be handed out to Jerusalem (vv. 31–35).

Ezekiel 23:36–49 is a continuation since the two sisters continue still with the sins of prostitution and idolatry. Both women here are addressed at the same time despite the fact that Oholah's punishment is past. This then signals a move away from the chronological to a more holistic view of events. Verses 36–39 describe their sin as adultery involving child sacrifice and idolatry. Verses 40–44 return to the theme of prostitution. In verses 45–49, unbiased righteous men, that is, the Babylonians as instruments of Yahweh's righteousness, will now pass judgment. Israel and Judah were unable to remain true, lusting after foreign nations, not placing their trust in the God of the covenant, looking to military powers. Prostitution has been a habit for the two women that they have not been able to shake off since Egypt.

The chapters immediately preceding and following the oracles against the foreign nations (chaps. 24 and 33) deal with the siege of Jerusalem and its outcome. The siege commenced in December–January 589/588 B.C., and the city fell in the summer of 587/586. This structure offers some clue to the manner in which the oracles against foreign nations function in the Book of Ezekiel.

Jerusalem is presented in the parable of the cooking pot (24:3–14) as under siege. To the difficulties and sufferings of the period, a mute reaction like Ezekiel's response to the death of his wife is demanded from the exiles (vv. 15–24). With the fall of Jerusalem (vv. 25–27), Ezekiel's dumbness will cease; that is, from that point onward prophecies of hope can be expected.

Oracles against Foreign Nations (Ezek. 25–32)

The pivot on which the book turns as a whole is the block of oracles against the foreign nations in chapters 25–32. This section is framed by references to the fall of Jerusalem in chapters 23–24 (cf. 24:1–2, 25–27; 33:21–22). This positioning of the oracles against the foreign nations has two purposes. First, it fills the chronological gap between the revelation that the siege has begun 24:1–2, and in so doing it maintains the prophetic suspense. Then these chapters remind that the Lord who is judging Jerusalem extends his moral government to the world. These oracles are against the nations that had sought to take advantage of Israel's distress. Such nations fall within the sphere of the Abrahamic curse on Israel's despisers (Gen. 12:3). Israel's restoration must be preceded by the judgment of her world. Ammon, Moab, Edom, and Philistia are summarily dealt with in Ezekiel 25. Tyre, which sees the removal of Jerusalem as opening the way for further commercial expansion, is singled out for special attention in view of her political importance and seeming impregnability in Ezekiel's day (chaps. 26–28). Oracles against Egypt occur in chapters 29–32.

Ezekiel 28:1–10 portrays the king of Tyre saying, "I am El." He is described as being in the seat of the gods, in the heart of the seas, reinforcing the allusion to El whose Canaanite dwelling place was the springs of two rivers, midst the channels of the two deeps. The thrust of the oracle lies in the description of how Yahweh reveals the fallacy of the king's pride. The oracle functions to assert the correct relationship between the king of Tyre and Yahweh; the king is created by, and subservient to, Yahweh. It has been frequently noted that the list of stones (Ezek. 28:13) on the king of Tyre's vestments bear a strong resemblance to the list of stones on the high priest's ephod described in Exodus 28:17–20. Carol Newsom (1984) shows that the king is thus presented as a priest in Yahweh's temple.

There is an extensive use in chapter 28 of Eden traditions. The prince of Tyre is cast into the role of the primeval man in the garden of God, the priest-king in the Garden of Eden. Ezekiel is saying that even if the king of Tyre were in Eden, he would be cast out. Even if he were full of beauty and wisdom, he would still go. There is no link with Zion in the passage. Sidon, as an adjunct to Tyre, is briefly dealt with in 28:20–24. Attention then switches to Egypt, which survived the Assyrian period intact but will be broken by Babylon (chaps. 29–32). Egypt will share the fate of Assyria, which has entered Sheol.

Content and Structure of Chapter 33

Repetition of the watchman theme in Ezekiel 33:1–22 begins a new phase in the prophecy with a return to Ezekiel's original commission. It is now noted that the judgment foreshadowed in the earlier announcement has been carried out (vv. 21–22); the capture of Jerusalem relieves Ezekiel's dumbness and permits him to begin the prophecies of hope in chapters 34–39. Six prophecies, all introduced with "the word of the Lord came to me" (Ezek. 33:23–33; 34; 35:1–36:15; 36:16–37:14; 37:15–28; chaps. 38–39), follow in unbroken succession without any indication of a time lapse between them. They thus connect the fall of Jerusalem with the hope that must flow from such destruction. By implication, the first prophecy (33:23–33) explains the apparent discrepancy between the Abrahamic promises (v. 24) and the judgment to be exercised upon Israel, which includes loss of the land. The prophet replies that the physical enjoyment of the land was conditional upon obedience. Quite naturally, the notion of the Promised Land figures prominently in the material that follows.

Chapter 33 begins, in verses 1–9, with a passage in which Ezekiel is told again that he has been made a watchman for the house of Israel. There then follows a section (vv. 10–20) in which Ezekiel speaks as a watchman to his fellow exiles. A brief report (vv. 21–22) about the news of the fall of Jerusalem reaches Ezekiel and his fellow exiles. In verses 23–29, Ezekiel delivers a further oracle, this time addressed to those who still remain in Judea, concerning illegal land appropriation. The final part of the chapter (vv. 30–33) concerns the way Ezekiel is now treated by his fellows exiles as a mere performer. The Book of Ezekiel will end with God present with his people in restoration, and chapter 33 begins the move to the end. We move now into what will be the chapter's predominant concern with restoration. The repetition of the watchman passage seems to signal a significant turn in the movement of the book.

Divine Leadership and Restoration (Ezek. 34–36)

Ezekiel 34 is an extended metaphor in which the people of Israel are represented as a flock of sheep pasturing on good land. Verses 1–16 deal with oppression inflicted by the shepherds whom Yahweh had set up over the sheep, resulting in the apostasy and scattering (i.e., exile) of the sheep (vv. 1–6). The shepherds are arraigned for a lack of fidelity to their office (vv. 7–10). Yahweh will now gather them, that is, restore them to their land, the good land, the mountains of Israel, and feed them (vv. 11–16). Verses 17–24 deal with injustice propagated by the sheep amongst themselves, the stronger upon the weaker. In the reconstruction, there is room for a Davidic under-shepherd, but only as a minor figure (he is called "prince" in v. 24 and not "king"). As a result of divine leadership, conditions of paradise-like peace follow (vv. 25–31). The blessed nature of this land is explicitly described in verses 25–28 in the stereotypes of blessing, fruit, and security. This elaboration of the land suggests again that the land awaits such a gathering event for its restoration.

Ezekiel 35–36 and Edom's Possession of Yahweh's Land

Redemption of the Land (Ezek. 35:1–36:15)

Ezekiel 35:1–36:15 deals with the elimination of any threat to the Promised Land and thus the removal of all enmity, symbolized in chapter 35 by Israel's old enemy, Edom. The address of 35:1–15 is to the land of Edom, that of 36:1–15 to Israel. Following on from 6:1–14, these sections draw heavily upon the notion of the land as the deity's residence. Ezekiel 35:3–4 is a proleptic announcement of judgment that is then formulated in two parts (vv. 5–9 and 10–15). Ezekiel 36:1–15 is addressed to the mountains of Israel, that is, the Promised Land. The enemy had thought they would take possession of the land (vv. 1–4). Edom's ravaging of the land had exposed the land to the reproach of the nations (vv. 5–7). Ezekiel 36:8–15 is an address to the land informing it of the complete character of its restoration.

The New Covenant (Ezek. 36:16–38)

Ezekiel 36:16–37:14 concerns the manner of Yahweh's redemption of Israel and her restoration to the Promised Land. Ezekiel begins by reviewing the defilement that led to the loss of the land (36:16–20). A restoration will come about solely through God's clear intention to vindicate his holy name through Israel (vv. 21–23). Ezekiel 36:24 speaks of cleansing and blessing following the return from exile. The land is to be restored to fruitfulness as it receives Yahweh's blessing (cf. Lev. 26; Deut. 28–30). This cleansing will mean a complete negation of sinful conduct enabling the people to live in security. In 36:24–38, a new exodus will bring together people and land (v. 24). Israel will be ritually cleansed, that is, the covenant will be restored, and a new heart will be given to her (v. 26). The parallel gift of a new divine Spirit (v. 27) facilitates obedience since it will mean a new heart or mind. In this way the ultimate gift of the Spirit, previously reserved in the OT for Israel's rulers, democratizes leadership so that presumably all become priests and kings in the new age (cf. Isa. 55:3). Unlike Jeremiah 31:31–34, it is not said here that the law will be placed in the heart, though in the theology of covenant renewal, familiar to the exilic prophets, this step would have been assumed, since the human heart was regarded as the volitional and emotional center of the person. National repentance is not mentioned, only national defilement (36:17), so that the imposition of the new covenant is a movement of grace. Ezekiel 36:28–38 leads us to the consummation of the program, namely, the restoration of the land or, in Eden terms, the renewal of creation so that the regeneration of the land parallels and depends on the transformation of the people.

The Valley of Dry Bones (Ezek. 37)

In Ezekiel 37:1–14, the restoration is looked at from another point of view. The prophet is taken to the valley of his call (cf. 3:22 with 37:1), where he witnesses the results of the prophetic ministry of judgment, namely, a charnel house of dry bones, what was once the house of Israel. By the divine power to re-create (note the allusion to Gen. 2:7 in Ezek. 37:5 and thus the link between Adam and Israel), a mighty national resurrection occurs. Which comes first in the OT, personal resurrection or national resurrection, is still disputed. However, there does seem some warrant for suggesting that the hope of personal immortality is always present in the OT. Yahweh is always seen as being able to kill or make alive (1 Sam. 2:6), and this belief issues into various statements about a personal resurrection (Isa. 26:19; and possibly Job 19:26). The doctrine of personal resurrection receives prominence, however, when the emphasis shifts from the state to the individual after the fall of Jerusalem.

The significance of the national resurrection is shown in the next address (37:15–28), where a new Israel is reconstituted from the previously warring factions, Judah and geographic Israel, with the entire nation once more in the Promised Land under Davidic leadership. In these new and changed circumstances, a covenant of peace, an eternal covenant, is made with Israel. The Abrahamic (and creation) promises of being blessed and multiplied are then reinvoked (v. 26). God now indwells God's people in this new relationship (v. 27). Ezekiel 37:23 likewise speaks of the cleansing of the people, which indicates their gathering, their comprehensive restoration in preparation for their proper and holy relationship with Yahweh. Among its results are a witness to divine sovereignty and confession thereof by the whole world.

The Last Battle (Ezek. 38–39)

The relationship of chapters 38–39 to what precedes and follows is somewhat difficult to gauge. They deal with an assault by Gog from Magog on the reconstituted people of God dwelling in peace, the defeat of Gog, and his elimination. On the one hand, the chapters seem to operate as an apocalyptic commentary upon and as a restatement of the principles underlying the oracles against foreign nations (chaps. 25–32). On the other, they deal with threats to the newly restored people of God which must be overcome before the onset of direct divine rule through the establishment of the temple age, to which Ezekiel 40–48 points (Niditch 1986, 220–23).

Chapters 38–39 are unusual, since the detail in Ezekiel is normally anchored in history. In these chapters, the elements of fantasy and exaggeration prevail, unlike the more sober reporting of the prophecy as a whole. The figure of Gog cannot be identified. His association is with the north, a perpetual threat to Israel. The theme of Ezekiel 38–39 is the attack by Gog on Israel, which is living peacefully, presumably, in unfortified towns and villages as a result of the restoration promises of chapters 34–37. A hint of the size of the invading forces is given in the time taken to bury Gog's dead (seven months) and to burn his weapons (seven years). Overthrow of the forces is accomplished in typical holy-war patterns, with Yahweh intervening for Israel, but with Israel not physically involved. Geographically, the prophecy is vague, and it is difficult or impossible to pinpoint localities mentioned; there is no reference to Jerusalem.

Ezekiel 39:21–29 is often thought to have no reference to the Gog prophecies, and it is thought to end the prophecy as a whole. But (1) these verses provide the Gog prophecies with a satisfactory conclusion, since they highlight the revelatory character of Gog's defeat, first in its effect on the nations and then on Israel, both of whom witness Yahweh's justice and power. (2) In verses 23–29, the particular context fades from view and the implication of Yahweh's more immediate dealings with Israel are taken up. Nations will now see the reasons for Israel's exile, namely her covenantal transgression and they will see the exile as an expression of God's wrath. (3) This epilogue summarizes God's mercies in creating the conditions which had preceded Gog's invasion (v. 27). (4) The covenant relationship among deity, land, and people has now been reinstituted. Yahweh will never leave the Israelites again. (5) Finally, verse 29 emphasizes the role of the Spirit in covenant maintenance, for to pour out the Spirit on Israel is to sign and seal the covenant renewal.

The New Temple (Ezek. 40–48)

Following the removal of all opposition to the people of God with the onset of the new age, the new temple—the symbol of divine rule—commands attention in Ezekiel 40–48.

Underlying the chapters is the thought that in temple service will be a new relationship made possible by deliverance. The temple on the mountain is the centerpiece of the new world. Chapters 40–48 implement the program of Ezekiel 37:24b–28. On the holy mountain, God will accept the worship of God's reconstituted people. The finale of Israel's history will be the dwelling of God in the midst of his people. This will climax the Sinai event and, like the Sinai event, provision will be made for God's residence. Chapters 40–48 have three major divisions: (1) 40:1–43:12: the vision of the future temple; (2) 44:1–46:24: rules governing access to the temple and activity within it; and (3) 47:13–48:35: apportionment of the land among the people. Two passages serve as transition: Ezekiel 43:13–27 concerning the altar, attached to what precedes, linking the first two sections, and 47:1–12 on the distribution of the land, formally attached to what follows.

The cosmic character of the temple vision is underscored by its being presented on the world mountain, the "very high mountain" of Ezekiel 40:2, which is usually identified as Mount Zion (Levenson 1976, 7). In 48:9–16, however, the temple is not part of the city. The citylike structure (40:2) is situated on the south side of the mountain. As 43:12 makes clear, the top of the mountain is most holy, for the mountain's height represents the holiness of the land. The special status of the temple in 48:9–18 stems from its being the land's holiest part. Thus, the temple must be on the summit. If 40:2 provides a geographical perspective of the land of Israel, it is also a mythic perspective, for the "very high mountain" and land are the same.

These chapters draw their theological stance from the remote past, particularly the exodus and conquest. Sinai characteristics are also to be associated with this mountain, so the blueprint for the new temple emerges from heaven, as the pattern for the exodus tabernacle had (cf. Ezek. 43:10–12 with Exod. 25:9). The older sacral traditions of Sinai and Zion intersect, both of which emphasized divine kingship. As the building of the tabernacle completed the exodus, so the eschatology in Ezekiel 40–48 is dominated by the construction of the new temple. In addition, as the meaning of the exodus was proclaimed by the cultic response of Israel to divine kingship expressed through tabernacle and temple, here the new temple functions as Yahweh's kingly location in the holy city.

The vision begins with a detailed description emphasizing the writer's absorption with the temple. Moving from the outer wall (Ezek. 40:5–16) to the outer court (vv. 17–27), and from the inner court (40:28–41:26) to the outer court (42:1–14), the tour concludes outside the wall (vv. 15–20). At the center is the structure of the house itself (40:48–41:26). We are moving, in these pictures, from what has been historically experienced to an eschatology in which the central notion of worship will characterize the response of the perfected people of God. The elaborate symmetry, its continuity with and yet distinction from the temple of Solomon, and the use of symbolic numbers all support this view. Thus the temple vision states more emphatically the tenor of Ezekiel's eschatology to this point. The temple becomes the most prominent feature of the land. The temple is described in great detail in the temple tour (40:4–42:20). The sanctity of the new temple is expressed by its measurements. Although there is no mention of ark, cherubim, or lamps, no mention of a wall around the inner court, and no equivalent of the lavers and the bronze sea, the altar is emphasized (43:13–27). The details are not a plan for physical rebuilding. The city, in contrast, is mentioned only in passing. Its significance is to be estimated in terms of the temple's presence within it.

Ezekiel is brought back to the east gate to behold, as of old, the deity's awesome approach (Deut. 33:2; Judg. 5:4–5; Ps. 68:8; Hab. 3:3–4). God passes through the east gate and fills the temple (43:1–5). The east gate is locked forever, since God will never leave again (cf. 44:1). The return is explicitly related to chapters 1–3 and 8–11, for 43:3–4 takes us back to the prophet's earlier visions, recorded in chapters 1–2 and 9–10 (Parunak 1980, 72). Like Moses, Ezekiel sees the pattern of a new sanctuary on the mountain and describes it twice (chaps. 40–42; 43–46). The holiness of the temple is emphasized by Yahweh's glory filling the temple (vv. 4–5). This event culminates in the restoration, inaugurating a new era characterized by holiness. To seal the temple's holy status, Yahweh reaffirms the mountain peak (v. 12) as his dwelling place (v. 7). The temple's situation at the center of the land means that Yahweh's presence overflows into less holy areas, so the entire land benefits. Holiness is thus seen as spread over the entire land. Then a series of oracles is pronounced in the temple proper (43:6–46:24). In the inner court, two prophetic pronouncements are delivered concerning the temple restoration (43:6–44:3) and its use in worship (44:4–46:24).

The building's influence on the land is outlined in Ezekiel 47:1–12, in terms of its purifying and sanctifying effects (cf. Exod. 15:17–18). The temple's high state of holiness, however, does not result in a uniformly high level of holiness throughout the land. Rather, holiness becomes less intense in the surrounding areas. The presence of intervening levels of holiness tends to accentuate the highest level and to protect the lower levels from contamination. In Ezekiel 40–48, this principle is manifested in the setting apart of a central strip of land, called the *terumah,* from the other tribal portions. This *terumah* is described in more detail in 45:1–8 and 48:8–22. The arrangement of the plots of land indicates in a stylized manner the relative hierarchy of holiness. The temple itself was graded into areas of holiness: the Holy of Holies, the sanctuary, the inner court, and the outer court. Moving out from the temple building, there are areas for priests, the area for Levites, the city, the environs, and the land for the prince's inheritance (Zimmerli 1980, 1010–17, 1144–46, 1221–33). In this way, the land around the temple is shown to be part of the arrangement that emphasizes the high point of holiness at the sanctuary, while also showing the rest of the land to be holy. Indeed, even the city that is designated as profane (48:15) has Yahweh's presence. This is not a contradiction, for *profane* does not mean defilement. It means, relative to other regions set aside for priests and Levites, that it is further removed from Yahweh. Thus, elevated purity exists even in the city (Greenberg 1984; Allen 1990, 285).

Ezekiel 47:1–12 describes a walk on which the prophet is taken along a miraculous stream of water issuing from the temple and fructifying the desert. A trickle of water runs down the steps toward the east gate. The waters of life flowing from the sanctuary heal the land and change it into a paradise, making it a garden of God. The celestial figure, who has reappeared to lead Ezekiel from the temple, measures the stream until it becomes unfordable. In just over a mile, the water increases to a deep river. Ezekiel 47:6b–7 serves as a climax by describing an oasis of trees growing in the barren wilderness of Judah, between Jerusalem and the Dead Sea. Trees of life (Ezek. 47:12) are planted on either side of the stream. These trees will be for food (v. 12), and, unlike an earlier time, one may eat of their fruit in this new age without fear of judgment. The land, cleansed and renewed by divine possession, is then divided (vv. 13–23). No conquest is needed, merely purification. The healing effect on the Dead Sea (47:8–10) is the removal of salt. It becomes a symbol of chaos healed.

The prophet is then instructed fully regarding fulfillment of the land promise in 47:13–48:35. In the first section (47:13–23), the boundary markers are fixed. These markers reflect the ideal Promised Land of Numbers 33:50–34:15. The regions conquered during David's reign or settled in Transjordan are omitted. By the explicit mention of the promise in 47:14, Yahweh declares that he finally will fulfill his promise (Allen 1990, 285).

The place of the house is fixed in chapter 48. The twelve tribes are mentioned by name, and the expression "tribes of Israel" is used explicitly at 47:13, 21, 22; 48:29. Allotments are given to the seven tribes to be located in the north (Ezek. 48:1–7). The tribe of Levi surrounds the sacred shrine as a further protection from contamination. Attention after the first allotments is directed to the holy site, which is set apart for the Zadokites, the purified priesthood (Ezek. 48:8–12). The Levites, the public, and the prince then receive attention (vv. 13–22). Finally, land is allotted to the five remaining tribes (vv. 23–29). The handmaid tribes (Gad, Asher, Naphtali, and Dan) are furthest from the temple.

In the redistribution of the new temple age, Reuben and Gad had moved back over the Jordan—Reuben to the north of Jerusalem, Gad to the far south. In the new order, the sons of Jacob's two wives, Leah and Rachel, are given proximity, and the sons of the concubines Bilhah and Zilpah are set at a distance. As a stepson, Gad is set in the far south, and the other three stepsons, Dan, Asher, and Naphtali, are placed in the far north. Of the other eight full sons, four are moved north (Manasseh, Ephraim, Reuben, Judah) and four south (Benjamin, Simeon, Issachar, Zebulun) of the sanctuary. Manasseh and Ephraim are placed north, true to history and for balance. Issachar and Zebulun are moved south. Reuben, the first son, fits below Manasseh and Ephraim. The placement of Judah north of Yahweh's territory and Benjamin to the south—obliterating the old north-south division—is surprising. The name Benjamin—"son of the south"—establishes his position. Each tribal strip included coastland, highlands, and Jordan Valley. The royal palace and temple no longer adjoin (43:7–8), and city lands are to the south of the temple area.

The third section (48:30–35) is concerned with the twelve gates of the city, one named for each tribe. The west side is the least significant, and the gates are named after three concubine children (Gad, Asher, Naphtali), the south gates after three of Leah's sons (Simeon, Issachar, Zebulun). Rachel's two children, Joseph and Benjamin, share the east side with Dan. Reuben, Judah, and Levi share the north. The temple and land are thus closely related. To worship in the temple carried with it the privilege of living in the land. If chapters 40–48 began with theological architecture, they end with theological geography. The eschatological name of the city (v. 35) emphasizes it as the city of Yahweh's rule. Israel's God is thus firmly placed in both city and temple.

In these temple chapters, the temple is carefully removed from former political associations, throwing the failures of the past into relief. The movements of the prince in regard to the sanctuary are circumscribed. The ideals of the Davidic period have been passed over in the interests of older sacral conventions, particularly of the exodus-conquest theology. The former temple servants will be replaced by Levites, the apostate priests who will now serve as gatekeepers and general helpers for the laity. Only the descendants of Zadok will serve the altar. The Levites now must do all that Levites, along with laypersons, had done formerly in the inner court, for the temple is purely a priestly domain, which the prince may not enter (45:4–8). The emphasis is clear. Yahweh is the sole ruler in the new age (cf. 20:33).

The tribes probably share equally in the distribution of land, since tribal allotments are equal. The interests of smaller tribes were never again to be overlooked. Thus the new society seeks to redress the economic and political imbalances of the past. There is a return to the ideals of the time when the promise was made, and loss of the northern kingdom is ignored. All twelve tribes are safely returned to the Promised Land, as Yahweh had promised in Egypt. Chapters 40–48 fulfill the ancient promises. The account concludes with the name of the city, Yehowa Shamma ("the Lord is there").

Having begun with a vision of judgment directly related to the temple, Ezekiel ends with a vision of a new society that is temple-controlled and theocratically centered. That the shrine and the city are no longer in Judah and that Zion is not referred to appears to be an explicit rejection of the Jerusalem royal theology. In short, what we have is a symbolic presentation of a return to the patriarchal promises—land allotted to a new people of God. No pattern from Israel's history accounts for the order of the tribes, another fact pointing to a new beginning. The tribal arrangement, foursquare around the sanctuary, reflects the older exodus structure and its theology. That there are no Levitical cities also implies a pre-conquest structure. In short, Ezekiel has returned to a time before the monarchy. In strongly criticizing the monarchy and holding it responsible for the political and religious breaches described, Ezekiel implicitly rejects any doctrine of the inviolability of Jerusalem and the Solomonic temple.

The emerging new-temple theology is not a blueprint for postexilic restoration. Rather, if Israel is to have a future, Yahweh himself will bring about a new beginning, with himself at the center. He alone will be responsible for the future of the people of God. Ezekiel 40–48 makes no provision for Davidic kingship. Indeed, instead of "king," the term "prince" is used for the political ruler of the future age (see 44:3; 45:7–8, 16–17; 46:2; 48:21–22). This terminology is consistent with the diminished role assigned to David and to kingship generally in this book, and with Ezekiel's clear theocratic aims. The book has taken us grandly from the picture of Jerusalem's temple under judgment to the heavenly temple from which that judgment emerged, a temple that has become the world center around which the new society will be constructed. We have viewed the process of renewal that the people of God must undergo, their vindication, and their final occupancy of the Promised Land. Ezekiel thus presents the hope of the people of God and God's final presence among God's people, the theme to which Revelation 21–22 is devoted.

13

Hosea

The dating of the prophecies of Hosea is fairly well defined by the introduction to the book (1:1). This introduction, which refers to activities from Jeroboam II of Israel (Hosea seems to refer to the turbulence in the north that followed his death in ca. 746 B.C.) until Hezekiah (probably a reference to his coregency with Ahaz, which began in about 727). Thus, they span the period of decline in the north to shortly before its exile, which Hosea anticipates but does not mention. The book is divisible into two broad sections, chapters 1–3 and 4–14.

Chapters 1–3 are a general indictment of Israel under the image of a marriage relationship; to this indictment has been added a conditional promise. This opening section is characterized (as is the book as a whole) by the bold adoption of Canaanite Baal imagery and language, appropriated in the interests of condemning the syncretistic fertility cults. Hosea presents Yahweh as the bestower of the blessings previously associated with the cults. In general terms, the book ends (Hos. 14) on the note of a covenant return which is presented in terms of an abounding fertility which trumps Baalism. Thus the book moves from covenant breach to covenant renewal, while exposing the full range of national sins along the way, showing itself to be covenant-centered and in contact with the Sinai traditions. Allusions to Israel's past—the patriarchs, exodus, and conquest—abound in the book. In summary, it is a recall to Israel's beginnings and to covenant fidelity. Unlike Amos, Hosea emphasizes Israel's religious deviations. Social sins are mentioned only in passing. It is covenant-centered, and most of the mainstream covenant themes (loyal love, knowledge, and fidelity) occur frequently.

The Unfaithful Wife (Hos. 1–3)

The opening material of Hosea most naturally divides itself into two elements, each introduced by "Yahweh said" (1:2; 3:1). The command to Hosea to marry an adulterous woman (1:2) is offensive to modern readers, but probably anticipates what will happen within the marriage. Between 1:2 and 2:1, three oracles relating to the children of the marriage offer a progressive review of the history of Israel. The birth of Jezreel ("God sows") is an indication of divine sowing. God has "planted" Israel in the land, but with a further "sowing," an act of judgment, God can and will take it back (1:3–5). This judgment is consequent upon the sin of Jehu (either his dynasty, ca. 841–752 B.C., or his realm, Israel) but has in mind a divine restoration and thus the normal prophetic presentation of salvation through judgment. The sin of Jehu turns out to be Israel's entry through Jehu into an alliance with Assyria, to which in its enduring form Hosea, more than a century later, is implacably opposed (Sweeney 2000, 11). The birth of a second child, "Not pitied," spells the end of the northern kingdom; the future hope lies with Judah (vv. 6–7). However, the birth of the third child, "Not my people," spells the end of the covenant with Israel as a whole (1:8–9). The name is the ultimate word of judgment, the ultimate breach of the marriage relationship.

After these three oracles dealing with the dissolution of the nation, a citation of the Abrahamic promise (Hos. 1:10–2:1) heralds a new exodus (in v. 10 Israel is again called "sons"), an Israel formed by the unification of the two kingdoms, the constant prophetic dream (v. 11). The name Jezreel is here used positively to represent the in-gathering that these promises foreshadow. Again, the divine expectation of blessing to follow necessary chastisement is evident.

Hosea 2 presents an allegory of covenant renewal under the traditional prophetic imagery of marriage. The children, who seem to be divided Israel, are introduced in verse 1 only to be dismissed and to reappear in the eschatological restoration of verses 22–23. The wife seems to be identified alternately with Israel and her land (Andersen and Freedman 1980, 124). Perhaps this personification of the land at various stages of the address is intended to heighten the implied comparisons and contrasts with the Canaanite Baal (i.e., fertility) worship that underlie the passage.

A separation of mother Israel from her husband has taken place (Hos. 2:2), though divorce is not in view (cf. Andersen and Freedman 1980, 222). The attempt to make vivid the enormity of her cultic apostasy through the intimate series of images in verses 2–5, which in itself suggests the closeness of the covenant relationship and its personal nature, ends only in a declaration of self-interest by Israel (v. 5b) to pursue the fertility deities. A sentence of judgment follows in three parts, each introduced by the word "therefore" (vv. 6, 9, 14). Yahweh will prevent Israel from pursuing the Baals, and the shallow determination of Israel to return to Yahweh will founder on lack of knowledge of the Yahweh who is to be sought (vv. 6–8). The deprivations that follow (vv. 9–12) are a visitation of the covenant curse upon the land for the reasons described in verse 13, namely, the commitment to Canaanite syncretism.

The judgment theme appears to continue with a further "therefore" (v. 14), but with an unexpected twist. Without any motivation for a change of lifestyle within Israel, the subject turns to covenant renewal. The theological idealism with which the Israel of the Sinai period was surrounded appears in verses 14–

15, evoked by the unmerited free will of Yahweh, who has remarkably turned Israel from depravity to dependence. Hosea is not a Rechabite and the wilderness is not for him the ideal. The cultivated land is God's gift to Israel (Hos. 9:3), and this attitude is reflected in 2:17. The wilderness experience was a prelude to prosperity. Deprivation however, must precede restoration. By Yahweh's own deliberate action Israel will suffer the loss of the blessings of the land in pursuit of which she had forgotten Yahweh and devoted herself to Baal (Hos. 2:5; 9:10; 13:6). However, the purpose of this deprivation is a saving one. It is that Israel may know that Yahweh is the sovereign Lord of nature. No weak loving relationship and no condoning of sin are contemplated. Yahweh's action in Hosea 2:14–17 is not envisaged as dependent upon Israel's return in penitence. Hosea does not anticipate Israel's reform and repentance but knows the measure of Yahweh's grace. Because Israel has forgotten Yahweh (v. 13), he will cause her to remember him (v. 16). So the nation's response in verse 16 issues from salvation; it does not precede it. The initiative in repairing the broken relationship lies within Yahweh's persistent love. We are to understand that these effects will be produced by the impending separation from the land, which is the clear punishment for covenant breach.

Only after this restoration, reported in detail in a series of oracles in Hosea 2:16–23, does Yahweh directly address Israel. The threats of the earlier part of the chapter are now removed, and the marriage metaphors are boldly resumed. God brings the mother into the wilderness now to allure her, to create a new covenant in which the harmony between God and Israel will be reflected by the harmony to be found within creation itself (v. 18). There will be a new marriage (vv. 19–20; cf. v. 16), and Israel will now "know" Yahweh (v. 20), just as she did previously. Israel's new recognition of Yahweh is because Yahweh has intervened to break off her relationship with Baal. This declaration of the renewed relationship forms the climax of the chapter, while the variety of covenant terms in verses 19–20 (righteousness, justice, steadfast love, mercy, faithfulness) indicates the depth of the renewal. Courtship, betrothal, covenant making, exchange of vows, and giving of new names are the renewal components in verses 14–23. Israel's restoration is described as a betrothal. Emphasis is laid on the moral aspect of Yahweh's relationship to Israel in which Israel's knowledge of Yahweh is not seen as a prerequisite but as a result. Israel, with blessing viewed from many perspectives, is presented as the people of the new covenant (see Andersen and Freedman 1980, 284–86). From concern with the name Baal (v. 16) we move to the covenant of peace (v. 18), to the theme of betrothal (v. 20), to the cycle of nature and the land's fertility. A new relationship will be established on the basis of Yahweh's own attributes, not on Israel's efforts and her uncertain loyalty.

The reinterpretation of the symbolic names in the saying (2:22–23) proclaims a reversal of judgment, a replanting of Israel in the land. Hosea draws on the etymology of Jezreel, here used positively. Verse 22 is concerned with the renewal of the earth's fertility; reconciliation and the blessings of the land go together; verse 23 is concerned with the settlement of the people in the land and their reinstatement as the people of God. Symbolic names were also in chapter 1, implicit reminders of the possibility of salvation. This picture is consistent with 733 B.C., when the hostile incursions of the Assyrian king Tiglath-pileser III resulted in the deportation of the population from the valley of Jezreel.

In Hosea 3:1–3, Israel's history of infidelity is again reviewed in a chapter which seems to be a continuation of chapter 1. Hosea 3:1 seems to command continued love of a wayward woman, not remarriage. But this time the narrative is in the first person, as opposed to the third-person account of Hosea 1. A total suspension of married life for a defined period is required (3:3), which verse 4 interprets as a suspension of cultic life, making it clear that the cultic apostasy is the great deviation with which these first three chapters are dealing. Hosea 3:5 contemplates an exile, after which a new era corresponding to the mood of 1:10–2:1 (and to the renewal of 2:14–23) commences. Hosea 3:1–5 anticipates the restoration of Davidic rule over a united Israel, destined to have its fulfillment only in Christ.

Thus, through the sustained play on the marriage metaphor, the covenant relationship between Yahweh and Israel, to which the response was Israel's worship, has been reviewed in Hosea 1–3. Hosea is the first to use this highly personal metaphor of marriage, which thereafter becomes a frequent one in the OT prophets. His book reviews Israel's history, institutions, and religion by employing the language of marriage, which draws attention to the initiation, development, and present state of the covenant relationship. He takes pains to contrast the idealistic beginnings (or the sinful beginnings in the case of the northern kingship) with what is now the empirical reality. Marriage is thus the vehicle used to illustrate the nature and the continuance of the Sinai covenant relationship. Its suitability is obvious. At Sinai, as in marriage, two parties not naturally related were yoked. The relationship was initiated by the husband, Yahweh. In this relationship there could, by its very nature, be no divorce. At the same time there were contractual notes about it that gave the relationship a legal status and made it inviolate. A wide range of terms was employed to depict its deep intimacy and highly personalized nature.

Clearly, then, the message of this prophecy in chapters 4–14, where chapters 1–3 will be expanded, will underline Yahweh's unfailing constancy and adherence to the Sinai relationship in spite of constant provocations by the human partner. Israel will ever be in breach, but Yahweh will not give her up. He will give her over to temporary punishment through exile, a result reached by a great struggle within himself between his compassion and his sense of justice. However, beyond that there will be a new creation. There will be the fulfillment of the commitment dating back, as Hosea understands it, to the patriarchal promise and the Sinai relationship in which Yahweh gave himself in free choice to Israel. A love that will not let Israel go finally brings us from covenant breach to a covenant renewal (Hos. 14) involving both Israel and her world.

General Indictment for Covenant Breach (Hos. 4:1–5:7)

Hosea 4–14 explains how the result of Hosea 1–3 will be achieved. Hosea 4 begins with the general indictment against Israel. Chapters 5–14 will take up the issues outlined in chapter 4. Covenantal values, expressed in three important terms, are lacking (v. 1). The absence of "faithfulness," "kindness," and "knowledge of God" (this last term comprehends the whole relationship; cf. 2:20) has resulted in the sorry condition of the nation. In particular, this absence threatens the gift of the covenant, life in the land. This is the note on which the indictment begins and ends (vv. 1–3). Yahweh's lawsuit against Israel rests on this statement of the disarray of the relationship. (The word *rib* 'controversy' in v. 1 is frequently used by the prophets as a technical term for an arraignment of Israel on the grounds of covenant breach.)

The three terms in 4:1 have been carefully chosen and progress in importance and intensity. "Faithfulness" is solidity and firmness, adherence to what has been established as normative. The covenant relationship is in view here, and faithfulness in this connection is virtually a synonym for righteousness—the maintenance of an accepted form of the relationship. Faithfulness therefore is not a propositional, but a personal, exercise, not an active searching for what is consistent, but a fidelity to norms that have been given.

Especially covenantal is the Hebrew word *hesed.* "Kindness" provides a good rendering. In a human context, the word refers to a specific action taken by one party in behalf of another on the basis of a close personal relationship. Such action, motivated by *hesed* and designed to respond to a need, is undertaken in a spirit of faithfulness to a prior obligation. If performed, this act does not arise from a sense of mere obligation (i.e., from the legality of a commitment), but from a sense of personal loyalty that the relationship involves. *Hesed* does not apply to the establishment of a relationship, but reflects fidelity and loyalty to an existing relationship. Its aim is to preserve the tenor of a relationship that already exists. When used of Israel in the Old Testament, it means faithfulness to the spirit of the covenant, not merely to the letter. When used of Yahweh, it speaks of his willingness to go beyond the strict legalities of the relationship and to preserve it in spite of the fault of the erring partner (Sakenfeld 1975, 324).

Emphasis is placed on the final term, "knowledge of God." Again we have a deeply personal term. It points to the manner in which God reveals God's self—in Israel's case, through covenant. (Usually in the context of covenant the wording "knowledge of Yahweh" appears.) "Knowledge of God" (*'elohim* is a general word for deity) will, in Hosea's prophecy, mean trust in the general providential superintendence of Yahweh. That such trust does not exist in Israel means covenant breach in the specific terms of rejection of the covenant commandments, notably the Decalogue of Exodus 20, which seems to be alluded to in the five Hebrew infinitives in Hosea 4:2. In its turn, this rejection means the withdrawal of the Abrahamic benefits (v. 3a), which inevitably affects the structure of creation itself (v. 3b).

I cannot present this prophecy in detail, but what follows are specific illustrations of the summary statement of 4:1–3. Hosea 4:4–5:7 is a sustained attack on false religiosity stemming from a lack of knowledge of God—ignorance of the covenant and its demands—in both north and south. Verses 4–10 indict the priests, who, in their wealth and degeneracy, have exchanged Yahweh for Baal and are responsible for the spiritual decline of the nation. In verses 4–6, they have neglected their ministry and the Torah, rejecting the covenant. In verses 7–10, it is said that the priests will suffer as do the people. They have promoted sacrifice for their own gain (v. 8), exacting sin-offerings in return for forgiveness. Therefore, by verse 9 they are virtually deconsecrated. Hosea saw his task as the reformation of the cult, not its removal. Yahweh will punish the priests, as well as the people, by hunger and infertility (Hos. 4:9–10). The Yahwistic priesthood had not instructed the people in what knowledge of God involved. Verses 11–19 turn to the implications for Israel of the apostasy of its sacral leadership. Israel has mingled her worship with fertility practices (vv. 11–13), producing faithless worship.

In Hosea 4:11–14a, those responsible for their deeds are addressed, and their apostasy, which is more than a passing phase (v. 12), is rebuked. The cult (v. 12) has prostituted itself, and the multiplicity of shrines, at which debauched worship is conducted (v. 13), attests to this fact. Verses 15–19 offer a fourfold warning against worship at deviant cult centers. Hosea did not reject Bethel (v. 15) as evil, but sought to reform it so that it would become a place of true worship. Hosea does not speak of a breach of the covenant, but puts forth a demand for exclusivity and knowledge of God. Sacrifice within this relationship has a legitimate place; however, the wind of judgment is coming (v. 19).

In Hosea 5:1–7, Israel's leadership—priests, the cultic leadership and kings, the political bureaucracy—are summoned, arraigned with all Israel, and condemned. But captivity and exile are just around the corner (v. 2b). Worship is busy, religious zeal is fervent with performance, but worship is without reality at what may have been old historical shrines (v. 2). False worship is a dereliction from covenant obligation. The real sin of Israel and Judah (v. 5) is their arrogant adoption of pagan worship. When the entire nation recognizes its folly and seeks to redeem it at their sanctuaries by legitimate sacrifice (v. 6), Yahweh will not heed. Festivals are being kept (v. 7), but they will be turned against Israel. A generation of non-Israelites has been born as aliens, in possession of alien values, with no claim on the Promised Land.

The Disastrous Effect of Foreign Alliances (Hos. 5:8–7:16)

Hosea 5:8–11 declares divine war against Israel and depicts God's threat to Ephraim and Judah, in which God is portrayed metaphorically as an infection and as a lion (5:12–15). In 5:8, the position of the watchman seems to indicate invasion from the south, by Judah. Gibeah was only three miles north of Jerusalem, Ramah five miles north, and Bethel eleven miles north. These cities had been captured by Abijah of Judah in the ninth century (2 Chron. 13:19), but control of them had been fluid. They may have reverted to Israel during Jehoash's reign (798–782 B.C.) or, more probably, during the Syro-Ephraimite War (ca. 734 B.C.). Assyrian expansion under Tiglath-pileser (745–727 B.C.) seems indicated in verse 9, resulting in Ephraim's desolation. Ephraim must wait for its doom. Judah, as a result of political ineptness (Hos. 5:10), will be under attack, with, it seems, the loss of territory, perhaps referring to the fluid situation between north and south during the Syro-Ephraimite War (733 B.C.). Yahweh's judgment on north and south is announced by two telling metaphors of himself as an insidious instrument of inner destruction for Israel (moth) and Judah (rot). Two more metaphors of Yahweh are expressed in verse 13, depicting Yahweh as the cause of infection (Israel) and assault (Judah). Israel, ignoring the real problem, the inner loss of its spiritual strength, will appeal to Assyria (ca. 733 B.C.), and would sue for peace as Hoshea did later, in 732. Yahweh, however, will be the real foe. Yahweh as lion will carry off the spoil of the north to his lair (vv. 13b–14). After their punishment, they will seek Yahweh in a national repentance of 6:1–3.

Hosea 6:1–3, a famous song of penitence, reflects a belief in Yahweh's ability to resurrect the nation's life. The two resolutions, "let us return to Yahweh" (v. 1), and "let us strive to know Yahweh" (v. 3a), which may be a pledge of repentance and covenant submission to Yahweh's lordship, are followed by assertions that Yahweh heals and restores. However, their seeking has only been cultic (Hos. 4:15; 5:6–7). Their return to him will be rendered impossible by their continued rebellion (6:11–7:2; 7:10, 14–16). Repentance cannot stem from incorrect theology, which is indicated clearly by the national dependency on the Canaanite fertility cult and on other apostasies. Yahweh's frustration is emphasized by the double question in verse 4 and in the divine displeasure; it is also emphasized by the caustic comparison of Israel's fickle love to mist and dew, while Israel expects Yahweh to appear as steadfastly as the dawn. But indications in 6:3 are that true repentance, which Israel was unable to offer, will mean the restoration of blessings on the land.

Yahweh struggles within himself. Israel's loyalty was fleeting and evanescent, like a morning cloud; genuine loyalty must be constant in faithfulness. So Yahweh (v. 4) rejects Israel's profession. Yahweh will come, but to judge, a further oblique reference to the Syro-Ephraimite War. Israel has brought the prophetic condemnations upon itself. Faithfulness and true knowledge of God (6:6) are required, not the sacrificial cult. The system is not repudiated, but reform must take place.

The denunciation continues in 6:7–7:7. Three national sins seem to be in view in Hosea 6:7–9. If, in verse 7, "Adam" refers to the fording of the Jordan in Joshua 3:16, as is likely, then Hosea says that the covenant has been transgressed continually since the entry into the Promised Land. Verse 8 may allude to the assassination of the Israelite king Pekahiah (ca. 740 B.C.), carried out by men of Gilead on Pekah's behalf (2 Kings 15:25), thereby relating these lines to the conspiracy against the throne in 7:3–7. Shechem (v. 9) was a famous cultic center (Josh. 24). "Murder" here may be metaphorical; nevertheless, the priests are perhaps involved as participants in the struggle for gain and power. Such iniquity has made the family of Israel unclean. Judgment, for which Judah's history has been preparing, is also about to be reaped by the south (v. 11).

Even when Yahweh seeks to restore his people, he still faces covenant infidelity (7:1–2). At this point, the prophecy becomes decidedly political, with successive oracles directed against Israel's kingship and against the international politics in which Israel has been involved. Hosea 7:3–7 is especially difficult. Kings rise and fall (Hos. 7:7), reflecting the instability of the northern kingship following the death of Jeroboam II, in approximately 746 B.C., as the nation vented its political passion. Some have connected 7:3–7 to Hoshea's coup against Pekah (2 Kings 15:30), some to Pekah's revolt (2 Kings 15:25). "Day of our king" in Hosea 7:5 is vague and could be his birthday, coronation, or the day of his death. The passion of the plotters is depicted vividly with the metaphor of a heated oven. Hosea 7:7 ends with "and none of them calls on me," confirming the nation's inability to seek Yahweh. Both in domestic (7:3–7) and foreign policy (7:8–11), Israel's leaders had scrambled to protect their power.

The message of Hosea 7:8–16 is that, although foreign alliances constituted Israel's death knell (7:8–16), the people in their extremity failed to turn to Yahweh and continued to indulge in fertility practices (vv. 13–16). These verses could be related to the general political instability after 733 B.C., although verses 8–12 seem to refer to Hoshea's appeal to Tiglath-pileser. But, within a few years, Hoshea had ceased tribute and had turned to Egypt for support (2 Kings 17:2–4). Hosea likens Ephraim's exposure and vulnerability to her surroundings—lacking strength or consistency—to half-baked bread or to one debilitated with age (v. 9). In this turmoil, Israel, shackled by pride, neglected to do the one thing that could have saved the nation—namely, to return to Yahweh and to offer obedience to the covenant (7:10). In her shifting alliances, Israel vacillates between the powers like a silly dove (v. 12), but Yahweh will bring this bird into his snare. In verse 13, Yahweh takes up a funeral lament for Israel. Verse 14a describes how the Israelites cry out in their sacrifices, but without true loyalty. Their cry, engendered by Canaanite practices, was to Baal (reading *lo' 'el* in v. 16; Andersen and Freedman 1980, 447). Israel's punishment will be foreign subjugation in a reverse exodus (vv. 14b–15, 16).

Thus, the fall of Israel is traced to Israel's inability to understand her covenant mandate. Israel had been run merely as a political state, but this approach ignored the Sinai commitment by which Yahweh's kingship had been recognized. The role of prophecy in all this was to point Israel back to her covenant obligation as the sole source of her life. Like his successors, Hosea brings no new demands, simply a call to be faithful to the platform, by which Israel's national life in the Promised Land could be secured.

This basic message is repeated on a different level in Hosea 8. If Hosea 7 has been set around the Syro-Ephraimite War of 734, the war's aftermath is the most likely setting for the oracles of chapter 8. This section, with the theme of rejection and transgression—including a general description of Israel's sin in verses 1b–3—introduces a catena of evidence and curses. The passage ends at verse 14 with a description of the judgment of fire that will befall Judah. Prediction of punishment for Israel's covenant transgressions and rejection of Yahweh (vv. 1–3) gives way to condemnation of political intrigue and religious idolatry (vv. 4–6), agricultural curses and their implications for Israel (vv. 7–8), a description of Israel's plight internationally (vv. 9–10), condemnation of the corrupt cult (vv. 11–13), and the futility of defense against destruction by fire (v. 14).

Turning to the specifics of chapter 8, the enemy is Assyria. The vulture is about to seize its prey (v. 1b), the Promised Land, but the ultimate enemy is Yahweh. Yahweh has now declared war because of covenant breach (vv. 1–3). Israel will appeal to Yahweh when disaster comes, but Yahweh's judgment will be effected through Assyria and the exile to follow (722/21). While still flirting with other gods (vv. 3, 4–6), Israel blatantly attempted to remind Yahweh of his national connection, presuming on its religious past in the time of the post–733 B.C. national distress. Covenant breach was evident at the political level. Internal instability was also evidenced by the fact that the people had set up their own form of kingship (v. 4a). In the volatile political situation after 746 B.C., the people arrogated to themselves what was Yahweh's right to install his representative. Their real allegiance, however, was exhibited at the religious level (v. 4b). Yahweh had rejected their exodus emblem, the calf of Samaria (vv. 5–6), made by human hands. Presumably only one is mentioned, that of Bethel, since Dan and its shrine had previously been captured.

The people must also be punished (v. 7), for they have sown the wind of whoredom, by which they expected greater fertility; the result, however, has been greatly diminished harvests. Three brief agricultural metaphors of futility denote expectations to be denied. What is left of Israel's crops Assyria will "swallow up," and Israel will eke out a miserable existence among the nations (v. 8). Israel's national disloyalty, clear in its appeal to Assyria, will mean international isolation, like a wild ass devoid of contact. Yahweh's punishment is coming (v. 9). Israel is to be gathered up for judgment, regardless of the alliances it has sought (v. 10).

Multiple altars violating the stipulation of a single sanctuary (Deut. 12) and a flagrant disregard for written laws, as well as a love of sacrifice and feasts, characterize Israel's religious life. In so doing, altars to expunge sin had become the means for sin (v. 11). The exodus will be reversed, and the nation will go back to Egypt (i.e., into slavery). Israel had forgotten Yahweh, committing the cardinal sin of which the Book of Deuteronomy had warned (v. 14). Yahweh will bring destruction by fire; the coming enemy will burn Israel's cities.

Israel's Long History of Covenant Default (Hos. 9:1–13:16)

Hosea 9:1–13:16 is a lengthy overview of Israel's sorry history of infidelity (Sweeney 2000, 93). Hosea 9:1–7a may reflect the breathing space between 733 and 721 B.C. The address is probably directed to the fall festival, the most important of the three annual Israelite festivals. It should have drawn Israel's attention to Yahweh as provider. Verses 1–4 emphasize the end of religious rituals and forecast the coming exile. Verses 5–6 seem a direct address at the festival, calling Israel to account, and predicting captivity and desolation. Verses 7–9 present Israel's arrogant degeneracy and Yahweh's punishment. Punishment is imminent. In verses 7b–9, Hosea also reflects on the ineffectiveness of other prophets' weak attempts to guide the nation. Set up as an offset to kingship, the prophetic office had been locked in combat with kingship since kingship's inception ("days of Gibeah" in v. 9 is probably a reference to Saul's election; cf. 1 Sam. 11:4).

Israel (9:1) is celebrating its feasts but integrating them, like prostitution, into the mechanisms of the fertility cult. Israel also worshiped Baal alongside Yahweh at multiple sanctuaries. Crop failure thus will come, and the people are about to be exiled (v. 3). They can no longer live in Yahweh's land, whose productivity they have blighted by their apostasy. Their exile will, in effect, reverse the exodus. They will serve as Assyrian slaves, eating unclean food in an unclean land. No cultic performances will be possible (v. 4), and festivals will not be celebrated (v. 5). Carefully laid plans (v. 6) are of no avail when Yahweh's punishment is unleashed. Israel is to be taken captive and killed. Those who escape death will go into exile. Gathering for mass burial will occur, along with a loss of wealth. They have now (v. 7) entered the evil days. In 9:7b–8, Hosea directs his scorn against the popular prophets, who have failed to alert the nation to the divine visitation. Hosea (v. 8) is the watchman of Ephraim and ought to be regarded, but instead he is thwarted. Israel's sin is so extensive (v. 9) that it demands punishment. Hosea's words are not merely a threat. National corruption is as bad as that of Gibeah in the time of the judges (Judg. 19–21).

The fall of the north is a foregone conclusion, presuming a setting in the 720s. Hosea not only expects the fall, but invites it (vv. 14, 17). Hosea 9:10–17 is an oracle of judgment that has its point of departure in election terminology. Through rich metaphors, the chosen people's original loveableness is described at the time they were found and chosen in the wilderness. As long as the subject is election, the terminology is metaphorical—mythical, not historical. When apostasy is described, we find concrete history. The mention of the time in the wilderness (9:10a) is the natural point of departure. Yahweh presents himself as surprised by delight, finding reason for deep joy and satisfaction in the early relationship—a delight soon to evaporate. Hosea, in turn, reflects on Israel's defection since the wilderness days (9:10–14); Baal-peor (v. 10) serves as the model of that defection (Num. 25). What happened at Baal-peor is now happening at Gilgal, which will necessitate return to a virtual wilderness situation (cf. Hos. 9:15–17). The consequences of devotion to Baal will bring the opposite of what was desired, namely, extinction instead of fruitfulness. This will occur when Yahweh abandons Israel (v. 12b). Emphasis is thus given to the miseries of a siege in 725–722 B.C. The dreadful threat is summed up in verse 13. Ephraim has been the cause of its own collective suicide. Verse 13 states that the judgment is already at work, in which Ephraim will produce children, but only for the executioner. The prophet prays to Yahweh to carry out this decision (v. 14). Hosea, in verse 14, chooses for Israel the least-dreadful punishment, childlessness instead of war and destruction. Verse 15 details further apostasy, and verses 16–17 deliver the merciless conclusion that Ephraim—the once beautiful plant, now withered—must perish: the chosen people will be rejected by their God. Verse 16 alludes to the death of the children, and verse 17 interprets.

Hosea 10–12

Every significant institution in the north (altars, high places, king, the bull image of Samaria, and the cult associated with it) will be dealt with as the land becomes desolated by Assyrian aggression (Hos. 10:1–8). The fate of the nation's cultic symbols (altars, idols, sacred stones, high places) is on view. In verses 1–2a, Israel's cultic sin since her early days had increased so that her altars, the product of a heart divided and which identified Yahweh's blessings as gifts of Baal, are marked for destruction. Israel has radically renounced Yahweh, her king (v. 3). Israel probably had entered a covenant with Assyria. Prevailing injustice in Israel will produce poisonous results (v. 4). Israel's corruption (v. 5) manifests itself in its idolatrous worship, since the two are interrelated. In fact, Israel will bewail the idol it venerated as it goes into the hands of her captors. The Assyrians will carry the bull-idol back as an item of booty when Israel is conquered and its possessions taken. The sorry history of Israel's disobedience in cultic practices will bring the nation shame and disgrace (v. 6b). Verses 7–8 chronicle the destruction, desolation, and death into which Samaria, the capital; Bethel, the cultic center; and kingship will go. The land will strike back at the fertility altars, covering them with thorns and thistles. The last king of the north, Hoshea, similarly had gone into captivity in 723 (2 Kings 17:4). The helplessness of the king carried off like a twig borne on water is portrayed vividly.

Kingship wrongly used ("days of Gibeah" in vv. 9–10, or perhaps the reference is to Israel's conduct since Judg. 19–21) has led Israel astray. The sin in Gibeah is the remote cause of the war (v. 9b) that is on the way. Verse 10a states the kind of war, verse 10b the cause of war. In Ugaritic religion, the heifer (10:11) was the symbol of the goddess Anat, who, previous to Baal's descent to the underworld, enters into a sacred marriage with Baal in the form of a bull. After his death she fights Mot (god of death), whom she defeats. The struggle is described in a way that one describes the ripening of grain. Perhaps a threshing rite is being described, which at the time of harvest illustrated the victory over chaos powers. No doubt Yahweh was worshiped under the figure of a bull or calf in the northern kingdom. If Hosea is using Canaanite imagery in 10:11–13, he contradicts it in his use. The fair heifer is removed from the threshing place (i.e., the fertility cult) and placed in Yahweh's service. Yahweh wants election service in righteousness and *hesed,* loyalty, in the preparation of the earth, which he will bless with righteousness. The heifer, that is, Israel, the people chosen because of their fair neck, beauty, and usefulness for the yoke, must live and work in a way (10:12) that meets the requirements of the relationship to Yahweh; Hosea describes proper relationship to God in the categories of the fertility cult. Israel's stay in the cultivated land (v. 13a) has been marked by sin from the beginning. That is why punishment is now taking place by the war that will destroy her. Verses 13b–15 sharpen and specify what had been threatened in verses 9–10. Israel had trusted in its military machine, but this machine will be overwhelmed by Assyrian aggression, apparently by Shalman (v. 14, a reference to the campaign of Shalmaneser V against Samaria in 724–722 B.C.). In the tumult of battle, no city will escape destruction, and fortified walls will not withstand invaders. The destruction of the north (723–721 B.C.) is likened to that of Beth Arbel, whose fate is otherwise unknown. In this storm, Israel's king will be eradicated; that is, the political destruction of Israel will occur.

In chapter 11, Hosea again recalls Israel to her past. Verses 1–4 proclaim God's care exercised through the exodus, and Israel's subsequent and longstanding refractoriness. Israel's history only provided evidence of the childish rebellion and the worship of Baal in the face of love and care. The fault was in no way Yahweh's (v. 3), for he had held little Ephraim's hands as he took his first steps, but ingrate Israel was unconcerned to fulfill their calling. Verse 4 compares Yahweh's love to a concern for a dependent beast led gently. Then comes a sentence of judgment (vv. 5–7). Disaster in the form of a reversal of the exodus is now about to break upon them (vv. 5–7). Destruction (v. 6), exile, and servitude (vv. 5, 7) lie before Israel, who is to go back into captivity, implying the end of national sovereignty. Admah and Zeboim (v. 8) were obliterated with Sodom and Gomorrah. This is not a prospect, however, in which Yahweh takes delight; wrath will not be the last word. It cannot be, given Yahweh's nature. Thus, verses 8–9 indicate the inner disposition of Israel's God, who struggles with the necessity to punish the object of his love. Yahweh has every right to eliminate Israel (v. 9), but he decides to limit punishment. So Yahweh changes his mind and decides not to destroy utterly (the punishment for a rebellious child in Deut. 21) but to restore. Reversing the destructive lion image, Yahweh will roar for Israel (i.e., dramatically redeem Israel from exile), and there will be a new exodus (vv. 10–11). Like the exodus generation (Exod. 4:22), those who return will be "sons," having prefigured in exile a radical new movement, though no further details are advanced. God's profound love for Israel is the thought of chapter 11. God will not do what legalities and logic demand. Yahweh cannot forget the covenant promise of mercy for the descendants of the remnant to come. Matthew's use of Hosea 11:1 (Matt. 2:15) has the sequence, until 11:11, in mind. Jesus in an incarnational descent into Egypt undergoes oppression with his people, to whom, although they do not deserve it, the possibility of a second exodus will be granted.

Hosea 11:12–12:2 takes up a new reproach against Israel and Judah as faithless and unrepentant, because of their Canaanite idolatry. Judah is on view (11:12b), where Judah still roams with Canaanite El and keeps faith with the "holy ones" (i.e., of El's Canaanite court) by their policy of foreign alliances. Israel is on view at 11:12a and 12:1 as the inveterate liar. It is extreme folly for Ephraim (12:1) to seek security from any other source than Yahweh. The prophetic propensity for comparing present conditions with history is brought into play again in 12:3–14, in which the patriarchal conduct of Jacob is compared to the present conduct of Israel and Judah. The prophet reminds the nation that Jacob strove for preeminence and power, first in the womb in conflict with his brother, and then in his maturity in conflict with God. But the encounter with God showed him where true strength and resources were to be found. Jacob found God at Bethel where God spoke to him. The success of their father Jacob was due entirely to divine favor and the closeness of the relationship that was his with God.

The theme of Hosea 12 is that the nation is consumed with the pursuit of wealth and power through injustice and oppression. Hosea 12:4 does not denigrate the sanctuary but reminds Israel of its true significance, for the word spoken to Jacob at Bethel was of future blessing for Israel. The prophet is reminding his hearers that only in encounter with God and in laying hold of God's promise can their future be secured. He makes no attack on the Bethel sanctuary. God's quarrel (v. 3) is with his people who, forgetting the ground of their hope in God's promise, have turned to oppression in order to secure wealth. To them the prophet brings a reminder of the honorable origins of the sanctuary at which they are worshiping, and of the God who is there to be encountered. Jacob does not appear in Hosea as a deceiver but as one within whom two possibilities can be found. He can appear as a warning or an example. But he had turned at Bethel to Yahweh, and the divine plan was revealed for him as a special nation. The nation could also use its sanctuaries as Jacob used Bethel—to return to Yahweh (v. 6). However, later in the passage, after a biting reproach has been delivered to the north for identifying with the inhabitants of the land (12:7–11), Israel, in verse 7, is identified with Canaan, the greedy merchant with the immoral cult. This merchant rejoices in wealth and security, but is characterized by immorality and religious infidelity. But wealth is worthless, for Israel cannot buy its (v. 8) way out of punishment. Ephraim is reminded that Yahweh had been Israel's only benefactor (v. 9). But Ephraim's lack of trust will again put the nation back into the wilderness situation when they will live in nomad's tents, the homes of the exodus and wilderness wanderings. Yahweh reminds Israel that they are without excuse. He had continually revealed his expectations to them through the prophets (v. 10) whom Israel had refused to hear. References to Gilgal (v. 11) in Hosea are related to cultic occasions that fit 12:12, and the rest of verse 14 has a cultic content. We can only guess from 12:12 what the sin of Gilead and Gilgal was, but no doubt it was cultic, and the punishment, in the case of Gilgal, is destruction of the shrine. There is a derogatory reference to Jacob, who left the land (v. 12) to serve a wife, not to serve Yahweh. In spite of such behavior, Yahweh did not give up on Jacob's descendants; for by the prophetic ministry of Moses (v. 13), Israel came up out of Egypt, and by the ministry of the same prophet, Israel was preserved (12:13). Just as Jacob once guarded sheep for his father-in-law after he fled, so God guarded Israel with the help of the prophet. That Moses is not named may be because the emphasis is upon the event. Jacob's servitude was in some way the equivalent of Israel in Egypt. In verse 14, the judgment comes.

Covenant Renewal (Hos. 13–14)

Finally, chapters 13 and 14 present both negative and positive assessments of the future. Hosea 13 ranges over the past, present, and future of Israel. Baal worship was characteristic of its early history (v. 1), and has continued (v. 2), but it will be removed. Four examples of disappearance—mist, dew, chaff, and smoke—are given in verse 3. The nation will vanish from the world scene. Israel's election (v. 4a) took place in Egypt and it involved a demand for exclusivity (v. 4b). Israel is reminded of the first commandment. The survival of the nation depends on their keeping it, for polytheism denied Yahweh's uniqueness. In verses 5–8, Israel is again referred to her past (cf. Exod. 20:1). Verse 5 refers to Israel's election again, the reason for the present altercation. At that time in the wilderness, and from the exodus, they were sustained by manna and quail. Then, God had met their needs, but Israel (v. 6) quickly forgot God. Yahweh will become (vv. 7–8) like a wild animal and will kill the flock. Israel is described as a flock that grazes and is satiated and forgets Yahweh. Israel is thus beyond rescue, a condition that her political institutions—especially kingship—have produced (13:9–11). It is likely that verses 9–11 refer to the capture of Hoshea (733–723 B.C.), which left Israel without a king and defenseless before the Assyrians (2 Kings 17:4). Kingship in the north had been a manifestation of God's anger since Saul's days (ca. 1031 B.C.). Ephraim is guilty (v. 12), and the sin will not be forgotten or forgiven. Israel will be like an unborn child who refuses to break out of the womb and thus perishes. Hosea 13:14–16 is to be taken as the ultimate threat. Yahweh, who has power to protect from death and hell, will deliver Ephraim and Samaria. Although Samaria may look prosperous, Yahweh's "east wind" (i.e., Assyria) will destroy it (v. 15). The destruction of the state and the demolition of the political fabric of the north were necessary precursors to renewal. Israel, north and south, was a nonpolitical concept stemming from Yahweh's election. Her history is a record of the failures that came from relying on institutions and of the degeneration of religion into formality and syncretism.

Yahweh's Appeal to Return to the Covenant (Hos. 14)

Since a strong emphasis in Hosea is on the land and the means by which it is to be retained, it comes as no surprise to find that the prophecies of return in Hosea 14 are couched in terms of abundant fertility and fruitfulness. In verses 1–3, Hosea invites Israel to turn back to Yahweh ("return" is a familiar Old Testament idiom for covenant renewal), a return which Yahweh himself will make possible ("I will heal their backsliding"). Hosea 14:2 may be read with the RV: "so will we render as bullocks the offering of our lips." "Bullocks" and "lips" stand in opposition, for Israel's altars have not been a means of expiating sin but of multiplying it. Political alliances or handcrafted gods will not save Israel (v. 3). In verse 3, Yahweh will respond to true confession, heal the relationship, and restore Ephraim's loss of sonship, disowned by rebellion and destined for death (Deut. 21:18–21; 14:3). "Freely" in verse 4 indicates the spontaneity and generosity of Yahweh's love for Israel. His love does not correspond to her deserts, but to his nature. He will heal their backslidings and, thus, will take the initiative. The pronounced use of fertility images in this section (vv. 4–8) indicates the degree of congruity that will then exist between Israel and her land. In Hosea 14:5–8, the emphasis is on God's sovereign freedom. Israel is depicted as a flourishing tree nourished by Yahweh, the dew showing the positive effects of God's sowing (cf. the mention of Jezreel in Hos. 1:4). Yahweh, who had sown chastisement, punishment, and exile, will revive his people once more in their land as the prophecy has turned full circle. But in verse 8, Yahweh himself is presented in the fruit-bearing tree imagery unique in the Old Testament of Yahweh. Hosea, by likening Yahweh to a green tree, boldly sees him again as the source of fertility. These are resources that Israel attributed to other deities in its paganized cult. So the restored Israel is presented as a luxuriant tree under whose protection agricultural life again will prosper. Yahweh is sovereign over the forces of nature, the proper dispenser of all that had been attributed to Canaanite deities. Verse 8 asserts that there is no place for any other deity beside Yahweh. Finally, in verse 9, an editorial note summons the reader to observe how Yahweh acts in regard to his gifts. Adherence to covenant—that is, acceptance of the right way—should be the result.

Summary

The first three chapters of Hosea pivot around chapter 2, an allegorical interpretation of Israel's history from the exodus to the coming exile and pending restoration. Hosea conceives of Israel as living between two eras. The first era stretches from the exodus to the exile. The second, beginning with a new captivity, will climax with a second entry into the Promised Land by way of a new exodus. The restoration of the covenant relationship will make the land an Eden and will bring Israel into harmony, not only with her land, but with her world.

The moral problems of the community do not engage Hosea in the way in which other preexilic prophets take up the questions of social reform. Hosea sees clearly that it is Israel's spiritual adultery, her harlotry, which has undermined and drained the nation's moral fiber. Israel is self-judged, and exile will be the occasion for purging and reflection and the basis on which Yahweh can begin again with her.

What ought to have been the good life in the land is the essential theme of the book. This good life is clearly the great covenantal blessing to which the Book of Deuteronomy points, a book bearing a marked relationship to Hosea. By Hosea's time, the land by which Israel was virtually identified was about to become desolate. How could it be recovered? Hosea's answer is that it will be recovered only by a fresh initiative from Yahweh, who made it available in the first place. Yahweh will not desert his people. With that hope, the faithful in Israel must be satisfied. Hope for the future can be built upon the unchanging faithfulness of Israel's Redeemer. In the most tender of terms, employing the richest imagery, Hosea has stated the intentions of the covenant, the manner in which they ought to have been implemented, and the punishment that must result from failure in this area. Nevertheless, the marriage, which began at Sinai, will continue, for in the ideal depiction of this relationship, Yahweh permits no divorce.

14

Joel

The first half of the Book of Joel deals with what is best understood as an actual plague of locusts, pictured in the form of an approaching army. Presented as a literal plague in Joel 1:2–14, it is then seen in 1:15–20 and 2:1–11 as indicative of a much deeper reality than the opening description seems to suggest. In short, we are faced with a natural evil in chapter 1, which is then theologized in 2:1–11, in terms of "the Day of the Lord."

In Joel 1:2–12, the approach and significance of the plague are described. The effect of the plague on various groups of the community is gauged: on the unresponsive, the "drunkards" (vv. 5–7); on the people of Zion (vv. 8–10), called upon to lament for the cultic dislocation and the deprivation of offerings, which the plague will cause; and on the farming community, whose holdings and livelihoods will be threatened (vv. 11–12). The priests (vv. 13–18), being responsible for the spiritual welfare of the nation, are then to proclaim a public lament for the coming day. Priests are addressed directly in verses 13–14, while verses 15–18 may be their response, as in a communal lament they recognize that the locust plague indicates "the day" of a divine visitation. A brief prayer from the prophet sums up the magnitude of the disaster (vv. 19–20). Human being and beast, fields and brooks, animate and inanimate have been exposed to the devastating effects of the locust onset. It is clearly a major disaster, which causes the prophet to look further at the underlying reality of what has been involved in this attack upon the land.

Joel makes his examination in 2:1–11, a unit that is encased by the ancient and theologically pervasive notion of the Day of the Lord, which is reflected in the natural disaster experienced. This is not an independent description of a disassociated event, for Joel senses that the plague contains features of, and is a precursor to, Yahweh's final, decisive visitation upon Judah. Traditional "Day of the

Lord" language is used here (e.g., the day is a day of darkness [v. 2]; cf. Amos 5:20; Zeph. 1:15). The approaching day is to be signaled by the sound of the trumpet, indicating that it is a type of counter theophany, since its chief features (gloom and darkness, mountains, fire, terror-struck populace) are typical of the OT theophanic presentation from Exodus 19 onward. This fearsome army marches on Jerusalem, reducing the land to a wilderness in its wake (vv. 3–9). The sobering reality underlying all this destruction is that Yahweh's hand is turned against Judah. This visitation is his coming in judgment (vv. 10–11); the reason for this divine action against Jerusalem, which figures prominently in Joel 1 and 2, seems to be the cultic degeneracy of the community. We gain no more than hints in this regard—certainly Joel does not detail social and ethical issues—but we are told that previous cultic repentance (see 2:13) may have been superficial (cf. the demand in 1:13–14 to repent thoroughly).

The phrase "Day of the Lord" is found about twenty times in the OT prophets. In evaluating its significance in Joel, much depends upon the date we assign to the book. (The older expositors suggested a ninth-century date, early in the reign of the boy-king Joash, ca. 837–800 B.C.) The book seems to fit most naturally, however, into the period covered by the ministry of Jeremiah (627–582 B.C.). The common factor in all day-of-the-Lord references is Yahweh's presence, but the manner of that presence is ambivalent. In Joel 2 and 3 it is certainly a day on which Yahweh will do battle with his enemies, as it is in Zephaniah 1:1–2:3.

Following Joel 2:1–11, and perhaps arising out of it (Prinsloo 1985, 49–61), verses 12–17 issue a clear call from Yahweh to repent on the basis of his long-suffering character; the priests are then urged to translate this call into national action. It seems to have had its effect, for Yahweh responds by driving back the fearful northern army (vv. 18–20). Blessings from the land ensue (vv. 21–23), betokening harmony once again between Israel and her world, and thus covenant restoration. Barns are now full and vats overflow as the land responds in superabundant productivity that reverses the ravages of the locust-ridden years (vv. 24–27) and thus the disaster of 1:2–14. Israel views all this as a manifestation of covenant fidelity (see v. 27, where the note of "your God" and "my people" dominates).

The Outpouring of the Spirit (Joel 2:28–32)

The famous passage on the outpouring of the Spirit, taken up by Peter in Acts 2, forms the centerpiece of the prophecy. It draws to a conclusion the theme of covenant renewal, effected after judgment, which 2:1–27 has taken up. Its eschatological tenor, however, indicates that it too has moved beyond a position of particular judgment to one of final judgment upon the people of God. As the centerpiece of the prophecy, Joel 2:28–32 operates as a fulcrum connecting both halves. It takes its rise from reflection upon the act of particular judgment, effected through the locust plague, yet it has in view the final judgment upon the people of God, which is effected by the last great assault (this will be the subject of Joel 3).

The outpouring of the Spirit upon all flesh (Joel 2:28) clearly has immediate reference to the fortunes of Judah, but equally clearly, Peter's use of Joel in Acts 2 gives the passage a much wider dimension. Spirit and flesh (divine nature and potential; human limitation) bring opposites together in a great anticipation of the new creation. Like the last Adam (1 Cor. 15:45), all flesh become partakers of the life-giving Spirit. What is natural gives way to what is thereafter spiritual. As an immediate consequence of this transformation, and with all social divisions and social barriers removed, all become recipients of the divine mind through the Spirit. All will be in immediate communication with Yahweh, and all will directly reflect the Word (i.e., will prophesy). This complete renewal, this regeneration of the people of God, brings into force Moses' wish for Israel (Num. 11:29), and fits her vocationally to become the community she has been marked out to be (Exod. 19:3–6). The description of the intervention to occur on the Day of the Lord—"portents . . . blood and fire and columns of smoke" (Joel 2:30–31)—has undeniable exodus connotations. The transformation of the heavens (sun and moon in eclipse) points to the cosmic upheaval by which the final "day" will be preceded. The community of salvation to emerge is identified with the remnant (v. 32).

Judgment and Blessing (Joel 3)

After the preliminary announcement of final salvation for Judah and Jerusalem (Joel 3:1), the unit which follows is encased by judgment features, with a satirical invitation offered to the nations to prepare for holy war, using whatever implements may be pressed into service (vv. 2–12). Judgment, which began earlier in the book with the household of God, now extends to the whole world. With the oscillation between eschatology and particular application that we have noted so far, Joel switches in verses 3–8 to offer paradigmatic examples (Tyre, Sidon, and Philistia) of tyrannical oppression inflicted on the people of God in his own time, an oppression that will be requited. In harvest terminology, verses 13–21 describe the fate of the Gentiles, thus returning to the locust-plague language of 1:13–20. Joel 3:15 repeats 2:10, confirming that the locust plague is an anticipation of the final "day." God the Warrior (note the image of divine involvement in holy war—v. 16) intervenes in judgment in both episodes.

After considering the nature of the divine intervention by which the Gentile world will be judged (3:15–17), the prophecy concludes with the promise of a restored paradise for God's people. Jerusalem, as the world center and font of blessing, dispenses fertility (v. 18). Nothing is said about world pilgrimage and thus about world submission in all this. The message concerns only world judgment (vv. 19–21), and thus divine vindication of Judah's (and Israel's) election.

Cleansing and restoration, comfort for God's people, is the theme of the last passage in Joel. If the prophecy was written in or around the exilic period, the theme binding the book together—the desolation of Judah followed by restoration and covenant blessing—echoes the new-covenant theology of the exilic period. Joel is more particularistic than Isaiah 40–66, but this is simply to say that the centrality of Jerusalem in Joel echoes the typical emphasis of southern prophecy, which Isaiah 40–66 transcends. Yet, with his note of God's redemptive act for the people of God, followed by a world judgment that ushers in paradise regained, Joel is at one with typical prophetic eschatology.

15

Amos

Amos seems to have been written about 750 B.C., since (1) Jeroboam II of Israel is still reigning; (2) there is no hint of the disruption that characterized the end of his reign; and (3) only general prophecies concerning the exile of the north are advanced. The prophet's introduction to his mission occurs in Amos 1:1–2. His material is concerning Israel, that is, the total entity in Palestine, as the following reference to the reigns of southern and northern kings indicates. The book presents his career as finished and Amos as a figure of the past, presumably dead. The two years before the well-known earthquake of recent memory perhaps refers to the earthquake occurring at the shrine Bethel in Amos 9:1.

Amos 9:7–10 returns to 3:1–2, the election of Israel and its consequences, while 9:11–15 takes up the themes of chapters 1–2, the relationship of Israel and Judah to the nations and to Yahweh's eschatological purposes.

Introduction to Amos's Mission (Amos 1:1–2)

Amos describes himself as a shepherd (1:1). This term may designate a status higher than an ordinary shepherd, perhaps an estate manager. Perhaps he engaged in mixed farming, since in Amos 7:14 he describes himself as a dresser of sycamore (fig) trees. The important feature of these initial verses is their Zion orientation, which stamps Amos's prophecy. The roaring of Yahweh from Zion indicates that some problem relating to the northern kingdom's stance toward Jerusalem requires attention (cf. the roaring lion on the move in 3:4). Since Zion and the Jerusalem temple are the prophetic symbols of divine government, Israel's failure to acknowledge Zion's position constitutes a basic flaw in their doctrine of God, in effect, a denial of Yahweh's sovereignty. It is suggestive that a reference to Carmel is associated with the introduction, for that name is evocative of the contest over the question of divine sovereignty, which had been fought by Elijah in 1 Kings 18. This reference raises suspicion that the north may have reverted to a position of syncretism somewhat similar to that which Elijah had challenged. Zion and Carmel represent cultic confrontation, and indeed the contents of Amos depict him as declaring war on the northern sanctuaries and proclaiming implicitly the sacrosanct character of Jerusalem. Moreover, that the book ends on the note of restoration, which is Zion-oriented, presenting Jerusalem as the divine mountain with implications for the wider world, causes us to conclude that, by Amos's time, the contours of Zion theology had been fully developed, even if the expanded expression of them occurs in the south slightly later (in Isaiah). We may surmise from the Jerusalem concentration of Amos 1:2 and 9:11–15 that Yahweh is moving from Zion in judgment against the north on the probable grounds of false cultic stances—postures that, because of their assertions of sovereignty, are a denial of his rule.

Oracles against the Foreign Nations (Amos 1:3–2:3)

The eight units fall into two groups of four parts, which then naturally divide into two pairs. The nations are all contiguous, and they number seven, with Israel, the eighth, at the climax. With the third and fourth transgressions, the full number, corresponding to the traditional number of the enemies of Israel in the Promised Land, has been reached and judgment must fall. These oracles against the foreign nations can be placed in no one historical context, but may be a review of relationships between Israel, Judah, and their neighbors, extending over hundreds of years. All eight pronouncements have the same three essential elements of a judgment oracle: an opening formula, a charge, and punishment (except for number 8, which follows the pattern only through the charge). Numbers 1, 2, 5, and 6 have a simple charge and complex consequences. In numbers 3, 4, and 7, the charges are amplified, but the consequences are simply stated. No two are the same. The first two threaten punishment on the ruler, the second two elaborate on the crime, but not on the punishment. The next two fasten on the rulers again. Ammon and Moab are also a natural pair, as are Judah and Israel. Amos 2:6–8 is addressed to northern Israel, but verses 9–13 speak to the classic Israel of the exodus. Amos 2:14–16 could apply to all, rounding off the unit. Amos has adapted the ancient list of seven nations to a present purpose.

Not all of the oracles have reference to Israel (or Judah), since the crime of Moab does not concern Israel, and that of the Philistines may not. This fact lessens the possibility often raised that the nations are censured in these oracles as members of the former Davidic empire for crimes committed against that kingdom.

The order of the oracles is not merely geographical. It has been proposed that in Amos's oracles we have an alternative listing of the enemies of Israel and Judah. However, it is doubtful whether the interest Amos displays in them is purely national. Marvin Sweeney (2000, 103) suggests that the order conveys an army's advance from the Fertile Crescent. More to the point, in terms of the interrelationship of the oracles, is the suggestion that the link between the oracles is literary (Paul 1971a, 399). Commencing with Aram, Israel's principal enemy, there is a link with the oracles against Philistia in the punishment envisaged (1:4, 7), while Aram and Philistia are also linked in Amos 9:7. Philistia and Tyre are linked at Joel 3:4–8; Jeremiah 47:4; Ezekiel 25:16–17, and here in Amos 1, by a leveling of the identical accusation (vv. 6, 9). Edom, Ammon, and Moab are frequently linked (e.g., Deut. 23:3–8; Isa. 11:14; Jer. 48–49). In Amos 1, the notion of fraternal attitudes connects Tyre and Edom (vv. 9, 11), while the three southern states complete the list with appropriate linkages. Edom and Ammon are linked by the nature of the offense (both presumably wrought with the sword; see vv. 11, 13), and then Ammon and Moab by the nature of the punishment (by fire; see 1:14; 2:2).

Oracles against Judah and Israel (Amos 2:4–16)

Judah and Israel are then surveyed. These two oracles break with the literary pattern that controls the previous six. Judah is reproached for a general covenant breach (2:4–5), but Israel is treated at length, and clearly, this oracle forms the climax to the sequence. Amos's audience may have listened approvingly to this point, even to the oracle directed against Judah, but punishment for them would have come as a surprise. The logic of the climactic denunciation presumes that Israel would have conceded the connection between sin and punishment, even upon Judah, for a covenant breach in which Israel did not feel involved. However, a particular covenantal basis for the denunciation against Israel could stand only if Israel saw the foreign nations as involved, or included in Yahweh's Sinai covenant with her; but clearly they were not. Since Judah is denounced for covenant breach, it may well have been Amos's assumption that Israel and the nations were included in a wider concept of a universal covenant. The application of covenant promises to Israel (and Judah), in any case, exacted more in responsibility from her.

The final oracle against Israel (2:6–16) is the longest, and the climax of the series. It shares many features with the others. Thus, Israel is placed on the same level as the surrounding nations, but for different reasons. It is noteworthy that there is no mention of a national covenant. (The word "covenant" occurs in Amos only in 1:9, where it is used in another connection.) Perhaps the concept of covenant had become so distorted that the word was best avoided. However, Amos sees the north as having rejected the covenant, which he indicates by using the more formal language of justice and righteousness. Covenant, in Amos, is everywhere presupposed as the relationship binding Yahweh and Israel, for the mere fact that a prophet raised the issues of social abuses, class distinctions, judicial partiality, and oppression of the poor meant that he acknowledged a covenant ethic, which did not permit such offenses. The new focus of the prophets was the judgment message directed against Israel (e.g., about a holy war organized against the nation), but they were not theological innovators. Prophetic theology came from the history of Yahweh's dealings with Israel, and on that basis, the prophets called Israel to account.

In claiming that the personal will of Israel's God is binding upon Israel, and should govern her moral response in just the same way that the nations should recognize a principle of universal morality operating in Yahweh's world, Amos is advancing to new ground (Barton 1980, 49). He expands the covenant concept to indicate that the special privilege accorded to Israel under covenant is a particularization of a more general posture of response that should control the created order. This accounts for the novel twist that Amos gives to the doctrine of election. Israel is not indemnified by it, but is made all the more culpable. How much worse, then, is the sin of elect Israel? How logical is the "therefore" in Amos 3:2?

In the climactic oracle against Israel, it is noteworthy that the expulsion of the Amorites comes first in the review of Israel's history (v. 9, after her pressing social sins have been exposed [vv. 6–8]). Only then does mention of the exodus follow (v. 10), while the third item in the review is the prophetic ministry by means of which the Sinai covenant was to have been preserved (vv. 11–12). Amos's thrust is thus directed against Israel's possession of the land, with, perhaps, the implication that exile (vv. 13–16) must result.

Witnesses Summoned against Israel (Amos 3)

After presenting the responsibilities of election (3:1–2), Amos, by deft use of rhetorical questions (vv. 3–6), compels his listeners to pay attention and to frame a reply. The sequence of thought that becomes increasingly ominous, moving from animals to animals and humans and then to humans alone, seems broken by the prose of verse 7 (as opposed to the poetry of vv. 3–6). However, this change from poetry to prose simply serves to throw verse 7 into clear relief as the dominant verse of the chapter, revealing to the audience that Amos's ministry is one of compulsion. The language of Amos 3:7 also points to Amos's prophetic authority as an auditor of proceedings of the heavenly council, whereby the history of Israel has been determined, and thus lays the basis for his claim to prophetic integrity. (In v. 7, note the use of *sod* 'secret', which by extension points to the prophetic membership of the heavenly council, the royal body with which Yahweh surrounds himself; cf. Jer. 23:18; Isa. 6.) The mention of the roar of the lion (Amos 3:8) signifies the inevitability of punishment (cf. 1:2). The tenor of 3:8 indicates, however, that Amos did not approach his task with particular relish.

In a somewhat mocking reversal of the holy-war motif, the two great powers of the day, Egypt and Assyria, are then called upon to witness the inner corruption of Israel (vv. 9–10). They are to assent to her punishment, vindicating its fairness, even when viewed from the basis of their lesser ethical connection to Yahweh. The description in verse 10 is still general. The mention of violence "stored up" gives us a clue as to its location. It is stored in the palaces, the royal buildings. The sociopolitical situation itself is condemned (Carroll 1992, 192–96). Exile will result as well as great devastation (vv. 11–12). Verses 13–15 provide an epilogue ("punish" in v. 14 returns us to 3:2), reinforcing the message of the chapter (Gitay 1980, 295). Bethel's destruction is emphasized, and those who have fled to it for refuge will be swept away (cf. the "horns of the altar," v. 14). There is now no escape for the north. Election must, if disregarded, lead to exile (v. 15), and any asylum will be denied to Israel (v. 14). Amos 3 thus provides the basic message of the prophecy, building upon the careful argumentation of chapters 1–2 and directing us to the inevitable consequences in store for the north.

Israel's Impending Judgment (Amos 4–6)

Amos 4 begins somewhat strangely, as an exposition of the outline of Amos 3, with an attack upon the indulgent behavior of the noble women of Samaria (vv. 1–3), who will be prominent in the march into exile. In commencing with them, Amos is referring to the reversal of relationships in public order that their lead in sinfulness has helped to bring about (cf. Isa. 3:18–26). In the highly structured series of five successive stanzas (vv. 4–6, 7–8, 9, 10, 11), Yahweh reviews successive disasters he has brought to Israel to provoke a return. The identical conclusion, "yet you did not return to me," conveys the comprehensive character of the judgment. The formula "oracle of Yahweh" closes each individual stanza within the unit.

In Amos 4:4–6, the inner reason for this public collapse is given, namely, the mechanical approach by Israel to the cult, the heart of the nation. The devotion to the cult in the north is actually rebellion against God. Notably in Amos, the cult is referred to disparagingly as "your cult" ("your sacrifices," "your tithes," etc.). Amos 4:6–11 deals with the covenant curses, which have been operating and have as yet been unperceived (hunger, drought, crop failure, etc.). The blessings of Leviticus 26:3–13 (the chapter to which Amos seems to be referring in this material, though undertones of Deut. 28 are also present) have been reversed. The threatened plagues must come after the message in chapters 5–6 when the situation is still open, but before chapters 1–3, when it is too late. The key verse, 4:12, is therefore most likely a warning and not an invitation. A fragment of a hymn brings the chapter to a close, emphasizing, by its content, Yahweh as Creator and then Judge. (Amos 4:13; 5:8–9; and 9:5–6 all seem related hymnic fragments used by Amos to sum up or to focus his argument.)

Amos 5–6 is a warning rather than a judgment. Amos 5 has a clearly perceptible structure (de Waard 1977, 176). The two sections—verses 1–17 and 18–27—are connected by the thought-patterning of the chapter. The theme of verses 18–27 is that ritual substituted for right worship will lead to ruin, a subject that builds upon verses 1–17, where correct worship is defined. The dirge of verses 1–2 has the prophet looking into the coffin of virgin Israel, her promising life cut short, fallen on the Promised Land. The measure of destruction foreshadowed in verse 3 grounds the lament of verses 1–2. The reason for all of this disaster seems provided in verses 4–6, in which Israel is urged to seek Yahweh, and not the northern sanctuaries. The message "seek the Lord and live" seems ironic, since the sanctuaries are condemned in verse 5 (see Hunter 1980, 70–71). Verse 7 turns the argument to social injustice, the outward demonstration of the inward malaise, while verses 8–9 (the hymnic fragment) form the midpoint of the chapter. Verses 10–13 return to the theme of verse 7, while verses 14–15 echo the thought of verses 4–6. Finally, verses 16–17 take up the lament of verses 1–2.

The midpoint of verses 8–9, and perhaps the key phrase of the prophecy, is the note on which verse 8 concludes: "Yahweh is his name." In the context, this statement is not an assertion about Yahweh's person or nature, but a reminder that this name had been given to enable Israel to call upon God (Exod. 3:13–15). By rejecting this name in worship, Israel has invited Yahweh's judgment. Yahweh, as Creator and Judge, threatens (vv. 8–9), perhaps with a reference to the flood in verse 9. In short, the central demand that the Book of Amos makes is that the Israelites in the north put the character of Yahweh and their response to him in worship at the very center of their national life.

Given this background, it is difficult not to imagine that the reference to the Day of the Lord in 5:18–20 has cultic connections. Since the "Day of Yahweh" had not yet acquired a technical meaning, it is possible to have different views about it, as Amos and Israel had. The Day of Yahweh, at this time, seems the expected day of his manifestation.

Perhaps, as some have suggested, 5:18 is a reply by Amos to a popular expectation of Yahweh's manifestation (theophany), cherished by the north and bound up with some northern cultic celebration, perhaps some New Year festival. While the connection between the "day" and Yahweh's intervention in holy war is often made in the OT, this is not a necessary or universal connection. The common element in all the references to this day is the dramatic appearance of Yahweh to bless or to judge. If the reference in 5:18–20 has cultic connections and responds to popular expectation, then verses 21–27 follow naturally. However, this section is not a call for Israel to repent for her covenant social breaches. It rather presages the divine judgment that must flow as their consequences. The translation of verse 24a, with older expositors, should read "justice will roll," a Hebrew imperfect, not a Hebrew imperative/jussive, "let justice roll." The context provides a reference to divine justice and righteousness as about to come, rather than as a reference to a jussive form, that gives the audience a direct command to perform justice and righteousness (Berquist 1993, 54–67). With the older expositors, who understood the water imagery as a reference to the flood, the reference to cascading water (v. 24) points to a time of disaster and destruction (cf. Isa. 10:22b), a time of overflowing divine righteousness. Verse 24 becomes the pivot in the unit 5:18–27, as the members (5:18–20, 21–24, 25–27) move from statements of human miscalculation (vv. 18–20), to divine displeasure (vv. 21–23), to punishment (v. 24), to apostasy (vv. 25–27). That Amos 5:21–24 is an attack on the cult is lessened by the observation that the only cultic acts mentioned are the voluntary acts performed in addition to basic cultic obligations. The wealthy could provide gifts to the deity beyond the mandatory offerings, perhaps in lavish attempts to secure divine favor. To seek divine favor through cultic excess is futile. God thus asks the people to desist (v. 23), emphasizing the utter impossibility of cultic influence upon divine actions. It is hardly likely that these verses operate as a complete rejection of sacrifice. It is probably an indication that, even in the wilderness—at the initiation of the sacrificial system—corruption had already entered. Israel's idolatrous worship will lead her into exile (v. 27).

In Amos 6, the prosperity of Israel as a whole is reviewed. The woe extends from verses 1–6 and is addressed to seven groups. The woes are being directed at the leaders of both countries (v. 1). In verses 1–2, complacent people are invited to draw an object lesson from the Assyrian treatment of Israel's neighbors; the moral and religious reasons for this warning are given in verses 3–6. Verses 7–11 foreshadow exile as a judgment, just as 4:1–3 did when the same question was discussed. Amos 6:12–13 points to the lack of reality that characterizes Israel's political life. They have had minor political successes, but an Assyrian exile is pending (vv. 13–14).

Amos's Five Visions (Amos 7:1–9:6)

The last major section of Amos runs from 7:1 to 9:6. The five visions of 7:1–9:6 reflect chapters 5–6, in which he delivered the exhortations to repentance, which were not heeded. Amos then received visions 3 and 4, and proclaimed their consequences in oracles of doom upon the nations (chaps. 1–4). Even the plagues recorded in chapter 4 did not bring repentance. These prophecies provoked Amaziah and vision 5 (9:1–4), which resulted in even more dire threats (9:7–10) within the disaster described in 8:4–14. Hope for the future was then framed in vague terms (9:11–15) (Andersen and Freedman 1980, 65–70). The visions are interrupted by the clash between Amaziah, priest of Bethel, and Amos (7:10–17).

All five visions have a similar form: they consist of two pairs (7:1–3 and 7:4–6; 7:7–8 and 8:1–2) and a fifth vision (9:1–4) to complete the sequence. The first four visions follow the same pattern, with only minor variations, but the fifth differs widely in form, length, and content. In the first four of two pairs, with each member resembling the other closely, the second of the pair seems intended to reinforce the first. The first four visions begin with exactly the same words, while the fifth conveys essentially the same idea but differently. The first two visions permit intercession and emphasize the effectiveness of Amos as a mediator, while the following pair allows no opportunity for intercession, but speak of God's decision to judge. The final vision exhibits the nature of that judgment. The first three visions also form an introduction to the confrontation between Amos and Amaziah, which leads to Amos's expulsion from Bethel. The fourth adds nothing new, but reinforces the third and sums up the effect of the first four visions by its closing remarks. Silence (8:3) can be the only response to the completeness of the judgment. The juxtaposition of visions and the biographical note of 7:10–17 seems to indicate that Amos's preaching caused his expulsion.

The first two visions portray a dramatic action. In each case, the prophetic response to the divine threat is to plead the smallness of Jacob. As Walter Brueggemann (1969, 386–89) has noted, the word "small" is used in the Jacob traditions (particularly in Genesis—see, e.g., 32:10–12), and in covenant traditions in the OT, to underscore Israel's election—she has no rights or credentials when called, and thus is unable to help herself. In the appeal to Jacob as small, then, there is contained a covenant plea to restore helpless Israel.

The movement to the third vision brings us into difficulty, for the word, usually translated "plumb line" (v. 7), seems not to fit. The Hebrew phrase is, literally, "wall of tin, with tin in his hand"—plumb lines in antiquity were made of lead. The fourth vision, which is directly related in type to the third, is based on a word play. One might thus expect word play in the third vision as well. With a slight rearrangement of the Hebrew consonants we may read verse 8 as "I am setting you in the midst of my people Israel" (instead of "I am setting a plumb line in the midst of my people Israel"). That is, the prophet himself is the "wall of tin," the impenetrable wall, of verse 7 (see Petersen 1977, 77–78).

Verse 9 is a transition, linking by the note of "high places and sanctuaries" the third vision to the dialogue of 7:10–17. At issue in this section is Amos's authority to operate in the north. Amaziah improperly labels the content of his message (v. 11) as conspiracy. The Hebrew term *amaziah* normally refers to sedition by a person legally subordinate to the country and its ruler—as Amos was not. Verses 10–11 summarize the matter reported to Jeroboam. Amaziah's immediate reaction is contained in verses 12–13, in the exchange between Amaziah and Amos (note the connections among vv. 9, 11, and 17, which seam the passage together).

Perhaps in the use of the word "seer" (7:12) Amaziah is raising the question of the legitimacy of Amos's ministry as a Judean in the north, since it is claimed that "seer" is a term normally associated with prophetic connections at the royal court (Paul 1971b, 1155). Amaziah's demand that Amos "eat bread" in the south would therefore seem to be a call to exercise his ministry gainfully in his own recognized domain. The hypothetical character of these two suggestions, however, must be recognized, for "eat bread" occurs nowhere else in the OT in the sense of "earn a living," and the terms "seer" and "prophet" are broadly interchangeable.

In Amos 7:14, it is uncertain whether the verb to be supplied should be present or past. If a present tense is supplied ("I am no prophet"), then Amos may be advancing a denial of official connection with the professional guilds. Yet such a general denial may contradict the connections with the prophetic movement that Amos implicitly claims in 2:11. In view of the clear commission appealed to in 7:15, it seems better to supply a verb in the past tense in verse 14: "I was neither a prophet, nor a prophet's son."

In any case, Amos supports his right to minister (as OT prophecy always supported its rights) by an appeal to Yahweh's direct intervention in his life (7:15). His ministry is a clear threat to the establishment in the north, as Amaziah recognizes. Amos not only defends his ministry, but also pronounces the same judgment upon Amaziah (v. 17), as he has pronounced upon Israel and the house of Jeroboam.

The fourth vision (Amos 8:1–2) offers a clear message. Israel looks secure and in full bloom, but really is ready for dissolution; she is ripe and about to decay. Amos 8:4–6 returns to the question of social justice to draw a direct connection between the way of life of the exploiters and their judgment (vv. 7–8). The reference to the rising and falling of the Nile (v. 8) comments on the earthquake of verse 8. Verses 9–10 address the same exploiters of verses 4–5. Verses 9–10 foreshadow a divine intervention. Verses 11–14 indicate that Yahweh will withdraw the prophetic word, which they had refused to hear.

The vision of Amos 9:1–4 differs from the previous four, in that Yahweh himself reports it. By its size and position, this vision seems the climax of the five. The fourth vision (8:1–2) announced the end; the fifth tells us how it will come. Cosmic upheaval (perhaps figurative language) directed at the (Bethel?) sanctuary will attend the end (9:1). Verses 2–4a consist of a series of five conditional sentences, growing in the intensity of the divine resolve to judge. The announcement of the fixed divine intent occurs at verse 4b ("I will set my eyes upon them for evil and not for good"), while in the hymnic conclusion of verses 5–6, the order of Yahweh as Judge and then Creator puts greater emphasis on the pending judgment. Yahweh's judgment will be thorough, but no righteous person needs to fear (no pebble of grain will fall to the ground).

The Future Hope (Amos 9:7–15)

Amos 9:7–8 deals with Israel's election and the responsibilities that stem from it. Other people, such as the Philistines and the Syrians, have had their own exodus, for God has dealt with them historically in a way appropriate to each. This fact does not in itself imply that Israel is reduced to their level, but simply that God acts in a sovereign manner in the history of nations. However, Israel is now a "sinful kingdom," and thus has negated the concept of a kingdom of priests, the vocation to which God had called her (Exod. 19:6). Judgment must therefore come (Amos 9:9–10).

Finally, Amos 9:11–15 deals with restoration after judgment. This final unit climaxes the linear progression of Amos's words of condemnation, warning, and pleading—all spurned by Israel. The final unit focuses on the future, with Yahweh's coming toward Israel presented as inevitable and final. These actions are both negative and positive. On the one hand, the present generation of Israelites will be surely and severely punished. On the other hand, a righteous remnant will be spared and one day there will be a glorious restoration, not surprisingly, at the end of the book. These verses do not come as an afterthought, but complete the Zion eschatology implicit at Amos 1:2. Yahweh will restore devastated Israel (9:11–12). The "booth of David" to be repaired is best taken as the Davidic house. The genders of the Hebrew suffixes in verse 11 must be closely noted; perhaps all the eschatological components—Jerusalem, temple, and Davidic dynasty—are being alluded to. ("Its breaches!" is feminine plural, and "it" in "rebuild it" is feminine singular; these could be references to Jerusalem and the temple, respectively. "Its ruins" is masculine plural and thus seems to refer to the Davidic dynasty.) Edom (v. 12) seems to be a paradigm for the repentant Gentiles, who will finally share in the covenant promises. To complete the book, Yahweh will restore his people Israel and fertility to the land; the mountains and hills will flow with wine (9:13–15). Verses 13–15 display the themes of a second exodus, with the Promised Land once more inhabited as Eden recaptured.

The Book of Amos moves from the Lord "roaring" from Zion, to the restoration of Zion. It is thoroughly Jerusalem- and temple-oriented. Its major plea is for right worship that reflects a right doctrine of God. The north had developed a syncretistic Yahwism, reflected at its shrines and in its feasts. The cult of the people thus had become theirs and theirs alone, since it failed to put Yahweh at the center. Amos calls on them to remember Yahweh, to hallow his name (see 5:8), to offer right worship, and thus to reject the mechanistic approach to the cult, which has sapped the strength of the north. To heed that call would rebuild the kingdom of God (9:11–15). But we know that, received without honor, the somber predictions of Amos were fulfilled within thirty years in the final destruction of the north.

16

Obadiah

The dating of this small book is uncertain. Most would agree that to date the book shortly after the fall of Jerusalem in 587/586 B.C. is most natural. It is clear from the eschatological stance of the conclusion of the prophecy—Edom will be judged in a process which emanates from Zion—that Edom has assumed the features of the exilic paradigm of the enemies of the people of God. In typical OT presentation, a historical incident is seen in terms of wider eschatological dimensions.

Verse 1a forms an introduction to the book, which begins, as it concludes, with a threat directed toward Edom. Obadiah 1b–4, in which the pride of Edom and her confidence in her remoteness are repudiated, is very similar to Jeremiah 49:14–16, and thus indicates the use of traditional material. The message is clear: seemingly impregnable arrogance will be brought down. The thoroughness of this judgment is then illustrated by the analogy of the pillagers, offered in Obadiah 5–6. Edom, in the day of her distress, may expect no help from outside friends, and even her famed wisdom will not avail her (vv. 7–9). In verse 8 the hint of divine intervention serves to heighten the mounting tension of the passage. Edom will receive what she has meted out to Jerusalem (vv. 10–14).

However, Edom's punishment will merely be an example of Yahweh's typical holy-war intervention (vv. 15–16). The movement toward eschatology grows more direct with the mention of the Day of the Lord, and the prophecy now turns from history to final prospect for the people of God. When that day comes, the remnant of the people of God will be gathered on Mount Zion (vv. 17–21), acting as an arm of God's judgment on Edom, Israel's initial (and typical) enemy. The return of the Promised Land, particularly that portion affected by Edomite predations, and the gathering of the scattered people of God are the themes of verses 19–20. Verse 21, by its terminology, harks back to the pre-monarchical period ("saviors" who will "judge," KJV), underscoring the final theocratic rule of the kingdom of God to which the conclusion of the verse points. Thus, the program of the restoration of Israel, the judgment upon the Gentiles, the return to the Promised Land, and the end-time divine rule demonstrate Obadiah to be a carrier of mainstream prophetic eschatology.

Despite the destruction of Jerusalem and the exile, the future for the people of God is secure. Edom is to know this truth. This is the burden of Obadiah, who, in addressing historical reality, typically sees in the events of his time the foreshadowing of the in-breaking of the kingdom.

17

Jonah

Perhaps no other book in the OT has proved so difficult to classify as the Book of Jonah, and doubtless the argument will continue. The forms of prophetic narrative appear at the beginning of the book and then again at the middle of the book (Jonah 3:1–3). The prophetic tone continues with an allusion to Elijah in 4:3, 8, and to the nature of his ministry, with which Jonah's can be compared. (Note the clear parallels between Jonah and Elijah: both flee, both are faced with death, both fall into a deep sleep, both sit under a tree and ask to die, and both are associated with a forty-day activity.) If the book is a parable, its point is not clear. It does not seem to be an allegory, since none of the available details that might have been exploited are pressed. There seems no reason to deny its prophetic status, though consideration of its purpose must be deferred until the details have been considered. On the whole, however, its message is clear. The word of God, once announced to a prophet of God, will not return void, and to engage in debate with God is fruitless (Bolin 1997, 177). Finally, the identification of the hero with the court prophet of 2 Kings 14:25 seems secure. We do not enter into the difficult question of the dating of the book. The matter must be left open.

Jonah's Flight (Jonah 1)

The Book of Jonah is characterized by the frequent repetition of key words and phrases as well as by its wealth of allusions to OT contexts. The book is divisible into two clear halves, chapters 1–2 and 3–4, with fine parallelism obtaining between (and within) the two sections. Jonah 1 focuses on Jonah's flight from the presence of the divine word (cf. Gen. 4:16), not simply a desire to quit Palestine. Verse 1 explains that Yahweh's word was given and that it was given to Jonah. Jonah may have been acquiescent as an acclaimed court prophet in the days of Jeroboam II (2 Kings 14:25). Verse 2 provides the content of the message in an imperative followed by an explanation of the imperative. The command implies Yahweh's worldwide sovereignty. Was he being asked to preach against Nineveh because Yahweh intended to judge the city for its evil, or in the sense that Yahweh had allowed some great trouble to come up against it? Alternatively, was Nineveh an evil city that had suffered misfortune? Several coastal areas on the Mediterranean have been identified as Tarshish. Given this interpretation, it is clear that God had not closed the door even on Nineveh and her people.

In 1:4–16, a storm begins (vv. 4–5a), continues (vv. 5b–10), worsens (vv. 11–15), and then concludes in verse16. The sailors are not far out to sea (v. 13). In verse 4, developments are stated simply: Yahweh caused a wind, which caused a storm, which caused the ship to sink. In verse 8, five questions are put to Jonah. Until the sailors know his identity, they can hardly know the God whom he serves. Is God (*'elohim,* a general word) a personal, family, or national God? It turns out that this God is the covenant God of Israel, Yahweh, and that his domain is the universe (v. 9); the sailors are terrified (v. 10)

Jonah has attempted to abandon his call and to move to an area beyond the present reach of God's word, Tarshish. Isaiah 66:19 lists Tarshish—Sardinia, Carthage, and Spain have all been suggested as locations—as a place where Yahweh's fame is yet to be made known.

As Jonah moves away from the divine presence into the boat (1:3), down to the hold and into sleep (v. 5), and presumably into death (v. 12), the mariners, who at first are depersonalized sailors ("salts," v. 5), move closer to Jonah's God. In Jonah 1:5, the vague term *'elohim* 'deity' is used; in verse 6, the captain calls to the universal deity, *the God (ha 'elohim);* verse 10 reports the sailors' recognition that Jonah was fleeing from Yahweh; finally, verse 16 includes a confession.

The sailors are represented as typical Gentiles, generally God-fearing (on the basis of an intuitive knowledge) and compassionate. Jonah, by contrast, flees before the knowledge of God that he has through direct revelation. He displays throughout the book a total lack of compassion. Through prompting by the sailors (representing the pagan world), Jonah is, in effect, forced to consider his commission (v. 8). The sailors' questions elicit from Jonah a statement of faith as a "Hebrew," in avowedly Abrahamic terms (cf. Gen. 14:13), that has at its center a basic confession of fear before Yahweh, now identified as the Creator.

Thus, the theme of the first chapter is the unconscious success of Jonah as the embodied word. The Gentiles' general factual awareness of God is gradually transformed into a reverential awe as they move from a deistic conception of God to a particular faith in Yahweh (Jonah 1:16). Their "fear" moves from an elemental fear in verse 5, to a fear of the divine messenger (v. 10), and finally to a fear of Jonah's God (v. 16). This emphasis through the sailors sets the tone for a major theme of the book—the reaction to the word by the Gentiles.

Jonah's Psalm of Thanksgiving (Jonah 2)

The psalm of Jonah 2 underscores Yahweh as the one who reverses circumstances and functions rhetorically as a kind of musical pause. It is to be divided into four sections: (1) an introduction (v. 2); (2) an initial stanza lamenting Jonah's banishment from Yahweh's presence, his temple (vv. 3–4); (3) a second stanza (vv. 5–7) in which the theme is descent into Sheol, and prayer from there to the heavenly sanctuary; and (4) the conclusion (vv. 8–9), in which Jonah expresses confidence of being heard (a customary ingredient in the thanksgiving psalms), rejects idolatry, and vows to renew his relationship with Yahweh and (presumably) thus to fulfill his commission (Walsh 1982). The centrality of Yahweh is indicated by the position of that divine name at the beginning and conclusion of the psalm, with Jonah's experiences being concentrated in the middle section (the divine name or an allusion to it occurs in every line of the psalm except for vv. 5–6a). This confessional psalm of thanksgiving moves Jonah from storm to calm, as the sailors in Jonah 1 have moved from calm to storm to calm (Cohn 1969, 78–83). The purpose of the psalm is to fit Jonah, by forgiveness, for the mission to Nineveh. The psalm recalls the episode of the fish as past, Jonah presumably having been returned to Palestine. It is thus preparatory to and anticipatory of the new beginning of Jonah 3.

Jonah's Renewed Commission (Jonah 3)

The commission is renewed in Jonah 3:1–3. There is no thrust or parry by Jonah this time, but mere obedience. Commissioned to go to Nineveh, he arrives and announces the sole words of prophecy in the book, "Yet forty days, and Nineveh shall be overthrown!" As elsewhere in the book, there are echoes of definite biblical contexts that import an element of ambiguity into the statement (here by the verb "overthrow"). "Forty days" and "overthrow" in verse 4 connote, respectively, the flood and the fate of Sodom and Gomorrah. Yet the verb "overthrow," which reminds us of the fate of the cities of the plain, is essentially neutral, pointing simply to a change in the condition of a person or object. Ironically, in this prophetic announcement of doom there is the nuance of repentance as a possibility; the later movement in the chapter confirms this. As in chapter 1, Jonah is the unconscious catalyst who, in contact with pagans, brings them to repentance. In both instances, their situation is reversed by the pronouncement of the divine word (cf. 1:9). Led by the king of Nineveh, the city repents (vv. 5–10), accepting that its future is bound up with God's free grace (see 3:9—"Who knows, God may yet repent and turn from his fierce anger, so that we perish not" RSV). Clearly, this reversal is a key to the book, for the narrator promptly records the divine response in verse 10.

Jonah's Anger (Jonah 4)

We have in chapter 4 somewhat of a parallel to Jonah 2. The prophet is again in a crisis situation (4:1; cf. 2:1), leading him to pray (4:2a; 2:6a). He refers to a distressing situation in Palestine, his own premonition of Nineveh saved by Yahweh's graciousness (4:2b–3; cf. 2:6b–7, by which he had been saved by the same grace from the depths of Sheol itself). The freedom of God, expressed here in salvation, creates for Jonah an intolerable situation, to which verses 4–11 respond. The salvation of Nineveh indicates that Yahweh's extension of grace cannot be predicted or manipulated, and that it cannot be confined to Israel. This reflection (v. 2) upon the old creedal formula of Exodus 34:6 (Magonet 1983, 36), restricted there to the covenant relationship, provokes a personal crisis for Jonah. He is not able to live with such a concept of Yahweh's grace, and he begs Yahweh for death, an indication of his utter powerlessness (Jonah 4:3).

Jonah 4:4–11 provides the resolution of the book. Questioned by Yahweh as to the grounds for his anger (v. 4), Jonah retires to watch, under the shade of a gourd, whether or not Nineveh will fall (note the repetition of the question of v. 4 in v. 9). Jonah, unrepentant, cherishes the hope that Nineveh will still be overthrown. The change of divine name within this chapter bears noting. As used by Jonah, Yahweh is to be associated with covenant compassion, *'elohim* with punishment and discipline.

The withdrawal of the protective gourd that God had created for Jonah is followed by the divine word, which spares Nineveh (4:11). God points out that Jonah has no grounds for anger in the matter of the gourd that God had given and taken. It is a thing of the night, brief, frail, and meaningless, like human life in general, seems the implication. Much less so, then, should Jonah be angry over Nineveh. Jonah had no claim on the plant and thus no right to talk about justice or injustice (Fretheim 1978, 234). The book concludes where it begins—with Yahweh's invincible word.

Some have pointed to divine freedom as the major issue in the Book of Jonah. Indeed, the emphasis in the last verse of the book is on God's sovereignty and his ability (as opposed to human inability) to make the best choices. However, divine freedom is everywhere asserted in the OT. The Book of Jonah could also be read as a condemnation of Israelite particularism. Such a theme, however, is nowhere pronounced, and it detracts from the more general issues to which we have referred. Equally, the book is not intended to resolve the difficult problems of the exilic period (i.e., mixed marriages and collaboration within the land with foreigners), for these matters are not taken up. Nor was it written to demonstrate the possibility of repentance in the most unlikely of circumstances, for repentance, as a possibility, is the presupposition with which the book commences. God is the initiator of crises in human experience, and God resolves them. God's ways are beyond human understanding and depend on a grace that cannot be anticipated or expounded, just as it cannot be measured. On that note, as a fitting summary of the whole, the book concludes.

18

Micah

Micah was a stirring preacher of judgment. His book begins and ends on that strong note (1:2–4; 7:7–20). He preached in the last third of the eighth century B.C. (during the reigns of Jotham, Ahaz, and Hezekiah), slightly later than Isaiah but generally overlapping with him chronologically. He shared most of Isaiah's basic concerns, probably also witnessing the fall of Samaria and the Assyrian visitation upon Jerusalem of 701 B.C. The book is divided into five parts: (1) 1:1; (2) 1:2–16, in which Samaria's punishment is to provide a paradigm for Judah; (3) 2:1–5:15, dealing with the punishment and restoration of Israel, and the emergence of Zion and the Davidic ruler; (4) 6:1–16, which appeals to Israel and Judah to return to Yahweh by showing what Yahweh requires in covenant relationships; and (5) 7:1–20, which presents Micah's confidence that Yahweh will move beyond punishment and act for Israel's blessing. The book begins with an international summons to judgment, a proclamation of the descent of Yahweh from his holy temple in heaven to the world (1:2–3). It concludes with this mission accomplished (7:14–17); the final doxology, however, relates to the immeasurable nature of divine forgiveness and a restatement of the Abrahamic promises (7:18–20). The book proceeds with a stern indictment of Jerusalem and Samaria. Social corruption, rife in Micah's time, is constantly referred to; leaders of north and south are accused. At the same time, the book, like Isaiah, exhibits a strong confidence in the future, associated with Yahweh's kingship to be exercised from Zion; and much of the prophecy is given over, in the hope sections, to the exposition of traditional Zion eschatology.

Judgment and Salvation (Mic. 1:2–16)

The descent of Yahweh in judgment is universally announced as affecting the whole earth (1:2–4). The particular reason for this coming is the failure of both north and south, Samaria and Jerusalem, to be centers of right worship (v. 5) and thus to be points of witness to the wider world. Verse 5 makes clear that Micah thinks Jerusalem and Samaria are responsible for the ills of the nation, but greater responsibility lies with Samaria. While Jerusalem will retain her children (v. 16), Samaria will be completely destroyed. Jerusalem is presented sympathetically, as a victim of Samaria, and also as a victim of the sins of Lachish (v. 13). Micah thus sees restoration for Jerusalem beyond judgment. The doom of Samaria, for idolatry, is then pronounced (vv. 6–7). The lament that follows anticipates, by its geographical references, the approach of an unidentified enemy, and, thus, the devastation of the land of Judah (vv. 8–16), with the loss of the Shephelah cities. Micah 1:10–16 presupposes a situation in which Jerusalem has lost the support of a number of towns. Though these verses are cast as a dirge, they make accusations against these towns (Stansell 1988, 40–47). The Shephelah cities were not lost through destruction, but disloyalty, which would have made their loss the harder to bear. This may not point to Sennacherib's invasion of 701, but to the tensions between Israel and Judah, following the death of Jeroboam II (ca. 749 B.C.; Shaw 1993, 64–65). The lament closes with a summons to Jerusalem to join in acts of mourning (v. 16), and this provides further emotional impact by the personification of Jerusalem and the cities, which have left her. The reason for everything is covenant breach (v. 13), through sin (v. 5) and idolatry (v. 7). The similarity of this material to David's lament over Saul and Jonathan (v. 10; cf. 2 Sam. 1:19–27) also underscores the poignancy with which the prophet views the approaching disaster, which he is powerless to avert.

Micah 1 does not seem to indicate a siege of Jerusalem, but a time of divided allegiance within Judah, when many of the Shephelah towns were at odds with Jerusalem policy. The time of the Syro-Ephraimite War (734–732 B.C.) seems indicated, and we will note how much of the prophecy seems rooted in this time period. Alternatively, Shaw (1993, 224) suggests a period in Jotham of Judah's reign, when the pro-Assyrian policy of both Samaria and Jerusalem may have been popular.

Israel's Punishment and Restoration, and the Emergence of Davidic Leadership (Mic. 2:1–5:15)

The activities of monopolistic landowners, which provide a more specific cause for the approaching disaster of chapter 1, are the subject of the prophetic lament in Micah 2:1–5 (cf. Isa. 5:8). The woe oracle that opens the speech commands attention and indicates, if derived from the mourning cry, the certainty of judgment. Punishment appropriate to the crime on the principle of requital is anticipated. The leaders who viciously prey on the people will receive their deserts in the loss of their property (vv. 1–4). They will be bereft of the land that they have filched. The judgment will be permanent and irreversible (v. 5), involving dispossession (v. 4) and humiliation. Micah 2:6–11 provides a logical response to verses 1–5, anticipating the objections that the prophet's message will encounter. Verses 6–11 continue the dialogue with the landowners, or with false prophets speaking on their behalf, as some suggest, and rebut them. Micah parodies their false assumptions (v. 6). For having made women and children their victims (vv. 8–9), they themselves will be denied enjoyment of the Promised Land (v. 10). The accused have violated covenant standards (vv. 8b–c, 9). This dismisses their claim to walk uprightly (v. 7). Because they have not acted as Yahweh's people should act, they have become Yahweh's enemy (v. 8a). They have forfeited the right to the patience and protection of Yahweh that he promised his people (v. 10). While his opponents say "do not preach" (v. 6) to a prophet of God, they are willing to listen to a charlatan (v. 11). Micah 2:12–13 is generally taken as an oracle of salvation, but Sweeney's suggestion (2000, 366–67) that it is a judgment oracle better fits the context. In this interpretation, the verses refer to the loss of the Shephelah cities in King Sennacherib of Assyria's campaign in 701 b.c., in which inhabitants were led away as sheep for the slaughter. That Yahweh stands at their head indicates the he is the cause of the exile.

Chapter 3 is moving toward a clear goal—the destruction of Jerusalem. Leaders, probably military leaders (Heb. *qatsin*), failing to render just decisions (v. 1) and inverting values (vv. 2–3) in acts of terror and violence, are bringing on the coming disaster. Prophets have been (vv. 5–8) complicit with them in preparing for war. The civil leadership (vv. 9–12), priests, and prophets accept bribes that deter them from carrying out their responsibilities. They foster a false hope (vv. 11–12) that Yahweh will protect Jerusalem. Micah is convinced that Yahweh has withdrawn his protection. When judgment comes, Yahweh will ignore cries for help (vv. 4, 7), and the military destruction of Jerusalem impends. Beyond judgment, however, there will be a transformation and world influence (4:1–5) for Zion. Micah 3:1–12 could fit the period of the Syro-Ephraimite confrontation with Judah (734 b.c.), when Ahaz's decision not to support Samaria was popularly disputed (cf. Isa. 8:6; Mic. 3:1–4). As the result of Ahaz's deceit, Micah sees the destruction of Jerusalem as a future certainty.

Micah opens his discourse with a summons to hear, addressed to the heads and commanders of Judah and Israel (both cf. 3:9–12). Micah 3:2–3, in which Micah sets forth a rapid series of accusations against them, is designed to develop the accusation against the national leaders. However, the reality has been their cruel and violent conduct (vv. 2–3). Acts of terror and violence (vv. 2–4) directed against the oppressed people of Yahweh (vv. 3, 5) are suggested. The rulers, of all people, should know justice. He seeks to shatter his audience's confidence in Yahweh's protection of Jerusalem. In verse 2, they hate the good and love evil; values are inverted, as demonstrated by their refusal to abide by the decision, perhaps made by King Ahaz, to remain neutral in the conflict. Cries for help when the reversal comes (vv. 4, 7) will not be heard. These leaders have undertaken action harmful to the nation, and they will bring about the destruction of Jerusalem. The prophets (vv. 5–8), who spoke for payment, appear to have been accomplices. Prophets who expect fees will be denied spiritual gifts—unlike Micah, who points to the power resident in him (v. 8). In 3:8, Micah, to win the confidence of his audience, gives a description of his character and mission that stands in sharp contrast to those of his opponents. True prophecy, he claims, is only possible through the Spirit of Yahweh, a traditionally correct observation (cf. 1 Kings 22). Leadership, based upon bloodshed and corruption, will be the ruin of Jerusalem and the temple (vv. 9–12). They, like the leaders (3:9–12), accept bribes that prevent them from faithfully executing their authority, and they seem to propagate the false hope that Yahweh will protect Jerusalem in spite of their deeds. The oppressors appear to hope to build Jerusalem by these deeds (3:10), but the result will be the destruction of Jerusalem (v. 12). Finally, the military destruction of Jerusalem will be the sure sign that Yahweh has withdrawn his help and protection from the city

Micah 4–5 has in view the eschatological divine rule over a restored people. Each of the seven oracles in the section takes its rise in doom and passes on quickly to hope. While the oracles lack formal connection, by repetition their message is clear. Jerusalem and the people of God will be vindicated.

Micah 4:1–8 assumes the impending disaster of 3:9–12. The message of 3:9–12, the building up of Zion, is continued in 4:1–5, but while this is by bloodshed and violence in 3:9–12, it is Yahweh (4:1–5) who builds Jerusalem up so that she receives world acclaim (cf. v. 8). Human efforts to build a New Jerusalem will fail, but God will succeed. The judgment upon the priests, prophets, and heads of Israel will result in their removal by Yahweh (3:9–12), and then in Yahweh's restoration (4:1–5). Micah 4:1–5 strikes the note familiar from Isaiah 2:2–5: Jerusalem will be the world center to which all nations will flow in pilgrimage. Yahweh's law will regulate the affairs of nations. Against the claim that 4:1–5 stems from the postexilic period, the notion of a glorious Zion would hardly have developed in postexilic times.

Micah believes in a restoration beyond the judgment. He invites his audience in verses 6–8 to look beyond the destruction that must happen. In Micah 4:6–8, shepherd imagery is used to depict the final state of the remnant people of God—they will be shepherded by Yahweh, after having been abused by corrupt Jerusalem leadership. Verse 8 and its promise underscore further the certainty of the Davidic dynasty's future. The series of ancient names used in verse 8 for the Davidic house is the climax of the speech. Micah 4:8 makes clear that a Davidic king will again rule over Jerusalem. "Tower of the flock" in 4:8 parallels "Ophel of the daughter of Zion." Ophel is probably the hill, the original Canaanite town, the ridge, on which the old city of David was built. The future monarchy will rule a transformed Israel.

Micah 4:9–5:15 assumes a time of distress (4:9–11) to be followed by a time of salvation (4:12–13), through a messianic intervention and victory (4:14–5:4a; Eng. 5:1–5a). The victorious remnant (5:4b–8; Eng. 5:5b–5:9) is then refined and the nations judged (5:9–14; Eng. 5:10–15). The section including 4:9–5:14 appears to depict the conditions of the Syro-Ephraimite siege of Jerusalem (ca. 734–733 B.C.; Shaw 1993, 156–57). The prophet, however, seems confident of Jerusalem's ability to deal with the invasion.

Jerusalem's present predicament (vv. 9–10) will be exacerbated by exile from the city, even as far as Babylonia (v. 10; cf. Shaw 1993, 135). The population is in panic and distress, with doubts, perhaps, about the adequacy of the leadership, even though the king (whom some take to be Yahweh) is in their midst (vv. 9–10). The presence of the Davidic king in Jerusalem was a sign of God's choice of Zion, for whom Yahweh pledged to defeat the king's enemies (Ps. 2; 89:20–23; 110; 132). Micah 4:9 reproaches Jerusalem for its unbelief. The severity of these doubts and fears may be indicated by the questions of 4:10, which contemplate capture and then exile of the people. But Yahweh will rescue them from Babylon.

Now, however, nations as confederates are gathered around Jerusalem, whose situation is hopeless, but Yahweh intervenes. This passage seems to reflect the belief that Yahweh gathers the nations to Jerusalem in order to defeat them. This defeat will occur on Zion itself. The leading questions of 4:10 remind the people of this theology, which Micah then articulates in verses 11–13. The present siege will result in victory, not defeat. The time beyond the destruction will be the time when an earlier oracle concerning Jerusalem will be fulfilled, and Yahweh will rule from an exalted Jerusalem, to which nations will come to learn of him (vv. 11–13). This will be a time when Israel will be gathered and reunited.

Verse 14 (Eng. 5:1) points to the victorious outcome of the siege, with the concept of the siege enveloping the section (4:9; 5:1). The city is besieged and seemingly without hope (v. 1). The invading king, the judge of Israel (i.e., the northern king, Pekah), will be humiliated. For Micah, the present siege will conclude with a dramatic demonstration of Yahweh's will and ability to rescue Zion.

Micah 5:2–6 seems to refer to a dramatic new beginning as in David's time. Verse 2 concerns the choice of a great ruler from a small or insignificant place. He stands for Yahweh and will rule in the strength of Yahweh; his will is subordinated to Yahweh. This one shall be the one of peace (v. 5). The humble origins of the Davidic king, as well as the emphasis on the divine initiative, remind us of 2 Samuel 7. However, the ideal ruler comes from among the descendants of David, so this passage is not a rejection of the dynasty, as some allege. Yahweh is generally agreed to be the subject of "he will give them up" (v. 3), that is, into the hands of the enemy. When the ideal ruler materializes, there will be a restoration from a prior punishment. The worldwide rule of the messianic king is the subject of verse 4. These verses provide prophetic assurance to Judah in the perilous times of the Jerusalem siege of 701 B.C. Not only will Yahweh lift that siege, but the time will come when Yahweh's Davidic representative will reign universally. Judaism still hopes for a fulfillment of that assurance—one that Christians find in the death and resurrection of Jesus of Nazareth.

Micah 5:5b–8 returns to the present situation of a threatened attack by Assyria, likely to occur as an intervention into the disordered political situation of the time. By the seven shepherds and eight principal men (v. 5), the prophet is using a traditional formula to refer to a multiplicity of instances (cf. Amos 1:3; Prov. 30:8; Sweeney 2000, 390). He may, as Sweeney suggests, be referring to the many Israelite revolts that will break out at the time of Assyria's final overthrow.

Appealing to national and religious pride, Micah paints a picture of a powerful, restored Israel, able to turn back a hostile invasion and unchallenged among the nations. The climax of the refutation is the exhortation of verse 9, which once again calls for Israel's victory over all her enemies. The inclusive phrase "all your enemies" ties with a future possible situation. The remnant is thus like a lion among the sheep. The remnant represents the divine victor and, on Yahweh's behalf, assumes the role of a lion among the nations. The prophet assumes that if Assyria attacks Jerusalem, the remnant of Jacob will assume its place among the mighty nations of the coalition, as a nation empowered by Yahweh himself, and thus be able to repel an Assyrian attack (5:9). The discourse has proceeded from the call for the defeat of Judah's enemies 4:9–5:1, to the description of a future transformed Israel, united and secure among the nations and protected by Yahweh's power. Micah 5:1–7 (v. 6) indicates a cataclysmic defeat for Assyria.

In 5:10–15, the situation is summarized, and these verses indicate the conditions necessary for Yahweh's victory. The nation is under threat from powerful foes. She takes refuge in her defenses, which Yahweh will destroy as well as the idols that stand behind them. He will then become the nation's strength, turning his power against the nations. Micah 5:10–15 indicates that, stripped of weapons, certain religious artifacts, and religious practices, the Israel of the future will be better able to trust in Yahweh alone.

The prophet, in 4:9–5:15, thus has an optimistic look at current events. He does not deny the difficulty of the present, but confronts it with the well-established Zion traditions. This leads to the conviction that Zion will triumph and an ideal ruler will emerge. Micah 5:10–15 unites two ideas that have furnished the proof for Micah's discourse. Both the ideology of Jerusalem and the royal ideology include the destruction of weapons and the coming of peace. Yahweh's declaration in verses 10–15, that the weapons of war will be eliminated, draws together the concept of the tradition of the ideal ruler, and the tradition of Zion, and points to the results of Jerusalem's victory and the emergence of the Davidic ruler. These verses unite the theme of judgment and transformation. Each of these carefully compiled episodes in Micah 4–5 has in view some threat to Zion and the eventual removal of that peril.

Yahweh's Appeal to Israel and Judah to Return (Mic. 6:1–16)

In the famous passage of 6:1–8, Yahweh contends with his people. The issue at stake is the conduct of the people of God within the covenant. The case against Israel is presented in lawsuit fashion in verses 1–5. The repeated summons "to hear" (vv. 1–2) is intended to provoke the audience to attention, and the summoning of the natural elements as witnesses adds a dramatic quality. Micah 6:3–8 describes the elements of the dispute. The verses set forth the position of the participants in the case. The use of dialogue heightens the dramatic effect, and thus holds the attention of the audience. In reply, Yahweh recites his deeds of kindness toward Israel, particularly her deliverance from foreign oppressors (v. 5). Israel asks what will avert the judgment (vv. 6–7). The accusing questions of 6:6–7 also suggest a sense of desperation. In an endeavor to gain

Yahweh's favor, increasingly costly sacrifices, perhaps including child sacrifice, have been scheduled. Micah responds with what is already known, namely, that obedience is better than sacrifice (v. 8). Micah is not rejecting sacrifice but the view that Yahweh's favor is to be obtained by costly and elaborate sacrifices. The present efforts to obtain Yahweh's favor are both desperate and misplaced. The prophet is ridiculing the suggestion that Yahweh's favor can be won by elaborate sacrificial rituals.

To establish justice is to uphold what is right, according to Yahweh's will, both in legal proceedings and in life. To walk wisely with your God involved obedience and the employment of discretion, prudence, and wisdom in the religious life. *Hesed* is the more difficult middle term. It signifies goodness and kindness beyond what could be expected. The heart of the matter is generous and beneficial action that could not be required. Verses 9–12 take up the reasons for the indictment: the familiar social sins, commercial exactions, and extortion. The series of rhetorical questions in verses 10–11a is designed to point to clear violations of Yahweh's will. It is not clear what city is on view in 6:9–16. It does not seem to be Jerusalem, since Davidic and Zion traditions are lacking in this section. It may be Samaria. The judgment sentence follows in verses 13–15; the economy will be stricken (a punishment that again fits the crime). However, the audience seems recently to have experienced great misfortune (cf. 6:13). They have been sick with smiting, made desolate on account of their sins. A summary, and repetition of and reasons for the punishment complete the chapter (v. 16). Judah and her leadership are likened to the days of Omri and Ahab in the northern kingdom. The reference to statutes of Omri and Ahab could refer to economic misdeeds, or idolatry, or apostasy. Or, it might be a reference to the continuation of the Omri dynasty policy of foreign alliances. Punishment is inevitable.

Micah's Confidence in Israel's Future (Mic. 7:1–20)

The lament tones in 7:1–7 begin with the harvest imagery of 7:1 that echoes the picture of judgment of 6:11. Micah 7:1–7 underscores the main point of the total prophetic address, prophetic distress over the calamitous collapse of society of Micah's day and its destructive effect upon personal relationships (vv. 2–6). His search for a righteous individual is as useless as the search for harvest fruit when even the gleanings have gone. In fact, even the best leaders of society are briers and thorns instead of desired fruit. The picture of society as an empty, thorn-infested field makes vivid Micah's case and creates an emotional response of horror in his audience (Shaw 1993, 187). Micah 7:3 underlines the failure of leadership in which the actions of the prince, judge, and great ones have been responsible for the failure of justice and order.

The song of trust in verses 8–10, which focuses on divine intervention expected for a defeated people, reasserts Israel's relationship with God. Micah 7:8–20 looks beyond possible destruction to some sort of divine intervention and restoration. In 6:16, the city is put to shame, but, in 7:16, the nations are to be made ashamed of their deeds.

The community has been defeated and is powerless to act on its own. The action envisioned by Micah is not resistance and struggle but a quiet bearing of the wrath of Yahweh, and a waiting for Yahweh to restore the community and to exercise justice. In 7:11–13, the community dwells in apparently much reduced territory. Thus the immediate future calls upon the people to bear patiently the wrath of God. Restoration and rebuilding, for which Micah hopes, will come in Yahweh's time, when he intervenes. Many, it seems, want to rebuild defenses and repudiate decrees, but this, says Micah, will result in greater destruction and defeat. The plea that God's people may dwell in Bashan and Gilead (v. 14c) seems to indicate that Transjordan has been lost. While verse 14c is clear, verse 14b is difficult. The image of verse 14b is that in which people are confined to forest and upland that are surrounded by fertile land occupied by others. The metaphor of sheep and shepherd (v. 14) reiterates the relationship established in verses 8–10. Yahweh can be trusted, but they must wait for him to act and depend on his guidance. A second reason why Yahweh can be trusted is found in verse 15. Here Yahweh promises his intervention, announced in verses 9–10, which recalls his exodus action. Verses 16–17 show the results of causing the enemy to see wonders. The results are fear on the part of the hostile nations and deep humiliation when Yahweh acts. Verse 17 depicts the enemy as humiliated, like a serpent licking the dust.

Undergirding the prophet's belief that restoration will come about as a result of Yahweh's actions is his belief in the faithfulness of Yahweh (v. 18). This confidence makes it possible to bear the present, and to wait patiently for redemption. This view of Yahweh enables Micah to conclude with a vow or an exclamation of praise (vv. 18–20). Yahweh can be trusted, since his nature is to have compassion and not to remain angry (cf. Exod. 34:6; Neh. 9:18; Ps. 86:15; 103:8; 145:8). The ground of this prophetic appeal to Yahweh is the immeasurable capacity of God to forgive and his steadfast adherence to the Abrahamic covenant (vv. 18–20).

This prophecy of Micah, the elder from Moresheth (note Jer. 26:17–18), breathes the passionate conviction of a man who, in his own town gates of Judah, has witnessed much of the social inequities and the partialities in leadership to which he refers. He offers no new solutions for them, and his message is still the unpalatable prophetic conviction that offenses against the covenant will be responded to with appropriate punishment. Unlike his contemporary, Isaiah, he offers no reassurance of the inviolability of Zion. He relies greatly, however, upon the character of Yahweh, recognizing that Yahweh will preserve Israel in spite of herself, although judgment from Yahweh will come. Yahweh's commitment, given to Israel's forefather Abraham, will finally be translated into the reality of Yahweh's rule over a purified remnant people from Zion, and the order of creation will be affected.

19

Nahum

The subject matter of this superbly artistic book, whose wealth of imagery must not be entirely reduced to historical specifics, is narrowly directed to the impending fall of the Assyrian capital, Nineveh, which fell in 612 B.C. Like Obadiah, Nahum singles out a Gentile power as the incarnation of world evil.

Judgment and Salvation (Nah. 1:1–14)

After the superscription, Nahum 1:2–8 offers a broken alphabetic poem (acrostic) that is a theological reminder to Judah of Yahweh's character as judge of his world. The word "avenging" is the controlling word in verses 2–3a, which depict the attributes of the Divine Warrior, who is about to arrive with universal judgment (vv. 3b–8). Verses 2–3 present a complete witness to God's covenant presence in obedient Israel. While the word "jealous" (v. 2) indicates the disposition of Yahweh to brook no rivals, to demand recognition of his universal sovereignty, "avenging" indicates the practical implications of Yahweh's jealousy. "To avenge" is used in biblical contexts in which the sense demanded is "punish" or "vindicate," depending on the subject referred to. (In Josh. 10:13, "punish" is required, while "vindication" for Yahweh's people is intended in Judg. 11:36; 2 Sam. 22:48. The "day of vengeance of our God" in Isa. 61:1–4 is the day on which Yahweh intervenes to rescue the elect and to bring them salvation.) Although God is slow to anger (v. 3), and Assyrian tyranny had tormented Judah for more than one hundred years, God is now about to intervene and destroy the tyrant.

After the manifestation of the divine character, expressed in terms of the older cultic confessions (cf. Nah. 1:3a and Exod. 34:6; Num. 14:18; etc.), the Divine Warrior's judgment occurs (Nah. 1:3b–8). The effects of this judgment are expressed in typical poetic imagery as a reversal of the creation victory: the sea is rebuked, sterility replaces fertility, and the world and its inhabitants are convulsed and unable to face Yahweh's fury (vv. 4–6). God will bring chaos, in the shape of Assyria, under control. Assyria will be burned up (v. 6) by Yahweh's anger. This act of judgment (vv. 7–8) is viewed from the two perspectives involved in our earlier representation of Yahweh, as destroyer of the wicked and, in demonstration of his grace, the vindicator of the faithful.

The judgment oracle in Nahum 1:9–11 becomes a particular application of these eschatological and general truths, as it declares the senselessness of Assyria's pitting herself against the controller of history. A divine pronouncement follows in verses 12–14, apparently foreshadowing salvation for Judah, who is never again to be afflicted by Assyria.

Announcement of Assyria's Fall (Nah. 1:15–2:13)

Nahum 1:15–2:2 reflects what was predicted in Nahum 1, commencing with a heraldic announcement of the fall of Assyria (1:15), the return of the exiles (perhaps the dispersed north), and the siege of Nineveh (2:1). The difficult verse 2 is not a parenthetical statement, nor should it be joined to verse 3, but more probably refers to the return of the northern exiles following the Assyrian collapse, and the restoration of the glory of Israel, the people of God.

This summary is then developed in the remainder of Nahum 2. The attack by the divine army, the defense of the Assyrian capital, Nineveh, and its final ruin are the subject of Nahum 2:3–10. Verses 3–4 describe the onslaught against the outer suburbs of Nineveh. The Assyrians stumble as they group to defend the walls of Nineveh. Finally, the river gates of Nineveh are opened and the attackers pour through, with the distress of the city personified in verse 7. With the opening of the river gates (v. 6), Nineveh is inundated. The lionlike Assyria, who had filled its cave with prey, is then depicted as desolate in the taunting poem with which the chapter concludes (vv. 11–13).

The Fall of Nineveh (Nah. 3)

In Nahum 3:1–7, the fate of Nineveh, doomed by God, is detailed in the woe oracle. Verses 1–3 survey the city as attacked by the military juggernaut. The reason is advanced in verse 4: the international harlotry of Assyria has enticed her world to ruin. Verses 1–4 advance the accusation: Assyria is an international harlot, outwardly beautiful but inwardly repulsive. Assyria's beauty is to be shown as sordid and ugly (v. 6), pointing to the merciless treatment she will receive. When Assyria is done to death (v. 7), no one will mourn. In verses 8–10, Nineveh is compared to the magnificent Thebes, the first great city in the Orient. Assyria's Ashurbanipal sacked Thebes in 663 B.C. History thus seemed to show that Nineveh was superior and better. Human might, however, is nothing when compared to the might of God. Like Nineveh, Thebes (v. 8) was also protected by water. Nineveh will stagger helplessly, mocked by Yahweh's prophet. Nineveh's forts, when shaken like ripe figs, will fall (v. 12). Nineveh's vaunted warriors will become like weak women (v. 13).

Nineveh is taunted to prepare for the siege (v. 14). She will prepare in vain, for the fire of divine judgment will engulf her, as will the traditionally associated judgment of sword and plague (v. 15a). She can multiply her defenses, but armies and riches will not save her (vv. 15b–17). Her vaunted resources (v. 16) and her organizational leadership (v. 17) will all be swept away.

The dirge of verse 18 finally ends the book. Assyria is now scattered like sheep without shepherds. Nahum considers Assyria's epitaph, as the prophecy concludes (3:18–19). Her kings are dead, her armies scattered. There is a sound of thunderous clapping from the world at Nineveh's fall. Assyria's passage from the scene of history provides the occasion for universal rejoicing.

The narrow range of this book seems particularly nationalistic, but it is not merely so. Nahum paints a very broad scenario of history. His concerns are not the state of Judean religious health, nor even the ultimate future of the people of God. Thus the book airs no social problems or, indeed, Zion theology. Rather, Nahum is drawing our attention to the ultimate security for the people of God that divine control over history affords. That this truth is particularly applied to a problem manifest in his day does not lessen its generality. God, the righteous judge, surveys human affairs. This fact alone ensures the comfort of his people. Nahum (whose name means "comfort") conveys this truth.

20

Habakkuk

The prophecy of Habakkuk is set between the rise of the Babylonian power (626 B.C.) and the fall of Jerusalem (587/6 B.C.). Habakkuk 1:1 designates what is to follow as a "burden" (Heb. *massaʾ*, 1:1), a designation argued to be a specific type of prophetic discourse intended to explain how Yahweh's intention is to be manifested in human affairs (Sweeney 1991b, 65).

The key to understanding the book appears to be the psalm of chapter 3, in which Habakkuk is encouraged to see the events of his own day through the perspective that the history of salvation offers. This will provide an attestation for divine fidelity, the major theme of Habakkuk 2.

Dialogue between Habakkuk and Yahweh (Hab. 1:1–2:4)

The first chapter is structured around two prophetic laments (1:2–4, 12–17), to which divine responses are given (1:5–11; 2:1–4, the second reported by the prophet). Habakkuk's complaint arises from the fact that a plea for divine intervention to remedy social breakdown caused by Chaldean oppression (cf. 1:12–17) has so far gone unheard. How long (v. 2) must he cry out concerning injustice, before God will acknowledge the situation and correct it? Why is he forced to regard the commotion and strife they generate (v. 3)? As a result (v. 4a), social order has broken down; Torah and justice are dismissed (v. 4b). In this breakdown of order, the wicked oppress (v. 4b) the righteous, perverting justice.

His complaint centers upon the apparently ineffective character of the prophetic proclamation of Torah. The second major section (1:5–11) is delivered in second-person-plural address. Verse 6 identifies the speaker as Yahweh. A description of the Chaldean invasion to come follows in verses 6–11 as a response to the previous complaint. These verses seem directed to the prophet and his adherents, that is, the righteous (cf. 1:2–4). God has raised up the Chaldeans (vv. 5–6), but not as the means of correcting the injustice. Rather, they may be viewed as its cause (Sweeney 1991b, 67). The imposition of Babylonian authority is concomitant with the breakdown of justice for the righteous (Hab. 1:2–4). The Chaldeans are an apostate and guilty nation, attributing their success to their own strength rather than to God. But the reality of the divine word will be seen in the impending world change, which will judge the wicked conduct of Judea. Babylon is about to move to the center of the political stage, replacing the oppressing Assyria, under whom Judean wickedness apparently flourished, a fact that will astonish the Judean population (v. 5). Verses 1–11 tell Judah that it will survive and that justice will ultimately prevail.

Habakkuk 1:12–17, which elaborates the complaint of 1:2–4, begins with a rhetorical question, addressed by the prophet to God (v. 12a), establishing Yahweh's antiquity and immortality. The statement *lo namut,* "we shall not die," is one of the *tiqqune soperim,* the corrections of the scribes, which should actually read *lo tamu,* "you shall not die," a confession of Yahweh's eternal nature and control of history. Habakkuk 1:12 is not expressing a hope for deliverance by the Chaldeans. The *qedem* 'antiquity' (1:12) is a word often used to refer to Yahweh's role as creator and master of the world. This question establishes the premise for the following material that Yahweh, as creator and master of the world, is capable of intervening, either to establish the Chaldeans or to remove them. This is made clear by the two statements that follow in verse 12b and verse 13a. Verse 12 states that Yahweh has appointed them for justice/law and arbitration (*hokiah*), that is, they have been established to rule, to punish previous Judean injustice, but not to provide justice in itself. Verse 13a asserts that Yahweh is incapable of looking upon wrong, that is, of injustice. Why, then, in the light of this admitted divine control over history, can God (v. 13b) maintain inaction while the wicked (Babylonians) consume the righteous? Will not Yahweh exercise control over his own creation, as he clearly can (v. 14)? Attention then seems to return to the Babylonians (vv. 15–17), who, limited and unaware of the role they play, worship the implements of war by which they impose their might. The Chaldeans are pictured as fishermen ensnaring the nations in their nets, worshiping their nets, that is, military power. The section ends with the prophet reiterating the question to God: how long will the Chaldeans have free reign in the world to continue this destruction and slaughter? Habakkuk 1:12–17 thus indicates prophetic disquiet with the divine answer of 1:5–11. How can the Chaldeans be the answer? We know, of course, that they are not. They bring one era of injustice to an end, only to promote another.

Habakkuk 2:1–20

Habakkuk 2:1 provides the context for the report/explanation of Yahweh's response in verses 2–20 (Sweeney 1991b, 71). The prophet is now at his watch station, needing only to wait (v. 1) for the turn of events (2:2–20) to come in answer to his complaint (v. 1b). The section comprises two basic parts: the report of Yahweh's response in verses 2–4, and Habakkuk's explication of that response in verses 5–20.

The answer comes, reported by Habakkuk from Yahweh (v. 2), to record the vision plainly so that the runner or messenger may proclaim it. Habakkuk must wait for the vision, for it will surely come at the appointed time. The second response of Yahweh (v. 4) states the basic meaning or principle of the vision: the righteous shall live and the wicked shall fall, that is, the righteous will ultimately triumph. Habakkuk 2:4b portrays the stability of the righteous and provides the necessary contrast with those whose life is unstable due to arrogance (cf. the meaning of Heb 'pl 'proud' at Num. 14:44b). Habakkuk 2:4a refers to the Chaldeans puffed up by their international successes (cf. 1:13), and verse 4b refers to trustful Judah. In sum, the verse promises that oppression will end with the downfall of Chaldea. This is supported by what follows in 2:5–20 (Sweeney 1991b, 70).

Habakkuk's explanation of Yahweh's response appears in 2:5–20. Habakkuk 2:5 explains verse 4 by comparing the instability of the wicked to the behavior of a drunk progressively overcome by wine. The report then proceeds by use of a second-person taunt song of the nations (vv. 6b–17), presupposing an international situation (vv. 6a, 8a, 10b, 13b). The appearance of the oppressive Chaldeans is an act of God. They will fall as a result of excessive greed and oppressive policies. The four woes constituting verses 6b–17 are those of the plundering oppressor (vv. 6b–8), which show that exploiters' attempts to insulate themselves against disaster will not avail; woes of those "who get evil gain for your houses" (vv. 9–11); woes of the vaunted city-builder (vv. 12–14) who ignores the real purpose of creation—society founded on mutual justice; and woes of Babylon as world seducer and idolater (vv. 15–17). Finally, the root cause of oppression is Babylon's human pride, which refuses to acknowledge the lordship of the Creator (vv. 18–19) and to admit the divine reality of Yahweh's rule over all creation as he sits enthroned in his holy temple (v. 20). Babylon's attitude—her abuses of power, political and social—will not go unpunished.

Habakkuk's Prayer (Hab. 3)

The psalm of chapter 3 provides the vision for which Habakkuk was bidden to wait. The form of the prayer is a petition (vv. 2–19a). The prayer is introduced (v. 2) by a plea to Yahweh on the basis of former divine acts, to manifest his power in present-day intervention. The psalm concludes in verses 16–19a with a profound statement of confidence. Verse 16 refers to the psalmist's nervous anticipation that waits for the day of distress against the invader, Babylon. Verse 17 refers to the present desolate state of the land, and verses 18–19a conclude with an expression of confidence in Yahweh.

By its survey of the past history of Israel's salvation, the psalm furnishes a demonstration of divine fidelity that assures the future of the righteous. It is characterized by the use of mythological motifs, particularly of divine defeat of chaos. The theophany report (vv. 3–15) refers to the manifestation, in time past, of the Divine Warrior (vv. 3–6) with the battle report (v. 7). Yahweh comes from Sinai as Lord of creation (v. 3), as the Divine Warrior, who is armed with supernatural weapons and will intervene for his people (v. 4). He convulses animate and inanimate creation (v. 6). Verses 8–15 are addressed to Yahweh and concern the purpose for which he will come. This section celebrates again the basic victory of the exodus, by which Israel's place within history was established. Poetic artistry and fact are mingled. Perhaps there are allusions to the plagues in verse 5 and to the wilderness march in verse 6 (compare the crossing of the sea and the Jordan in vv. 8–10 and the conquest's long day in v. 11). It is typical for descriptions of divine appearance to have mythological touches.

The purpose for which Yahweh had come (and is coming) is then explicated in 3:8–15. He is coming to defeat the primordial enemies—the river, the sea, the floods—which are to be riven (read v. 9b as "thou didst cleave the rivers of the earth" RSV) as the chaos dragon (Tiamat in the Babylonian epic *Enuma Elish*) was split asunder in the creation battle, and is now personified in some new historical encounter. Creation (the mountains, sun, and moon in vv. 10–11) stands appalled at the prospect of this intervention, which recalls the primordial battles, but which is directed to the present threat facing Judah. The threat is personified in sea-dragon terms (read "tail to neck" in v. 13). This is the earth-shattering vision for which Habakkuk has waited. It does no more than simply insist that Yahweh is consistent; as he dealt with one threat in one crucial era of history, so he will meet another in this present era.

After this vision, we read of the response of the prophet. Awe (v. 16) turns to quiet commitment (v. 17), irrespective of events, to patience and confidence in God's strength (vv. 18–19). The life in which one must patiently wait has now been received through the vision delivered.

Habakkuk 3 expresses the confidence that the vision in 2:1–4 and Yahweh's righteousness will be realized when the people are delivered from oppression.

Habakkuk 1–2 explains that Yahweh has raised the Chaldean empire as part of a divine plan not immediately explained. Babylon, the cause of Judah's oppression, will be punished. This punishment will demonstrate (chap. 3) Yahweh's sovereignty over the world and, ultimately, divine righteousness as well. The book is affirmation of Yahweh's control of history, designed to convince Judah that Yahweh is maintaining fidelity in a crisis situation.

The Book of Habakkuk reveals to us this prophet's spiritual pilgrimage. He is finally moved to his position of 3:16–19 by the promptings of inner conviction in response to prayer. Habakkuk can now see that the power in Israel's past history is available to the righteous who shall live by faith. This book reveals a genuine sharing of a doubt that assails all believers, a feeling that God stands aside from the moral struggle of the believer. This doubt is removed not by the addition of new facts, but simply by the addition of a new perspective; not new revelation, but new insight into old revelation. The key verse, 2:4, is taken up repeatedly in the New Testament, admittedly in different contexts than the present, but nowhere more significantly than in Romans 1:17. There, the righteousness of God, which in that context appears to be divine fidelity to the patriarchal promises, is to be responded to by trust in the gospel that reveals God's righteousness, a gospel providing further attestation of the unchanging character of God in salvation and judgment. Habakkuk needed this reassurance, as did his times. Doubtless, having ascended to the heights (3:19), his ministry provided the confidence that the faithful of his day needed to capture his vision.

21

Zephaniah

Zephaniah prophesied concurrently with the early ministry of Jeremiah, but seemingly before the Josianic reforms of 621 B.C., since there are abundant references to syncretism.

Yahweh's Declaration of War on Judah (Zeph. 1:1–2:3)

After the superscription, the book opens with a threat from Yahweh to destroy everything on the face of the earth (Zeph. 1:2–3). This introduction sets the tone for both the prophecies and the conclusion of the book. This tone is seen in prophecies of sweeping judgment, under the broad orbit of the advent of the Day of Yahweh on Judah and on the nations mentioned thereafter. The book concludes on the same note, with the expected eschatology of Zion's world significance.

False worship, a typical prophetic theme, is the reason advanced for the initial attack on Judah and Jerusalem (1:4–6). The remnant of Baal (v. 4) would be the last vestige of Baal worship following the collapse of Assyrian authority. The accusation stems from the three national sins, exposed in verses 5–6: idolatry, syncretism, and indifference toward God. These had been attitudes fostered by the long reign of Manasseh and the short reign of his son, Amon. The cultic overtones of the Day-of-the-Lord theme that follows are thus clear (1:7–2:3), but the concept of the day transmutes into the imagery of holy war. In this great Day of the Lord, when the cultic acts are to be reversed (Judeans are to be Yahweh's sacrificial lambs; see v. 7), the Lord's sacrifice, preparatory to declaring holy war, has been prepared (v. 7).

Zephaniah 1:7–13 begins the prophet's command for silence before Yahweh. There can be no defense of their actions, and no protest is allowed. Yahweh will attack Jerusalem for its leaders' assimilation of foreign customs (v. 8), manifested particularly in their adoption of pagan religious practices (v. 9), which is naturally associated with social injustice. The statements directed against government officials and cultic functionaries (vv. 8–9) would support a purge of elements that were not loyal to Yahweh (v. 5b).

Ominously, Yahweh will enter from the north, the area of numinous threat (v. 10). Jerusalem's entrepreneurs and the economy that supports them will be removed (v. 11). In Jeremiah-like fashion, Yahweh will search Jerusalem with candles to expose the offenders (vv. 12–13; cf. Jer. 5:1), who, for too long, have been undisturbed in their view that God no longer governs the world (v. 12). Verse 13 contains four lines of covenant curse (Deut. 28:30, 39). No offense will escape divine scrutiny. Conditions at Bethel in Amos's time have been duplicated in Jerusalem (cf. Amos 6:1). People are at ease, theoretically holding a doctrine of Yahweh, but in practice denying his reality (Zeph. 1:12).

Verses 14–18 turn more narrowly to the theme of the Day of Yahweh. Zephaniah 1:14–18 consists of two basic subunits. Verses 14–16 contain the prophet's description of the day. In verses 17–18, the prophet describes the consequences of the Day of Yahweh for its victims. It is a day of cosmic distress and anguish (v. 15). Yahweh's battle cry is heard, and no fortifications can withstand his assault (v. 16). The dependency upon Amos 5:20 is clear. It is a day on which Yahweh will roar against Zion, a day when the universe is plunged back into primeval chaos. Warrior Yahweh advances upon his creation, beginning with his own household. Desolation, distress, and a terrible end await Jerusalem. Judah's population will grope in the dark like blind people (v. 17). No ransom can suffice to buy Yahweh off; God's jealousy will consume them in their rebellion (v. 18). Prominent in this first chapter is the divine word directly spoken by Yahweh himself (1:2–6, 8–13, 17); it is punctuated only by prophetic asides that add a graphic and vivid note to the nature of the divine threat.

Zephaniah 2:1–3:20

Zephaniah 2:1–3 is the introduction and premise to what follows, and is not connected with what has preceded (Sweeney 1991a, 397). Zephaniah 2:1–3 exhorts people to seek Yahweh, and the *ki* that follows gives the reason—the impending downfall of the Philistine cities. If people do not seek Yahweh, shown in their exercise of justice and humility, they will meet the same fate. The nation without shame is called to an assembly of repentance (2:1–3; there are reminiscences of Joel here). Whereas 1:2–18 focuses on the actions of Yahweh, 2:1–3 focuses on the actions of the people. The only hope advanced, however, is that by heeding such a call, the humble—that is, the obedient remnant—will be delivered.

Yahweh's Declaration of War on Judah's Enemies (Zeph. 2:4–15)

The remainder of chapter 2 is given over to oracles delivered against foreign nations (vv. 4–15). The book is not universal in its assessment of the nations, for those listed do not provide a universal model but form a comprehensive list of King Josiah's enemies (Christensen 1984). Zephaniah 2:3 provides the basis for the entire exhortation that follows (2:4–3:20). Statements concerning the four Philistine cities are grouped in pairs: Gaza and Ashkelon (v. 4a), Ashdod and Ekron (v. 4b). The following material in 2:5–3:20 explains the effect of this disaster. The first section (2:5–15) is primarily concerned with the nations, with a secondary focus on the remnant of the house of Judah/my people. The second section (3:1–20) is primarily concerned with Jerusalem and Israel, with a secondary focus on the nations. When taken together, they explain the significance of the impending events for Jerusalem and Judah among the nations, beginning with the Philistines (Sweeney 1991a, 400). Zephaniah 2:5–15 contains a series of four prophetic announcements of judgment against Philistia (vv. 5–7), Moab and Ammon (vv. 8–11), Cush (v. 12), and Assyria (vv. 13–15) as Yahweh's punishment. The reason for the selection of these nations will become apparent in the light of the historical context of Zephaniah.

Unlike the situation confronting Amos, who needed to establish plausibility before turning to Judah and Israel, Judah, at this point in history, needs no convincing of the reality of the threat, and Zephaniah thus begins the chapter with her. The world-shattering character of her judgment has a ripple effect on the surrounding nations—the traditional enemies of Judah to the west; Philistia (vv. 4–7), whose busy commercial cities will become grazing grounds; and to the east, on boastful Moab and Ammon (vv. 8–11). After their judgment, the remnant of Israel will possess the territory of the enemy. Brief oracles against Ethiopia (which would include Egypt), a power to the south (2:12), and, in language reminiscent of Nahum, against Assyria exulting in her independence in the north (vv. 13–15) conclude the chapter.

Jerusalem's Destruction and Her Future (Zeph. 3)

Zephaniah 3:1–20 begins with a prophetic announcement of salvation for Jerusalem, in 3:1–13. Jerusalem becomes the subject of the lament in 3:1–5. While verses 1–4 focus on Jerusalem's guilt, verse 5 focuses on Yahweh's response to that guilt. Again, the problem is corrupt leadership. Princes, judges, prophets, and priests have all perverted their roles, while the ideal leadership of Yahweh, available continually to the community, has been ignored (v. 5). Yahweh's speech in verses 6–13 also focuses on the situation outlined in verses 1–4. The first subunit (vv. 6–7) describes Yahweh's past action against the nations. Judah's negative reaction is reported in verse 6b. Jerusalem had not responded (v. 7) to such divine interventions (cf. Assyria's defeat in 701 b.c.).

This prophecy ends on a note of great hope. Verses 9–10 announce Yahweh's action to the nations, calling them to serve him (v. 9), and the reaction, the offering by the exiles (v. 10). The judgment of Babel will be reversed (v. 9), and the foundation of human unity will be Yahweh. The centrality of Jerusalem is implied in verse 10. Pride will depart from Jerusalem (v. 11). The return of the scattered people of God, whose tongues will demonstrate the new gift of pure lips, in covenant-keeping obedience, will characterize this New Jerusalem (vv. 11–13). Verses 11–12 describe Yahweh's removal of arrogance from Jerusalem (v. 11) and from the remaining humble people (v. 12). Verse 13 then describes the righteous members of the remnant of Israel who will dwell there.

Following this (3:14–20), the prophet summons Jerusalem and Israel to rejoice, a summons that provides assurance to the audience, that the promises previously mentioned will be realized. The summons (v. 14) is provided with the basis (v. 15) that Yahweh has removed the judgment, and now reigns as king of Israel in Jerusalem. The prophet reports this assurance to Jerusalem in 3:16–20. Verses 16–17 contain the assurance reported by the prophet, followed by the basis for it in verse 17, which announces Yahweh's rejoicing over Jerusalem. Verses 18–20 report Yahweh's assurance speech. The speech begins with Yahweh's statement concerning his purge of the wicked from Jerusalem (v. 18), followed by his statement concerning his exaltation of Jerusalem in verses 19–20. Verse 19 (second-person, feminine-singular objects) is directed to Jerusalem, which will receive the returning exiles, and verse 20 (second-person masculine plural) is directed to Israel, which will return to Jerusalem, reestablishing the unity of the people of God.

In Josiah's time, there was a concern for the reunification of Judah and Israel, and the concept of the remnant here is positive. They are survivors of past punishment who represent the divine pledge of national restoration. The "remnant of the house of Judah" indicates that Judah represented the hope for all Israel following the fall of the northern kingdom in 722/21 B.C.

The intention of the book is to exhort the audience and to convince it to alter its behavior in order to avoid the announced punishment and to be counted among those who enjoy the future restoration. The prophetic announcement of the Day of Yahweh, in 1:2–18, prepares for Zephaniah's exhortation to seek Yahweh in 2:1–3:20.

Zephaniah brings to the south Isaiah's message of the security of the faithful under the kingship of Yahweh, the fidelity of Yahweh to his Abrahamic promises, and the dominant centrality of Jerusalem/Zion, where Yahweh's throne will be established. The prophecy has thus moved from universal judgment to the universality of salvation in a judged world where the Abrahamic promise of a great name for his descendants has been realized in the gathered remnant, through whom the world, at large, is to be blessed.

22

Haggai

Haggai's four oracles are dated within the book as ranging between August and December 520 B.C. After a period of uncertainty within the Persian Empire, Darius I had recently come to power. The aim of this brief prophecy is clear: to persuade the returned exiles in Jerusalem and in what remained of Judah, to rebuild the temple. There is some superficial difficulty in reconciling the accounts of Ezra, Haggai, and Zechariah as to the date of the commencement of work on the Second Temple, and the identity of the temple builder. Ezra 3:8 suggests that the work was begun by Zerubbabel, which is supported by Haggai 1:12–14 and Zechariah 4:9. Ezra 1:8 and 5:14–16 indicate that it was Sheshbazzar, the prince of Judah and Persian-appointed governor. We note that Zerubbabel's name is mentioned when the religious implications of the building operations are in view (Ezra 3), and Sheshbazzar's when the secular. If we accept the further suggestion that the verb underlying the somewhat puzzling phrase "lay the foundation" (Ezra 3:6, 10; 5:16; Hag. 2:18; Zech. 4:9) is more generally used to refer to progressive stages in the building operations (Andersen 1958), then the problem is solved. In Haggai's day, the statement that "this house lies in ruins" (Hag. 1:4) would then mean that the building was partially reconstructed, but not frequented by worshipers (i.e., that it was desolate).

Israel's Repentance (Hag. 1)

The political situation in the Persian Empire may have contributed to the lethargy that Haggai addresses. Cyrus, the conqueror of Babylon, died in 530/529 B.C. and was succeeded by his son Cambyses, who later died by his own hand in 522. After several revolts, Darius I (522–486 B.C.) followed him. Darius's position was not fully secure until 520 B.C., about the period when Haggai writes. Haggai 1:1–2 identifies the prophet, the people, and the problem he will address. Speaking on the first day of the month, perhaps on the occasion of a festival or holy day, Haggai addresses his first charge to the community leaders Zerubbabel and Joshua, Davidic representative and high priest, respectively. Although the returnees have been restored in their land (v. 4), they continue to insist that conditions are not yet conducive to the rebuilding of the temple.

The ground of difficulty between the prophet and the community is quickly established in Haggai 1:4–11. Although work had apparently begun upon the temple in the initial period of the return (538 B.C.), it had not been undertaken with any degree of thoroughness. Although the temple was seemingly standing in Haggai's time (the comparison in 1:4 between the state of the temple and the manner in which the people are housed, i.e., in "paneled houses," suggests that the temple is nearly completed but requires roofing), it was not the focus of public attention. The site, as a worship center, seems to have been deserted (I am taking the Hebrew word *hareb* 'desolate' in the sense of "unfrequented"). Haggai's argument in 1:4–11 may be reduced to the community's need to "seek first the kingdom of God." The difficulties of the times to which the people have referred have been caused by the community's dispiritedness and lack of commitment. If the people put the building of the temple first, the difficulties of the period, depicted in verse 11 in the familiar terms of Deuteronomy 28 as the operation of the covenant curses, would vanish. This lack of obedience to the primary requirement of the return, this lack of recognition of Yahweh's sovereignty over the returned community, Haggai correctly construes as covenant defection.

Haggai's message has its intended effects: in 1:12–14, the community's attitude changes. An appropriate covenant response (v. 12), that the people "obeyed the voice of the Lord their God, and . . . feared before the Lord," is greeted by the prophet with words of encouragement and covenant renewal, "I am with you" (v. 13; cf. Exod. 19:3–8). Note that in 2 Kings 17:7–23 and 2 Chronicles 36:15–16, the reason for the fall of the north and the south is given as the failure to hear the prophetic word. The pattern of Haggai 1 has thus been (1) the traditional presentation of the people's sin (vv. 2–5); (2) prophetic preaching in response, with attention drawn to the covenant curses which have been operating because of national failure (vv. 6, 9–11); (3) the repentance of the people in reaction to the prophetic word (v. 12); and (4) covenant reaffirmation (v. 13; cf. Beuken 1967, 27–49). The substance of Haggai 1:14–15 resembles the commissioning of Moses to build the tabernacle (Exod. 35:29; 36:2). Thus, the rebuilding of the temple will stamp the returnees as the people of God.

Rebuilding the Temple (Hag. 2)

The address of 2:1–9 occurs a little more than one month later (in September 520 B.C.), and is designed to meet the derogatory comparisons that have been drawn between the first temple and what is being erected (v. 3). Verses 4–5 are reminiscent of the older charge to Joshua to be strong and of good courage (the charge here is to Zerubbabel and a different Joshua; cf. Deut. 31:7; Josh.

1:6). The returned community, like the community of the conquest period, is to take heart in the provision of the divine Spirit, who had operated in the exodus community (Isa. 63:14) and would similarly overcome all obstacles arising in the present period. The account continues with the eschatological promise that would be attached to the rebuilding of the temple. The depiction of divine intervention leading to the pilgrimage to Zion by the nations, in verses 6–9, and the double entendre in verse 9, bound up with the word "place" (indicating both temple and Promised Land), make clear the benefits that Haggai expects to accrue to the returned people of God as a result of the temple building. The building of the temple would, by its placement, bring peace to the Promised Land. Haggai sees its erection as a necessary preamble to the ushering in of the eschatological age, which for postexilic prophecy was a matter of imminent expectation (cf. the New Testament view of the second coming). Since what is being built is, in the mind of the prophet, the eschatological temple, its glory will surpass the Solomonic temple (v. 9). God will rule from it, not merely dwell in it, and God's shaking of the nations will draw the wealth and submission of the world to Jerusalem.

After the conversion call of Haggai 1 and the tenor of 2:1–9, it is difficult to feel that the people addressed in 2:10–14 (on the twenty-fourth day of the ninth month, 520 B.C.) are the returnees. These verses may provide a general warning to the population that repentance without performance has no significance, yet the change in tone seems abrupt. All the people spoken of in this passage are "unclean." This fact seems to rule out the return community as being in view, as does the pejorative use of "nation" in verse 14 (such a use of the word only rarely applies to OT Israel). It is better to suppose that the people addressed are the opponents of the temple building, of whom we hear in Ezra 4:4. There "the people of the land" appear to have been the occupants of Palestine who had not been exiled; their request to participate in temple building with the returnees was rejected by Zerubbabel, presumably on the grounds of their cultic defilement. Accordingly, the "work of their hands" (Hag. 2:14) would be not what they offered in sacrifice, but participation in temple building. Verses 15–19 are best seen as offering encouragement to the returned community, in spite of opposition, to continue to carry out the charge to build. They are to remind themselves of how they have been blessed since the decision to begin work again (vv. 18–19). There were intervening difficulties, to be sure, but they have been overcome.

The oracles of this prophecy have a balanced character. The first and third oracles refer to the condition of the returnees and the need to take positive steps to rebuild the temple, while the second and fourth detail the eschatological consequences that will flow from the rebuilding. The fourth oracle (2:20–23), given on the same day as the third, is addressed to Zerubbabel as temple builder. It is no accident that this address immediately follows the rejection of semi-pagan participation in temple building. The language used of Zerubbabel in this section ("servant," "signet ring," "chosen") was used earlier to express rejection of Jehoiachin, a preexilic member of the house of David (Jer. 22:24). General continuity with Davidic tradition is thus being expressed, but in the absence of more definite historical evidence, it would be too much to suggest that Zerubbabel is being addressed messianically, or that the prospect is being entertained of a Davidic restoration. Zerubbabel is a continuity figure only and is addressed primarily as the Persian-appointed governor (Hag. 2:21). However, his role as temple builder does stress Davidic continuity, a theologically important detail.

Certainly, Haggai is in continuity with the program of Ezekiel and with the general message of restoration that Ezekiel offered (Ezek. 40–48). But his prophecy is no mere return to preexilic nationalism, nor is it given over to petty or cultic concerns. If it were, prophecy would be in its demise. On the contrary, Haggai argues that from the small and disillusioned postexilic community will arise the eschatological people of God. God has not forgotten his promises, delivered through Moses and David, and God will honor them by the ushering in of God's kingdom.

23

Zechariah

Zechariah exhibits much the same range of concerns as Haggai, namely, the rebuilding of the temple, the return of Yahweh to Jerusalem, and the role of that city as world center. His prophecies were delivered over slightly more than two years—from October 520 B.C. (Zech. 1:1) to December 518 (7:1). In view of the clear theological connections in the book, there is no good reason for theories of multiple authors. Zechariah 1–8 is oriented toward rebuilding the temple and the subsequent role of Jerusalem. Zechariah 9–14 is more enigmatic. It is noteworthy, however, that chapter 1 begins with the return of Yahweh to Jerusalem and the temple (9:1–8), while Zechariah concludes with the role of Jerusalem as the world center (14:16–21), as does chapter 8. It is possible, therefore, that Zechariah 9–14 offers theological comment on the more historically oriented first section, particularly since chapters 9–14 are often considered to be what later came to be called apocalyptic or protoapocalyptic literature.

Covenant Renewal (Zech. 1:1–6)

Zechariah 1:1–6 introduces a sustained note of covenant renewal as a precursor to the temple-building theme in Haggai. Note the emphasized use of "return" (vv. 3–4), a term often used theologically in covenant contexts in the OT to signify "repent" (cf. v. 6). The returnees in this section are carefully separated from their fathers (v. 4) so that the issue of a new beginning, after the return from exile, becomes clear. The exile had atoned for the past, and a new beginning is offered through the series of visions that follow.

The Visions of Zechariah (Zech. 1:7–6:8)

Zechariah 1–8 contains a series of seven visions (I am excluding Zech. 3 because of its style and content). These visions are largely temple-oriented (Halpern 1978, 180), with the fourth vision (4:1–4) forming the centerpiece. Visions are a normal component of prophetic literature, but this formal arrangement of seven (or eight, if Zech. 3 is included), together with the bizarre imagery, points toward the emergence of apocalyptic visions as part of the thought of this period, although in Zechariah 1–8 we are still formally in the domain of OT prophecy.

Accompanying each vision is interpretation by an angelic presence and commentary. That no interpretation is supplied in Zechariah 3 reinforces the opinion that this chapter stands outside the sequence. In the first vision (1:7–17), four patrolling horsemen emerge from "the myrtle trees in the glen" (an uncertain reference—perhaps the entrance of heaven is in view). Having patrolled the earth, they report, disturbingly (since the prophet is looking for the shaking of the nations), that all is quiet. In the ensuing heavenly council, the prophet is commissioned to carry a message of consolation to Jerusalem (vv. 14–17). To the previously raised question of when the exile will really end (v. 12), the divine response is anger to be vented against the nations and comfort extended to Jerusalem. Verse 16 makes clear that Yahweh's return to Jerusalem alone will guarantee its security. Therefore, the temple, the emblem of divine protection and government, needs to be built.

The second vision (1:18–21) is of four horns that four craftsmen are to cast down. Although horns usually suggest an altar, here they are symbols of power. No succession of world empires seems in view, simply the more general message that world authority will not prevail against the kingdom of God. The degree to which world power is to be kept in check is seen in the third vision (2:1–5), which speaks of a measuring line to be cast around measureless Jerusalem (cf. Ezek. 40:3). Yahweh himself will provide a wall of fire around Jerusalem, suggesting the flaming sword of Eden (Gen. 3:24). There may also be notes of the new exodus here (cf. Exod. 13:20–22; Isa. 4:5–6). Following this vision is a call to return from exile (Zech. 2:6–7), since the rebuilt Jerusalem will provide warrant for the return. One may conjecture either that a series of returns following 538 B.C. has taken place or, more probably, that this vision offers a theological interpretation of the nature of the return from exile. Verses 8–9 are difficult but may mean that, after having been commissioned by Yahweh (i.e., after having seen the glory), the prophet is certain that his ministry will be vindicated by events. Zechariah 2:10–13 completes the theological presentation by announcing the coming of Yahweh as world king to Jerusalem, to which the nations will now come in pilgrimage.

Zechariah 3 is concerned with the purification of the high priesthood, and thus with the recommissioning of the postexilic priesthood, with the new age in view. In what seems to be a heavenly council setting, Satan, as a kind of prosecuting attorney, accuses Joshua (v. 1). God, however, has decided for Jerusalem (v. 2) and has plucked Joshua from the fires of exile, purified and refined, thus rebutting Satan's charge. Being clad with new garments suggests a change of fortunes and new fitness for office, and thus Joshua is a symbol of the new age (vv. 3–4), while the placing of the turban on Joshua's head indicates the last act relating to his investiture. Additionally, the gold plate on the high priest's miter signifies Israel's holiness (Exod. 28:36–38). The prophet's personal notation on the importance of the turban (Zech. 3:5), which in Exodus is the vestment signifying the high priest's representative character, is designed to underscore the reconstitution of Israel as the people of God in the person of the high priest. Verses 6–7 express that Joshua's access to the heavenly council depends on the removal of his representative guilt and on the institution of right worship in Jerusalem. Verses 8–10 guarantee the restored priesthood as a sign of the prophet's effective word. The stone of seven facets (v. 9), representing totality or completeness, probably is to be connected with the ancient Near Eastern practice of ceremonially engraving the foundation stone of the temple. The coming of the branch (v. 8) will coincide with the removal of Judah's guilt and punishment. The building of the temple will achieve the Solomonic concept of rest, for all Israelites (v. 10) will sit under their own vine and fig tree (cf. 1 Kings 4:25).

Zechariah 4 offers the central vision of the seven visions. This chapter is concerned with the blessing of God to come through the leadership of the community in the new age. The meaning of the lampstand, with its seven lamps, is not clear (vv. 2–3). At its top are the seven bowls and seven spouts proceeding from each of the bowls/lamps. The whole seems to symbolize Judah as the illumination of Yahweh's worldwide dominion. Two olive trees flank the lampstand (vv. 3, 11–14), or two "sons of oil" (not, as mistranslated in v. 14, "anointed ones," since the word used for oil in this context is not otherwise used in the OT for anointing). Joshua and Zerubbabel symbolize community blessing. The two are, in their own ways, representatives who usher in the new postexilic age. Verses 6–7 seem to point to the removal of a stone from the ruins of the former temple, the site of which is cleared. This stone is then laid as the first stone (vv. 8–10), the foundation stone of the new temple, thus signifying continuity between the temple ages.

The fifth and sixth visions both denote the removal of wickedness from the land and are thus cultic and purifying in tenor. In Zechariah 5:1–4, the scroll on which the curse is written has the dimensions of the porch of Solomon's temple, probably an indication that the building of the new temple will remove the curse that the scroll contains. In the sixth vision (vv. 5–11), wickedness in the form of a woman—perhaps a Canaanite Asherah figure in a measuring basket (an ephah), typifying preexilic apostasy—is removed from the land and fittingly consigned to Shinar (i.e., Babylon). There, an anti-temple, the house of verse 11, is built for it. The land must be holy and its inhabitants holy. The seventh vision (6:1–8) is clearly parallel to the first; the four chariots come out, this time from between the pillars that provide the gateway to the heavenly palace (the "mountain" of v. 1). The combat wagons sent out toward the north presage judgment; any threats to God's people in the postexilic period were thought to come from the north. Cosmic peace is thus reestablished by a movement from heaven.

All seven visions take place on the same evening. The structure of each of the seven visions is identical: introduction, what is seen, prophetic questioning, and communication from the interpreting angel. The first and seventh visions are clearly related as expectation and result, and are related in their details. The third vision follows the political liberation that the second vision foreshadows. The fourth vision is central, while the fifth and sixth visions are related by naming the cleansed land as a prerequisite for temple rebuilding.

Coronation and Deliberation (Zech. 6:9–8:23)

Zechariah 6:9–15 deals with the crowning of Joshua. Two crowns, however, appear in the text (vv. 11, 14). Is Joshua to be crowned twice, once for himself and once for the absent Zerubbabel? More likely, verse 13 is to be taken as a complementary address by Zechariah to the two leaders (Ackroyd 1968, 198–99). The prophet alternately addresses Zerubbabel and Joshua, telling the former to build the temple and rule, and the latter to put on splendor and be priest. Perhaps Zechariah is thus signifying the dual control of the postexilic period. Verses 12–13 probably signify a ceremonial coronation of Joshua that looked forward to an ideal age of the new temple and messianic fulfillment. Since the rebuilding of the temple by Zerubbabel was by this time well advanced, verse 12 can hardly refer to the Jerusalem temple. Moreover, the association of branch with ideal messiahship (Isa. 11:1) looks beyond human kingship to the age of fulfillment, of which the return from exile was a foreshadowing.

Chapters 7–8, as one long address, are largely given over to a discussion of moral and social issues facing the returned community. A question about the validity of exilic fasting (7:1–7) finds its answer in traditional prophetic summarization of the righteousness that God requires of God's people (vv. 8–14). External observances (vv. 5–6) are pointless. Messages of hope presented in 8:1–8—the return of Yahweh to Zion, its repopulation, and then covenant renewal—are followed by encouragement to the people on how to live in the light of Jerusalem's future (vv. 9–17). The present task is to build the temple (vv. 9, 13). Covenant curses are to be replaced with covenant blessings. Verses 18–23 conclude the first section of the prophecy, indicating that the previous fasts will now be replaced with festivals directed toward the prospect of Jerusalem reestablished as the world center. Zechariah 8 ends with the note of the Gentiles' reaction to all these developments: in the new age they will repeat the old confession made by Abimelech to Abraham, "God is with you" (Gen. 21:22), as foreign nations spread the news of the kingdom. They will be compulsively drawn to Jerusalem, summing up the blessing to be extended to the world through this New Jerusalem.

Theological Commentary (Zech. 9–14)

The details of these chapters are extremely complex and will be referred to only briefly in this survey. The historical references in 9:1–7 have proved particularly difficult to interpret; it is best to regard the geographical references as typifying the traditional foes of Israel (Hanson 1975, 292–324). This passage deals with the march by Yahweh from the northern borders of the Promised Land to Jerusalem and the temple, securing his people from oppression. God will encamp at Jerusalem, acting as its sentry (v. 8). There, Yahweh will reign through the eschatological messianic king (vv. 8–10; cf. Ezek. 37:22, 24; Jer. 33:14–22; 23:5), with war ended and universal peace declared. Israel's ideal borders will be reestablished. In 9:11–17, Yahweh addresses Zion in amplification of 9:1–10. In fidelity to his covenant undertakings (v. 11), Yahweh will redeem Zion's prisoners (vv. 11–13), using Judah and Ephraim (i.e., all Israel) against world enemies (Greece), fortified with the theophanic appearance of Yahweh as the Divine Warrior (vv. 14–15). The victory will be followed by the fertility of the new order (vv. 15–17).

Zechariah 10:1–2 is a critique of false leadership, which can turn fertility into drought. The people seek counsel from diviners, not Yahweh (v. 2). Fertility and faithfulness are linked. The rest of the chapter continues this attack, but concludes with the imposition of Yahweh's leadership. Verses 3–5 speak of judgment for the false shepherds, but salvation for the misled flock. The cornerstone and "tent peg" (v. 4) are basic to the stability of the people, perhaps royal leadership through which the successes of verses 6–10 will be effected. Verses 6–10 pledge Yahweh's restoration of the northern and southern kingdoms, including the return of the scattered exiles. So many will return that areas outside of the Promised Land (v. 10) will be required to accommodate them. Processional notes, referring to the second exodus from Egypt and Assyria and the unity of the strengthened people of God under Yahweh's authority (v. 12), conclude the chapter.

Zechariah 11:1–3 is a taunt song using familiar imagery for arrogance, and sings against proud leadership, whose authority, continuing the theme of chapter 10, will be lost. All human pride will be vanquished. In verses 4–17, Zechariah's commission (vv. 4–6) and its execution (vv. 7–14) are reported. The prophet is commissioned to fatten the community for slaughter, since nothing can be expected of them (vv. 4–6). Verses 7–9 indicate beneficial action for the sheep. Three shepherds, probably community leaders in the employ of the base sheep merchants, are destroyed. The flock will not receive the prophetic message (v. 8), and they are left to their own devices (v. 9). This opens the way for the disaster announced in verse 6. The section is framed by the role of the staff (vv. 7, 14), indicative of north/south restoration (Ezek. 37:15–18) that had been attempted and frustrated. The flock is slain, and the kingdoms are again divided. Verse 8 is admittedly difficult. Does it mean the elimination of all false leadership, with three as a symbolic number? In verses 11–13, the prophet is given his hire, since his mission has achieved the purposes of the sheep merchants. He contemptuously designates it for temple use, presumably the sheep merchants' point of control, pointing to the problem in the chapter of corrupt priestly leadership. In verses 15–17, the prophet is recalled to represent false leadership, since divine leadership will have been repudiated. False leadership will be concerned with its own gain, which indicates its eventual destruction. The message of the chapter is clear: Yahweh has offered good leadership to bring about covenant renewal and unity between north and south. This leadership has been spurned, and the community must now accept the results of this rejection.

Chapters 12–14 concentrate our attention on the end-time conflict, from which Jerusalem will emerge as the center of the new creation. Zechariah 12:1–9 describes the conflict that engulfs inviolable Jerusalem. The nations attack, but reel (vv. 1–3). Divine victory comes through Judah (vv. 4–7), Jerusalem is delivered (v. 8), and the enemy is destroyed by God through Judah (v. 9). The reception of the Spirit and the regeneration in the people of God are noted, including the national weeping that betokens heartfelt repentance (vv. 10–14). The phrase "him whom they have pierced" in verse 10 may open the way for seeing vicarious, servant-type suffering in this passage. The text reads "me whom they have pierced," but is commonly emended to "him whom they have pierced." In this case, it is Yahweh who has been "pierced," but perhaps through his servant representative. At any rate, the christological application of this text in the New Testament makes the point clear (see Rev. 1:7). The lamentation, like the mourning that accompanied the death of Josiah (the reference to Hadad-Rimmon is to the place where Josiah died), indicates the strength of the repentance (Zech. 12:11–14). So this is lamentation for the death of a royal person; its scope indicates that the community had been involved in the rejection of verse 10. The fountain cleanses all of the community's leadership—royal, prophetic, and priestly (13:1). The shepherd's death has thus cleansed the house of David and of Jerusalem's citizens.

Eschatological cleansing, together with the removal of all idolatry, is again the emphasis of 13:2–6, a reinforcement of the previous passage. Verses 7–9 resume the imagery of Zechariah 11. God's own shepherd has been smitten, and the sheep scattered. From the scattering, however, the surviving remnant of verses 8–9a will emerge as the product of the shepherd's death. In them, the covenant relationship (v. 9) will be fulfilled. In the New Testament, Jesus applies to himself this theme of the smitten shepherd who preserves the remnant by his death (Matt. 26:31).

Finally, Zechariah 14 presents a symbolic picture of the eschatological day (Hanson 1975, 369–401). Impelled by Yahweh, nations fight against Jerusalem (vv. 1–2), and the city is captured. Half of the city goes into exile, half stays. Yahweh intervenes and victory is divinely given (vv. 3–5). The Mount of Olives is leveled to construct a processional route for Yahweh into Jerusalem, as Yahweh comes with his holy ones, the remnant, in return (cf. Isa. 40:3–5). A new created order results (vv. 6–8), with the transformation of the earth by living waters flowing from Jerusalem (cf. Ezek. 47:1–12). Verses 9–10 proclaim the universal reign of God from Jerusalem (the geographical description is remarkably similar to Jer. 31:38—a foreshadowing of the operation of the new covenant?). Surrounding territory is flattened and Jerusalem is elevated, thus throwing her into clear relief as a world symbol. Jerusalem's security is sure (vv. 11–15), but covenant curses will afflict her enemies. The text describes the battle against Jerusalem, in which even the people of God (Judah) were involved. In verses 16–21, the nations come yearly as pilgrims to Jerusalem, under the threat of withheld fertility, bringing the world's wealth. Jerusalem becomes identified totally with the temple as a sacred site (vv. 20–21).

Like the Book of Haggai, the prophecy of Zechariah lays heavy stress on God's purposes for temple rebuilding and the eschatological era expected to result. Chapters 1–8 weave these expectations with the history of the postexilic return. Chapters 9–14 seem to lift the prophecy to a higher pitch, with chapters 9–11 reflecting on the quality of Judean leadership, while Zechariah 12–14 poses the end-time threat to Jerusalem and describes its removal. We conclude with Jerusalem as the center of the new creation, the royal city from which Yahweh reigns. Revelation 21–22 brings us the same picture in the New Testament as the biblical canon closes.

24

Malachi

Underlining the Book of Malachi is the covenant note at the conclusion: the return of the Elijah figure. Malachi is devoted to the task of covenant renewal. The book raises what it sees as the inhibiting factor for the community, namely, its willful approach to covenant observance (McKenzie and Wallace 1983, 549). It concludes on the note of covenant recall through an Elijah, which can only be an eschatological possibility. The book is set within the Persian period and must date to later than 516 B.C., since the temple is presupposed as having been built. The book probably could be viewed as the precursor to the Ezra-Nehemiah reforms, since by its indictments it seems to prepare the community for reform.

Malachi is composed of six prophetic disputations (1:2–5; 1:6–2:9; 2:10–16; 2:17–3:5; 3:6–12; and 3:13–21), all of them bearing on a covenant traceable to the Abrahamic covenant. Each disputation is structured in the same manner. Each begins with a statement by the prophet or Yahweh, followed by an objection from the people, seeking clarification; each ends with an explanation that clarifies the issue and leads to a conclusion. The passages seek more to convince people of a position than to dispute with words. The prophet then gives a short response. The name of the prophet himself, Malachi, which means "my messenger," may be a veiled reference to the figure expected in 3:1, or it could be an abbreviation for "messenger of Yahweh."

God's Constancy (Mal. 1:2–5)

The opening dialogue, which revolves around the choice of Israel and the exclusion of Edom, takes up the old patriarchal basis of election, as the personalized language of the section (Jacob and Esau) suggests. Whether this theme was prompted by some incident of the time—perhaps a gradual incursion by

Edom from the south—or whether Edom is universalized to represent nations outside the covenant, the point is clear. These verses serve as a reminder that Israel stands in covenant with Yahweh, and affirm that Yahweh has remained faithful. Because Yahweh has been in covenant with Israel, he has destroyed Edom and will do so again if needed. The fate of Edom is described in curse language; Edom has been made a dwelling of jackals, and any attempt to rebuild will be futile. In common treaty language, the people will recognize this futility and will profess the greatness of Yahweh's name. The covenant with the ancestors, since it was based on the elective concept to which Malachi appeals, is thus still operative. Malachi 1:2–4 is a tightly structured chiastic element; 1:5 is the climax of the unit. Malachi 1:2–5 proceeds from an improper to a proper attitude to Yahweh, to a negative attitude to Edom, while the Jacob-Esau traditions are acknowledged. Malachi 1:2–5 refers explicitly to Obadiah, and Malachi 1:4 quotes Obadiah 3–4 in stating Edom's resolve to rebuild.

Condemnation of the Priesthood (Mal. 1:6–2:9)

The section begins with language recalling the covenant relationship—father and son, master and servant (see also "great king" in v. 14). Indifferent worship, sanctioned by priests, is this section's major consideration. The people have profaned the exclusive relationship between parties that the covenant demands. If the blemished offerings are unfit for the Persian governor, what an impertinence to offer them to the great king! A declaration of guilt in 1:10b–11 follows the accusation. Yahweh declares that he has no pleasure in them and will accept no offering from them (v. 10b). Such worship denies the specific nature of divine rule over Judah, and the prophet counters by pointing to the day when divine rule will be universally acknowledged (v. 11, in which future verbs should be supplied). Therefore, the Lord invokes a curse on any who bring an inferior offering (cf. Jer. 11:3), for Yahweh is a great king and his reputation is acknowledged by all nations (1:12–14).

A covenant emphasis emerges in 2:1–9: priestly conduct is seen to contravene the covenant with Levi (referred to in Jer. 33:20–26; Neh. 13:29; Num. 25:11–13; and Deut. 33:10–11, in which the covenant referred to is wider than the tribe of Levi). Perhaps a reference to the reestablishment of the priesthood under Joshua after the exile is implied (Zech. 3). The priests are now confronted: if you do not honor me, I will curse you. Indeed, they are already cursed (2:2–3). We cannot be sure from the context of verse 4 if Malachi rejects the priesthood in favor of a more general covenant with Levi. The Ezra-Nehemiah reforms, which challenged priestly authority, sought to cut across narrow priestly privilege. Levi had feared, had walked in peace and uprightness, and had respected the deity's name (vv. 4–6). But the priests had failed to show Yahweh respect. As punishment for not obeying the deity, the priests are made to be despised and debased.

Infidelity of Israel (Mal. 2:10–16)

Malachi 2:10–16 raises covenant issues of a different character. The message addresses the people as a whole and their infidelity to the Abrahamic relationship. The "one father" to whom appeal is made in 2:10 seems to be Abraham; the people are related to God by a covenant that he had instituted with their father Abraham. The spiritual nature of that relationship is under review, and the language turns fairly naturally to the marriage relationship that Judah has profaned. The Sinai covenant, as we know, is often depicted by the prophets in terms of marriage, and the reference in verse 11 may be to Judean apostasy (as it may be to intermarriage with foreigners, a pressing matter of the times). The subject of the prophetic rebuke of verses 13–16 is difficult to determine. The text of verse 16 is uncertain, and the use of the Hebrew verb meaning "to put away" for "divorce" is unusual. It is unclear, then, whether divorce is in the prophet's view here, or whether he is making a further attack upon idolatry. In any case, the people's covenant breach of the Sinai arrangement is clearly in mind.

Messenger of Judgment (Mal. 2:17–3:5)

Such covenant breach invites response. The people have wearied God with their doubt. God will come to judge those who ridicule the absence of God's judgment (Mal. 2:17). The identity of the messenger of Malachi 3:1, who seems to be equated with the messenger of the covenant in the same verse, is difficult. The covenant character of the messenger is noteworthy. The messenger acts as God's agent for punishing covenant violators. The verse contains references to Isaiah 40:3, and also to Exodus 23:20, both positively indicating divine direction to the Promised Land. Malachi 3:1 points to the land's retention, although this messenger delivers a threat to the community's existence. There is a hint that the messenger of 3:1 is to be identified with someone already on the scene, although his role will clearly be taken up in the Elijah figure of 4:4–6. The "Lord" of the verse is clearly Yahweh, who is about to visit his temple. He will purify the priests to restore temple worship. That the messenger functions as the alter ego of the sovereign explains the grammatical fusion of the *mal'ak* (messenger), the *'adon* (Lord), and the *mal'ak habberit* (messenger/angel of the covenant). The statement of 3:1, that the Lord is entering the temple, may be appropriate to the covenant lawsuit.

This passage may include an allusion to the ministry of Ezra, who, as a covenant-renewal figure (Neh. 8), would then anticipate the Elijah of chapter 4. Since the offerings of Judah and Jerusalem will be acceptable only when cleansed, the social malpractices to which 3:5 refers must be judged. In verse 5, the Lord reveals that he will bring punishment against adulterers and those who swear falsely, against those who mistreat the hireling, orphan, and sojourner, and against those who do not fear the Lord. All the categories describe covenant violation, and prohibition of such actions appears in the covenant-obedience passages (cf. Exod. 22:21–23) on the sojourner, widows, and orphans. The one who does not fear the Lord (3:5) is a general description of the covenant breaker.

Call to Repentance (Mal. 3:6–12)

If Malachi 3:6 is taken with what follows, then the section refers to God's covenant constancy, despite the continued defection of God's people (v. 7). Yahweh, who does not change, stands in direct contrast to Israel as described in 3:5. Yahweh does not renege on his word. God has kept covenant, while Israel is faithless. Israel's covenant violation has had a long history (3:7a); however, (3:7b) the Lord offers the chance of repentance in spite of long faithlessness. But the people immediately question the Lord's words, and this leads to a further indictment that they are robbing God (3:8–9). How? By their tithes and offerings; therefore, they are cursed. If they honor him, God (3:10–12), as Malachi refers to the covenant-blessing formulas (Deut. 28:11–12), would make them prosper. God would open the heavens and pour forth an agricultural bounty.

Judgment and Salvation (Mal. 3:13–4:3)

No response to the previous calls seems to have been made. The people's words have been harsh against God: "You have spoken harsh words against me" (v. 13 RSV). Therefore, the charge is explained further. The people have doubted the importance of serving God, saying, "it is vain to serve God" and "what is the good of keeping his charge?" They have denied the necessity of obeying the covenant. They see no reason to serve him and to keep his charge. The precise meaning of "walk as mourners" is unclear (v. 14; cf. Ps. 38:7; 42:10; 43:2; and Job 30:28 for the expression). Perhaps this means that they have not secured their requests for aid. The people decide to disregard God's standards and deem happy (compare 2:15 with 2:12) the ones who scoff at God.

Verses 16–18 are strongly covenantal in character and respond to the issues raised in 3:13–15. In contrast to the speech of the doubters (3:14–15), God heeds the conversation of the righteous in 3:16, hearing and rewarding them. The book of remembrance may be analogous to the text of the ancient Near Eastern treaty (Exod. 24:7; Deut. 28:58). The Lord will also make them his *segullah* (special possession), the word used to describe the special status of the vassal (cf. Exod. 19:5 of Israel), that is, the Lord will recall Israel to its vocation as a light to the Gentiles. In 3:17, the Lord promises a reward to those who serve him (contrast 3:14–15, where the people have deemed it vain to serve God). In the final ultimatum (3:18), the Lord reiterates his determination to punish the wicked and to reward the righteous, so that when God acts, the distinction between the righteous and the wicked will be clear. Then Yahweh will treat the righteous as a man pities a son who serves him.

The contrast between judgment upon the community and salvation for the elect, in terms of the Day of Yahweh, is then made in 4:1–2, with the final destruction of the wicked promised in verse 3. The language abounds with the themes of the book and the terminology of the lawsuit. The reference to a sun of righteousness to arise with healing in its wings (4:2) refers, probably, in a nonspecific way, to the dawning of a new era, the coming of a righteous day for Israel. Although the meaning is general in Malachi, we may take this as fulfilled in the ministry of Jesus. Yahweh reveals that the goal of Elijah, the messenger par excellence, will be to reunite fathers and sons—language similar to that of treaties. If this reconciliation is not made, the Lord will smite the land with a curse. The Lord will declare complete and total war against the guilty.

Faithful Obedience Required (Mal. 4:4–6)

The point of the book is thoroughly brought out in this appendix. Yahweh is faithful to his covenant, but he requires a response from the community of the day. Before the final Day of the Lord comes, there will be an Elijah-type prophet who will declare the real issues set before the people of God. The coming of this Elijah (in terms of 1 Kings 18–19) will mean a restating of the covenant demands. After this Elijah, the Day of the Lord or the coming of God will occur. If the Elijah initiative should fail, then the final covenant curses will fall on Israel for covenant breach. These closing verses were fulfilled in the ministry of John the Baptist, which was followed by the Day of the Lord, coming in the person of Jesus.

Malachi concludes the prophetic corpus, and closes the Greek (and thus our English) OT canon on this fitting note—of the cleansing required by the community as a prelude to covenant renewal. Israel is potentially under a curse, for assent to the covenant only in name will destroy her. This has been the essential message of Israelite prophecy from Samuel onward. In Malachi, the prophetic movement concludes with the coming Elijah figure, its witness to Israel ending on the high note of pronounced covenant emphasis on which it had begun, with the inauguration of the monarchy.

Part **4**

The Books of the Writings

25

Psalms

The third and final division of the OT canon, the Writings, contain miscellaneous material (poetry, wisdom literature, and history). Some of these works undoubtedly contain old material, and some of them (e.g., Psalms and Proverbs) are anthologies. Liturgical influences account for the presence of certain books within this division of the Hebrew canon. Each of the five *megilloth* ("scrolls") is associated with a specific Jewish festival: Ruth with Pentecost, the Song of Solomon with Passover, Ecclesiastes with the Feast of Tabernacles, Lamentations with commemoration of the fall of Jerusalem, and Esther with Purim. Books such as Daniel, Ezra-Nehemiah, and Chronicles owe their presence in the group either to the date of their emergence (after the canonical process of history and prophecy had been completed) or to their form (Daniel). The collection is headed by the Book of Psalms, to which we now turn. The canonical order of the Masoretic Text will be followed in the remainder of our OT presentation. The Septuagint numbers the Psalms differently, joining 9 and 10, and 114 and 115, and splitting 116 and 147 in two.

The Structure of the Psalms

The Book of Psalms is an anthology, whose movement or structural unity cannot be analyzed precisely. The title is from Greek *psalmos* 'song', 'hymn'. Originally, the book appears to have lacked a title; later the Hebrew word *tehillim* 'praises' was applied. Psalmody in Israel was, of course, much older than this collection; indeed, some of the most theologically significant literature in Israel appears early in poetic form (e.g., the "Song of the Sea" of Exod. 15). Whatever the origin of the individual psalms, they finally all became cultic in the sense that Psalms represents in its final form the hymnbook of the Second Temple. This fact alone cautions us from relying too much on historical-critical approaches as we endeavor to understand the meaning of particular psalms. The function of many individual psalms within the cult may, however, be inferred from their form. Any analysis of particular psalms, or of the book as a whole, must, of course, emphasize function. It is equally clear that the Book of Psalms reflects the experience of believers, and thus the household of faith. It may therefore be expected not to initiate particular theological themes or emphases, but rather to seek to preserve them. Caution must be exercised when liturgical material of the Psalter is used to postulate an emphasis (such as a theology of kingship) that differs from, or that is nowhere else attested in, the rest of the OT.

Psalms is divided into five books (Ps. 1–41; 42–72; 73–89; 90–106; and 107–50). The first four books conclude with a doxology, while Psalm 150 is a doxology that concludes the entire Psalter. Perhaps this division is as old as the time of the Chronicler, for 1 Chronicles 16 draws upon Psalm 106 and follows with what amounts to a doxology, a reflection of the use of that psalm in the Psalter. The age of this fivefold division and the reasons for it are disputed. Perhaps it reflects the Pentateuch, a suggestion supported by the fact that the Pentateuch was divided into 153 sections for synagogue reading. Certainly, however, this somewhat artificial division indicates the anthological character of the whole and its gradual compilation.

Hints as to the way the whole book came into being are offered principally by the psalm titles (G. H. Wilson 1985, 155–62). Authorship seems to have been a predominating concern in the arrangement of Books One through Three. Almost every psalm in Book One is either expressly or implicitly ascribed to David (this is known from the superscription or, in the case of Ps. 10 and 33, by their relationship to the preceding psalm); here the preponderating divine name is Yahweh. Book Two opens with Korah psalms (Ps. 42/43–49), while the transition to the additional Davidic psalms that follow is heralded by the intrusion of an Asaph psalm (Ps. 50). Psalms 51–65 are Davidic, as are 68–70, with which the untitled Psalm 71 seems closely connected. The transition between the two small Davidic collections is made by the repeated use of the title "choirmaster" in the psalm headings (Ps. 64–70). Book Two ends with Psalm 72, which is dedicated to Solomon and concludes with a doxology. Noticeable also in Book Two is the preponderance of the divine name Elohim.

Book Three also heavily features individual authorship. It begins with an Asaph collection (Ps. 73–83), while the subsequent Korah collection (Ps. 84–85 and 87–88) is split by a solitary Davidic psalm (Ps. 86). The book concludes with a single psalm ascribed to Ethan (Ps. 89), but this one is similar in type to Psalm 88. In Books Four and Five, authorship is less prominent (only nineteen are credited, seventeen of them to David).

Psalm 90, which begins Book Four, is ascribed to Moses, a title that seems to act as a bridge between Books Three and Four. The name of Moses appears no less than six times in Book Four (99:6; 103:7; 105:26; 106:16, 23, 32); otherwise, it occurs only once, at 77:20. Only Psalm 92 in Book Four has a superscript, but the LXX provides one for each of these psalms. Among these psalms in Book Four are Yahweh *malak* psalms ("Yahweh reigns"), identified by a similarity of content. Psalms 92–99, with Psalm 91 as introduction, show concern for God's kingship and enthronement. Battle terminology is frequent in these psalms. Psalm 96 is considered a Yahweh *malak* psalm, with verse 10 celebrating his victory. These psalms (92–99) are victory psalms concerned with the holiness of God and God's praise, God's victory over enemies and God's continued rule. Psalm 93 seems (cf. the LXX superscription) to celebrate David's conquering of the land. Psalm 97, a Yahweh *malak* psalm, also has an LXX superscription similar to Psalm 93, relating to the land. The two psalms could well be Davidic, as the allusion to the ark in Psalm 99 indicates. Their victory-song type argues for David's and not Solomon's time (Anderson 1994, 239). These psalms have been seen as the answer to the Davidic king's problems in Psalm 89 (G. H. Wilson 1985, 215), in which Yahweh is exhorted to remember his covenant with David, although the Book Four psalms are seemingly of a much later date. Common beginnings and endings connect Psalms 103 and 104. Psalm 104 also connects to Psalms 105 and 106 by its hallelujah conclusion.

The boundary between Books Four and Five is very fluid. The first psalm of Book Five, Psalm 107, lacks a superscription, so that no change in authorship marks the boundary between Books Four and Five. Psalm 107, however, seems by its opening verse to be related to Psalm 106. Book Five, presumably the latest, is editorially interesting. The book begins and ends with a psalm of praise (Ps. 107, 150), and small collections within the book may be detected: Psalms 108–10 seem connected by their promise of universal dominion to the Hebrew king. Psalms 111–12 are acrostics, each introduced with "hallelujah," responding, it seems, to Psalm 110 (Zenger 1998). Psalms 113–18, traditionally associated with the Passover, are a liturgical unit. Psalm 119 is a magnificent prayer for grace and faith to keep the Torah. Psalms 120–34, the psalms of ascents, are so called because of their apparent association with liturgical pilgrimage to the Jerusalem temple. Psalms 135–36, forming the climax to 120–136, strike out in a new direction in praise of Yahweh as king. They are functionally related also by their apparent use during Israel's major festivals. Psalm 137 introduces the Davidic collection of Book Five (138–45). Psalm 145:21 concludes the Psalter, with Psalms 146–50 a fivefold liturgical hallelujah. Psalm 150 brings the Psalter to a definitive conclusion with a hymn of totally unmotivated praise.

It seems that the editing was chronological and not topical or liturgical, since the statement at the end of Psalm 72 that "the prayers of David, the son of Jesse, are ended" indicates a collection earlier than our fivefold division. We may infer from 1 Chronicles 16:4 that Levites were preparing hymn collections in David's time, and from 2 Chronicles 29:30 that Asaph and Davidic collections existed by Hezekiah's time. No satisfactory account regarding the detailed order of our present numbering can be advanced; indeed, the Hebrew and Greek texts differ on the numbering.

Titles of the Psalms

Only a small minority of the psalms lack a title or some descriptive information. Many of the titles appear to describe function: for example, *mizmor* 'psalm' occurs more than fifty times; *shir* 'song' thirty times; some are clearly musical directions (e.g., *lamenasseah,* "to the choirmaster," occurs some fifty-five times); some refer directly to cultic use (e.g., Ps. 92, "for the Sabbath"); some advance historical information on the setting of the psalm (Ps. 3, 7, 18, 34, 51–52, 54, 56–57, 59–60, 63, 142); still others ascribe authorship or indicate relationship. This matter of relationship is difficult, since the Hebrew preposition *le-* can have several meanings. The phrase *ledawid,* for example, can be translated "for David," "belonging to David," "by David," or "concerning David." In the last analysis, we are dependent on the content of the psalm, the particular type of Hebrew poetry, and probability. If the titles are not original, they are at least a useful aid as to how the Jewish community interpreted individual psalms.

Psalm Types

Psalm types can be reduced to two—prayer and praise. The laments (petitionary prayers) of the Psalter are of a fixed form. The first section of the lament psalm is the address or invocation of the divine name (cf. Ps. 3, 4, 5, 80). Often an introductory plea for hearing and answering is added (5:1; 59:1, 2; 83:1). The next section is the occasion for the psalm—the problem involved, whether inner sorrow or despair, threat of death, and so on (10:2–11; 57:4; 58:3–5). Then follows the petition, which reveals the purpose of the psalm—usually for Yahweh to answer the worshiper (13:3; 86:6; 142:6). The lament is concerned with the removal of suffering or personal or national distress; this is evident in that lament flows into petition, although in some cases petition is implied.

Motivation, as a fourth element, follows, which gives reasons why Yahweh should answer, normally in response to the trust of the worshiper, but perhaps also for the sake of Yahweh's honor. The certainty of hearing is then stated, and this sudden change in mood in the psalms has evoked much attention. A vow, usually of praise or thanksgiving, typically closes the psalm. The general character of these psalms makes them adaptable to particular needs. The lament seeks change. But no formal lament psalm stops short with lamentation, which has no meaning of itself, but which functions as an appeal. The final goal of the lament is the praise of God, and this is how the normal lament concludes.

The psalm of praise has a fixed form and consists of three parts. Almost always it begins with a call to praise, an exhortation to sing to the Lord. It usually names the person or group to whom the exhortation is directed. It mentions the mode of praise (cf. Ps. 149:1–3). Some psalms intersperse such calls to praise throughout the psalm. The main element in the psalm is the actual praise of God, recalling God's acts and attributes. God's praiseworthy acts occur in three main arenas: nature or creation, history, and the personal life of the believer. The final element in a typical psalm of praise is the resolution that ends the praise on a note of closure, generally as a prayer or a wish (Ps. 30:12; 67:7; 97:12).

Interpretation of the Psalms

Up until the middle of the nineteenth century, the psalms were classified by their titles or by their content. At the end of that century, Hermann Gunkel (codified in *Enleitung in die Psalmen,* 1933) classified them by what he judged to have been their relationship to the cult, that is, their intended use in a recurrent social or liturgical context. He defined five major types: hymns of praise, thanksgiving psalms, community laments, individual laments, and royal psalms. Minor types included songs of Yahweh's enthronement, wisdom psalms, pilgrim psalms, victory songs, community psalms of thanksgiving, and prophetic Torah psalms. For the most part, Gunkel's classification has been adhered to. In particular, many Scandinavian scholars (led by Sigmund Mowinckel) have insisted on a cultic origin for psalmody. The problem with such views is the distinction that must be drawn between origin and function. Undoubtedly, many of the psalms were of individual composition. Such psalms eventually acquired a liturgical function that provided the occasion for their collection. In the last analysis, similarity of psalm types refers to the similar way in which certain psalms were used in worship.

Attempts by other scholars to find a major cultic connection such as a fall festival or a royal Zion feast to provide a basis for most or much of the content of the Book of Psalms are called into question by the special pleading that such attempts intrinsically contain. In the case of Hans-Joachim Kraus (1966, 203–5), for example, the supposition is that Israel's confession of divine kingship could not have been early, even though the acknowledgment of the divine kingship of a deity was fairly universal in the ancient Near East.

Note should be taken of the major modifications that Claus Westermann has made to Gunkel's thesis, again with general acceptance. Westermann (1965) has shown that Gunkel's division between the hymn of praise and the thanksgiving psalm is too forced (1965, 18), since the basic character of the thanksgiving psalm is praise—a report of what God has done and a reaction to it. Westermann (1965, 22) rightly points out that the *Sitz im Leben* of the hymn of praise and the thanksgiving psalm (for which his own terms are descriptive praise and declarative praise, respectively) is not the cult, as Gunkel had argued, but Yahweh's intervention in the form of national or individual salvation. The backbone of the Psalter, suggests Westermann (1965, 115ff.), is the lament. This type of psalm is a petition, and thus a prayer for a change of the condition described. The design of the lament is therefore to secure God's intervention. Understood this way, the lament is a powerful witness to God's activity, and thus anticipates psalms of praise for deliverance from the adversity described.

Admitting that there are various subtypes, Westermann (1965, 34–35), in the main, divides the ingredients of Gunkel's classification into two ways of praying: plea (lament) and praise (hymn and thanksgiving). Thus, he retains classification but with the important difference that he emphasizes the function of a psalm in liturgical use rather than its formal literary type.

The Major Emphasis of the Psalms

The Book of Psalms is a compendium of biblical theology, and issues touching every aspect of OT thought and life are discussed. There is, however, an overriding emphasis, broadly suggested by the introduction and conclusion.

It is agreed that Psalm 1 provides a formal introduction to the book. The concern of this carefully structured psalm is the two basic ways to live. The right way is the way that delights in Yahweh's *torah;* it will ensure that "blessedness," the note on which the Psalter opens, will be realized in one's personal life. The Book of Psalms thus places before us the theme of how life is to be lived. This is the life of obedience, required by those within the covenant. When we consider further that the Hebrew title of the book is "praises" *(tehillim),* we are left with the conviction that Psalms praises Yahweh for having left us an indication of the correct way in which life is to proceed, no matter what our circumstances. This concept of the book as praise is reinforced by the fact that the Psalter, divided editorially into five books, concludes with a fivefold flourish of hallelujah psalms (Ps. 146–50), introduced and concluded by "Praise the Lord!" The final psalm is a litany of praise to Yahweh as Creator and Redeemer. The movement in the Book of Psalms is thus from obedience to praise, indicating that obedience, exemplified by Psalm 1, leads finally to undivided praise (Ps. 150), although much human experience lies between the beginning and the end. Psalms, a book written by people to God, has become canonized through its use in general worship to depict the experiences of life.

The Psalter is thus a book of praise, proclaiming that God, as Creator and Redeemer, has given to Israel through the Torah, through the revelation of God in history, the possibility of new life and a complete indication of how it is to be lived. By this witness of OT saints and the presentation of their experiences in all facets of life, we are encouraged to trust Yahweh for the future as we have trusted him in the past. Of course, not all the psalms have reference to what God has done; many of them are eschatological, referring to what God will finally do. But, here again, OT eschatology rests on the character of Yahweh and his interventions in history.

Enthronement Psalms

Gunkel (1998) suggested that psalms such as 47, 93, 96–97, and 99 were composed to celebrate the annual enthronement festival of Yahweh as universal king. Mowinckel (1967) translated *yahweh malak,* the liturgical formula occurring in these psalms (though *'elohim* is the divine name in the phrase in Ps. 47), as "Yahweh has *become* king," and postulated analogies with the Babylonian New Year festival. This festival celebrated the victory of the city-god of Babylon, Marduk, over the elements of chaos, a victory that had brought creation into being. Mowinckel concluded that the New Year festival was the occasion on which Yahweh's control over the universe was reasserted. In addition to Gunkel's enthronement psalms, Mowinckel associated approximately another forty with the group.

Two points, however, deserve attention. The first is that the contested phrase *yahweh malak,* which gave rise to the hypothesis, ought to be translated "Yahweh is king." The verb is durative, not ingressive. In Israel, Yahweh was understood to reign eternally. Practical problems exist about an annual enthronement theory, for who should enthrone Yahweh, who has all power? Who should transfer royal authority to him? We thus have an acclamation formula celebrating Yahweh's eternal kingship, clear from his lordship over creation (to which the core psalms in this group, 47, 93, 96–97, and 99, all refer).

Second, a pattern in these psalms points to Yahweh's eternal kingship: (1) through mythic analogies, creation is presented as a cosmic victory; (2) there are references to the history of salvation, or to deductions to be drawn from it. Creation and history in all of these psalms are thus narrowly tied together. It is therefore invalid to refer to such psalms as enthronement psalms, since such a notion suggests the loss of authority and then its renewal. The eternal kingship of God was an OT postulate and a major focus of worship. It would be strange indeed if liturgy did not reflect this emphasis.

What was celebrated in the enthronement psalms was not the New Year itself, but Yahweh's continuing kingship. Since Yahweh's kingship for Israel was not secured through an annual battle against the forces of nature or of chaos, one could not expect that the New Year would receive prominence. A cultic event that celebrated Yahweh's kingship in connection with the autumn festival seems to make the best sense. True, the only text to link enthronement and the autumn festival is Zechariah 14:16, but why would the linkage have been made unless it was well established?

Zion in the Psalms

The central feature of the Jerusalem cult tradition, and what bestowed on Zion its sacral character, was the belief that Yahweh dwelled among his people in Jerusalem, enthroned in some sense in the Jerusalem temple. Among the variety of ways that Yahweh is represented as present on Mount Zion, the most prominent is as king. Already, in the entrance liturgy of the early Psalm 24, Yahweh is described as king of glory (vv. 8–10) who enters his sanctuary at Zion, described as the mountain of Yahweh, the place where his glory dwells. Similarly, in Psalm 68, Yahweh is depicted as king in connection with a procession of the tribes into the sanctuary (vv. 25–28). Psalm 132, celebrating the dual election of David and Jerusalem, does not explicitly call Yahweh "king," although the language is royal. In verses 7–8, the ark is conceived as, or in association with, the throne of God. Placement of the ark in the Zion temple thus signified the dwelling of God as king in Jerusalem.

Royal Psalms

Gunkel also pointed out that many psalms give prominence to the place of the Israelite king (Ps. 2, 18, 20, 21, 45, 72, 101, 110, 132, 144:1–11). He argued that such psalms were used on important occasions in the life of the king. This point has been so thoroughly developed that some scholars take many, if not most, psalms to be royal. Indeed, without any corroborative evidence in the OT beyond the Psalms, the involvement of the Israelite king as Yahweh's representative in an assumed New Year festival is, as we have noted, only a postulation. At the New Year festival the king combated and was overcome by the forces of chaos, an ever-present threat to Israel's stability. In a process of ritual humiliation, the king was delivered over to and then rescued from Sheol, betokening as representative of Israel the nation's passage through this threat. But this postulation makes too much of kingship, which arrived relatively late in Israelite history.

It is possible to hold a view of "sacral kingship" that sees the Israelite king, like his ancient Near Eastern counterparts, as the regulator and dispenser of blessing as Israel's corporate head (see Ps. 22, 28, 61, 63, 71, 89, 144, all of which may refer to the king). It is clear that the king is regarded as a divine appointee, assured of divine protection and blessings (Ps. 2:6; 18:50; 21:3; 78:70; 89:18). The thought of several of the psalms, however, goes well beyond historical kingship and is clearly messianic. In such psalms, the king's role as an adopted son, his spectacular victories, his priestly prerogatives, and other messianic motifs are extravagantly presented (e.g., Ps. 2, 45, 72, 89, 110, 132). These avowedly messianic psalms explain the extreme interest in historical kingship that the Psalms betray, providing a religious understanding of the king as an ideal figure, which ran contrary to historical experience.

Finally, we note briefly that many theories have gathered around such terms in the Psalms as "wicked," "righteous," "poor," and "I." These terms have been variously interpreted as corporate or individual, as lay or royal designations. However, the Psalter is a comprehensive book of Israel's experience, an anthology drawn from her religious history. Further, there can be little doubt that earlier psalm settings have been changed by liturgical function. Thus it may well be unwarranted to assume that such terms are applied consistently or unequivocally. Creation, exodus, Zion theology, the law as God's light to the redeemed, God in various roles (warrior, judge, shepherd), the Sinai and Davidic covenants, and eschatological expectation all find their place within the compendium of the Psalms. But most of all, the Book of Psalms provides the great description of the life of faith, its blessings, its struggles, and its prospect. As Westermann has pointed out, the various types of psalms point us to a circle of faith. Descriptive praise for what God has done leads to the lament, in which attention is drawn to the condition of the psalmist, which is contrary to what the history of salvation might suggest for a member of the people of God. Lament changes to plea and then to the certainty of being heard—a typical movement in the lament psalms. Answered prayer in turn leads us into the declarative praise of thanksgiving, which gives expression to our experience of the character of God, to whom all praise is due.

Traditional approaches to the Psalms have been too theological and conceptual. Theology will come to us from them indirectly and implicitly; we expect the psalms to reflect theology, but hardly as liturgy to initiate it. The exposition of biblical poetry depends on our ability to empathize with the mood and emotions of the writer, doing justice to the richness of meanings that figurative language, especially metaphor and simile, conveys, understanding by such study the logic of the comparison.

Wisdom Literature

The Solomonic authorship of Proverbs and Ecclesiastes and Wisdom of Solomon is perhaps better understood as royal patronage, perhaps as in the case of the Davidic authorship of the Psalms. Perhaps the movement had its origins in family and tribal wisdom, although it is likely that there were foreign contacts, particularly from Egypt, where wisdom was the work of a royal or scribal class.

Unlike the prophetic books, which assume special revelation, the wisdom literature is general and almost universal in its pronouncements. Most of the events of salvation history (exodus, conquest, etc.) are absent from this material, which concentrates on the regular rather than the unique. There are hardly any national references beyond those pertaining to the king. The absence of these themes is occasioned by the fact that the wisdom literature relates people to their world more generally than the books of salvation history. In short, the wisdom movement operates within a wider framework than that of redemption. It is finally concerned with the harmony of orders that the created structure, animate and inanimate, must exhibit. We have drawn attention to a series of biblical covenants operative between God and God's world since creation, covenants in which God's purposes for the world are revealed. The wisdom literature of the Old Testament is a broad call for individuals to operate within limits, which a theology of creation itself provides.

The Books of Job, Proverbs, and Ecclesiastes all share an interest in the development of pithy sayings, and all concern themselves with common intellectual problems relating to people and their world. While the difference among such books is great, they do seek to observe human character on the widest plane and to study its consequences. Since the interest in these books is anthropological, the neglect of the concerns of salvation history is understandable.

However, the integration of wisdom and salvation history is easily effected since both stand within the broad horizons of creation theology. In the wisdom books, creation is presupposed rather than expounded, as the search for order and regularity within the world goes on in a manner displaying the necessity of such a presupposition. As for salvation history, we know that those who have been redeemed, God created, and they are living in this world. They are challenged to live out life in this world as part of God's order of creation. God has made the same universe available to believer and nonbeliever. The facts do not change, but there are differences in construction that one's worldview places on the facts. Challenged by one's world, each individual is confronted with personal limitations, unpredictability, and his or her own misuse of creation. It is not the case, however, that no distinction is drawn in these books between the secular and the sacred. For it is made clear in Job, Proverbs, and Ecclesiastes that the fear of Yahweh provides the context within which wisdom will operate. As such, fear of Yahweh is the beginning of wisdom.

26

Job

The atmosphere of the Book of Job is non-Israelite and patriarchal. Its dating is unsure—certainly no criteria for dating are afforded by the fairly widespread use of Aramaic forms within the book, since these could point equally to an early as well as to a late date. The book exhibits the epic form, in which prose and poetry may naturally be mingled.

To regard Job as an epic may well do justice to the form of the complete book, though the word "epic" must be used cautiously, for Job betrays an intensity of personal feeling foreign to the detachment of the earlier epic. To see the book as offering a parallel to the laments of the Psalms speaks only to the form of the dialogues of the book. It ignores the fact that the poetic dialogues of the Book of Job do not function as the lament psalms do, to engender confidence and praise, and it ignores the place of the epilogue and prologue as providing the key to the book. The category of drama has often been adduced for the book, but this is to apply a literary anachronism, since Jewish drama appears much later as a form. To apply the term "comedy" to Job is to misunderstand its theological purpose. None of the comparable materials of the ancient Near East offer proper parallels for this stimulating OT book. Certain judicial features are present, but to regard it as an extended legal dispute is to account for only a fraction of its material.

Most of the prose in the book is found in the introduction (chaps. 1–2) and conclusion (42:7–17). A lament from Job (chap. 3) connects the prose introduction to the ensuing dialogues of chapters 4–26. In them, Job's three friends (Eliphaz, Bildad, and Zophar) speak in turn and, with the exception of the last round of the debate (in which no speech by Zophar is offered and thus no answer from Job given), are in turn answered by Job. Job 27–28 appears to be a new movement by Job, a presentation of his own theological credentials kept intact during the heat of controversy. In chapters 29–31, Job reviews his case, appealing for a divine verdict. This is followed, however, by the judgment of Elihu, a final human summation from a detached onlooker (chaps. 32–37). The divine speeches of Job 38–41 then introduce Job's response in 42:1–6.

The Prologue and Epilogue (Job 1–2; 42:7–17)

Since the prologue and epilogue provide the understanding for the book, we first consider their content. Job 1:1–5 introduces us to this revered patriarchal figure, prosperous and yet righteous. We are then moved to the heavenly council, where Satan seems to be more than merely the council's roving advocate. Indeed, as a cynical accuser of the brethren in this parable (cf. Andersen 1976, 79), Satan issues a challenge to God regarding the basis on which Job's righteousness rests (vv. 6–12). That two conflicting opinions exist in heaven underlies the issue that will be debated in this book. The Satan figure (the prosecuting attorney in the heavenly council) asserts that Job is righteous because he is blessed; God counters with the insistence that Job has been blessed because he is righteous. We shall see that the friends put forward Satan's case, while Job argues the divine case. The stage is now set for the contest that will work itself out in the dialogue. The issue is whether God will be vindicated in God's judgment of Job, whom God has declared to be righteous and blameless (1:8). Will the divine reputation hazarded on Job be preserved? We know that it will, and we know now that in the dialogues that follow, even though Job is overthrown by calamity, he will retain his uprightness.

The challenge to Job is sharpened progressively by the loss of his property and family (1:13–22) and, after Satan's cynical assertion that Job would recant if smitten physically, by his affliction with terrible adversity to his body (2:7). The reader clearly sees the issues. This suffering of Job is unmerited. It is not retributive; there is no connection between an antecedent offense and its consequence. We expect the dialogues that follow will reflect, not only Job's innocence, but also that, under remarkable adversity such as Job has experienced, he will not break. At once, we are led also to see that the book is not concerned about suffering as such (since the basic issues are raised in 1:9–10, before Job's suffering begins), although faith upheld under adversity is a major theme. A still broader theme broached by Job is the existence of evil in our world and proper reactions to it.

The prose epilogue in 42:7–17 completes the book. Satan does not appear, since the test has been concluded. Indeed, the friends have taken Satan's place in the epilogue. We are told that the friends stand condemned, but that Job is right. We are not told in detail how these judgments have been worked out, but we guess that, by Job 42:6, he has come up with an appropriate personal response to his difficulties. We gather, judging from Satan's cause-and-effect view, that righteousness follows blessing, that in the dialogues the friends have largely taken a position of self-interest, and thus they are clearly wrong.

Job is then restored, as an act of grace, to a position twice as prosperous as he had occupied before God exposed him to testing. What is more, the narrative, which elevates Job at the end to one who, as intercessor, influences the councils of heaven, does not offer a doctrine of reward. Rather, what is being affirmed is the generosity of God.

Three Cyclic Addresses (Job 3–26)

The point of Job's lament in Job 3 is not to curse God's part in creation, nor is it a call for the destruction of creation. Job already has declared that he is prepared to accept good or evil from the hand of God—in effect, to trust, though he be slain. In chapter 3, he merely calls for release from the life in which he has ceased to see further opportunity. Sheol has become the place of rest and repose for Job, and offers a new threshold of hope (v. 17). Three cycles of addresses follow, in which Job's friends, as the representatives of current wisdom, speak in order of age. While slightly different approaches to Job's problems are evident within the cycles, the speeches are somewhat repetitive and will not be traced in detail here.

Starting with the premise that God protects the lot of the righteous (4:1–6), Eliphaz and then Bildad and Zophar develop the inference that, since Job is unprotected from adversity, he must be unrighteous. Within the first round, the friends skirt the issue, which is the magnitude of Job's sufferings, and urge Job to come to terms with his hidden, but unconfessed, sin. From this position they never retreat, thus advocating an ironclad doctrine of retribution that, in its firmest presentation (see Bildad in 8:1–7), binds God to the world, leaving God no room to move.

Job's position, however, needs more discussion. Job, for his part, claims in this first round no more than that his sufferings are incommensurate with whatever fault may lie behind them (chaps. 6–7, 9–10, 12–14). He himself does not claim blamelessness (as Zophar asserts in 11:4), and by the end of the second round of speeches (chap. 21) Job has reached a position that categorically denies his friends' position on retribution. The facts of the case, Job maintains, do not support the friends' cause, and he pushes the illogic of their attitude to its ridiculous conclusion.

Job asks only that his friends understand his plight. He agrees that an individual is accountable for conscious sins, but Job is not aware of having sinned (6:24–25) in such a manner as to deserve what has befallen him. In a poignant parody of Psalm 8, Job asserts that God has become his enemy, evoking the need for a personal audience with God (Job 7:11–21). No notion of a lawsuit to bring God to the bar is developed, not even in Job's response to Bildad, in the controversial chapter 9. Job is concerned as to how he might be vindicated, for he is certain that if he had the opportunity to confront God, he would be cleared. At the very least, he would find out why he has been afflicted (9:16). At issue in this densely packed chapter is understanding right relationship with God. Once that is understood, the difficulties of life will vanish, for they also will be understood. Of God's power and God's goodness, Job is convinced. He would be content if only God would tell him why he is suffering (see Job 7:20–21). The lawsuit issue is raised in Job 9 (see vv. 1–4), only to be dismissed by Job in this long speech (chaps. 9–10), which reiterates his basic confidence in God as a faithful Creator. Yet in his longing for death (10:18–22), Job has not moved from his position of chapter 3.

In his final speech of the first round, Job asserts that were God to slay him, yet would he trust (13:15 KJV, NIV), affirming not only his basic commitment but also his acceptance of the underlying goodness of God. Job is thus all the more puzzled as to why God has acted as God has (vv. 24–25). Job 14 reflects on the brevity of life and its purposelessness, outside of the possibility of a life beyond the human dilemma. The primary theme in Job's second round of speeches (chaps. 16–17, 19, 21) is not hostility to God (16:6–17), but what seems to be the reverse. Job remains confident of final vindication (16:18–17:16), for he has a heavenly mediator (16:19) and does not rely upon the favor of his friends. He can understand neither why God has forsaken him (19:7–22) nor the attack of his friends (vv. 2–6). In 19:23–29, Job contemplates death, confident that, after death, there will be the possibility of contact with God, the experience that he has sought.

In the last round of speeches, Job's arguments are longer (chaps. 23–24, 26), while those of the friends are curtailed, an indication of the direction in which the narrator is moving. Job still wishes to come before God (23:1–7), but God is inaccessible (vv. 8–17). Only Eliphaz, in this round, offers an effective speech (chap. 22). Bildad has virtually nothing to add (chap. 25), while Zophar does not enter the ring. Clearly, the friends' arguments have been totally rejected by the author. Job 26 is Job's final response to the three friends. After a short reply to Bildad (vv. 2–4), the chapter paints a magnificent picture of God, anticipating the theophany of chapters 38–41.

Job never denies that he is a sinner. He affirms only that he cannot see any particular sin that has brought on this present crisis. He never retracts from his position of absolute trust (Job 2:10), although he is tormented by the strange posture that God has, evidently, adopted toward him. The friends are inflexible in maintaining that Job's hidden faults are responsible for his present plight. Only occasionally throughout the dialogues do these representatives of traditional wisdom address the real issues. (See, e.g., the suggestion by Eliphaz in 5:17–27, taken further by Elihu, that suffering is pedagogic.) We have reached the end of the dialogues, convinced that some personal encounter between God and Job is required.

Job's Final Speech and the Author's Answer (Job 27–28)

Job insists on his personal integrity and hands over his case to God, asking for vindication in the face of his friends, who must, in terms of their doctrine, be subject to the fate of the wicked, which Job graphically depicts in 27:13–23. The ensuing magnificent poem on wisdom clearly reveals Job's impeccable orthodoxy. In chapter 28, Job meditates on the illusory search for wisdom (vv. 1–11) and its inaccessibility (vv. 12–19). Only God knows wisdom, and God alone can reveal it (vv. 20–27). Extremely significant is that the fear of Yahweh, which is the beginning of wisdom (and the traditional formulation of theological wisdom), is characteristic of Job (28:28; cf. 1:1). Such fear is the sole context in which knowledge of God can be developed. The use of the divine name Adonai (but many manuscripts read "Yahweh") in verse 28—its only occurrence in Job—may underscore Job's uprightness and link him with orthodox wisdom.

Job's Dilemma and Elihu's Speeches (Job 29–37)

Job 29–31 reviews his past, acknowledging the great blessings he has received (chap. 29). These favors have all been lost, however, and his friends now mock him (chap. 30). In his dilemma, Job utters a great oath of innocence and places his case before God (chap. 31). We are now ready for the theophany of chapters 38–41, preceded by the speeches of Elihu in chapters 32–37.

There is a wide range of opinion on the speeches of Elihu. Some judge their style to be pedestrian; others see them as artistic. Some regard them as mindless repetition of previous arguments; others think they offer the final solution. It is generally agreed, however, that their tone of command is a human anticipation of the imperative judgments to be delivered by the divine speeches that follow. They appear to be the author's last presentation of secular wisdom's attempt to refute Job—a final human judgment preceding the divine.

Only in the fourth speech (chaps. 36–37) is new ground broken, and this speech directs us to the divine speeches that follow. God's dealings with human beings are not simply in terms of rewards and punishments. They are also remedial and pedagogic (a position which Eliphaz earlier anticipated—5:17–27). Calamity in life brings its opportunity for trust, and thus the full answer to Job's problem cannot be found in the appeal to justice. The argument moves from the wisdom of God to God's power, and thus to the astonishing control of God over a universe from which, for Elihu, God is somewhat detached, and in which humankind is only a passive spectator of divine events. Elihu is right to emphasize that men and women should stop to ponder the works of God. But Job has done that (chap. 26). What Job needs now is the encouragement that can be given only by personal confrontation with the Creator.

God's Solution (Job 38–41)

God reveals himself in a storm, reminding us of the beginning of Job's difficulties (Job 1:13–19) and, thus, hinting that this appearance will lead to their resolution. In the magnificent assertion of creative power that follows, God says, indirectly, that he does not choose that human beings should know all the factors operating in this present world. We may see the results of God's handiwork, but we do not know God's purposes. There is no hint in these speeches that Job is being treated as a sinner; rather, he is being treated as one whose horizons need to be expanded. God has appeared in answer to Job's appeal. Thus, at the end of chapter 39, Job is challenged to respond. His response to this first divine speech is subdued. He confesses ignorance, but not sin (40:3–5). As Yahweh had spoken twice in the prologue, a second divine speech now ensues (40:6–41:34). Moral issues are now much more prominent. Job can no more pronounce judgment in the moral realm (40:10–14) than he could control the natural realm, the subject of the previous speech. He must, therefore, be content to leave his life and its issues with God. He dare not provoke God any more than he would provoke Behemoth (40:15–24) or Leviathan (chap. 41), denizens of land and sea.

Job's Response (Job 42:1–6)

The limits of traditional wisdom have been explored by the dialogues, the addresses of Elihu, and the divine speeches. In the last divine speech, a solution has been pronounced. Job has received assurance that divine justice and power are established over all creation. He is now content, and says so in 42:1–6, although specific answers to his questions have not been given. He has seen that human events are part of a larger whole, while his friends have argued within the tight contours of a cause-and-effect chain of sin and punishment. The Book of Job has not solved the problem of human suffering. That is not its intent. Rather, it has demonstrated the intimate connection of God with God's world, and God's careful and detailed superintendence. It has dispelled all mechanical views of God and thus liberated the doctrine of God's sovereignty. God gives life, and God withdraws it. Meaning in life cannot be understood within the human compass, but only within the framework of a vision of God that looks for justification of the present puzzles of human existence in a life yet to come. In saying all of this, however, the real problem of the Book of Job has been left untouched, and to this we now turn.

The divine verdict of verse 42:7b, "You [the friends] have not spoken of me what is right, as my servant Job has," has been rightly asserted to be a guide to our understanding of the purpose of Job. The verdict is emphasized by its repetition in verse 8. But to what section of the book do the words refer? To the divine speeches or the dialogues, or both? The contrast between Job's words and those of the friends seems certainly to refer to Job's speeches in the dialogues. The friends are absolutely condemned, and Job commended, and this is a divine assessment of the dialogues' total course, not of particular aspects. The forgiveness of the friends now becomes dependent on Job's intercession. This is a measure of the divine confidence in Job, echoing the divine verdict in 1:8. Job seems not to require forgiveness, and we appear to be put in a situation in which Job's contribution in the dialogues has been consistent with his character presentation in the prologue. We would expect that such a divine assessment, once uttered in chapters 1–2, would be sustained throughout the whole book. The theophany of chapters 38–41 has not altered that assessment; it has simply pointed to the general human problem of the limited horizons of knowledge. The theophany had been revelatory, not corrective, since the issues of dispute in the dialogues had not been broached. Job had been rebuked by the theophanies, but not condemned. The divine speeches had resolved the problem of theodicy in the book, and Job had seen that. But with all the additional information provided by the theophanies, Job's basic problem had remained. His fortunes were not restored until after the issue between Job and the friends had been resolved in Job's favor, indicating that the competing attitudes of Job and the friends constituted the basic problem that the book addresses.

Job had suffered unjustly, and his friends had responded with traditional, but unconvincing, theological views. But God in the theophany did not address this problem. Further, it seems in 42:7b–9 that Job was right to question God in the dialogues, that he was acting correctly in raising the question of divine justice. Job knows that his suffering is undeserved, but he does not know how it is possible for undeserved suffering to exist. But God allows, in his second divine speech, for this fact to exist in a universe over which he is sovereign, and Job now understands this, solving for himself the problem of suffering, but probably not solving his theological questions.

That God's commendation of Job relates to the dialogues does not make the divine speeches unnecessary. Job must also learn that no neat human investigations can unfold the character of the inhabited world. Job, after the divine speeches, admits his limited understanding (42:3b). The changed attitude of Job in 42:2–6 makes it possible for God to render a more complete verdict on the whole affair.

A Review of the Dialogues

There is no development in the friends' theology in the three cycles of speeches. Their minds are set in familiar patterns. Even in their styles of argumentation, the friends provide a static, stylized background against which the tortured but adventurous hero of the book excites our imagination and sympathy. The friends, the resolute defenders of orthodoxy, are wrong about Job. Job maintains that he has not denied the words of the Holy One (6:10), and that he is just and blameless, so why is he suffering? He does not regard himself as sinless and seems, at times, to admit minor sin (cf. 7:21 and 13:26, where he speaks of the iniquities of his youth). Job repeatedly asks his friends, and then God, as to the nature of his wrongs or the charges against him (6:24; 10:2; 13:23–24). If the charges were known, he could clear himself of graver wrongs and repent of lesser sins, since he could have sinned in some way of which he was unaware. But he denies sins such as violent wrongdoing or straying from God, which would merit the present punishment and the suggestion that sin merits graduated punishment. God, who makes Job appeal for mercy (9:15), knows that Job is innocent. Job is willing to accept punishment for proven sins, but he is convinced of his integrity and innocence and that, if there were a trial with a heavenly witness, he would be acquitted (9:32; 16:19–21).

The Book of Job and the Problem of Evil

The problem in the book is that the prologue has made God the author, albeit permissively, of a particular evil. The doctrine of God as the author of permissive evil seems biblically correct. As it must, if dualism is to be avoided, the Bible asserts the responsibility of God for evil (cf. Isa. 45:7, which in context must refer to creation, not to the historical circumstance). God is often the architect of national misfortunes, and we understand that this is part of God's providential control. But the Book of Job has made God the author of specific personal problems. The problem of suffering generally can be left to one side, since that is not taken up in Job. What comes up in the book is not the question of natural evil, but the question of the anguish of faith derived from suffering. By the prologue, God has become the agent of specific suffering and death. Job has become the pawn in a heavenly power struggle, losing his possessions, family, and his standing. The prologue has presented a doctrine of God that seems difficult to us and against which Job in the dialogues rightly protests. We would judge that Job's protests, laments, calls for justice, and demands to see God have all been right.

Much then depends on our assessment of the book's purpose and on its character as we understand it from the prologue. One approach is to see that the prologue has all the elements of a folktale. The "there was once a man in the land of Uz whose name was Job," with which the prologue commences, may be a genre indication. The perfect character of Job, his complete family, his unparalleled commercial, agricultural, and pastoral success, the folksy account of the heavenly scenes, and the detail of his family's death all point in this direction. We may also add the restitution in the epilogue of what was lost. If this approach is valid, then the prologue erects a doctrine of God against which the book will argue and on which God himself, in 42:7–9, will finally pronounce. While God may be accepted as the general author of evil, and creation itself be seen to be moving to a final order from a contingent beginning, God reveals himself biblically as one who may test, but not tempt, by imposing specific evils. We understand that if incidents such as those that Job undergoes do not express the divine intention, the nature of such incidents are known to God. In the face of this presentation, the dialogues of Job present the language of protest. The Book of Job then becomes a progressive undoing of the prologue, even to the replacement—and more—at the end, of Job's losses. In short, the doctrine of God in the prologue flies in the face of the revelation of God to Israel and to us all.

The alternative is to regard the prologue as necessary in correcting a cause-and-effect understanding of divine operations. On such a view, the conceivable resolution of the book would have been the divine speeches, without need of Job 42:7–9. The dialogues thus indicate what God expects from us all within baffling human experience, fortified as we are (and as Job was not) by our informed knowledge of the divine plan (chaps. 38–41). Such an approach to the dialogues, however, robs them of the purpose of highlighting the dispute of the prologue. The Book of Job then becomes an illustration of the language of Romans 8:28, that all things work together for final good for those who love God. But our problem would still be the divine endorsement of Job in 42:7, in the face of Job's verbal assault on God in the dialogues. Why in the face of this extreme language of protest was Job declared to be in the right?

The Book of Job is one of the great puzzles of revelation. It is clear that, in itself, it does not merely correct a misplaced doctrine of retribution carried too far. For it is Satan who holds the view that God runs the world in this tit-for-tat way. We know that this is not so, and we look for its denial within the book.

That comes in the divine speeches, which are an answer to this question but not to the essential question raised by the prologue. The puzzling presentation of God in the prologue is the book's essential problem. It seems that to the problem of divine consistency, which the prologue raises and that is aired fully in the dialogues, only the forthright divine statement of 42:7b–9 is the solution. Perhaps the purpose of the Book of Job will continue to elude us. But from all the information available, we must attempt to construct a viable biblical hypothesis.

27

Proverbs

No detailed arrangement seems to prevail in the Book of Proverbs after Proverbs 9. Sometimes collections are evident, and sometimes a catchword provides a framework of order. The last section on the virtuous wife (31:10–31), however, clearly balances the earlier warning contained in chapters 1–9 against "the loose woman," and is an obvious epilogue, the more so since the woman of 31:30 is one "who fears the Lord" (Blocher 1977, 5). These details and that Proverbs 10:1–22:16 contains 375 lines (the numerical value, in Hebrew, of the name Solomon) point to the book as a very careful editorial compilation. The topic of the Book of Proverbs is wisdom, not just wise behavior or wise teaching but wisdom itself, the human intellectual power, both as knowledge and as a faculty. The Hebrew word *hokmah* 'wisdom', as we have noted, refers broadly to some skill or expertise, a natural endowment that one may possess, intelligence of a most general kind. In addition, it seems to be used more technically in the Book of Proverbs for what can be acquired or enhanced by instruction (see 21:11), or by observation of one's world (see 6:6–8). We will consider the definition further after surveying the contents of the book. For the time being, we will define wisdom as the theory of knowledge that equipped individuals in the OT to understand themselves and their world. The notions of both technical excellence and moral competence are included in Proverbs' usage. Wisdom thus not only offers philosophic insights into one's world, but also is basic to scientific method. Wisdom is and always has been, in all its forms, however, the gift of God (cf. Deut. 4:6).

The Book of Proverbs is not simply about doing, but also about knowing. The most intensive reflection on wisdom comes in Proverbs 1–9, a hermeneutic preamble to the rest of the book. The chapters include a varied cast of characters, chiefly a father figure and his son, which, in ancient wisdom teaching, are metaphors, perhaps for a teacher and pupil. We find conflicts regarding choices between good and evil and wisdom and folly. The presence of so much conflict makes moral choice the unifying action. Faced with competing values and lifestyles, the "son" (and, by extension, the reader) is repeatedly urged to choose one and reject the other.

Various subordinate themes occur in Proverbs 1–9, such as the origins of wisdom, the benefits and rewards of wisdom, the tragic results of rejecting wisdom for folly, and the necessity to choose wisdom and the characteristics and acts of wisdom. We also find a unifying viewpoint and tone. The repeated address to "my son" gives these chapters a single viewpoint. This viewpoint is that of a narrator, an old person, an authority figure, who has seen life and is qualified to explain its meaning to the young person whom he addresses. This wise man often speaks in the imperative as he gives instructions and advice. We find repeated formulas that in one way or another command the listener to be attentive. The effect is to instill in us the conviction that the narrator possesses urgently needed information. Even the imagery of Proverbs 1–9 falls into unifying patterns. The master images are two personified abstractions named Wisdom and Folly. But, in the midst of this, the writer has incorporated diverse literary techniques and forms. His artistry is seen by his ability to handle variety and, at the same time, to achieve unity.

Purpose and Theme of Proverbs (Prov. 1:2–7)

A series of key terms is densely packed in Proverbs 1:2–6, all of which contribute to understanding the book's purpose even before the theme is explicitly stated in verse 7: "The fear of the Lord is the beginning of knowledge." The precise arrangement of key terms in verses 2–4 indicates the purpose of the instructional material to follow, while verses 5–6 indicate the effect upon the wise. Verse 7 sketches the general context in which this process must operate.

Wisdom, *hokmah* (1:2a), is linked with the series of terms that follow (Nel 1982, 109). Verse 2 lists *musar* 'instruction' or 'correction' (see 1:8; 3:11; 4:13), and then *binah* 'understanding', a term that in Proverbs carries the sense of a basic insight into life and the ability to respond properly to life's experiences (see 1:5; 2:2; 3:19; 4:5, etc.). A collection of three interrelated terms follows in verse 3b: *sedeq, mishpat,* and *mesharim.* The term *sedeq* 'righteousness' in Proverbs seems to mean the ideal order and harmony to be appropriated and expressed by the wise (8:8; 12:17). The term *mishpat* means "justice," or the action by which *sedeq* is expressed, mainly by judicial means (2:8; 24:23; 29:4). Finally, *mesharim* 'equity' is a subjective term indicating the personal stance to the ideal order that *sedeq* connotes (8:6; 23:16). These three terms imply a defined order to be brought into being and expressed by official and personal action. One who is untutored—the "simple" (*peti*) of verse 4—may thereby deal "prudently" (*'armah*) on the basis of knowledge now available to him. To the uninstructed (*n'aar* 'youth', parallel in v. 4 to *peti*), "knowledge" (*d'aat*, used seventy times in Proverbs) and "discretion" (*mezimmah*) are both now available. This knowledge involves an objective content, a subjective reception, and a decision to act on the content received (Nel 1982, 110–15). There is a close relationship between "knowledge of God" and "the fear of Yahweh" (cf. 1:7, 29; 2:5; 9:10), while "discretion" indicates the pursuit and demonstration of what is good (2:11; 8:12).

Attention to the implication of these terms assures the wise person of an increase in basic understanding (1:5). One who is insightful will be able to reconcile the tortuous problems of life and to understand the material that the remainder of the book presents (v. 6). The book takes the simple facts of life and puts them in the form of proverbs (*mashal*, v. 6). Compared or contrasted with other facts or experiences, these aphorisms, models, or paradigms have an incisive effect. The word *melitsah* 'figure' in verse 6, a parallel to *mashal*, indicates a cutting word that can penetrate by the starkness of its presentation.

The introduction leads to the key statement in the book: "The fear of the Lord is the beginning of knowledge." This statement appears in 1:7 (with "knowledge" for "wisdom") and 9:10, thus forming a frame for the determinative first section of the book (see also 15:33; 22:4; 23:17). "The fear of the Lord" illuminates the intelligence and thus makes the acquisition of divine wisdom possible (note the parallel of wisdom with "knowledge of the Holy One" in 9:10); it provides the context within which wisdom can operate. A range of meanings is possible for *re'shit* 'beginning', but the word most probably means "what necessarily comes first in a sequence." In Proverbs, it is best translated "principle" or "essence" (Blocher 1977, 15). Since "fear" is the proper attitude to be taken before God as God reveals himself (Deut. 5:29), the total phrase conveys the idea that wisdom, which is the theme of the Book of Proverbs, is not merely a set of maxims to control human behavior, but rather a worldview. It is a rule of life that brings us into contact with the principles of order which control reality.

Proverbs 1–9

The remainder of Proverbs 1–9 is composed of ten discourses (1:8–19; 2:1–22; 3:1–12; 3:21–35; 4:1–9; 4:10–19; 4:20–27; 5:1–23; 6:20–35; 7:1–27) formulated as father/son instruction and five interludes (1:20–33; 3:13–20; 6:1–19; 8:1–36; 9:1–18) occurring between or concluding the discourses. In the discourses, the father, an authoritative figure, is the dispenser of wisdom who offers life as opposed to death. All the discourses are directed to the young man on the brink of manhood, and concern the temptations to which he is exposed. The goal of the discourses is to develop moral character, but the author generally avoids topics treated elsewhere in Proverbs. The primary function of wisdom is to protect against temptation. The youth is on the threshold of full adult life, for which he must now be prepared.

The discourses are comprised of an address, exhortation to hear and remember, a motivation to commend the teaching, the teaching itself, and a conclusion summarizing the lesson (Fox 1997, 614). Their message is plain and unambiguous, yet wisdom means something more than simply knowing the moral options. Wisdom is attitudinal or emotional as well as intellectual. The son is thus not only urged to learn but also to love and desire wisdom (4:6–8). Wisdom seems a power for moral advance that, once achieved (as given by God), resides in the learner as a potential, the inner light that guides a person through life. This wisdom is identified with, though not identical to, the fear of God, which is both the starting point and the culmination of wisdom.

Interspersed among the discourses and instructions are four or five interludes, depending on whether 6:1–19 is included. This section, although beginning with a father/son address, does not show the same formal structure as the instructions and seems to be four unconnected units offering social advice. In any case, the detail of 6:1–19 is not germane to the topic of the interludes. The remaining four (1:20–33; 3:13–20; 8:1–36; 9:1–18) present wisdom as a feminine persona, with all four offering a positive image of the personification (1:20–33) in Wisdom's condemnation of folly (3:13–20), Wisdom's worth and her link with creation (8:1–36), Wisdom's self-praise and her role in creation (9:1–18), Wisdom's (9:1–12) and Folly's (9:13–18) invitations. The personification probably has its origin in the ancient and universal mystique surrounding woman, and not, as often assumed, foreign or mythological sources. Folly in the interludes seems an abstraction or amalgamation of the "strange woman" in the instructions, finally offset by the book's acrostic conclusion (31:10–31). She is depicted in terms similar to those used of the adulteress in chapter 7, with the spread banquet (9:2, 5), analogous to 7:14, 16–17, in which it is the spread bed that lures the fool, and not the invitation of 9:15 (cf. 7:18, 21).

The four interludes (1:20–33; 3:13–20; 8:1–36; 9:1–18) present Lady Wisdom positively as the personification of mental power. She claims to have preceded creation and to exist in a daughterlike relationship with God. She transcends earthly reality and human minds individually and collectively, yet she is active in the busiest spheres of human existence. She interacts with human wisdom, but is not exhausted by human wisdom. Lady Wisdom is a heavenly creature, residing in proximity to God. She exists outside of the human sphere, but freely penetrates it. In this connection, the key passage is 8:1–36, in which Wisdom, as teacher, calls for attention. She is revealed in Torah but she is more than verbal revelation. On the other hand, the feminine persona is also prominent in the discourses in Proverbs 1–9, but is negatively presented. This difference in presentation of the feminine persona means that the negative/positive presentation is brought to a climax and summed up in chapter 9. That chapter puts the question as to which woman will direct the reader's lifestyle. Chapter 9 brings the two competing presentations together and asks for an evaluation and a commitment; the precise details that the commitment will involve are communicated in chapters 10–31.

Wisdom in Proverbs 1–9

Proverbs, in the interludes of chapters 1–9, asserts that all knowledge proceeds from a single source, beyond time and space, making itself known by communicating itself to human sages and through them. What the father says about Wisdom in the discourses, Wisdom says about herself in the interludes. The common element is that wisdom demands human attention. Wisdom realizes her potential only through human activity. Wisdom is not an inert body of knowledge, a mass of facts and rules. In the final analysis, wisdom is a gift, but it cannot be limited to the subjective apprehension of the gift. As a gift, wisdom is potentially available to all within the domain of creation. Underlining this potential universality, wisdom is conceived as playing an important role even before the cosmos came into existence, and as standing in a special relationship to the created world of people (cf. Sir. 1:9, God "has poured out wisdom on all his works"). This wisdom is to be found somewhere in the world, and it is there, but it is incapable of being totally grasped. Von Rad (1972, 156–57) in an influential modern interpretation, identified wisdom in Proverbs 8 and so on with primal order, the order-producing force with which God informs the world. A search for wisdom, however, is not a mere search for order. Wisdom cannot be primal order but must, if the identification is to be followed, be knowledge of the primal order. But to imprint such primal wisdom in the world makes the concept mechanistic, depersonalized, and attainable. In the final analysis, wisdom turns out to be separate from the works of creation, a principle that comprehends all insightful teaching and astute thought; wisdom turns out to be the meaning implanted by God in creation, which is not mere knowledge but which will issue in the doing of God's will. Thus wisdom is not merely God's order in this world, but knowledge of divine order and the implications of such knowledge, with a view to action. Wisdom is a word about the world, an objective truth that, as a gift, may be subjectively grasped. Israel partook of cosmopolitan wisdom, but complemented it by special revelation, necessary because it was not finally accessible within creation (Job 28). Sirach 24:1–22 asserts that wisdom lodged in Israel, where it took the form of Torah (24:23–29). It resides permanently and securely in Israel because it is part of Israel's revelation. Wisdom's teaching will appear in the subsequent chapters of Proverbs.

Critical for an understanding of wisdom in the OT is the statement in Proverbs 1:7 that the beginning of wisdom is the knowledge or fear of Yahweh. This makes it clear that the knowledge, and pursuit of it, must be pursued within the closed circle of revelation. Such a word is, however, available only to those who are willing to sit before it and submit to it. The fear of Yahweh, a worldview that puts Yahweh at the center, provides the context in which wisdom, as the revealed knowledge of God relating to existence within creation, will be given. Proverbs, Job 28, and so on mandate knowledge of Israel's God for the acquisition of wisdom. In the OT, wisdom can be taught and its effect seen from example, but it must be pursued, for ultimately it is the gift of Yahweh. Personified as woman in Proverbs 1–9, wisdom is a heavenly creature, residing in angelic proximity to God. But wisdom is also ubiquitous in everyday life, traversing the streets and speaking to all who, through faith, have the facility to hear. It is argued that Israel did not have a monopoly of wisdom, and that wisdom in its essence, rather than in its infinite particulars, is God's general gift to humanity. Israel partakes of this cosmopolitan wisdom, though her portion is greater. Again, there may be truth here on the general level, but this is *not* what the Bible finally calls wisdom.

So true wisdom is an understanding of God's purposes, particularized for Israel's conduct within salvation history. In this sense, Israel's knowledge of creation intersected her salvation history, since the summation of God's purposes for the world was to be had in redemption. Wisdom and revelation are thus overlapping terms, as are wisdom and Spirit. The christological movement of the New Testament, which links wisdom and the Word (*logos;* cf. John 1:1–18), is therefore not only understandable, but also demanded. The world is only able to understand within a framework of dependence on Yahweh's revelation. The fear of Yahweh that put Yahweh at the center of the Israelite worldview was later expressed in the Christology of the New Testament.

The Message of Proverbs 1–9

Wisdom metaphors are fivefold: evangelist (1:20–33; 8:1–21), tree of life (3:18), a way (4:10–19), a craftsman (8:22–31), and Lady Wisdom (chap. 9). A common thread in all of these metaphors is that choice is an essential component of life. This fact is then embodied in the notion of two ways, taken up in detail in 4:10–19. After the first instruction, a warning against seduction by sinners (1:8–19), wisdom as evangelist stands at the head of the streets and calls (vv. 20–33). Chapter 2 has a more obviously formal structure than the other chapters in this collection, and has been considered to be programmatic of the content of chapters 3–7. It can be divided into six stanzas (1–4, 5–8, 9–11, 12–15, 16–19, 20–22) making two balanced halves. Stanzas 1 and 6 form the introduction and conclusion, but, more important, the themes treated in stanzas 2–5 are taken up and developed in subsequent discourse. Stanza 2 relates the pupil's relationship with God (cf. 3:1–12). Stanza 3 discusses the pupil's possession of wisdom (cf. 3:13–24; 4:[1]5–9), stanza 4 the avoidance of evil (cf. 4:14–19), and stanza 5 avoidance of the adulteress (cf. 5:1–20; 6:20–35; 7:1–27). Proverbs 2 introduces the series of discourses that extends to 7:27. Wisdom must be desired (2:4), but it is the gift of God (vv. 5–8). Therefore, it will protect against adversity (vv. 9–11), although opposition will come from people of perverse speech (vv. 12–15). Verses 16–19 present the image of the seductive woman, which is probably to be related to fertility-cult practices and the sexual overtones associated with them. This image is balanced in verses 20–22 by the reward for fidelity: inhabitation of the ideal land.

Chapters 2–3 are the theological center of Proverbs 1–9. Reflection on creation and wisdom is there (3:19–20), but creation does not play a dominant role. The creation theme is used to enhance the status of wisdom by portraying it as closely associated with the Lord, as a witness or unique instrument of creation. Thus the creation motif turns out to be secondary. Creation faith is thus subordinated to wisdom speculation. Creation plays a slightly greater role in Job, and a significant role in Sirach, but a slight one in Ecclesiastes, as in Proverbs. The book assumes a creation theology, though this is not the main theological component of the wisdom tradition.

Chapter 3 contains two addresses introduced by "my son" (1–12, 21–35) that present the way to get true wisdom, which is devotion to Yahweh (vv. 1–12). The "my son" in verse 11 is not the beginning of a new section but is resumptive. Wisdom's blessing is life (vv. 13–18), since it provides harmony with the purposes of creation (vv. 19–20) and thus affords protection and confidence, noted in the second "my son" address of verses 21–35. Proverbs 4:1–9 offers the father's (i.e., teacher's) advice for life: get wisdom. Verses 10–27 introduce the celebrated motif of two ways: the way of wisdom (vv. 10–13, 18) and the way of folly (vv. 14–17, 19). The way of wisdom, which is clear and straight and leads to life, is the way of righteousness. By contrast, the way of folly is darkened with obstacles, and those who tread it live in darkness.

This theme of two ways continues virtually throughout the remaining addresses, as does the pattern of introducing each of the ten addresses with the words "my son." The eighth discourse (chap. 5) is a warning against adultery and the "loose woman." Proverbs 6:1–19 is a collection of four short units before Proverbs 7:1–27 concludes the series on the note of the call of the adulteress herself, who has occupied a central position in four of the instructions (chaps. 2; 5; 6:20–35; and now chap. 7). She is also featured in the didactic poem of contrasts in Proverbs 9. She seems to personify the fertility practices common in Israel. A love cultivated for Lady Wisdom, however, will keep the disciple from Folly's seductions (7:4–5). The theme of the two ways is designed to underline the compelling worth of choosing wisdom, also a matter of emphasis in the poetic and proverbial material which links or expands the ten instructions. Lady Wisdom protects her traveling companion from being preyed upon by the strange woman, who entices with inviting speech (5:1–4), but whose feet travel the path leading straight to Sheol (5:5–8). The actual author of this protection is Yahweh, who works through wisdom, the true source of knowledge (3:21–26). Ultimate deliverance from the loose woman (2:16–19) and rescue from all false paths that threaten covenant fidelity thus rest with him.

Proverbs 8 addresses the question of how the meaning that is implicit in the ordered world can impress itself onto the mind of human beings. The chapter serves to integrate the instructional material that has preceded. The relationship between wisdom and Yahweh has been clear since 2:1–6, where a search for wisdom is in fact a search for Yahweh, not for wisdom as an end in itself. Thus, this search leads to knowledge of God by which the world may be rightly ordered. In 3:19–20, we learn that wisdom was Yahweh's instrument in ordering creation. Proverbs 8 takes us further in this direction, discussing this key to ordered reality. On the one hand, wisdom provides us with an understanding of the nature of reality and is, in its essence, the provision of a right worldview, while on the other hand, wisdom and the knowledge she provides always remain elusive and mysterious.

Wisdom, as a teacher, begins 8:1–11 and concludes 8:32–36, providing an *inclusio* of self-commendation that encompasses two poems on Wisdom's role in providence (8:12–21) and creation (8:22–31). She stands not in a hidden, sacred place but on the heights, by the roadside, where the paths cross (Prov. 8:2). She speaks not from the sacred place of the sanctuary, but in the most profane public place, at the gate of the city, where instruction would normally be conveyed. Wisdom's presence at the gate points to her involvement in the life-giving and life-sustaining justice that is at the center of social and even cosmic life. The world to which Wisdom comes is thus a city teeming and bustling with the traffic of human life. Wisdom does not withdraw from everyday life in order to offer the quiet rest of meditation or rare encounters with God through mystical or cultic rituals that distinguished between the sacred and the profane. Rather, Wisdom goes in search of people in their customary pursuits and offers them instruction for life so that their various activities, from marriage to business deals, to the advising of kings, could help the follower live in harmony with the world and experience success. Proverbs 8 asserts that humankind is addressed from creation by a desire for order from which it cannot escape. Both the art of government and the conduct of personal life depend on this ordering power. In verses 12–21, Wisdom providentially directs the course of human history. She has intellectual capabilities—shrewdness, finesse, the ability to make plans (v. 14), insight, and, of course, wisdom itself. She has moral qualities; she hates pride, arrogance, and perverted speech, and she has power (v. 14). In verses 15–16, Wisdom is the patroness of high-ranking state officials and kings, those representing traditional authority, whose decisions in public affairs shape the course of the state. In verses 17–21, she asserts that, with them, she entertains a relationship of mutual trust and love, since through her a beneficial order of both creation and society results.

The central section (vv. 22–31) is divisible into four sections, in the first and last of which Wisdom speaks about herself (vv. 22–23, 30–31). In the first of the two middle strophes (vv. 24–26), the situation before creation is described, and, in the second (vv. 27–29), Yahweh's creative action. Wisdom speaks of her mysterious origins as God's darling child, which reaches back to the time when the world was created. Thus, the function of verses 22–31 is not merely to provide an additional rationale for hearing Wisdom's call, but to emphasize the primacy and importance of Wisdom based on her status as the sole witness to creation available to humankind. A key to the identification and understanding of Wisdom is the term *qananiy* 'created me' in verse 22. The vocabulary of the immediate context and the context itself support the translation "create." Wisdom in any case belongs to the sphere of things created. As the beginning of God's ways, she was the best element of creation. Wisdom is the child of the Creator, but only a spectator of creation. She watched the establishment of the universe and learned its secrets. Her joyful play in the presence of the Creator is an unmistakable sign of intimacy. Sirach 1:9 says that God poured out wisdom on all his works, and this seems an understanding of a cosmological process, namely the bestowal of something special on creation—something we have learned from Job 28—which now suffuses creation with immanence. What is objectified in Proverbs 8 is not an attribute of God or something analogous to the Spirit, but an attribute of the world, namely that mysterious attribute by virtue of which Wisdom can give order to people's lives.

Although it is clearly differentiated from the whole of creation, wisdom is an entity that belongs in the world even if it is the first of the works of creation, the creature above all creatures. This special position of wisdom over against created things is also the position of Job 28. The text of Proverbs 8 addresses Wisdom as a person who addresses humankind, who is created/born and who is in close fellowship with the Lord. The term "personification," and not "hypostasis," seems the appropriate term with which to label Wisdom in Proverbs 8 and throughout chapters 1–9. In Proverbs 3:19–20, Wisdom is referred to as an instrument of God, without any hint regarding her independence, and the literary presentation of Proverbs 8 must start from there. At Proverbs 8:32–36, Wisdom returns to her initial role as teacher. The goal of instruction is the cultivation of personal wisdom, in which piety and reflection characterize and form the sage's identity and being. Wisdom offers life to those who enter her dwelling. The contrast between life (happiness, prosperity, and success) and death affords a fitting conclusion to the poem.

Finally, in Proverbs 9, in which the first part of the book is summarized, Lady Wisdom and Lady Folly are pitted as rivals. Both sit at the highest point in the city and call out to the simple, seeming to represent the two possible worldviews: wisdom's invitation leads to life, and that of folly leads to death. Two alternative religious stances, two basic ways of looking at existence, are contrasted.

The Message of Proverbs 10–31

In Proverbs—and this is the book's main emphasis—wisdom is the motivating force in conduct within the covenant relationship. The wise teaching of Proverbs is a manifestation of the revealed wisdom to which a proper relationship to the covenant (the fear of God as the necessary factor) admits us.

The remainder of the book is given over, with little discernible structure, to proverbial admonitions that outline the shape of covenant conduct; the imperatival note of the first line is coupled with the motivation offered by the second. The admonitions demand orderly conduct, and the motivations, drawing on human experience, advance the argument. Put otherwise, while the admonitions speak of adhering to the order of creation, the motivations present this appeal as reasonable. Proverbs 1–9 has offered the framework for the implementation of chapters 10–31. The point from which the wisdom movement proceeds is the recognition of evil as a breach of the created order, reparable only by an insight into and an application of what wisdom can provide.

The definition of "proverb" is notoriously difficult. The Hebrew *mashal* has a wide range of meanings and seems to be connected with comparison and with rule or power. Proverbial speech is assertive, apparently self-explanatory, frequently paradoxical, and brief. The comparison is the basic feature. The basic wisdom saying is usually composed of two lines in parallelism, a common feature of Proverbs 10–31. Often there is simply a juxtaposition without a verb, as the following illustrates: "A son who gathers in summer [is] prudent, but a son who sleeps in harvest brings shame" (Prov. 10:5). A proverb may display many forms of parallelism. *Synonymous parallelism* occurs when the two lines are brought together, saying the same thing in different ways. The second line usually reinforces the basic idea of the first line (Prov. 14:19; 16:28). When the two lines provide a contrast, this is *antithetical parallelism* (Prov. 10:1, 10:5, etc.).

When the first line is an illustration or example and the second line distills a wisdom principle from it, this is *emblematic parallelism* (Prov. 10:26; 25:23; Mouser 1983, 56), drawn from nature. *Synthetic parallelism* places two sayings loosely together in run-on form. Proverbs, moreover, are pithy generalizations of experience, not inflexible laws and not promises.

There is little discernible structure in the collections, although chapters 10–15 tend to be pragmatic, and 16:1–22:16 religious. Nor does any particular social setting dominate (Nel 1982, 76–82). A court setting occurs on a few occasions, a wisdom-school background is sometimes suggested by many of the traditional topics, and there is some relationship with cultic interests. We cannot determine a setting-in-life from the form of the admonitions themselves. They do presuppose a structured society, but more than that we are unable to say.

Proverbs 22:17–24:34 consists of "sayings of the wise" given over to, among other things, instructions for administrators and present admonitions to industry and sincerity. Parallels to this section exist with the Instruction of Amenemope (twelfth century B.C., Egypt), known from 1923. But the correspondences are not thoroughly precise, and the themes of the Hebrew material are not in the Egyptian order; further, the correspondences do not extend beyond 23:11. Proverbs 23:13–14 is close to a pair of sayings from the Aramaic, "The Words of Ahiqar," found at Elephantine, but probably north Syrian in origin.

Chapters 25–29 provide the second miscellaneous Solomon collection. In Proverbs 25:1, the sense of the Hebrew *'atiq* 'copied' seems to be "moving material from one context to another," perhaps of transcribing it, although the material need not previously have been in written form. Hezekiah's officials may also have added editorial content if the material was based on oral sayings. A good case has been made that the approximately 130 lines in this section reflect the numerical value of the name of their collector—King Hezekiah. Proverbs 30:1–14 stresses the limitations of wisdom, and verses 15–33 provide a numerical poem. The sayings of Lemuel's mother (31:1–9) condemn lust, drunkenness, and oppression and prepare us for the artistic close of the book, an acrostic poem on the theme of the "good wife" (vv. 10–31), perhaps a counterpoint to the "loose woman" of chapters 1–9.

The Good Wife (Prov. 31:10–31)

Proverbs 31:10–31 draws together the major themes, motifs, and ideas of the book in a final summarizing statement about wisdom as an industrious, resourceful, and selfless wife. It is the final piece in a symbolic framework that unifies the whole book, including the individual sayings. If the woman at the end of the book is Wisdom, then we have come full circle from chapter 1. We see her now as self-sufficient, selfless about the many different tasks in which she helps and guides us. The poem's concentration of attention is on the wife and on all that she does, emphasizing her virtues as well as her prudence and ingenuity. Remarkable similarities between the portrait of the wife and various descriptions of wisdom indicate that the poem in chapter 31 is the book's final, masterful portrait of Wisdom. She was presented last in chapter 9 as a young marriageable woman, seeking one who would accept the gifts of life that she offers. Now that time of courtship is over. In chapter 31, Wisdom is the faithful wife and mistress of the household, fully settled. Wisdom is thus presented throughout, not as a mysterious, lofty ideal for the initiated, but as a practical, faithful, lifelong companion for those who would choose her way. Her origins are with God (8:22–30), and her teaching wins blessings from God (8:35). But her home is in this world.

Right living is the theme of Proverbs. True wisdom depends on an understanding of God's purposes in creation, which have been particularized, as we know, in salvation history. Whereas prophecy reflected upon and responded to salvation history, the wisdom movement directed its attention to what creation itself implied for human conduct. In this sense, God's providential government of the world intersects with salvation history (i.e., God's special relationship to Israel). Law, the subject of prophetic reflection, came to be seen as the revelation of the divine will in the most general terms, and was thus able to coalesce with wisdom. This did not take place as a demand, but as an explication of the right attitude to be adopted to divine revelation. For it became clear that ethical responses derive from the understanding that human beings must live as subordinate creatures in a world in which Yahweh intends harmony and order to prevail.

28

Ruth

The Book of Ruth is found within the Hebrew canon in the Writings, probably because of its liturgical use at the Feast of Pentecost. Its position between Judges and Samuel in the Greek OT was doubtless dictated by its content. That position seems appropriate, however, for the book is probably a product of the early monarchy, displaying the interests of that period. The question of its dating is contested; for example, the argument from the use of Aramaic forms is two-edged, just as easily providing evidence for an early dating as for a late dating. Its title is perhaps a misnomer, since the book is about Naomi's family.

The book exhibits a fivefold division (chaps. 1; 2; 3; 4:1–17a; and then the concluding genealogy of David in 4:17b–22). The message is simple. A family calamity is gradually reversed by a series of remarkable divine interventions, which are quite behind the scenes and whose nature must be inferred. The addition of the genealogy at the end makes it clear that the book is a demonstration of the mysterious way that God works through the processes of history, bringing fullness of life out of seeming hopelessness (a major theme of the book), and controlling the destiny of Naomi's family. The story runs its own course with intervention by the narrator only in 1:6 and 4:13. The book also displays the unobtrusive but active piety of the believer of the judges period; the divine name is prominent, occurring most frequently in the prayers (1:8–9; 2:12, 20; 3:10; 4:11–12, 14; cf. 2:4).

On the simplest level, Ruth concerns redemption of the plot of land that apparently still belonged to Naomi but had fallen into the hands of others after her departure for Moab. On a deeper level, the commencement of the book, which underscores the famine in the land, is to be contrasted with the conclusion of the book and the Davidic genealogy there. Such a contrast indicates that the book points in more general terms to Yahweh's covenantal *hesed* ("loyal love, kindness") as it serves to provide background for the later career of King David. Ruth is, then, the typical believer to whom rest in the land will be granted; at this level she symbolizes Yahweh's wider attitude toward Israel.

The general movement within the first chapter is from famine to harvest, from abandonment of the land to return. Verses 1–7 recount the migration to Moab and the decision to return to Judah. The unfortunate circumstances and the double catastrophe that prompted the return are described. In four dialogues (1:8–10, 11–14, 15–17, 19c–21), Naomi takes the issue forward, raising in 1:8–9 the key themes of the book, namely, a home, a husband, and kindness (Heb. *hesed*), which are to be provided for Ruth. The troubles of this chapter—the emptiness encountered in the famine and in the deaths of Naomi's husband and sons (vv. 3–5)—are countered by the note of hope on which the chapter ends. While Naomi remains the point of reference in the chapter, the confession of Ruth at verses 16–17 is central. The mention of Naomi's return in verse 22 underscores Ruth's ethnic background, and thus her conversion.

Gleaning in Boaz's Field (Ruth 2)

In 2:1, the important information is delivered, indicating in itself the conclusion that Boaz was a kinsman of Elimelech. The dialogic pattern of Ruth 2—Ruth and Naomi (vv. 2–3), Boaz and the reapers (vv. 4–7), Boaz and Ruth (vv. 8–15a), Boaz and the reapers (vv. 15b–16), and Naomi and Ruth (vv. 19–22; see Prinsloo 1980, 334)—places the exchange between Ruth and Boaz at the center. In this chapter about gleaning in Boaz's field, chance seems to play its part (2:3), but this is simply the narrator's manner of indicating that no human intervention had thrown Boaz and Ruth together. Ruth has now found favor (2:10) with the kinsman. Boaz, who has been informed of Ruth's background (2:11), is led to exclaim that her attitude indicates that she has taken shelter under the wings (Heb. *knp*) of the God of Israel, a pregnant phrase whose inner meaning is disclosed in 3:10, where Boaz's skirt (*knp*) is to be spread over Ruth. Chapter 2 closes with the end of the harvest period, and thus the end of the connection between Ruth and Boaz, with the connection between Ruth and Naomi now resumed.

Yet the dialogue between Boaz and Ruth demands that the narrative be taken further. In the presence of Naomi's kinsman, Ruth, in exodus terms, has declared herself to be a "foreigner" (2:10). Boaz then proceeds to define her position in Abrahamic terms (but with reference also to 1:15–18): she has left family and land (2:11). His benediction upon Ruth (v. 12) begins the process of fulfillment, which is taken further in verse 20, where Naomi sees Boaz's action as a demonstration of divine *hesed*, the keynote of the book. This kindness (cf. 1:8–9) will eventually issue in the rest to be provided under David (4:17b–22).

Rest for Ruth and Naomi (Ruth 3)

Home, husband, and rest remain to be provided for Ruth, but the processes of *hesed* have begun. Naomi once again takes the initiative in dialogue (vv. 1–6). Her words both begin and end the chapter (vv. 16–18), but the center of attention is the encounter between Boaz and Ruth (vv. 7–15). The close correlation of chapters 2 and 3 is shown by the comparable formats. In both, Naomi puts Ruth into contact with Boaz (in an opening scene); in both, Boaz, as kinsman, is the provider (gleanings only in 2:18, but in 3:17 a very substantial provision of food as a gift). Both chapters end with Naomi's comment on the implication of the meeting that has formed the center of each chapter.

While Ruth 2 deals with the establishment of the relationship with Boaz (note that his name frames the chapter [vv. 1, 23]), Ruth 3 identifies him as the one who will provide rest for Ruth (cf. vv. 1 and Heb. *manoah*). Ruth is simply to wait until the matter provoked by her offer of marriage (3:9) is resolved. Ruth in 3:9 (skirts, 3:9 = wings, 2:12) fulfills Boaz's prayer of 2:12. Boaz gives Ruth high praise for having put the family redemption before what may have been her personal predilections of marriage to a younger man (3:10). Ruth's redemption is now assured, either by Boaz or by a nearer kinsman (v. 13).

Resolution at the Town Gate (Ruth 4)

The town-council setting in Ruth 4 is fascinating. The meeting among Boaz, the kinsman, and the elders in verses 1–8 concerns Naomi's right to sell land, a unique reference in the OT. However, the right of inheritance accorded to the daughters of Zelophehad, who died without male issue (Num. 27:1–11), may provide some parallel. Ruth 4:5 is puzzling, but the use of "buy" (*qanah*) in reference to Ruth could mean "acquire by marriage" (E. F. Campbell 1975, 147). There are clear differences between the use of the Levirate law in Ruth 4 and the remainder of the OT. Verse 5 may therefore indicate a local application of a more general law. Perhaps the notions of redemption and marriage are to be separated, for Boaz takes up the matter of redemption in the presence of the elders (vv. 2–4) but takes up the matter of marriage before all the people (vv. 9–10; see Davies 1983, 231). The theme of emptiness and fertility is carried forward into the marriage between Boaz and Ruth, by the blessing called upon the marriage in 4:11, in which Rachel and Leah provide examples of barrenness followed by fertility.

As the one orchestrating all these events (4:13), Yahweh has made his own name famous in Israel (though v. 14 may also ambiguously refer to the child born to Ruth). The child is the real redeemer of Naomi, and in this sense, her son (v. 17). He (Obed) will also build Ruth's house, which will be definitively established by David. The Book of Ruth thus operates as a counterpoint to the Book of Judges. This indicates the type of kingship that was to operate as a result of covenantal fidelity, and the tranquillity that a true faith communicates, as opposed to the general disorder of the period of the judges.

The events of Ruth happened "in the days when the judges ruled" (1:1), that is, when the covenant was placed at considerable risk by Israel. Ruth indicates how Israel's future will be preserved, namely, by the extraordinary initiatives taken throughout her history by Yahweh. The book points to Yahweh as Israel's Redeemer, great in *hesed* (Exod. 34:6). Undoubtedly the genealogy at the end of the book reflects its intent—to record the divine intervention that protected the family of Naomi. At a time when the covenant was threatened, Yahweh's *hesed,* seen in this book as establishing and preserving personal relationships, was in fact establishing Israel's history. This was a history that would be consummated by the birth of David, the establisher of Israel's rest and the bearer of a famous name (Ruth 4:14; cf. 2 Sam. 7:9).

29

Song of Songs

Early disputes about the canonicity of the Song of Songs were virtually settled by Rabbi Akiba's pronouncement that "the whole world is not worth the day on which the Song of Songs was given to Israel; all the writings are holy, and the Song of Songs is the holy of holies" (*m. Yadayim* 3:5). The prevailing interpretation of this vexing book is literalistic, portraying it as a collection of love lyrics bound by related themes, refrains, and repetitions into a dramatic expression of love's experiences. Recent attempts to find precise structural patterns in the song—for example, chiastic devices—overlook the natural divisions within the song itself and have not proved convincing.

Largely discredited today is the allegorical interpretation of the Song of Songs. To avoid the difficulties that the song poses, Jewish and Christian expositors had viewed it as an allegory of Yahweh and Israel or of Christ and the church. Such allegorical approaches, however, tend to be impositions upon the material and not expositions of it. The cultic-mythological approaches, popular earlier this century, which saw the song as based on fertility-cult parallels, are also not appealing. The wedding-week theory makes the book a cycle of seven descriptive love songs (Arabic *wasfs*) in praise of the physical features of the partners, each song to be sung on a particular day of the wedding week. This founders on the fact that it is not agreed that there are seven clear sections into which the song is divided. In addition, there is a time gap between such relatively modern customs and the biblical period. The once-accepted dramatic theory, popular in the nineteenth century, presupposes the use of a form unknown to Israel in the biblical period.

The best approach views the Song of Songs as a collection of lyrics, linked by interrelated themes and characterized by repetition of motifs, a lack of progression, and abundant symbolism. Erotic images are commonly employed.

The song's lyrics seem to have been deliberately crafted and/or ordered to form seven (rather than six, though the matter is disputed) cycles or poems. The end points of these seven cycles are marked by refrains or concluding lines (2:6–7, 16–17; 3:5; 4:16–5:1; 7:11[10]; 8:3–4, 14; the refrain at 6:3 is exceptional). Scene shifts (the book has six) announce the beginning of each new cycle (2:8; 3:1; 3:6; 5:2; 7:12[11]; 8:5). The seven constituent units form a very obvious chiasm, the center of which is 3:6–5:1, the wedding scene, which contains the book's dramatic high point (4:16–5:1). While we must recognize Israel's restraints on premarital sex and adultery, the unabashed nature of the book indicates that the subject of human love could be presented with freshness and an absence of inhibition. The Solomonic associations may suggest the line of interpretation to be followed as we try to understand this book, namely, that it belongs to the reflective literature of Israel's wisdom movement. The assignment of the book to Solomon, however, would present no insuperable difficulties. The linguistic objections based on the occasional Persian or Greek word can be countered, while the association of the content with earlier Egyptian love lyrics might indicate that the book could be as old as the era of Solomon.

Structure of the Song

First Unit (Song 1:1–2:7)

The first unit commences at 1:2 with the lovers apart and the beloved expressing her desire to be with her lover. The unit continues with exchanges of expressions of admiration and desire; and it concludes with the two lovers united in 2:4–7, with a refrain marking the completion of the unit. The sequences—lover separated, expression of desire, lovers united—are used throughout the book as the pattern of all the cycles, except the last. The unit features the sevenfold alternation of speakers: woman (1:2–7), man (vv. 8–11), woman (vv. 12–14), man (v. 15), woman (vv. 16–17), man (2:1–2; reading 'at with BHS in 2:1), woman (2:3–7). Verses 2–4 (despite the internal change of person, which may be a stylistic feature) praise the lover. Verses 5–6 present the beauty of the beloved as seductive, but withdrawn and unconventional. The extremes contrasted in these two verses—country and city, simplicity and sophistication—typify much of the ambiguity and poetic fancy that are characteristic of this book (Landy 1983, 144–48). Whatever the reason, the beloved is the subject of rejection by her family; she has been forced into a controlled environment apart from her "own vineyard." Verses 7–8 project a rendezvous between the two lovers, whose different statuses in the world (as king and shepherdess?) separate them and threaten them. Verses 9–11 imaginatively liken the beloved to a royal mare, that is, to a beautifully adorned member of the king's entourage; in response, she likens their love to fragrance experienced (vv. 12–14). Verses 15–17 express the mutual admiration of lover (v. 15) and beloved (vv. 16–17), illuminating their relationship by reference to appropriate natural images. In the garden imagery of 2:1–7, the beloved presents herself as a chaste lily, and her lover as an apple tree, protective and yet desirable, under which the beloved shelters and feasts.

The Man's Invitation (Song 2:8–17)

Song 2:8 introduces the beginning of the second unit of the song. The commencement of this new unit is indicated by a scene shift. The previous unit featured the young woman desiring to be brought into the home of her beloved (1:4, 12, 17; 2:4). The young woman is now in her home, from where she sees her beloved approaching (vv. 8–10a). He is coming to invite her to join him in the freedom of the countryside (vv. 10b–15) and thus to leave the security of the home. Song 2:16–17 is the beloved's closing description of their union. The main speaker in this unit is the lover expressing his desire for her to come and be with him.

The Woman's Dream (Song 3:1–5)

The book's third scene is a dreamlike sequence referring to the beloved's search for her lover. The beloved is in her bed (dreaming?). She yearns for her lover and is unable to sleep (v. 1). She goes into the city to search for him (v. 2), where she is found by the watchmen (v. 3a). She questions the watchmen as to his whereabouts (v. 3b). Finding her lover (v. 4a), she returns with him to her home (v. 4b), and they are united. The refrain of verse 5 closes the unit. Again, the movement is from absence and desire to discovery.

The Wedding (Song 3:6–5:1)

In the second unit, it was the lover approaching, and now it is the beloved coming up from the wilderness, approaching with her wedding entourage wafting its fragrances and myrrh (3:6–11). The splendid vision of the approaching bride evokes naturally the lover's admiration and desire for her (4:1–15), expressed in two seven-part appreciations (4:1–5, 9–15). These are constructed around a summary of her beauty (v. 7) and an invitation to come with him (v. 8). The section is completed by the description of their union in 4:16–5:1. The unit is concluded by the poet's interpolation, "Eat, O friends, and drink: drink deeply, O lovers!" (5:1 RSV).

Song 5:2–7:10

At 5:2 comes another shift of scene. The young woman is dreaming (?) in her bed. She again searches for her lover in the city streets and meets the watchmen, by whom she is humiliated. The occurrence of a refrain at 6:3 suggests the end (Dorsey 1990, 88), but there is no scene shift. Song 7:10 seems to be the end, with the refrain, "I am my beloved's, and his desire is for me." The dream search for the absent lover by the beloved begins the unit. Then follows a refrain and question (5:8–9), which introduce a section (vv. 10–16) describing the lover's body from the head down (ten parts, including head, hair, eyes, belly, legs). Song 6:1–3 answers a question from the chorus, the daughters of Jerusalem, as to the lover's location. The central unit, 6:4–9, presents the young man's praise for the beauty of his beloved. At 6:10–6:13a, she goes down to a garden filled with flowers, where she fantasizes about her lover prince. Song 6:13b–7:6, corresponding to 5:10–16, is the lover's praise of the beloved's body from the feet up and finally the description of their union (7:8–10). Thus the unit begins with the lovers separated and ends with them united.

The Woman's Invitation (Song 7:11–8:4)

With 7:11 comes another change of scene. The scene is a round of deeply intimate encounters where the lover is both brother and outsider (8:1), and is led into the chamber of the beloved's mother (8:2–3). It is now springtime, and the beloved invites the lover to go with her into the countryside, where she would give him her love (7:12–14 [11–13]). If he was her brother (8:1–2), she could bring him into her house and engage in an intimacy with him as brother that would be unobjectionable (8:1–4). The unit begins with desire expressed in the invitation and concludes with the refrain of 8:3–4.

Closing Words of Love and Desire (Song 8:5–14)

We are suddenly transported back to the edge of the wilderness (8:5) as the beloved approaches. The beloved returns from the desolate land on the arm of her lover. Verse 5b shifts our focus from the arid wilderness to a verdant apple tree. The lover speaks (with *BHS,* following the Syriac) of awakening his beloved under the very apple tree (a symbol of the generative principle) where her own mother conceived. The third speech is from the beloved, asking that she be a seal upon his heart and arm, which would mark him as hers (v. 6), and she expresses the theme of the book—that the intensity of love is as strong as death and beyond all financial compensation.

Finally, 8:8–14 returns us to the scenario of 1:1–2:7. The beloved is restored to the family relationship, protected and unassailable, attractive and now to be defended. The beloved then speaks of herself in these terms (v. 10), confessing that she has found peace in her surrender. The extremely obscure stanza about the sister and her breasts (vv. 8–10) is so difficult that even the identity of the speaker(s) is unknown. Verses 11–12, from the beloved, cite the measure of her powerful love that again is beyond all reckoning. The lover prince is styled as Solomon. The metaphor of the vineyard of 1:5–6 resurfaces at 8:11. She is his vineyard, and she would recompense him if she could, with the same return he gets from those who tend his vineyards. Some see the vineyard of 8:11 as Solomon's kingdom (or harem?; see Falk 1982, 133), with the "keepers" as his officials into whose care the beloved was committed. But more probably the Solomonic allusions in the songs are symbolic, not literal. The beloved pictures the lover as "her prince." Now, in verse 12, she has her own vineyard worth a kingdom ("You, O Solomon, may have the thousand"). In verse 13, the young man is again the speaker beseeching the beloved, now in the garden, to let her voice be heard. The unit concludes with a sentence (v. 14) focusing on the beloved, who summons the lover to meet her upon mountains of spices.

This imaginative collection appropriately closes with the reappearance of the garden theme. But now companions occupy it, and the beloved sings of it, giving it meaning and tangibility (Landy 1983, 206–10). Love, stronger than death, will return us to Eden, or near to it.

Thematic Considerations

Successive chapters are locked together by common themes and motifs such as the vineyard, particularly the garden, flowers, trees, blossoms, and fruit. Character analysis is not possible, for the beloved and the lover are not distinct as personalities. We are dealing not with them but with the problem of love per se, which they illustrate. The garden as the primary setting for their love is most completely developed in the central poem (4:12–5:1) and in 6:2–12. These poems both describe the beloved, although such imagery abounds throughout, and sound the note upon which the book closes (8:13). The predominance of this cluster of motifs takes us back to Genesis 2 and to the theme of perfect love, which finds heightened expression in this idealistic situation. That the message of the garden dominates the opening and closing sequences (1:2–2:7; 8:8–14) indicates the degree to which the tone of Song of Songs is set by this imagery.

The basic message of the book appears in the major statement of 8:6–7 ("love is as strong as death"), which speaks for the preeminence of love and of its intensity and, perhaps, ultimate agony. We are thus dealing with an imaginative meditation on the relative perfection that is human love. The experiences described introduce the lovers to a newfound paradise in which love surpasses all that riches can convey, and for which Solomon's splendor and even a kingdom can be cast aside. The garden imagery identifies the experience as the summit of human joy (2:3, 13; 4:3, 13–14; 6:7; 7:2, 8; 8:5), while the imagery drawn from flora (2:1, 16; 4:5; 5:13; 6:11; 7:2; etc.) and fauna (2:12, 14; 4:5; 6:9; 7:3, with fawn and dove being the principal symbolism for the two lovers) appeals to the integration of nature and experience of which Genesis 2 and Eden speak.

Such human experiences virtually serve to reverse the effects of the fall (note how 7:10 reverses the language of Gen. 3:16), providing in this garden encounter a fountain of life (cf. 4:15). Yet the rapture of this human experience is inevitably balanced by the restlessness that is characteristic of all human relationships, and that ever threatens their dissolution.

The song has as its goal the human ideal that "the twain shall be one flesh." The book therefore serves as an idealization and commendation of human marriage, even though marriage is fraught with problems and is ever under stress. The frank character of the song's language echoes the somewhat similar language used by Israel's prophets in describing the covenant relationship. We may fairly conclude that the marriage relationship is being depicted as a microcosm of what the covenant was intended to produce within the people of God.

But love is possible only within the limits that the garden imposes and within the presuppositions that the Eden image conjures up—namely, within the partners' complete commitment to each other, united by the bonds of a common faith. In our real world, the song's garden motifs are necessarily mingled with threats to the garden, a motif which the book variously represents as wild growth, wilderness, hostile irruptions, drought, and the like. Only in the garden—an Eden ideal often interpreted in terms of the partners as well as in terms of their experience (see 4:12–5:1 and 6:1–12, in which the loss of the beloved turns the thoughts of the lover to the garden, and a descent into it recaptures love)—can human love reach the intensity of strength and commitment for which this book speaks.

Since the Song of Songs is a symbolic representation of ideal love, characters or figures cannot be pressed for literal correspondence to historical persons (e.g., to Solomon or to the daughters of Jerusalem). Such a view does not lessen the significance of the song's message. Indeed, proper evaluation of the type of language within a book must precede its interpretation. There is a pronounced subjectivity in such a task, but I agree with those who suggest that an excessively literal approach to the song (or an endeavor to find precise relationships between episodes) would rob the book of its evocative and haunting effect.

The theme "love stronger than death" reminds us of the perfect love that undergirds all human structures. Thus, while the interpretation of the book as an analogy of Christ and the church fails to deal adequately with its contents, the Song of Songs as an idyll of perfect love clearly points in this direction.

30

Ecclesiastes

The dating and the structure of Ecclesiastes, and the difficulty in reconciling some of its material with traditional biblical teaching, have provided the main areas of discussion that have arisen over the book. The title (1:1) and the epilogue (12:9–14), however, provide clues to its purpose. On the question of dating, the consensus that the book is late need not necessarily be accepted. The linguistic and stylistic evidence may be differently interpreted. The absence or breakdown of certain Hebrew syntactical constructions (or a stage before their development), as well as the use of language, could put the book either early, thus giving credence to its assertion of Solomon connections, or late. In Qohelet, we have the views of Israel's greatest and wisest king, presumably the one best able to master life and to know, by wisdom, the meaning of existence, undertaking to determine the good, the organizing principle for all human values in human life, by many quests. Thus, there is something of a progression of the voice, actions, and observations of the narrator in moving through the two major sections of the book, from doing to knowing, historically the twin poles of human existence. On the basis of what the king has learned from his experiences during his lifelong quest, he instructs his audience from the grave.

Prologue and Epilogue (Eccles. 1:1–2; 12:9–14)

There are clear connections between 1:1 and 12:9–14 (the person of the Preacher is discussed by the book's editor, who also intervenes at 7:27) and at 1:2 and 12:8 (referring to the Preacher's message), while the introduction (1:3–11) corresponds to the tone of the postscript (11:7–12:8). The thematic phrase, the Hebrew *hebel hebalim,* that sets the tone for the book and establishes its course occurs in 1:2 and is repeated in 12:8, thus framing the whole. It is followed by the categorical statement that all is *hebel. Hebel* occurs thirty-eight times and is the key refrain for the first half of the book. Customarily in the OT, *hebel* = breath (Job 7:16; Ps. 39:5, 11; 62:9). This also appears to be the major connotation of the term in Ecclesiastes (at 3:19; 6:12; 7:15; 9:9; 11:8). In conformity with such a basic meaning, C. L. Seow (1997, 47) suggests a meaning of "what cannot be controlled," which fits the contexts of Ecclesiastes well. There are cases in which *hebel* may imply futility (cf. 5:6; 6:4; 11), but these are few. The root meaning that underlies the term and this analysis of human existence is beyond human grasp or understanding (cf. 1:15; 2:11, 17, 26; 4:4, 16; 6:9).

We may thus discuss in detail 12:9–14 in order to have the purpose of the author well in mind as we pursue the theme of vanity raised by 1:2 and 12:8. The claim is made that Qohelet's work (this name may mean "assembler" or "collector") belongs to the mainstream OT wisdom movement, offers a proper framework for faith (he "taught the people knowledge," 12:9), and represents careful evaluation of and reflection upon the subject matter that he presents. The "proverbs" (*meshalim*) referred to in verse 9 are clearly the "words" of verse 10, that is, the substance of his presentation, which has taken the form of grouped poetical sayings that find their significance only within the worldview (12:8) that 12:9–14 presupposes. What has been written, it is asserted in verse 10, conforms to the norms of mainstream theological tradition, a point emphasized by the use of *yosher* 'uprightness' (i.e., what conforms to a standard) and *'emeth* 'truth'.

What has been put forward is meant to stimulate reflection (12:11), as does the thought of the whole wisdom movement. We notice the use of "goads" for the individual pronouncements, "nails" for the collected whole. The words of the wise are provocative, like the jabs of a shepherd's goad (Fox 1977, 103). Yet even wisdom teaching of this character must defer to the demand to fear God and to keep God's commandments (vv. 13–14). Beyond the limits of life to which Qohelet has referred in his teaching lies the fact of judgment to be encountered (v. 14).

The Preacher's thesis, that life is often beyond human control, is not a pessimistic survey of the human condition. Qohelet wants us to be aware that every experience is bound up with a temporary human condition (1:4–11; 3:1–8; 12:2–7). In this sense, activities motivated purely by human desires are a "striving after wind" (1:14; 2:11, 17, 26; 4:4, 16; 6:9). The implications of reading *hebel* as "outside human control" points to the limits on human life. True wisdom will then recognize the provisional nature of much of our experience, and will accept that our experience of a fallen world and the evil within is soon to pass. The book may then be read as a positive assessment of faith that is able to look beyond such limitations, and to conclude as it does that the duty of humankind is to fear God and to keep God's commandments.

The Introduction and Conclusion (Eccles. 1:3–11; 11:7–12:8)

Prompted by the search for human significance, the Preacher, in 1:3–11, develops the theme that nothing final results from toil. This conclusion is then illustrated by the endless repetition in the world of nature, in which nothing new happens. Toil is finally futile because of the finiteness of humankind and the limitations imposed by the worldly environment. Emphasis on, and the implications of, the limitations are returned to in 11:7–12:8. In view of the epilogue (12:9–14), the implications are obvious: humankind must operate within these limits because the limits cannot be changed. Qohelet, instead of regarding all of life's experience as meaningless—a vanity of vanities—laments in verses 3–11 that life is full of activity that is seemingly meaningful but to which human toil can make no contribution or alteration. The thematic statement is followed by the programmatic question for the first section, "What do people gain from all the toil at which they toil under the sun?" (1:3). In translating *yitron* as "profit" ("what a person has from") this question is often understood as rhetorical. Life's actions are without profit. This view would suggest that Qohelet regards all of life as meaningless.

But another derivation for the word is more likely. *Yitron* occurs in the OT only in Ecclesiastes 1:3; 2:11, 13; 3:9; 5:8, 15; 7:12; 10:10–11, and is usually translated to mean "profit" or "advantage." But the verb *yatar* in Hebrew means "to remain" (cf. 1 Sam. 25:34), in reference to those who survive after battle. Qohelet is obsessed with discovering what would enable one to live beyond the grave, at least in human memory. So the idea is not so much advantage but continuation or endurance. Thus, Qohlelet may be asking, "what continues to endure from the labor at which one toils during life?" This question serves as a programmatic inquiry that prompts Qohelet to launch his quest to find an answer—a question set forth in the internal structure of his testament narrative. *Hebel* in 1:2 is being adduced to the superlative degree. Everything is somehow vaporous or a mere breeze.

The contrast in the initial poem between the eternal cosmos and the cyclic character of the particulars (generations, sun, wind, streams [Eccles. 1:4–7]) is significant because the human generations, like individual humans, are ephemeral, while these activities independent of human intervention continue. The nature of the cosmos is characterized by three active and physical agents of reality: the sun, which rises and sets; the wind, which blows in circuitous rounds; and the streams, which run in an unending course to the sea. What characterizes these three active agents of the physical universe is their laborious and cyclical motion, without ending, independent of human intervention.

The second strophe (1:8–11) centers on anthropology, especially the two major features of human nature: knowing and doing. But just as God is not observably present in the workings of nature, so human senses cannot observe God working in human relationships. So the very process of shaping sapiential knowledge, deemed to be life-giving in its capacity to direct human lives, is now for Qohelet a wearisome and fruitless activity. Like the unending movement of the three natural forces, humans continue to search for meaning and insight, but to no avail.

Qohelet's Personal Experience:
The Futility of Human Wisdom (Eccles. 1:12–2:26)

This section, which pursues the limited advantage of human wisdom, begins with a statement of Qohelet's intention to investigate human experience (1:12–15) by the use of human wisdom (v. 13). In anticipating his conclusion, Qohelet observes that God has given humans an evil task with which to busy themselves (1:13). This ambiguous remark is then clarified by the observation that all that is done under the sun is *hebel,* ephemeral and ultimately beyond human control. So the gains of human wisdom not only fail to secure life, but also increase the anger and pain.

If considered strategies for the pursuit of human experience do not bring satisfaction, what about pleasure, fame, and wealth (2:1–11)? The royal person scans a great spread of human pursuits (2:4–9), looking for lasting results from experience and labor. After expanding on the pursuit of pleasure (2:1–3), the king mentions the constructing of houses and gardens (vv. 4–6; cf. 1 Kings 5–9), vineyards (Song 6:2; 8:11), gardens, parks, every kind of fruit tree (2 Kings 25:4; Neh. 3:15; Jer. 39:4; 52:7), and pools (cf. Neh. 2:14; 3:15). Most of these probably refer to Solomon's building activities on the sacred mount— the palace and temple complex replete with private and landscaped gardening, the groves of trees and pools of water (1 Kings 5–9). Then Qohelet outlines the fabulous wealth he acquired (vv. 7–8), counted in the form of slaves, flocks, silver and gold, provinces, and singers and concubines for the aesthetic and more physical enjoyment of kings (1 Kings 4:23–28; 10:1–11:3). He then claims (v. 9) that his wealth and accomplishments obtained by wisdom (1 Kings 3:28; 4:34; 10:7–9) surpassed all before him in Jerusalem (cf. 1 Kings 10).

This laudatory review of noble accomplishment and tangible signs of divine blessing echoes the grave biographies and royal instructions of Egypt and Mesopotamia. Prudent and righteous actions in traditional wisdom were thought to secure the stability and well-being of the cosmos and society, and they demonstrated that the deceased had lived in accordance with the dictates of world order. But by the time of writing, these memorable achievements, in Solomon's case, had all vanished.

When the royal voice assesses what his hands have done, and the labor expended in accomplishing these things, the conclusion is that all was ephemeral and pointless, for nothing remains. Such pursuits were splendid as far as they went, but they provided no final answer. They only sharpen the misgivings we felt about life (2:11). In this baffling world, enjoyment of what you have while you have it is the only course.

Death in Ecclesiastes

After what seems an endless pursuit, made relatively better only by the exploitation of human wisdom (1:13–16), we are brought to the theme of death as the negation of all human endeavor (2:17–23). For the first time in the book, but not for the last, the fact of death brings the search to an end. If one fate comes to all (2:14) and that fate is extinction, it robs every person of dignity and every project of its point. Qohelet does not deprecate the goals of toil, only its failure to satisfy. The one benefit that Solomon had obtained from his toil was the pleasure in his work. The more each of us toils at our life's work, the more difficult we find it to accept that the results of our toil fall into inappropriate hands. So in verse 21a he speaks of the failure of toil to achieve permanent results. The compulsive worker of verses 22–23, who overloads days with toil and nights with worry, has missed the simple joys that God was offering. Qohelet (v. 24) points out that the very toil that tyrannized him was potentially a joyful gift of God and joy in itself (v. 25), if only he had the grace to take it as such. In themselves, the basic things of life, if rightly used, are sweet and good. Verse 26 summarizes his thought. The wisdom God bestows upon those he favors is not the content of knowledge gained by experience. Such knowledge might well increase his misery. Rather, God has given the favored one wisdom from above to do what is beneficial. Verse 26 also indicates that life may hold more than we think—and the book will end on this theme—but, meanwhile, we are shown meaning in such glimpses as to assure us only that there is an answer and that the author is no defeatist. The vital contrast in verse 26 is between the satisfying gifts of God—wisdom, knowledge, and joy—which only those who please God can desire or receive, and the frustrating business of amassing what cannot be kept, the chosen lot of those who reject God (cf. Fox 1989, 188–89).

In the end, therefore, is there any choice between wisdom and folly?—for death, in both cases, has the last word. On this view, the two spheres of human dwelling are the earth, the place where humans live and act—the spatial context for 1:12–11:8—and Sheol, the end point of human destiny. While humans live on earth, God determines in secret the course of history. Sheol is humanity's eternal home (12:5), the one place to which all creatures go (3:20; 6:6), the abode of darkness in which humans dwell without conscious awareness (9:5–6, 10). Humans are made from the dust and to dust they return (3:20; 12:7; cf. Job 10:9), and the memory of them is eventually lost. In death they have no enjoyment, wisdom, knowledge, or memory. Dust is associated with death and is a synonym for Sheol. *Ruah* (spirit) is the divine, animating breath that returns to God at death (12:7). Qohelet is skeptical that life under the sun can distinguish between the life-giving spirit of humans and that of animals (3:21). So death is certain, its timing uncertain.

Thus a thoroughly rational examination of life is unable to find satisfactory meaning; everything within human experience ultimately is beyond human control, or, at best, temporary. God determines every event. Humankind by implication is unable to discern the works of God in the world. This fact, without faith that sees meaning in a life beyond this world, inclines us to limit our worldview to what we find under the sun. We reach the conclusion that we must live for the moment, accepting what comes from God, since we cannot exercise control over it. Nothing can be done apart from God, this somewhat remote figure (2:24). God disposes as God pleases (vv. 24–26).

For Qohelet, the search began, as it must, with wisdom (1:12, 16–17). But he says nothing of wisdom's first principle, the fear of the Lord, and we can thus assume that the wisdom of which Qohelet speaks is the best that we can do on our own, under the sun, purely on the basis of empirical judgment. This study leads Qohelet to deprecate, as a worthless end, the pursuit of human reflection on life (vv. 16–18). Qohelet praises human wisdom, spells out its benefits, and knows that it is superior to folly (cf. 2:13). Yet he sees that human wisdom is limited and cannot achieve its goals, and that, faced with death, human wisdom is as helpless as folly.

In all of this, Qohelet operates from an essentially empirical epistemology. He investigates the world by human wisdom, that is, by his powers of reason. He never invokes, as Israel's wisdom would, a priori knowledge—what he had heard from the authorities in the past—as an argument for his convictions. Unlike the older Israelite wisdom, he is less concerned to determine and discuss individual experiences than with life as a whole, and with passing a definitive judgment on it. Israel's teachers did not appeal to experience as the source of new knowledge and rarely invoked experiential validation of truth. Qohelet, however, conceives of knowledge as the product of human thought, and thus wisdom and its correlate knowledge are, for him, limited and vulnerable. The OT underlines the limitation of his method, since Israel's wisdom has commended wisdom that comes from the fear of the Lord by revelation. Job 28 presents the traditional Israelite view. Wisdom cannot be found; it cannot be bought. God alone knows the way to it. If it comes, it comes through God's mediation. Fearing God, people will do what is wise.

Qohelet's purely empirical investigations separate the human and the divine worlds. Even Jerusalem, which is the setting for the temple (5:1), the holy place (8:10), appears to be desacralized, for God dwells in heaven, not on earth.

What Does It Profit? (Eccles. 3)

Ecclesiastes 3:1–9 reviews the significant moments that come into each life. The two words for time that introduce this poem denote moments, or definitive segments of time, as opposed to indefinite durations. The doctrine of the proper time is taken up in 3:1–8. At its head, the thesis is formulated—the proposition itself. The body of the poem then illustrates this proposition in concrete terms. This illustration happens by means of fourteen antitheses that explain, clearly, how the proposition that has been boldly stated at the beginning is to be understood. Qohelet is aware of a force that mysteriously orders every event. He knows that every activity and every event is subject to determinism. In each recurring event, an individual is helpless, and the search for security is meaningless, given the unpredictable way in which life unfolds. Only God knows how events interact and have meaning. Humans can appreciate this truth only as a doctrine, not as a fact of experience (vv. 10–11). One can only react to what is presented, and everything comes within the time frame that God imposes. The times do not come as our choice; we are simply required to seize the opportunities as they come. Human activities are not equally successful and meaningful on every occasion; their success and meaning—indeed, all are tied to specific moments, the timing of which is beyond our control. This is a limitation imposed on human energies. We can do nothing but yield to this fact, for it is not capable of alteration. We cannot fail to recognize this limitation, but we can also meditate upon it, derive some profit from it, and perceive in it a mysterious kind of order.

Here then is the puzzling dependence of every happening upon an appropriate time. The Hebrew word *'et* tends toward the meaning "set time, right time," "moment of time," "time for." The world and events appear completely opaque. But on the other hand, Qohelet is aware that they are within the scope of God's activity, although the haphazard presentation of 3:1–8 suggests that there is no discernible pattern regulating events. The point at which the divine power becomes real for Qohelet is in the realization that there is a set time for every occurrence, a moment in which things are "beautiful" (3:11). To that extent, Qohelet is aware that the world is controlled, but, again, the best we can do in life is to enjoy the moments as they come (3:12). It is decisive for every human undertaking that it should happen at the right time. God has made this so, in order that people should fear before God (Eccles. 3:14). We are forced to conclude, therefore, that we can enjoy life only under the conviction that God has given us a vision of the future, that God has put eternity—the ability to move, in thought, beyond the limitations of our determined world—into our minds (vv. 12–15).

Justice cannot always prevail (3:16), given the inhumanity of men and women. But in verse 17, God is in control and, thus, injustices are finally God's concern. Humankind is, like the animal world, mortal (vv. 18–20). Who knows, however, whether death is the end (v. 21)? Presumably, if it is not the end, Qohelet's suggestion seems to be that divine justice will operate in an afterlife. Since death faces us, let us live our present life (v. 22) by making the most of current opportunities.

This section thus answers the question, raised in 3:9, of what remains at the end of life; nothing remains. Thus, the search for relative advantage (in toil, wisdom, etc.) that characterized chapters 1–3 has been consistently negated by the intrusion of death into the world and the basic unpredictability of life (see 2:14–16). All we can do is take the present as God-given (3:22).

The Trials of Life (Eccles. 4:1–16)

From chapter 4 onward, Ecclesiastes assumes a more impersonal note. The theme of social injustice is taken up in 4:1–2. Ecclesiastes 4:3–16 considers the relative advantage of courses of action or experience in a set of "better than" sayings. The conclusion is that we may settle for such relative good that is deducible from experience, but human effort is no guarantee of success (v. 4). So honest toil has value relative to slothfulness (vv. 4–6). Labor and loneliness are then drawn together as themes in verses 7–12, in which the creation of relationships is urged and is contrasted with the type of success that isolates, a motif illustrated by the example of rulers whom fickle public opinion abandons (vv. 13–16).

How Should We Act in This World? (Eccles. 5:1–6:9)

In a world in which everything is fleeting, how should we act? Qohelet enters a phase of instruction. A proper attitude to God in the matter of cautious speech and vows is commended in 5:1–7. Ecclesiastes 5:8–6:9 presents a series of injunctions. In 5:8–9, Qohelet offers the injunction to keep one's counsel in the face of obvious injustices that cannot be remedied. Likewise, life lived in moderation is the general theme pursued in 5:10–6:9. Wealth brings its own problems (5:10–12), is easily lost (vv. 13–14), must be surrendered at death (vv. 15–16), and breeds anxiety (v. 17). Ecclesiastes 5:18–20 advances the same conclusions as those offered previously (cf. 2:24–26). We are to accept what God has given. If that is wealth, then let us view it as a gift, not as the result of human achievement. Reflections upon the same theme continue until 6:9. Human desire for wealth produces toil; further, in the face of death, which mocks all desires, all gains must be handed over (6:1–6). In view of our insatiable appetites, let us enjoy the moment rather than long after a future fulfillment (vv. 7–9).

What Is Good for Humankind? (Eccles. 6:10–8:17)

Ecclesiastes 6:10–12 again sounds a common theme: If all things are predestined, what can one do in view of one's ignorance? These verses begin a new section. Most suggest that these verses divide the book, stressing humans' inability to know as the theme of the second half of the book, a theme also evident in 2:19; 3:21–22; and 5:1. Chapters 7–8 then emphasize our inability to discover what is good (Ogden 1979, 348). There is no discernible order in a world that we must accept. The theme "who knows what is good for people?" dominates the poem of 7:1–14. In typical fashion, Qohelet draws contrasts—death is better than life, wisdom better than folly, the end better than the beginning, and wisdom better than wealth. Attached to these statements, however, are countering positions that negate the relative advantage of wisdom. The problem is that the world is full of baffling contradictions. The poem concludes with a question relating to God's creation: Can we make straight what we see in life as crooked (cf. 1:15)?

As the theme of the search for the good continues, Ecclesiastes 7:15–18 dismisses the customary opinion that righteousness and longevity are to be yoked. No amount of righteousness or wickedness can change circumstances. One who fears God (v. 18) lives with life as it is. Verses 19–22 assert that there is a real advantage in wisdom, but the question is raised, Where can wisdom of this character be found (vv. 23–24)? A meditation on this search for wisdom continues in verses 25–29 and is illustrated by the traditional topic of the "strange woman" (i.e., folly) to be avoided. Only those favored by God will escape the perils of life (v. 26), while others will be caught. Human beings are indeed created uncomplicated, but they make life difficult as they continually contrive clever plans ("many devices"; v. 29).

Chapter 8 continues with this search for wisdom, which certainly is a good. In the face of this search, however, who is truly wise (8:1)? Yet, wisdom does have a role to play in tempering conduct to the circumstances. Thus, submission to royal authority, autocratic in its display, is reviewed (vv. 2–4). The king must be obeyed, for we live in his time and we are generally powerless (vv. 5–9). Jerusalem is not the *axis mundi* (the center of creation), securing order against the threat of chaos. Neither is it the sacred mount where God dwells and from which God rules the cosmos; rather, the city is the place of power where the royal voice once prevailed as king (1:12) and where the wicked now practice their evil deeds and are praised for what they do (8:10). The doctrine of retribution (v. 10) is dismissed, since it does not account for the circumstances of life. Even if justice is done, it is done slowly and thus does not check wickedness (v. 11). The orthodox statement is then made that judgment will finally come (vv. 11–13), presumably after death. But life is the puzzle, and we cannot count on retribution (v. 14). We must, it is concluded again, therefore enjoy our present life (v. 15). Life is a predetermined set of events, and an individual placed "under the sun" is simply exposed to its caprices (vv. 16–17).

The Value and Limitations of Wisdom (Eccles. 9:1–11:6)

Ecclesiastes 9:1–16 presents humankind as confronting life and facing the inevitable end—death. Life is predestined (v. 1), and death is the lot of all (vv. 2–3). But life is better than death, since hope and life are bound together (vv. 4–6). Since life only has possibilities, let us enjoy what time we have (vv. 7–10). We cannot know the timing of God's events, and we must operate within our limitations. Success is not guaranteed to the gifted (vv. 11–12). Wisdom is important, however, and, if recognized, can serve a valuable social function (vv. 13–16).

Next, 9:17–10:20 stresses the profitability but vulnerability of wisdom (Ogden 1980, 37). According to 9:17–18, wise words are better than the intemperate outburst of a ruler; still, a little folly may destroy wisdom's input (9:18). A little folly is all it takes to counter wisdom and honor (10:1). On the other hand, the conduct of a fool proclaims the lack of sensitivity (10:2–3). But at times wise action has its advantages (10:4). Society is always subject to perversion (vv. 5–7), and risks are associated even with customary actions (8–9). Wisdom and skills have value (v. 10). We must do what we can to control life while recognizing that life is always full of risks (v. 11). But there is a recognizable contrast between the words of the wise and the words of the fool (10:12–15).

Verses 16–17 deal with discernible political advantage. If verse 18 continues the thought, then the political state is only secured by industry. Verse 19 seems to affirm that pleasure is the only desirable end in life, but, as Seow points out (1997, 340), this verse, along with verse 20, may continue the criticism of the ruling classes, who do nothing but enjoy themselves. Verse 20 continues the thought that political advantage must be weighed. Finally, 11:1–6 is a call to adventurous living and liberality, notwithstanding the limitations of what can be known (Ogden 1983, 229). This section thus operates as a corrective to the overly cautious words of 9:17–10:20, in which alternatives are often carefully balanced. We must not let caution rule our life; rather, we must continue with what life has called upon us to do, remembering, however, that we are not in control.

Postscript: "Enjoy Life, but Be a Realist" (Eccles. 11:7–12:8)

Life is a wonder (11:7). In Ecclesiastes 11:8a, the theme of enjoyment is raised and is then expanded in verses 9–10, while verse 8b broaches the theme of death. The enjoyment of life is a pattern that should be set in youth, and then should control the way life is lived (11:8–10). The theme of death is taken up in 12:1–8 (Loader 1979, 108). Celebrate life when you are young, for youth quickly passes and old age robs existence of its vitality and joy. Then death comes to bring life to its end. Yet, even here, the metaphors used for life convey its value—that is, the metaphors of silver cord, the golden bowl, the pitcher at the fountain, and the water wheel. This does not mean that Qohelet does not recognize the ultimate tragedy that, while there is still an innate desire for life's continuance, it is impossible to grasp and retain the life-giving spirit (8:8). Death is the irrevocable destiny of each human being.

God as Creator (12:1) and Sustainer (the giver of "spirit," v. 7) determines life's outcomes. Readers are challenged to remember—and this is not a call to reminisce, but a call to conform their lives to the will of God. The interpretation of 12:1–8 is contested. The verses describe the ebbing of human vitality, but under what circumstances? Seow points out (1997, 376–77) that the passage may have in mind the collapse of human structures in what could be a cosmic end-time scene. It is a time for terror, sky darkening, and so on (v. 3), when human activity (v. 4) collapses and humanity goes to the everlasting darkness of death. From the perspective of human thought under the sun, the book proper closes with its insistence on the fleeting character of life's purposes (12:8). The message is pointed and clear. Life is swiftly ebbing away. Everyone must turn to God while there is still time.

From an examination of human experience, Qohelet sees no discernible moral order, and his doctrine of limits accounts for the strange series of ambivalences and contrasts that mark his work. But in taking this approach, Qohelet is not reacting against the need for piety and its expression. He, like Job, is merely taking the wisdom movement of his own day to task for its overemphasis on a cause-and-effect nexus between act and consequence. Traditional conclusions of popular wisdom are therefore pilloried throughout the book.

The consequent emphasis of the book has been on the transcendence of God, on God's detachment, aloofness, removal from and yet sovereignty over the human scene. This last item is necessarily emphasized, since the real danger that Qohelet combats is the human attempt to control the world, expressed by his phrase "under the sun/under the heavens," for such effort is essentially an attack on divine sovereignty and inscrutability.

A doctrine of creation, however, underlies the Preacher's thinking (see 3:11, 14, 20; 7:14; 8:17; 11:5; 12:7). We are reminded in this book that we are creatures. We live an existence that the book broadly defines as "under the sun." Thus no key to the meaning of life can be found within our closed circle of existence (3:10–11; 7:14; 8:17). Qohelet strongly affirms the transcendence of God, but links such presence with constant admonitions to find the purpose for life in acceptance of what God gives, and in the reminder that we stand under God's judgment. We are thus to live in the knowledge that God determines what happens (1:15; 5:8; 9:1–2).

By any standard, Ecclesiastes is a fascinating book, not easily interpreted in detail (the attempts at schematic analysis of its contents are legion), and probably only loosely structured. But the message is clear: the fear of God leads to life. Since the book ends on that note, the editor commends Qohelet's teaching, albeit with some reservations. Conventional wisdom, which stands implicitly condemned for having ignored this divine truth, is rejected. This fear of God, as we have noted in Proverbs, is fidelity to divine revelation and, thus, fidelity to the covenant relationship. From such wisdom flows axiomatically the further injunction enjoined on us as the book closes—to keep God's commandments.

31

Lamentations

Five poems compose the Book of Lamentations. The first four are acrostics (i.e., each verse begins with a sequential letter of the Hebrew alphabet). The authorship of the book, conventionally ascribed to Jeremiah (on the basis of 2 Chron. 35:25), is unknown. The fivefold structure of the book shows little or no progression, but offers a repetitive analysis (as the use of the acrostic device suggests) of the passions that the fall of Jerusalem aroused, and the significance of this fall for the history of Israel. The book centers particularly on a reflective analysis of the place of Judah within the history of salvation, a matter which had now been called into question. Chapters 1 and 2 are related, since each has twenty-two verses of three lines. Chapter 4 is an acrostic poem of two lines per alphabetic letter. That chapter 5 is not an acrostic serves to give it emphasis. The general structure of the acrostic pattern is preserved in chapter 5 to the degree that it also has twenty-two verses. Chapter 3 seems the climax of the acrostic structure, with three verses for each letter of the alphabet and thus sixty-six verses in all.

Zion, the Forsaken Widow (Lam. 1)

The theme of the first poem is the desolation of the holy city; the refrain "there is none to comfort her" is repeated five times (1:2, 9, 16, 17, 21). We gather that it was the divine intention that there should be no comfort, that the destruction of the city and the temple should raise a question mark over the place of Judah, within the purposes intended for the people of God. The whole book in fact makes this point through repetitive emphasis. Zion is spoken of in the third person in the first half of the chapter, thus setting the tone for the book (vv. 1–11, 17). Elect Zion has now been reduced to desolate widowhood (v. 1). That is, the divine covenant with her from Sinai, through David, now seems to have been broken, and the marriage dissolved. A powerful personification of Zion as a deserted and degraded woman begins the chapter, as present and past are contrasted (vv. 1–3). Her function as the city of God has ceased with the fall of Jerusalem, for none now come to her solemn assemblies (v. 4a). People and city grieve because of this severe affliction (vv. 4b–7). The reason for this condition is the depth of her rebellion (vv. 8–9). She has therefore been delivered to the adversary, the temple has been profaned, and its treasures pillaged (v. 10). The height of despair is depicted by reference to the famine, with which the first half ends (v. 11).

Zion herself speaks in 1:12–22, punctuated by an authorial comment in verse 17. The turning point in the chapter is a plea for pity from Yahweh (v. 11b) and from passersby (v. 12), for God has demeaned her (vv. 13–14), and her young men have been consumed (vv. 15–16). Verse 18 is the heart of her self-examination. Covenant involves obligation. Yahweh has been faithful; Jerusalem has not. Foreign alliances have been her undoing (v. 19). The confessional strain continues, with a plea to Yahweh to witness her sufferings (vv. 20–21a), a plea which gives way to a call to Yahweh to requite her enemies on their day (vv. 21b–22). Thus, what happened came from God's hand and was justified, but the hope is faintly expressed that it will not be the end, that God in due time will requite Zion's enemies.

God, the Destroyer of Zion (Lam. 2)

God is depicted as having sacked the city (2:1–9a); all relationships have been broken, for lines of communication through the leaders have ceased (vv. 9b–10). The Divine Warrior has turned his hand against his own city (vv. 4–7), cutting off all that seemed to identify Judah as the people of God (temple, kingdom, festivals, and cult). The speaker now empathetically enters into Zion's grief and is moved to tears by the distress that, as in chapter 1, culminates in famine (vv. 11–12). The second half of the chapter is his first-person meditation on a sorrow for which he can find no comparison (v. 13). But a word is required from him, for prophetic counsel has been false (v. 14). Enemies have mocked Zion's fall from her position as the world's center (vv. 15–16; cf. v. 15 with Ps. 48:2). Yet Yahweh himself has been the author of the tragedy (Lam. 2:17), as the fall of Jerusalem is presented in terms similar to those predicted of Babylon in Isaiah 14:12–21. What has happened has been the outworking of the covenant curses (Lam. 2:17). Zion is now called upon to articulate her grief (vv. 18–19), and she responds in the lament of verses 20–22, the theme of which—the affliction of the day—returns to the thesis of verses 1–2 (Johnson 1985, 64).

Patience through Suffering (Lam. 3)

The tone of this poem is heavily personalized, moving from a first-person singular depiction of the suffering endured, where the speaker laments over the distress of Zion that has been divinely induced (3:1–18), to a contemplation of the bitterness of affliction (vv. 19–20). A central middle section of the poem runs from verses 21 to 42 (Johnson 1985, 66). This section, the exact middle of the book, gives the theological solution to the riddle of the disaster. The steadfast daily mercies of the Lord engender hope (v. 23), and the thought is born that punishment is not a final rejection but has rehabilitation in view (vv. 31–33). God stands behind the whole course of events (vv. 37–39). Out of evil good will now come (v. 38), and Zion's inhabitants may now lift up their hands to heaven (v. 41). Verses 42–51 analyze the reasons for the disaster, which must move the Lord finally to pity (v. 50). In the chapter's closing section, the individual lament resumes with the description of the persecution at the hands of the enemy (vv. 52–54). God, however, takes up Israel's cause, having heard the plea of distress (vv. 55–57). This knowledge emboldens the speaker to call directly and confidently for the requital of Zion's enemies (vv. 58–60). In typical lament fashion, verses 61–66 close this strong chapter of self-awareness and affirmation by drawing attention to the attitude of Zion's enemies, to whom Yahweh will appropriately respond.

The Guilt of Zion's Leadership (Lam. 4)

Third-person address is used in 4:1–16, followed by a description in the first person. As in chapters 1–2, the distress of Jerusalem is climaxed in the horrors of famine and even cannibalism (v. 10). The unthinkable has happened—Jerusalem has fallen. The course of the tragedy is further reviewed in the second half of the chapter (vv. 12–22). Nobles, priests, prophets, and the search for foreign alliances have all contributed to Jerusalem's fall. This disaster has occurred despite a declared doctrine of Zion's inviolability (v. 12). Davidic kingship—the divine representative who incarnates life (cf. 4:20 and Gen. 2:7), the tree of life itself (Lam. 4:20)—has been brought to an end by the capture of its last representative. Enemies (typified by Edom) may triumph for a moment, but the day of their punishment will come (vv. 21–22).

Hope for the Future (Lam. 5)

The last poem seems a chorus piece in the first-person plural, a prayer of the community. The Promised Land is gone (5:1–5) because of a dependence on foreign alliances (vv. 6–7). The review of present troubles continues through verse 18: lack of law and order, famine, atrocities, and the sufferings of the people. The turning point comes in verse 19, which affirms God's eternal kingship. The book concludes with a direct call to Yahweh to forgive, though his people are undeserving (vv. 20–22).

Lamentations 3 forms the theological center of the book. The review moves, as we have noted, from suffering to conviction to hope. Such a frank admission of guilt was the platform upon which a theology of history could be built during the exile. Reliance on the externals of the faith had brought Israel to ruin. It would be the daunting task of exile to perceive that the election of Israel preceded all externals. Yahweh, who had selected her, would continue with her if he chose.

32

Esther

The rationale for the Book of Esther is found in 9:20–32, in which the institution of the Feast of Purim is narrated, a festival that celebrates the vindication of the Jews over a concerted attempt during the Persian period to eliminate them. Esther is the only OT book not represented at Qumran, and Talmudic disputes occurred over doubts about its canonical authority because (1) as the rabbis noted, the name of God does not occur in its 167 verses, although the name of the Persian king is mentioned often, and (2) no cognizance is taken of Jewish customs, law, or history. The author's familiarity with both general and specific details of the Persian life during the Achaemenian period lends credence to his story. But not all are convinced of the book's historical credibility. Yet, the number of Persian words in Esther and its numerous Aramaisms suggest the story's composition during a period not far removed from the events it describes.

Narrative Details

The setting is the Persian court during the reign of Ahasuerus (probably Xerxes I, who ruled from 485 to 465 B.C.). Though questions have been raised as to the historicity of the book, Esther exhibits a detailed knowledge of the Persian court, and it is clear from other sources that Jews did rise to positions of authority at Xerxes' court. The book opens with a lavish banquet, to which Xerxes' queen, Vashti, is summoned. Her refusal to appear leads to her being replaced by Esther (her court name; her Jewish name was Hadassah). Ironically, Esther controls the king more completely than did her determined predecessor. We are then introduced to Mordecai, whose ancestors were carried from Jerusalem in the deportation of 597 B.C. Mordecai is a "son of Kish," reminding us of the earlier Saul, while his antagonist, Haman, an Agagite (3:1), is connected to the

Amalekites by the Talmud. The Amalekites were Saul's opponents in 1 Samuel 15. Esther, doubtless involving some compromise on her part (with a tolerance of foreign customs, like the stance of Dan. 2–6), was ordered by Mordecai to conceal her Jewish background (Esther 2:10). By chance, Mordecai overhears a plot to assassinate the king (vv. 19–23) and is able, through Esther, to make the matter known.

Chapter 3 introduces us to Haman, and to Mordecai's refusal to bow before him (vv. 1–6). As a result of this decision by Mordecai, Haman seeks to eliminate the Jews; Haman, with whom the ascendancy remains until chapter 5, obtains by payment the right to put his proposal into practice throughout the empire (3:7–15). The fate of the Jews is sealed for the day before the celebration of the Passover, or the thirteenth day of Adar (v. 13). Esther is pressed by Mordecai to approach the king (chap. 4), and in the key verse 14, points to her fateful role. For this purpose and for this time she has come to power, a statement that clearly alludes to God's hidden control. Though not bidden by the king, Esther approaches Ahasuerus, is remarkably received, and is able to persuade both the king and his prime minister, Haman, to accept her invitation to two successive banquets (5:1–8).

Haman, elated by recent events, now resolves to hang Mordecai (5:9–14). A further chance happening intervenes, as the king, unable to sleep, discovers in the royal records his indebtedness to Mordecai (6:1–9). Haman is forced to honor Mordecai with the honors he ironically thought were intended for himself (vv. 10–14). By the second banquet, the initiative is with the queen (chap. 7). She is able to plead for her people, to identify Haman as the enemy, and, after the king ironically misconstrues his pleas for his life, to have him hanged upon the gallows constructed for Mordecai. The relationship of Mordecai to Esther is made clear to the king (chap. 8), the decree of Haman for the destruction of the Jews is reversed, and Mordecai, robed from now on as a king, moves freely in royal circles (8:15; note how 2:5 has previously hinted at his royal descent). Armed with the king's command, the Jews rise against their opponents, executing Haman's sons as well (9:1–19). Esther 9:20–32 tells of the institution of the Feast of Purim in two accounts (vv. 20–28 and 29–32; note also the earlier anticipation in vv. 16–19), recalling the slaying and hanging of Haman's sons on two successive days (vv. 10–15), and the deliverance from whose father the feast perpetuates. Esther 10:1–3 brings to mind the opening details of chapter 1, taking us back to the wealth, power, and courtly pomp of kingship—the note on which we began (Jones 1978).

Theological Motifs

The absence of coincidence in history (see Esther 4:13–14) is the major theme struck by this book, despite the lack of any direct reference to God throughout. History is divinely directed, and God will intervene for Israel as he has done in the past. This theme makes understandable the recurring allusions to the history of salvation, principally to the exodus and the Joseph narrative. It is the survival of the Jews that holds the theological significance of the account. Like Moses, Esther occupies a key position at a foreign court. Mordecai and Haman clash, as Moses and Pharaoh did. In both cases, the Jews are in the hands of a tyrant and are delivered. Several dangerous meetings with each king are necessary, and they enhance the prestige of the leader. The exodus events culminate in Passover, those of Esther's period in Purim, which recalls Passover. Both exodus and Esther present narratives of a great deliverance accomplished through a complex combination of improbabilities. Of course, there are differences (see Berg 1979, 31–35). Moses, however, works not through, but against the administration. The analogies between Esther and Moses and between Mordecai and Aaron cannot be consistently maintained; the Jews do not leave Persia. Nevertheless, the cumulative evidence favors the drawing of general comparisons (Loader 1978, 418).

As he is in the Joseph narrative, Yahweh basically remains concealed. There are other points of comparison, particularly the influence of a well-placed person (cf. Daniel and Judith) at a time of great difficulty for the Jewish people, together with the skill, wisdom, and decorum of that individual. Esther is also like Ruth in its concern with the way in which the hidden purposes of God order the future. The evidence of Yahweh's operation throughout Esther is available for the discerning, the faithful. Here the remarkable series of coincidences in the book may be noted. Mordecai chances to hear the plot against the king. Ahasuerus has insomnia at a critical time, and Mordecai is thus saved. Haman enters the court at a moment when the king is pondering a suitable reward. The king returns to the fateful second banquet just when Haman has fallen on Esther's couch in supplication.

Thus, though God saved the Jews through a series of natural events, the undercurrent of the account makes it clear that Jewish obedience to this higher power is the factor to which history bends. Perhaps the absence of direct mention of God heightens the emphasis upon human responsibility that the book appears to bring. But Esther is the account of a great reversal of fortunes, seemingly occurring through a conjunction of fickle circumstances—hence the feast name Purim, "lots," commemorating both the "chance" which the book underscores and the historical casting of lots by Haman for the destruction of the Jews (9:24). Reversal seems the most important structural theme in Esther, one that organizes much of the presentation and the wording of events, where measures intended to harm the Jews fail (Vashti and Esther; Haman and Mordecai, which Haman's wife and friends recognize as the turning point; Haman and the Jews, etc.). Repetition of the vocabulary in the antithesis is the most distinctive marker of their mirror relationship. In a few cases, vocabulary repetition is absent but reversal is there.

At the same time, the narrative is one of high artistry, making its message deliberate and not incidental. Eating and drinking motifs provide a structural link for key passages. There is a strong parallel between the relationship of Mordecai and Haman, and that of the Jews and their oppressors. The book begins and ends with the account of a feast (1:3, 5; 9:17–18). Two feasts occur at the center of the book, given by Esther for Haman and the king, with the point of transition in the book coming between the two. In each case the feast leads to rejection and elevation: Ahasuerus's involves Vashti and Esther, Esther's concerns Haman and Mordecai, and Purim affects the enemies and the Jews (Berg 1979, 31–35).

33

Daniel

The inclusion of Daniel in the Writings of the Hebrew canon does not necessarily mean that, by the time of its production, the prophetic canon had closed. Nor does Daniel's place in the canon necessarily mean that it must be dated in a Greek or even Maccabean period. It simply points to the book's use of another genre of biblical literature, apocalyptic, making its contents other than prophetic in the accepted sense of the word. Beginning with Daniel, the term "apocalyptic" is applied to material bearing the general character and features of that book. It is not my purpose to argue here that the origins of Hebrew apocalyptic are basically rooted in OT prophecy, with certain affinities as well, to the wisdom movement, or to insist that foreign influences featured little in the development of the medium. Although such arguments can be sustained, I am concerned to offer some background, explaining the very different theological outlook which is characteristic of Daniel, and which separates the book from the OT prophetic traditions.

The apocalyptic movement arose in Israel in response to a defined need, the catastrophe of 587/586 B.C. It was thus a form of literature, apocalypse, raised up to meet the crisis of the end of the nation and to deal with an exilic situation, where foreign powers exercised mastery and the people of God were in retreat under persecution. The worldview that is apocalypticism raises the question as to what course would the history of salvation, expressed to that point through the nation of Israel, now take in these changed circumstances. Apocalyptic, basically, involves the uncovering of the shape of this future by a narrative series of divine disclosures, usually through supernormal means such as dreams and visions. God promises to respond to the crisis that has afflicted God's faithful (no longer the people as a whole) in history. Salvation is now the promise held out to the faithful. Since nationalism vanishes on this level, universality, a world-encompassing judgment from which the kingdom of God will emerge, is an emphasis of the literature. History is now seen to bear a cosmic significance. There is a spatial dimension attributed to revelation, whereby we see the interplay of principalities and powers, with the decisions that control it, being taken within the heavenly session in which Israel's God presides. The temporal aspect of revelation concerns the nature of the eschatological kingdom of God as coming by divine and remarkable intervention. With that coming, there is bound up the nature of the heavenly being, who, as world ruler (note "one like a Son of Man" in Dan. 7:13), will implement the shape of the end. The apocalyptic literature thus offers the reassurance to Israel that God has not abandoned history; God's control over it is being exerted, despite other impressions that its course may suggest. No longer in this medium is national Israel the center of revelatory attention. Now it is the faithful and the wicked, the godly and the apostate. Appropriately, since the judgment of individuals is reserved for beyond time, a doctrine of resurrection also emerges in literature of this type (see Dan. 12). But since the development of apocalyptic has its roots deep in Israel's past and beyond, older traditional motifs are also featured in Daniel and in this literature generally.

Daniel, an extremely undervalued and sophisticated book, brings the message of the OT to fruition. Daniel 1–6, which establishes the context for Daniel 7–12, ignores Israelite salvation history and takes us back to the generalized worldview of Genesis 1–11, in keeping with Daniel's limited interest in things Israelite and more general concern with the totality of history and its outcome. The book's dating is often disputed, and it is regularly suggested that its extreme attention to detail in the matter of the Seleucid wars with Egypt (chap. 11) places this book in the early Maccabean period. This detail, however, is not so precise as is often alleged, and it is doubtful whether this feature of the book diminishes the probability of dating it in the Persian period. But the issue of dating and the complexity of historical references and cultural allusions within the book are not easily resolved. There is now a greater disposition to conclude that the material from chapters 1–6 (the so-called court tales) stems from the Persian period, even if (as the recent arguments go) it was revised in terms of other interests during the Maccabean period.

The Two Halves of the Book of Daniel

The book falls into two clear halves, chapters 1–6 and 7–12. Daniel 1–6 provides the background for the more pronouncedly apocalyptic visionary sequences of Daniel 7–12. The division of the book into these two formal halves, however, ignores the major exegetical problem of the book, namely, the use of two languages—Hebrew in 1:1–2:4a and chapters 8–12, and Aramaic in 2:4b–7:28. No analysis of the book is satisfactory that does not come to terms with the peculiarity of the two languages and the probability that the Hebrew interprets the content of the Aramaic. (Dan. 1 is introductory, and Dan. 8–12 depends on chap. 7.) The Aramaic sections appear to offer a sequence that is relatively self-contained and complete: chapter 2 corresponds to chapter 7, chapter 3 corresponds to chapter 6, and chapters 4 and 5 are interrelated. To put it another way, we have in these chapters a sequence of authority and deliverance (see fig. 2).

Daniel 2 Authority
Daniel 3 Deliverance
Daniel 4 Authority
Daniel 5 Authority
Daniel 6 Deliverance
Daniel 7 Authority

Fig. 2. The sequence of Daniel 2–7

The provision of Hebrew in Daniel 1 may have been required for canonical purposes, and we may say the same for chapters 8–12. Since, however, chapters 8–12 apply to the particular Israelite situation under review, the more universal truths conveyed by Daniel 7, the use of Hebrew from this point of view is highly appropriate. The use of Aramaic, the lingua franca of the Persian period, intrinsically carries with it a note of universality. It puts us in touch with the major purpose of the book, which is to survey the course of human history from the advent of the "times of the Gentiles" until the ushering in of the kingdom of God. In summary, we may see Daniel 1 as introductory and the Aramaic sections as self-contained, with their implications for Israel being drawn out in chapters 8–12.

Daniel's Exile (Dan. 1)

Daniel 1 introduces us to the Jewish captives, taken in a siege of Jerusalem in about 603 B.C., sixteen years before the fall of the city. The first two verses of the book are the only place where the name of a Jewish king appears, and there is little interest thereafter in a concept of national Israel. The unthinkable has happened—the Jerusalem temple has been profaned and the temple vessels taken. Nebuchadnezzar no doubt viewed them as deity symbols, and their capture as a demonstration that his gods were mightier than the God of Israel.

Babylon is interestingly designated in verse 2 by the rarely occurring term "land of Shinar." This phrase occurs only four times in the OT, three of them in remarkable contexts (Gen. 10:10 is a geographical reference of no significance for our purposes). In Zechariah 5:11, sin in the form of a woman in a measuring basket is consigned to the "land of Shinar," where, fittingly, a "house," that is, a temple, is built for it. Babylon is, then, the place where sin is deified. The other major reference is in Genesis 11:2, where the "land of Shinar" became the center for realizing what has been the persistent humanistic dream of one world, one common set of social values, and one language. This attempt to order the world without reference to the Creator, this misplaced search for the center, was then rejected. And now in the "land of Shinar" (Dan. 1:2) we find this common set of unities (one language, one social policy, one common bond of education, etc.) consciously revived as a tool of empire by Nebuchadnezzar. In this connection, young Hebrew captives are selected for training (1:3–7) for service at the Babylonian court. Since there is a remarkable degree of allusion, in these early chapters of Daniel, to the material of Genesis 1–11, we have probably, in Daniel 1:2, a deliberate reference to the Babel incident and to Nebuchadnezzar as the humanistic reviver of those policies. Daniel, in spite of all this (1:8–21), exhibits a faith that survives when every form of institutionalism has been removed. In the matter of eating food, probably previously offered to Babylonian idols, he refuses to compromise. He was willing, however, to make concessions where his covenant faith was not challenged. He thus becomes the example for the exiled Jew of how to live under foreign rule, and provides a very definite contrast with the figure of the last king of Judah, Jehoiachin in 2 Kings 25:27–30, with whom the physical Davidic hope dies. The laconic conclusion of the chapter (1:21), reports that Daniel outlives the Babylonian Empire and sees the ushering in of the Persian period. He has exhibited the uncompromising characteristics of the person of faith, whose life is able to sustain the effects of a changed world. He is thus the exemplary figure of the period.

Nebuchadnezzar's Dream (Dan. 2)

The highly significant Aramaic section begins at 2:4a. The chapter is devoted to the dream of Nebuchadnezzar and its interpretation. The paradox of this chapter is that, through the unlikely medium of a bizarre dream (2:1b–6), God communicates reality to Nebuchadnezzar. Neither the empire over which he presides, nor the decisions that he makes, provide reality for Nebuchadnezzar. The element of reality is the contact that the dream permits him with the controller of history (2:24–30). Now he needs someone to interpret the nature of reality, to put the wild shapes of the night into proper perspective. Daniel, as Joseph did before him in Genesis, can put the pieces of the puzzle together. There is a marked similarity between the presentations of Daniel and Joseph. Both were captives at the royal court, both succeeded where the professionals failed, both were promoted as a result, and most important, both operated in an Israel that stood before an exodus, a major impending change. In short, only Israel, only the community of faith, has the answer as to the direction history will take.

The interpretation of the dream (2:36–45) of a human image, clearly designed as the counter to the image of God in Genesis 1:26–28, involves progression, but deterioration, within four successive kingdoms (Babylon, Persia, Greece, Rome). It is characterized by a strange blend of sequence with simultaneity. Thus, on the one hand, the empires give way in a sequence of decreasing splendor though increasing strength (gold to silver to brass to iron). On the other hand, the image—composite and, thus, a human fabrication and unstable as to its base—is destroyed as one whole. Perhaps the four kingdoms represent a picture of the totality of human government, symbolic of the human power structure, of the power of the human image. The historical sequence of king-

doms presented offers variations on human power structures that are antithetical to God. Progressive human government will inevitably exhibit the same innate tendencies to search for the center within itself. But whatever changes may
be introduced, there is no substitute for the ideal kingdom of God's rule. This
kingdom will be brought in, the interpretation explains, with decisive sudden-
ness. The picture of a stone, cut without hands, which then fills the whole earth,
seems to have Zion overtones (cf. Zion as a stone in Isa. 28:16), perhaps pointing obliquely to the familiar prophetic eschatology involving the establishment
of Jerusalem as the ideal world center.

Defiance and Deliverance (Dan. 3–6)

Daniel 2 presents a clash of authorities: the kingdom of God confronted by
human power. Daniel 3, whose first sentence signals that we are to regard this
chapter as a continuation of Daniel 2, takes up the notion of dominion as displayed through the counterimage of man (cf. Gen. 1:26) that Nebuchadnezzar
constructs on the plain of Dura for his world to see. The image in this chapter
is clearly a symbol of his worldwide dominion. The identical word *selem,* the
comparable size, and the matching component of gold prompt the understanding that Nebuchadnezzar is duplicating, although with some variation, the
image he has seen in his dream. He is attempting what the Babel builders (Gen.
11:1–9) had attempted—to make a name for himself.

That the king is preoccupied with public perception, with the need to have
the nature of his reign understood, is clear by the next action, since all the authorities are summoned to the dedication of the image. No sooner is the extensive and pompous list uttered than it is repeated. All the people involved are
identified by political status. This is not an occasion for the general populace.
The extensive lists suggest a rather sophisticated political network. The repetition of this list shows the king's control of the network. Precisely what the king
wills, is what will take place. The precise people who are summoned are the precise people who assemble. Thus, although repetitive, the list repeated shows us
that conformity is the norm of the kingdom; disobedience is unthinkable
(Fewell 1988, 66). The dedication involves more than admiration of the king's
handiwork; it requires the swearing of an allegiance that is akin to worship. This
tremendous assertion of sole power by Nebuchadnezzar cannot go unchallenged. The remainder of the chapter deals with a counterdemonstration of divine power. The three Jewish captives who refuse to submit are rescued from the
furnace, in which a fourth "man" appears. Finally, Nebuchadnezzar acknowledges the power of their God to deliver.

The challenge to divine authority, implicitly posed by Nebuchadnezzar in
Daniel 3, is the theme with which chapter 4 proceeds. The chapter has a tripar-
tite outline of dream (vv. 1–18), interpretation (vv. 19–27), and realization (vv.
28–33). Again the king has a perplexing dream, and again Daniel presents its
meaning. The king is called upon to repent and remember his creatureliness.
The great tree of the dream, stretching from earth into the heavens, under which

all find shade and food, is clearly the tree of life (Gen. 2), the world tree, the Babylonian Empire of Nebuchadnezzar, under whose aegis all may find security and sustenance. It is an assertion of Nebuchadnezzar's Babylon as the new Eden, with the king as the center. The claim that to be related to this tree is to be related to the source of life (v. 12) is contemptuously denied by the detail of the chapter. Nebuchadnezzar, because of his pride, is reduced to the creatureliness that he has spurned when, twelve months subsequent to the dream, he is dismissed from his kingdom (vv. 29–33). Later he is restored on the basis of genuine repentance and acknowledgment of the true place of the kingdom of God (vv. 34–37).

In Daniel 5, Belshazzar, the eldest son of the usurper Nabonidus, is king. His reign is disputed, but Nabonidus was resident for much of the period immediately preceding the fall of Babylon in 539, at Teima in Arabia. If not king, Belshazzar was probably regent. The place of the temple vessels is important in this chapter. Their use in a Babylonian orgy, by a ruler who had not profited from Nebuchadnezzar's experiences, would have been the climactic affront for the Jew. We feel that, because of such hubris, the end of Babylon is near. This presumption must be punished, and the mysterious handwriting on the wall (three weights, mina, shekel, peres—*mene:* God has reckoned your kingdom and paid it out; *teqel:* weighed in the scale and found too light; *peres:* kingdom given to the Medes and Persians [Wolters 1991]) announces the demise of the Babylonian power.

Deliverance of the captives is the theme of Daniel 6, as it was in chapter 3. There is, again, an unreasonable royal command involving a religious practice, and again a pious Jew (this time, Daniel) refuses to obey. The conspirators implicate Daniel in chapter 6, as they had implicated his companions in chapter 3. Daniel, remarkably, is rescued from the lions' den, as the Jewish youths had been rescued from the furnace.

Judgment for the Saints (Dan. 7)

Chapter 7 falls into two halves (vv. 1–14 and 15–28). In the first half, the visionary emphasis dominates. Four beasts arise out of the inimical, primeval foe, the sea. The number four probably suggests the totality of the threat from the forces of chaos, although, in the later application of the material, the beasts are historicized in terms of four empires (as in chap. 2). Total opposition to the kingdom of God is thus represented in this bestial, semi-human form. From the fourth beast, to which special attention is paid, there arises a little horn (7:8). It is tempting to identify the little horn of 8:9 with this horn, although the former may be a historicization of this more general concept.

Clearly, the vision is not interested in strict chronology, since the fourth beast is destroyed before the remaining three lose their dominion (7:12). We may also note that the underlying imagery of the vision appears to lean heavily on the old, yet still widely current, mythology of the triumph of the hero deity over the forces of chaos (the creatures from the sea in chap. 7). The judgment scene unfolds in verse 9 as the heavenly council convenes; the opening of the books of destiny (v. 10) appears to make this judgment the final universal human event.

There now comes one who, with intentional ambiguity, is described as "one like a Son of Man" (7:13), a typically vague apocalyptic description of what appears to be in this context a human being. He comes on clouds (literally, it would seem), which are the attendants of deity in the OT. If the underlying Canaanite mythology is pressed, some triumph over the forces of chaos might seem indicated, but it is doubtful whether such neat parallels may be drawn.

We should note that the presence of the "one like a Son of Man" is generally to be associated with judgment, since his appearance in the heavenly sphere is virtually coincident with judgment's having been pronounced. Dominion (i.e., what had been promised to humankind originally), glory, and an everlasting kingdom are then given to this figure. To this man, the manifested image, all power is given. His appearing sums up all things while his coming ushers in an age of everlasting dominion.

In the second half of the chapter, this Son of Man does not appear. We do find there, however, the saints of the Most High (vv. 18, 22, 25, 27), who do not figure in the first half of the chapter. There is no need to see the Son of Man as other than representative for the saints. Since, in the OT, saints normally stand in for Israel, the Son of Man thus seems representative of Israel and enters into the power and authority structure meant for Israel in the OT, and, through her, for all humanity. We are not required to identify the saints with him or to presume that he suffers with them. Indeed, the second half of the chapter seems a historical application of the first half. Nor are the saints of the second half of the chapter heavenly beings, as some have argued (in the OT, "holy ones" encompasses both divine and human beings). The message of the second half of the chapter seems directed at the suffering faithful of any age. In Daniel's era and subsequently, they are to take comfort from the fact that the issues affecting the history of their day, for which they suffer, have already been determined. The die has been cast in their favor, the high court has convened, and judgment has been pronounced. All that is now required is to make individual application of this judgment.

Vision and Interpretation (Dan. 8–12)

Chapters 8–12 work out these details. The sequences of vision and interpretation that Daniel 7 has advanced are continued in these chapters. Chapter 8 seems to concentrate on the second and third figures of the vision of Daniel 7. Greece's replacement of the Persian power, and then the emergence of Alexander's successors (Ptolemy in Egypt, Philip in Macedonia, Seleucus in Syria and Babylon, and Antigonus in Asia Minor), provide the historical background. There is a concentration on the Seleucid kingdom, and on the little horn (8:9), Antiochus IV Epiphanes. His hubris reaches to an assault on heaven and God (vv. 10–11). This passage might be a foreshadowing of Antiochus's possession of the Jerusalem sanctuary from 167 to 164 B.C. Or perhaps, as some suggest, there has been a blurring of the boundaries in 8:1–12: Israel and the host of heaven attacked by Antiochus have become mixed or fused (see v. 24).

Daniel 9 begins with Daniel's prayer. The detail of verse 1 continues to puzzle, but "Darius the son of Ahasuerus, by birth a Mede" may be a royal title. He may have been Gubaru, the general who conquered Babylon, or he may be identical with Cyrus. Israel's offenses against the covenant are confessed in this prayer, touched off by Daniel's meditation upon the seventy years of exile of Jeremiah 25:11–14 and 29:10. It is now realized that the exile has become open-ended. Israel can only hope for God's forgiveness (Dan. 9:9), and Daniel finally prays that the holy city and sanctuary will be rebuilt (vv. 17–19). The answer comes from Gabriel, in 9:20–27. The particular details in verses 24–27 operate between two poles: (1) the people and their sins and (2) the future of Jerusalem. These concerns are alternately addressed in the verse structure that follows. The question of a precise approach to these verses has drawn three major responses:

1. The numbers are to be symbolically interpreted: history from Daniel's time to the Second Advent is being generally presented.
2. The calculations end with the desecration of the temple by Antiochus IV Epiphanes in 176 B.C.
3. The message refers to the advent and the crucifixion.

Of these three options, the first is to be preferred, since any attempt to establish a precise timetable leads to difficulty. The use of symbolic number in apocalyptic is, in any case, expected.

The device of vision and interpretation ties Daniel 10–11 together. Beside the Tigris, Daniel receives yet another vision (10:1–11:1). This sets the stage for the account of the Hellenistic wars that follows. In Daniel 10 we are taken behind the scenes, and it is indicated that the principalities and powers are, even now, waging the real conflict in the heavenly places. Angels representing both Persia and Greece (10:13, 20) are contending with Michael. In the explanation that begins in 11:2, Persia is quickly disposed of, and the remainder of the chapter turns to the fortunes of the Seleucids and the Ptolemies. Verses 6–20 deal with the wars between these two dynasties; verses 21–45 detail the fortunes of Antiochus Epiphanes (175–164 B.C.). This latter account merges into an antichrist presentation in 11:36, where Antiochus comes into direct conflict with God himself.

In Daniel 12:1, Michael, the protector of Israel, intervenes. The distress described before his intervention is the familiar one of apocalyptic woes, which precede the in-breaking of the final kingdom. This seems to be confirmed by the mention of the resurrection in verse 2. The interpretation of this verse is not easy, but the probable exegesis confines those resurrected to the righteous only; that is, a resurrection of the faithful is being described. The righteous shine as stars in the firmament, a reference to their heavenly character, and they are, in view of the terminology used (*maskilim* 'wise', in v. 3), to be related to Daniel himself (cf. 1:4, 17). And in view of Isaiah 52:13, where the Servant's activity has been characterized by the use of *sakal,* the related verb, they are to be seen as a servantlike community of the faithful, that is, a community of saints. The prophecy is then sealed until the appropriate period (Dan. 12:4).

The epilogue (12:5–13) is a revelation to Daniel himself of the time involved. How long, he asks (vv. 6–7), will it be to the end of these wonders? That is, how long will the distress of the end time last? This has no reference to Antiochus Epiphanes, since the events of the end time as they are described in 11:40–45 do not tally with what we know of his career and his death. The three and one-half times of 12:7 has in view the period from the beginning of the end to the end itself. In verses 11–12, yet another period is alluded to, namely, the desolation of the sanctuary by Antiochus Epiphanes (in 167–164 B.C.), referred to in 8:13–14.

The Book of Daniel has moved from the saints in chains to the saints triumphant. Its theme has been the survival and vindication of the people of God in the face of mounting world opposition. In this great struggle between the two imperia involved, the kingdom of God will prevail. History is firmly under divine control; and if it seems not to be, we are to take heart from what we know to be the case, from this revelation from behind the scenes. God is working all things out, the Son of Man will come, dominion will be given to him, and he will reign forever and ever. Of course, we recognize that in the ministry of Jesus, the advent of that Son of Man indicated the beginning of the end, with judgment announced by the very fact of his coming. The world and its structures have been judged by his ministry and by his death, but his resurrection has assured us that his second coming to enter into dominion will sum up history and ensure our final salvation.

34

Ezra-Nehemiah

The Books of Ezra and Nehemiah may be treated together, since their common authorship is generally accepted, although the question of their relationship to the Books of Chronicles is a matter of dispute. The view that Chronicles was the product of an authorship different from Ezra-Nehemiah has become more widely adopted. The absolute dating of Ezra-Nehemiah is contested, as is the relative order of the return of the two reformers. The difficulty is occasioned by the fact that there were two Persian kings of the period who bore the name Artaxerxes (see Ezra 7:1; Neh. 2:1), Artaxerxes I (Longimanus, ruled 465–424 B.C.) and Artaxerxes II (Mnemon, ruled 404–359 B.C.). On the grounds of probability and content, I adhere to the traditional dating of Ezra's return at 458 B.C. and Nehemiah's at 445 B.C., noting, however, that the question of dating or order does not materially affect the interpretation of the books. It is more likely that Chronicles was written after the close of the Ezra-Nehemiah period, and that it reflects the period of the two reformers, as I argue later. In my judgment, little hangs on the formerly argued close association of Ezra-Nehemiah and Chronicles.

Rebuilding the Temple (Ezra 1–6)

Both books are concerned generally with return from exile and restoration. Israel, despite the loss of all its institutions (land, kingship, priesthood, temple, Mount Zion), still looked to the future. It is noteworthy that Ezra begins and Nehemiah ends with detail relating to the temple. Indeed, it is not too much to claim that such a temple orientation, which is sustained throughout the two books, gives to them their inner consistency. This unity clearly prevails in the case of Ezra, which is almost entirely devoted to temple matters. The first six chapters of Ezra do not involve the reformer, but because of their temple orientation, they can be conveniently grouped under his name. These chapters are taken up with a temple-rebuilding program, and ostensibly do not prepare us for Ezra's coming or for the issues that he will confront. But we see how connections between Ezra 1–6 and 7–10 may be forged. When Ezra does come, he too is concerned with the regulation of worship in Jerusalem and with the rightful function of the temple. He thus continues the emphasis struck in chapters 1–6.

The Book of Ezra, whose opening verse presupposes connection with what has preceded, commences with the decree of Cyrus (538 B.C.), permitting the Jews to return to rebuild the temple in Jerusalem (1:1–4). An Aramaic form of this Hebrew decree is repeated in an official context in Ezra 6; thus the first six chapters, separated in time from the remaining four by almost a century, begin and end with this temple motif. The language of the edict in Ezra 1 is more theologically reflective and echoes the close of 2 Chronicles, while Ezra 6 is an official record. The language of Ezra 1:1–4 (as we note later when dealing with the similar 2 Chron. 36:22–23) sustains the second-exodus expectations that Isaiah 40–55 built around Cyrus. Cyrus was to be the architect of the second exodus, and, in effect, the restorer of the city of God, preparing in this way for the fulfillment of the exilic period's prophetic eschatology. This eschatology held that Jerusalem, restored, reintegrated by covenant, and the center of a cleansed land, would become the place to which all nations would rally in pilgrimage. The building of the community and the building of the house go together (cf. Cyrus's decree, 1:2–4). Being the people of God and building the house are interdependent. Impetus for the decree comes from God. God works indirectly, prompting humans to action. Cyrus has been appointed by God to build, and Cyrus delegates the task to all of God's people in his kingdom. Ezra 1:5–6 is a proleptic summary. The returned community rose up promptly to fulfill this call. What follows is the story of the heads of the father's houses, who act in obedience to Cyrus's summons. As God stirred the spirit of Cyrus, so God stirs the spirit of the returnees. The indication of 1:5–8, that the returnees were those whose spirit had been stirred, suggests a limited number, with the majority of Jews probably remaining in Babylon. Motivated by the decree are the key tribes of Judah, Benjamin, and Levi (Ezra 1:5), which assume an important role in the genealogies of 1 Chronicles 1–9. It is pointedly noted that Cyrus returns the temple vessels that Nebuchadnezzar had taken, thus indicating that the exile had ended (Ezra 1:7).

First Movement (Ezra 1:7–6:22)

This section depicts the return and the reestablishment of the cult, and opens in Babylon. Cyrus's own activities (1:7–8) indicate his initiation and compliance with Yahweh's intervention (v. 1). The return of the temple vessels, an important point establishing continuity between the Solomonic temple and the temple to be rebuilt (1:7–11), elaborates on 1:6. The list of the returnees indicates the importance of community. The people who will build are the focus; they are a great multitude from which leaders will emerge, while the early leaders, Zerubbabel and Joshua, vanish. The building of the walls refers to the building of the city, itself the total house of God, though Jerusalem at this time was small, confined to the temple and the older city of David (the Ophel).

Ezra 2:1–67 elaborates on 1:5. The purpose of the list is uncertain, and suggestions of a census document, or a list of several returns, have been made. Sarah Japhet (1983, 114) suggests that the association in Ezra 2 of those identified by family and those identified by domicile testified to a desire to amalgamate the two communities of the exiles and those who had remained in the land. Certainly, the books are concerned to stress the reestablishment of one Israel in the Promised Land. In view of the controversy arising over the rebuilding of the temple, the list may validate the builders of the Second Temple, and be that which was furnished to the Persian governor during the disputes of the Haggai-Zechariah period. We note that the Cyrus decree had given returnees the responsibility for building the temple (1:3). The further importance is emphasized by the repetition of the list in Nehemiah 7:6–72.

The list comprises various segments of Judean society. It is significant that the list begins with a lay group of eleven men, who head the list of returnees (2:1). Nehemiah 7:7 mentions twelve men, perhaps with symbolic reconstitution of the community in mind. Laypeople occupy the larger part of the list (vv. 3–35). Then come the priests, Levites, singers, gatekeepers, Netinim, and Solomon's servants (vv. 36–58). The sequence from priests to Solomon's servants follows a descending order. Servants of the community follow later, both male and female (vv. 65–66). The list is comprehensive, indicating a return of the whole people. The question of communal identity constitutes the first problem, as the people confront the necessity of ascertaining who belongs to the group (2:62–63; Eskenasi 1988, 40). It is not even certain who led the return. First Esdras names Zerubbabel, but Ezra is not clear. Sheshbazzaar is mentioned as *nasi'* in 1:8, but no other action is reported by him until 5:16, which credits him with laying the foundations, although 3:1–3 mentions Zerubbabel and Joshua with others who laid the foundations. There seems a reluctance to dwell on leaders. Zerubbabel, whose Davidic origin is never mentioned, is never elevated, but is paired with Joshua. Zerubbabel is never called governor, as he is in Haggai 1:1. Only Sheshbazzar, in 5:16, and Nehemiah, at Nehemiah 5:14, are so called; all of this is in contrast to 1 Esdras, who elevates Zerubbabel as governor, leader, layer of the foundations, and so on. If Sheshbazzar is included implicitly in the leadership list of Ezra 2:2, then there are twelve lay leaders in Ezra as well as Nehemiah 7:7. All members of the community assist in building.

The central task of the returnees is the building of the altar and temple, built in accordance with the decrees of Cyrus, Darius, and the Torah of Moses. Ezra 3:1–6 probably refers to the rededication of the altar (and nothing more), shortly after the first return (H. G. M. Williamson 1983, 23). There is a clear attempt, in the interests of continuity, to duplicate the dedication of Solomon's temple, since the rededication of Ezra 3 takes place at the Feast of Tabernacles (vv. 4–6), the period at which the first temple was dedicated. Ezra 3 makes it clear that the author is bent upon establishing continuity with Solomon's temple, arguing that it was no new temple that was to be rebuilt, but simply the

Solomonic temple reerected on its original site (Ezra 3:3). The chapter seems thus a typological account of the building of the Second Temple, juxtaposing, for this purpose, events in the reigns of Cyrus (vv. 1–6) and Darius (vv. 7–13). Ezra 4:7–24 indicates that the house of God is identical with the city as a whole, and is not synonymous with the temple (Eskenasi 1988, 54–55; cf. 3:8; Dan. 5:3). Building the altar is the first step, and initiative comes from the people as a whole (3:2a); only then do leaders emerge (Zerubbabel and Joshua). When building work is finished, then leaders disappear. But this new beginning was only tentative, for the foundation stone was not yet laid. The next phase of building operations (3:7–4:3) occurs at the instigation of the returned prophets, Haggai and Zechariah, at the beginning of the reign of Darius I (520 B.C.). In other words, they are not leaders who stand apart from the community, nor do they initiate action. Similar community involvement in the laying of the foundations occurs (3:8).

In Ezra 4:1–3, we learn that "the adversaries of Judah and Benjamin" opposed rebuilding in the Zerubbabel-Joshua period. The central conflict now concerns adversaries who request permission to build as well, but are rebuffed by Zerubbabel, Joshua, and the rest of the heads of the fathers' houses. The opposition during the entire period of Cyrus and Darius is summed up in verse 4 as coming from "the people of the land" (Ezra 4:4–5 seems to summarize the difficulties of the period; Talmon 1976, 323). "People of the land" is a common OT phrase with no unitary meaning, but it must be interpreted in the light of particular contexts. In view of this context of opposition, the term here may refer to the population of Palestine that had not gone into exile. Perhaps they were non-Jewish and included the Samaria nobility. They appealed to a continuity of sacrifice at the temple site since their arrival in Palestine in the time of the Assyrian king Esarhaddon (681–669 B.C.). Nothing is known of such a movement, but it would have been consistent with Assyrian policy. Certainly the later Samaritans cannot be meant by the reference, since that sect did not come into being until well after the close of the Ezra-Nehemiah period; they were impeccably orthodox and would not have appealed to such a syncretistic background. Whoever the adversaries were, the returnees saw themselves committed as a group to the rebuilding of the temple. (In v. 3, note that the word *yahad* 'together' here may mean "congregation"; see Talmon 1953, 133.) Ezra 4:6–23 (with v. 24 an editorial link that introduces the detail of chaps. 5–6) documents the community difficulties experienced from the time of Darius I to Nehemiah. Chapters 5–6 return to the rebuilding of the temple under Haggai and Zechariah. The first half of the Book of Ezra concludes with the temple rebuilt; thus, the theme of rebuilding has provided the continuity for these six chapters.

This Second Temple was five years in the building (4:24 and 6:15); thus, the total work, begun in earnest after an initial tentative period of two years (3:7–8), took seven years, as the first temple had. Work stops on the house of God in Ezra 4:24, resumes in 5:1 at the instigation of the return prophets, and the *hekal* is completed (6:15). The conflict is triggered and resolved via letters;

a resolution takes place and the temple is finally built. Tattenai, the local Persian governor, and his colleagues do not negotiate with leaders other than the elders (5:5a). Zerubbabel and Joshua have disappeared when or before the task was finished. Formerly the king built the temple (1 Kings 6:1–8:66 and in the ancient Near East generally). The edict of God and the edict of the three kings (6:14) combine to produce the results, but actual completion must await the decree of the Persian king, Artaxerxes. A conclusion with a proleptic summary closes the event (v. 15), and the movement ends with the community as a whole, celebrating its success (6:16–22).

The dedication of the Second Temple occurred in the month of Adar (6:15). The entire community oversaw the work of the clergy in accordance with the book of Moses (6:16–18). Passover festivities (6:19–22), which speak for the redemption of Israel once again in its land, appropriately follow the dedication. The festival was designed to exhibit the unity of the new Israel, a product of the returnees and those who remained in the land but who had separated themselves from pollution (6:21).

Return of Ezra (Ezra 7–10; Neh. 8–10)

The changed scene in Ezra 7:1 indicates a new action. Ezra 7 presents the return of Ezra himself, who gives his name to the whole book. Ezra 1–6 has established the theocratic basis of the new community, and Ezra 7–10, together with the rest of Ezra's memoirs in Nehemiah 8–10, continues with an emphasis on the person of the reformer.

The narrative moves from Jerusalem back to the Diaspora. Ezra's return parallels, replicates, but extends the first return. The central characters are Ezra (7:1–6b) and the children of the exile (7:7). Ezra 7:8 anticipates his arrival in Jerusalem. Ezra himself is a paradigm of effective leadership, a self-effacing man who transfers powers from himself to the community (Eskenasi 1988, 64). We expect from Ezra a major presence, but we find him an unassuming person who refused to ask for an escort (8:22). Ezra seems never in total control of community affairs (9:1), has great powers but does not readily use them, and lets others take the initiative. There is an obvious contrast between what he is entitled to do and what he does. In chapter 7, the narrator and king sing Ezra's praises. Epithets are heaped upon him (Ezra 7:6), and he is credited with a fourteen-generation pedigree, the longest in the book and the first to exceed a single generation (Eskenasi 1988, 63). Ezra's pedigree moves the opposite way from the genealogy of Ezra 2, from present to ancestor. Ezra's scribal role is stressed (7:6, 11). The book thus indicates an important new initiative about to take place under Ezra.

It is now clear that we may dismiss the traditional picture of Ezra as the father of Judaism, the beginner of a new movement that substituted a Judaism of obedience to the law for the older biblical picture of the nation of Israel. It is equally clear that the identification of Ezra as the imposer of the law, who brought back the canonical Pentateuch, is no longer a satisfying one. Both of these proposals of older research have undergone considerable modification in recent presentations. Certainly, Ezra's prominence in Ezra 7 is hardly based on any innovative restoration of law to the community, since the role of law in Ezra 7 is arguably subordinated to temple and cultic concerns. But the portrait of Ezra as a priest whose primary concern is for the Torah articulates the centrality of the rediscovered document. To take this point further, Ezra is presented as "a scribe skilled in the law of Moses" (7:6). This, however, is a reference to a law whose components the writer presupposes to have been in active use by the immediate postexilic community (see 6:18). Although the law was relatively unknown to the popular community (a common situation in the OT), there does appear to have been an upper stratum that knew it and that was encouraged to communicate it (7:25). The Torah and letter of Artaxerxes authorize Ezra (7:14) to implement the teaching of God that is in his hand (7:11–26). Concern for the house is at the very center of the king's letter, flanked by Ezra's credentials and the king's law. The Persian king acclaims Ezra (7:12–16). Ezra will disappear as soon as he accomplishes his goals, attested by 7:10: to study, to do, and to teach the Torah.

Artaxerxes' letter (7:11–26), perhaps reflecting Ezra's own wishes, begins an elaboration of the report condensed in 7:1–10. The letter contains four basic points. First, the king grants permission to all the people to go up with Ezra. Second, the king appoints Ezra to oversee or inspect Judah and Jerusalem according to the *dat* 'law' of his God (7:14). Then the king assures provisions for the care and furnishing of the house of God (7:15–24). The letter echoes Cyrus's decree, but extends it with rights and provisions for the house of God that go beyond what Cyrus and Darius have allowed. The house of God is to be completed (7:19). Finally the king directs Ezra to appoint judges and to teach the *dat* 'law' of his God, and authorizes him to impose severe penalties upon those who violate the *dat* of Ezra's God and the *dat* of the king.

Thus, Ezra is authorized to appoint, punish, implement, and spend according to his judgment and the book that is in his hand. He was also to appoint magistrates and judges (7:25–26). Probably he was to apply the OT law to now-changed circumstances of life regarding the temple. Ezra 7:26 linked God's law and the king's law in a harmonious diarchy. On the evidence of Nehemiah 8:1, we may suppose that what was being referred to was the Pentateuch. That the law was read by Ezra at the Feast of Tabernacles in 444 B.C., in connection with covenant renewal (Neh. 8:1), suggests that the writer had a return to older paths in mind in Ezra 7 (cf. Deut. 31:10–13). Indeed, the law may have been read regularly, following Ezra's return in 458 (Eybers 1976, 20, suggests every seven years, which would fit the dates). Certainly, the reading of the law in Nehemiah 8 was designed at that stage to operate analogously to the reading of the law in earlier periods, such as under Josiah (2 Kings 22–23).

At last, Ezra himself appears (7:27). Ezra first gives thanks and credit to God, the God of "our" ancestors. The focus on God comes first (Eskenasi 1988, 65). These opening words introduce the so-called Ezra memoirs. They are third- and first-person narratives, enabling us to hear Ezra himself and a narrative perspective on Ezra. He characteristically includes, invites, and involves (8:17–20).

He is the one who works with others, recognizes their importance, preserves their names, and gives credit where credit is due. Thus, his return is not a solitary affair. His concern for broad and full participation shines through in his appointment of Levites (8:15–20; Eskenasi 1988, 65–66).

The vast gifts for the temple are handed over to twelve priests and Levites to be transferred to responsible persons in Jerusalem (8:24–30). The journey itself receives minimal recognition, but much attention is given to what takes place upon arrival. Three days after their arrival, the gifts are transferred to the Jerusalem priests and full account is made, and, once again, we have the careful naming of names (8:33). The continuity of care is thus reported. Ezra and the returnees defer to the authority of those already in Jerusalem, demonstrating that Ezra does not use credentials to usurp power.

The arrival of Ezra and his company gives ground for a celebration affirming the oneness of the people as the totality of Israel. They (the returnees other than Ezra) disseminate the royal letter (8:36) to various officials who in turn aid the people and the house of God. The scene closes with reference to the documents of the king, with the people celebrating, and with the house of God supported.

Chapters 9 and 10 detail the central crisis of this return. The determination now must be made as to who participates in the holy seed (9:2), that is, the identity of the people of God must be established. Once the people have purified themselves, the narrative turns back to the Diaspora, in Nehemiah 1, to a new movement. But Ezra subjects only himself to repentance, fasting, and mourning. Ezra reacts to the reported news of the mixed marriages with self-castigation and a confession to God, in which he includes himself with the transgressors.

His behavior seems contagious. The initiative in dealing with the crisis of intermarriage with non-Israelites in the land comes from community and not from Ezra. Shecaniah, a layman—and not Ezra—proposes a resolution (10:3), and he virtually commands Ezra to take charge (10:3b–4). Only then does Ezra assume leadership, but this is translated into community participation. He engages all the community in commitment, and then withdraws (10:6), allowing the community to exercise authority (Eskenasi 1988, 69). On the mixed-marriages affair, Ezra remains in the background; he assumes the role he had been asked to take only after the assembly has convened. Then, at long last, he issues instructions. The community gives a resounding yes on the question of separation from foreign women. But Ezra, arising in his priestly capacity and issuing directives for the first time in the book, accepts a counterproposal (10:14–15) to ease the pressure. Ezra disappears from view once the committee has done its job.

The range of prophetic concerns that Ezra (and Nehemiah) displays is set in an Israelite state dominated by priestly influence. The reading of the law was probably designed to stir the populace at large to covenant renewal, rather than to provide for community regulation in itself. Such a renewal movement does take place later in Nehemiah 9–10. Even the alleged concentration on precise legal observance in Ezra 9–10, as well as the action taken against intermarriages between Jews and aliens, was not an end in itself. For it also involved a second-exodus motif (as did the processional character of the return in Ezra 7–8, strikingly reminiscent of the prophetic expectations of Isa. 52:7–12). This involved the cleansing of the Promised Land from defilement (cf. Lev. 18:24–30; Ezek. 36:16–36; see Koch 1974, 184–89). It instanced the operation of covenant law at work in the returned community. Thus the sequence of temple cleansing or restoration of proper worship, the reading of the law, reform measures, and the conclusion of a covenant in Ezra 7–10 and in Nehemiah 8–10 take up concerns similar to those that the reforming kings of Chronicles espoused. Platforms of this character were always within the mainstream of OT reformers' concerns.

Furthermore, one must not lose sight of the all-Israelite character of Ezra's activities. The point has been made that within the narratives concerning Ezra personally, the term "Israel" is used more than twenty times, while "Judah" occurs only four times (7:14; 9:9; 10:7, 9, all geographical references). Ezra is sent, as the terms of his commission make clear, to "all the people in the province Beyond the River" (7:25), that is, to virtually the entire population of the older cis-Jordanian boundaries of the Davidic empire. This all-Israel tone in Ezra (and Nehemiah) sustains prophetic concerns, and cautions us from construing action taken during this period as anti-Samaritan. This emphasis on the purpose of Ezra's return follows hard upon earlier material treating the unsuccessful character of the first return under Sheshbazzar, Zerubbabel, and Joshua (chaps. 1–6). The material may have been designed, therefore, to contrast what was achieved under the leadership of these two returns. We are probably being encouraged by this all-Israelitism to view the results of the Ezra mission as more determinative for the final shape of the community than results in 537 B.C.

Return, Rebuilding, and Reform (Neh. 1–13)

Nehemiah 1–7 describes the wall-building taking place despite internal and external opposition. A change of scene (Jerusalem [Ezra 10], Susa [Neh. 1]), time, and major characters separate this section from the preceding section. The incomplete date formula of Nehemiah 1:1 establishes connection with preceding material. Nehemiah 1–7 describes how Nehemiah and the Judeans built the wall, as Ezra 1–6 describes how the returned exiles built the altar and temple. Nehemiah 3 lists all the builders and their activities. Nehemiah 3:38 (Heb.) reports the completion of half of the wall, Nehemiah 6:1 that the whole wall, except for the doors, was complete. Nehemiah 6:15 records the date of completion. The final touches are described in 7:1–3. As in the earlier movement, adversaries precipitate the conflict. Like Ezra 4:1–5, Nehemiah 2:19–20 excludes opponents from building (cf. Neh. 2:20 with Ezra 4:3b; Eskenasi 1988, 79).

We should note the quasi-prophetic manner in which the Book of Nehemiah opens. True, God does not speak to him in a typical prophetic consultation, but the divine will is clearly indicated, and Nehemiah is equally, clearly charged to implement it (chap. 1; see Ackroyd 1970, 30). As the rebuilder of the city walls (chaps. 2–3), he is also cast into the traditional leadership role of the ancient world (Smith 1971, 129–30). We learn little about Nehemiah—no hint of family or tribe—and this is an odd omission in a book concerned with genealogical matters. Nehemiah speaks first and speaks constantly. Nehemiah's address to God typifies his relation to God and contrasts him with Ezra. Typically, Nehemiah asserts that he built the wall (6:1). That the list of builders in Nehemiah 3:1–32 does not coincide with previously named groups and individuals suggests that Nehemiah's cohorts, the Judeans, are a different group from Ezra's. The groups eventually combine, and the emphasis on people in Nehemiah 8, where Ezra and Nehemiah combine, is strongly developed. The significance of the wall as the thread that links the narrative is clear. From Ezra 4:7–24 we have seen that the house of God and the city walls are coextensive.

Nehemiah 2:5b requests permission to rebuild Jerusalem. In the past, Artaxerxes had forbidden this (Ezra 4:21). The last part of that letter had left the future open, and Nehemiah now seizes the opportunity in 2:7–9. So his actions essentially continue Cyrus's decree. We meet Eliashib, the high priest, a designation which first now occurs in the two books, as the wall is sanctified (Neh. 3:1). As the facilitator of political stability and the resolute upholder of the law (as the book presents him to be), Nehemiah in his mission evinces not only prophetic traits but also royal ones. He is thus a religious reformer who can be cast into the very best traditions of a Josiah or Hezekiah. Though he is a formidable figure whom a consortium of local rulers cannot daunt (chap. 4), he is not indifferent to the social plight of the common people. The economic measures he takes in Nehemiah 5 are designed to win popular support and thus to broaden the reform base as much as they are to check the power of the Samaria-based opposition (chap. 6).

Nehemiah in chapter 5 engages in fence-mending on various levels. Nehemiah 5 is a tantalizing chapter in its present location. As Eskenasi points out (1988, 148–50), breaches in the walls are paralleled by breaches in the social structure, and both require attention. But the social problems seem to be the other side of extravagant war efforts and building. Nehemiah appears responsible for the social depression that may have resulted from the community's over-commitment to wall-building. His first response in Nehemiah 5 is to quarrel with the leaders because they exacted interest from their own people (5:7), only to admit that he also has been involved in the same practice (5:10).

Nehemiah's amassing of power reaches a surprising apex in 5:14. Unlike the conciliatory Ezra, he pulls rank and refers to the king's mandate extended to him as governor, and institutes popular measures designed to stem the social crisis (5:14–19).

The problem of foreign opposition to the rebuilding of Jerusalem intensifies from chapter 4 to chapter 6. Here, the strong leadership of Nehemiah is seen to advantage. He refuses to be deterred from wall-building by the contrivances of Sanballat of Samaria, Tobiah of Ammon, and Geshem of Qedar. Finally the wall is completed in fifty days (6:15). Even the enemies saw the hand of God in this (6:16).

With the wall built, and protective measures taken for guarding the entrance to Jerusalem (7:1–4), a citizen list of the new Israel was compiled (7:6–72). The list, formally and structurally important in the two books, is practically identical with Ezra 2. The repetition indicates that different groups have been welded into one people. The list, beginning with twelve laymen, seems to define the new Israel of the return. The repetition forms an *inclusio* binding the material from Ezra 2–Nehemiah 7, compressing the three movements of the restoration into a unity, namely, the movements aiming at the rebuilding and refurbishing of the house of God, the bringing of the law, and the building of the wall. The activities of Nehemiah 2–7 have the effect of gathering all the people into one (cf. Neh. 8:1). Only the returnees constitute the new Israel, as Japhet (1983, 103–25) has shown. But Nehemiah's list goes a little further, mentioning the rest of the people alongside the leaders, emphasizing the total involvement (7:71–72). Ezra 2 leads immediately to the building of the altar and worship. Nehemiah 7 leads to the reading of the Torah. The Torah has now assumed a greater prominence than the temple and its sacrifices.

Community Celebrates the Completion of the House of God (Neh. 8:1–13:31)

For the first time in the two books, the people gather as one entity in Nehemiah 8:1, and the gathering adopts the rigorous implementation of the Torah (8:1–10:39), dedicating itself prior to dedicating the walls. The book of the Torah is literally placed at the center of a united people. The law was to be available to all and not to be the preserve of experts (H. G. M. Williamson 1988, 287–88), and thus it is significant that Ezra's reading took place, not in the temple, but in an open space in front of the water gate (Neh. 8:1, 3). To this public place the whole congregation, men and women and all that could hear with understanding (probably children), gathered. The law is presented as something that should serve as the foundation for community life. The community bound itself willingly to keep the law (10:28–29).

Nehemiah 8:1–10:39 elaborates on three assemblies (8:1, 13; 9:1) at which the reading of the Torah takes place. The section concludes in the production of a written pledge by all the people. Nehemiah 10:1–29 contains commands to observe the Torah, with detailed obligations for the house of God (10:31–39). The community progressively affirms and commits to the law. These commitments function as the culmination of what had preceded and as a necessary prelude to declaring the city holy (Neh. 11:1). The gathered people instruct Ezra to bring the book of the Torah. The public reading includes all men, women, and children, who are attentive and responsive (8:3, 6, 9). Leaders quickly merge back into the community, with a multiplicity of leaders doing the reading.

The pairing of Ezra-Nehemiah here is fundamental to the present understanding of the book. Ezra and Nehemiah combine their efforts in this momentous gathering, and each has an inextricable part in the other's life work. Levites speak, but Ezra/Nehemiah are left out. The second day of reading (8:13–18) begins like the first, with a smaller group who come to Ezra the scribe, that is, to Ezra in his scribal capacity, to learn Torah (Neh. 8:13). Ezra has disappeared, and the book now assumes prominence. They immediately implement the written instruction and celebrate Tabernacles. "He [who] read the book" during the seven days (Neh. 8:18) seems not to be Ezra, who has vanished, but probably the community. A third assembly (9:1–38) is convoked by the people, and also includes reading of the Torah (9:2b–3a). The people stand up, confess, and read the Torah. Only then do certain Levites rise to what approximates a leadership role, but they do so jointly with a verb in singular form (Eskenasi 1988, 100), emphasizing their unity. The lengthy prayer of 9:5b–38, emanating from the whole community (cf. 10:1), points to the effect of the third public reading.

Important in the Ezra materials in this connection is the covenant-renewal ceremony of Nehemiah 8–10. Ezra's reading of the law is followed by Levitical exposition (8:7–8); it is the Levites who draw out the implications of this covenant renewal in terms of the salvation history, reviewed in the long prayer of 9:5–38. The emphasis in this prayer is on the gift of the land as the fulfillment of the promise to the ancestors, while the concluding verses of chapter 9 indicate the position in which the people of God, now returned to the land, find themselves: they are slaves. That is, they are conscious that the real exodus of prophetic concern still awaits them, and for its blessings they pray. Striking in this covenant renewal of chapters 8–10 is the absence of general priestly support. Priests are not associated with the reading of the law, and their support for the reform movement seems to have been only perfunctory.

The fourth unit (10:1–39) testifies to the community's vow to follow the Torah. The pledge is another indication of knowledge, now of the Torah, and of its implementation. The community formulates obligations in writing, and Nehemiah carries them out (chap. 13). Laypeople dominate the list of signatories. An annual temple tax to maintain the institution is mandated. Temple provisions, the prerogative and responsibility of kings during the monarchical period, are now undertaken by the people communally (10:32–34). Again, the names of the signatories are meticulously recorded. Eighty-four names occur in Nehemiah 10:2–27, and the list is made comprehensive in 10:28–29 to include the rest of the community. Many of the names are new and differ from Ezra 2. Covenant ceremonies in the OT normally describe the event in terms of leaders, but this event is democratically focused (Eskenasi 1988, 103–4), and the emphasis has moved from temple to book.

The stability of the temple city remains a concern. Lots are cast to bring 10 percent of the people, a form of population tithing, into Jerusalem (11:1). A list of settlers occurs at 11:3–36 and a list of cultic personnel at 12:1–26. The city is now an all-encompassing holy place (Neh. 11:1) and contains the holy seed (Ezra 9:2). The last item in Nehemiah 10:38–39 was the commitment of the people to tithing for the house of God.

As the book closes, 12:1–26 leads us back to Ezra 2:1, recapitulating lines of cultic personnel, back to those who came up in the first wave of the return (cf. 12:1). Cyrus's edict has been implemented. Entrance, now into the holy city as the total house of God, demands purification of priests, people, gates, and wall (12:30). Typically, Nehemiah claims he orchestrated the movement (12:31; Eskenasi 1988, 118). There is a bifurcated procession to the temple, with Ezra and Nehemiah in opposite approaching groups, finally meeting at the house of God (12:40–42). The great joy of the day is heard from afar (12:43). The book of the Torah is read, and the people take charge, separating Israel from everyone of foreign descent (13:1–3).

Coda (13:3–13:31)

Nehemiah concludes by giving an account of the reform he initiated, punctuated by calls to God to remember him (13:14, 22, 29), reaching a crescendo in 13:31. Nehemiah took these steps after his return to Jerusalem, at an unspecified time, subsequent to his recall by the Persian king in 433/432 B.C. (Neh. 13:6). Some have supposed that the character of Nehemiah's political pretensions, aiming at kingship, led to the recall (see 6:7). Doubtless, however, such assertions were ploys of his opponents. The impact of the reforms in 13:4–22 clearly struck at priestly privilege. The measures concerned the purity of the house of God (13:4–14), the Sabbath (vv. 15–22), and purification of the community (vv. 23–29); these were followed by Nehemiah's final call for remembrance (13:29).

Nevertheless, that divisions within the community had been exacerbated by Nehemiah's reforms is evident from his bold measure expelling from Jerusalem the son-in-law of Sanballat, governor of Samaria. This son-in-law was also the grandson of the ruling high priest of the period, Eliashib (13:28).

At the conclusion to Nehemiah, the period ends on a note of profound disappointment, with the community wracked by divisions between the priesthood and the laity. The Nehemiah party is opposed by a Jerusalem officialdom, supported in turn by a powerful Samaria faction, whose Persian sympathies, we know from extrabiblical sources, are pronounced. Although the Ezra-Nehemiah period began with the high hopes attached to the Cyrus edict, it ends with a frank admission by the author of Nehemiah of the failure of an experiment and with the community divided.

This sustained attack on priestly privilege by these reformers was not to prevail. After 400 B.C.—that is, after the close of the Ezra-Nehemiah period—the power of the Jerusalem priesthood gradually became dominant, and the theology that had prompted the Ezra-Nehemiah movement became one of popular hope. It was taken up in about 150 B.C. in the rise of the Pharisaic movement. The pendulum was poised to swing against the reforms. With the advent, around 400 B.C., of direct Persian government, a Jewish state emerged that was dominated by the priesthood. This government would endure, with all its tight bureaucratic authority, until the Maccabean revolt. Against the background of this failure, and the despair in pious circles that it engendered, the Books of Chronicles, as I shall argue, were probably written. But with Ezra-Nehemiah the stirring of new and important lay movements within Judaism had begun. The wielding of entrenched priestly power, however, prevented the initiatives of the period from bearing fruit.

35

Chronicles

Chronicles ends the Hebrew canon. Since the Books of Chronicles probably represent the latest composition within the OT, this placement may be justified on historical grounds alone. Yet the shape of the canon seems to have been theologically ordered, and the similarity between Genesis and Chronicles has often been commented upon. Like Genesis, Chronicles begins with creation, tracing the human race from Adam before narrowing the divine choice, at the beginning of the second chapter, down to Jacob (Israel). Both Genesis and Chronicles end with a prospect of redemption and a prophecy of a return to the land. Moreover, Chronicles neatly summarizes the theology of the canon, ending its account at the exile, but maintaining an open-ended attitude to the future.

The closing verses of 2 Chronicles (36:22–23) inform us that the end of the exile, as prophesied by Jeremiah (Jer. 25:12), occurred in the first year of the Persian king Cyrus. Yahweh stirred up the spirit of Cyrus, who then made a proclamation throughout his kingdom, thereby putting his own realm into the context of a general world rule by Yahweh.

The decree, which is stated in terms of a commission given to Cyrus by Yahweh, directed the exiled Jews to return to Jerusalem to rebuild the temple of Yahweh. As we have seen, these closing verses of Chronicles appear as Ezra 1:1–3. This linkage suggests the continuity of the two works, a position held as axiomatic until perhaps the last three decades. On such an assumption, the Books of Chronicles were theologically preparatory for the work of Ezra-Nehemiah that followed. Thus, the purpose of Chronicles was traditionally assumed to be support for the community reforms that Ezra and Nehemiah endeavored to implement.

The balance of scholarship now seems to favor separation of the two works. Sarah Japhet and H. G. M. Williamson have both concluded decisively that

Chronicles and Ezra-Nehemiah come from different hands (cf. Kelly 1996, 15). Chronicles and Ezra-Nehemiah, however, have a special literary relationship. The narrative of Chronicles precedes Ezra-Nehemiah, but it would seem to draw messages from their reforms. Chronicles depicts the second stage in the return from exile and the establishment of cultic life. But while this had happened, it is ambiguously assessed in Ezra-Nehemiah. The temple is functioning again, but is not associated in Ezra-Nehemiah with the ideology of the Davidic covenant. Chronicles presupposes the work of Ezra-Nehemiah, and M. Selman (1994, 38) has shown that two of the three main sections of Chronicles—1 Chronicles 1–9 and 2 Chronicles 10–36—conclude with citations from Ezra-Nehemiah, both of which have to do with the temple and the return to the land (1 Chron. 9:2–17 = Neh. 11:3–19; 2 Chron. 36:22–23 = Ezra 1:1–2).

Over against Ezra-Nehemiah, a more positive note marks Chronicles. The time of Israel's punishment is past for Chronicles (2 Chron. 36: 21; but contrast Ezra 9:7–8 and Neh. 9:36–37), and we look for a greater fulfillment of the ancient promises that the temple mediates. Chronicles, as Japhet and Williamson have shown, has a more comprehensive notion of Israel than Ezra-Nehemiah (Kelly 1996, 232), so that the suggested theological differences in stance are not compelling. Our survey of Ezra-Nehemiah has indicated that these books deal with the formation of an ideal worshiping unit, Israel, centered on the present purified temple. The Chronicler shares these theological considerations, but he goes somewhat beyond Ezra-Nehemiah in the pronounced eschatological note that characterizes his work.

Any attempt to date Chronicles must come to terms with the material in 1 Chronicles 3:17–24, which seems to take the Davidic dynasty down to about 400 B.C. The majority opinion for the dating of the books between 400 and 350 B.C. may be sustained by an understanding of their purpose, a task that we now undertake.

1 Chronicles 1–9

First Chronicles 1:1–9:44 is almost entirely genealogies relieved only by a little extra information. Genealogies afford important insights into the character of biblical religion. The Chronicles genealogies are concerned with God's design for all Israel (as the concentration of interest indicates), but with special attention being given to Judah and Levi. The genealogies, therefore, in 1 Chronicles 1–9 provide clues to the purpose of the books. Chronicles through its genealogies affirms a divine plan for creation, within which humankind, especially Israel, enjoys a distinct place. The greater part of 1 Chronicles 1–9 is devoted to the ancestry of Israel as opposed to other nations (2–9). Even with Israel, an apparently disproportionate amount of space is devoted to the tribes of Judah (2:3–4:23), Levi (6:1–81), and Benjamin (7:6–12; 8:1–40). We contrast this with the few verses devoted to Ephraim (7:20–29). Within the tribes of Israel, Judah is given precedence because it was from this tribe that the Davidic dynasty later emerged. Specifically, the Chronicler's genealogies show how Israel's present arises out of the past, and how God's initial purposes for humankind are fulfilled in her. They condition us to see how Jesus ultimately brings to fruition God's plans for Israel. It follows that the genealogies are highly selective, making it pointless to attempt to construct a chronology from them. Their function, broadly speaking, is to show that the promises of God and God's purposes continue.

The first chapter moves from the broad base of creation. A linear genealogy connects Israel (v. 34) with Adam (v. 1), suggesting that Israel is the goal of God's purposes in creation. First Chronicles 1 then goes on to show how its interest in the line of promise is furthered by the way it deals with groups of sons. Noah's sons, Shem, Ham, and Japeth, are listed in that order but are presented in the reverse order, allowing the author to deal at length with Shem, through whom the line will continue (McConville 1984, 9). The genealogy enumerates the nations of the world according to the traditional pattern of Genesis 10. The nations are presented in a counterclockwise direction, from the perspective of Judah or Jerusalem. The line of promise (1:4–27) leads naturally to Abraham, then traces links to Israel through Isaac. Therefore, Israel's place in the world is the major point of the presentation of chapter 1. Here Israel, a small stateless community within the Achaemenid Empire, sets forth its place within humanity (Kelly 1996, 177). The implication of the opening chapter is that Israel may take confidence from its election and continuing divine provision.

First Chronicles 2–9 follows the order of world-Israel, Jerusalem-temple. The world of nations forms the first external circle, with Israel as the center. The tribes of Israel form the second circle in which Judah, Benjamin, and Levi form the definite centers of gravity, with Levi in the middle; the third circle is Jerusalem and its inhabitants. The temple, the dwelling of Yahweh, and its personnel stand in the center. So we have a series of concentric circles. The pattern is a well-thought-out one of concentric holiness (cf. Kelly 1996, 179).

Chapter 2 begins with Jacob, with concentration on the tribal development of Israel, as it will be displayed through the twelve tribes. The Chronicler thus asserts that the purposes of God in creation (chap. 1) are realized through Israel (chaps. 2–9). Thus the genealogies define the contours of God's government of the universe, both in terms of the election of Israel and in terms of moral order, covering, in chapters 2–8, the period from the origin of tribal Israel to the later monarchical period. Chapter 9 mentions the exile briefly (9:1) without emphasis, since its purpose is to complete the national presentation up to the postexilic return of Israel from exile. There is a brief genealogical attention to all tribes except Dan and Zebulun (both situated in the extreme north), but the major focus is on Judah and Levi, kingship and priesthood.

To the problems of the period, the Chronicler asserted that this small community was the heir of the promises, the successor of Israel at its greatest, and that all God's commitments to its ancestors still stood (McConville 1984, 12). The function of chapter 9 is that God's plans for the world, centered upon Israel throughout its history (chaps. 2–8), are now being taken forward in the unlikely looking remnant that clustered around Persian Jerusalem. The northern tribal details are sketchy, as if to say that their attachment to Israel is tenuous;

their Israelite status, however, is affirmed, and the genealogies are, in effect, an invitation to them to recognize the primacy of Judah and Jerusalem (Kelly 1996, 184). The message to all Israel is that there can still be a glorious future. Concentrating on Judah, Chronicles maintains the idea of a united Israel, the full twelve tribes constituted as something that, in principle, may be realized again.

There is no suggestion throughout the two books that Jerusalem and Judah represent the totality of Israel, and the hope is that there will once again be an integrated Israel in the land. The author is, however, equally concerned with the spiritual dimensions of the community to be integrated, and this emphasis is clear from his progressive assessments. The Chronicler defines the community in somewhat different terms from Ezra-Nehemiah. He depicts Israel functioning as a tribal unity; the northern tribes, though in a state of rebellion, were still part of Israel, whose restoration had begun. But the postexilic community is far from having been regathered. The survivors of the northern tribes (cf. Hezekiah's attitude, 2 Chron. 29–32) retain their status as legitimate members of Israel. For the Chronicler, Israel was a covenantal bond of land and people under the Davidic covenant (1 Chron. 17:9; 2 Chron. 7:14). The kingdom was at its most extensive and united shape, as in the time of David and Solomon (1 Chron. 11:1–3; 13:5; 2 Chron. 1:2). The old promises remained valid and were capable of increasing fulfillment through obedience to the demands of the covenant. Israel continues as the earthly form of Yahweh's kingdom (1 Chron. 17:14; 28:5; 2 Chron. 9:8; 13:8). The Chronicler holds an ideal Israel that is inclusive in its land and population, and that seems to reflect the conditions of the Davidic-Solomonic kingdom. The earlier promises relating to the land and people, in the Abrahamic and Sinaitic covenants, have found their confirmation and continuing validity in the covenant with David.

The Chronicler's view is that the Abrahamic covenant promised the land to Israel forever (1 Chron. 16:15–18; 28:8; 2 Chron. 20:7–8; cf. v. 11). The response to the gift of the land has been the building of the temple for God's name, that is, in recognition of his kingly sovereignty. Chronicles is not as concerned as Kings was with accounting for the loss of the land, but in stressing the resumption of Yahweh's saving activity toward Israel, and what the people's appropriate response should be. There is no suggestion that the concept of Israel has been reduced to that of a cultic community. Israel may continue to enjoy its inheritance through careful attention to the law, and the Chronicler holds out the prospect of a more extensive fulfillment.

The Monarchy from David to Solomon

The Reigns of Saul and David (1 Chron. 10–29)

The Chronicler begins his account of the monarchical period with the reign of Saul, showing how this disastrous kingship left the state bereft and exposed to the Philistines. Saul (1 Chron. 10) appears only in an account given of his death. Some suggest the Chronicler's aim was to compare the tragedy of Saul with the success of David. The portrayal contrasts the lack of salvation with Saul to the fulfillment of salvation in David. The cause of Saul's tragedy was his treachery (1 Chron. 10:13–14). He did not seek Yahweh and failed in relation to the cultus. He had a negative relation to the ark. He was dismissed, along with his dynasty. Saul's death was divinely willed ("the Lord killed him," 1 Chron. 10:14). King and dynasty could only be established by divine action or disposed of by such action. The Saulide genealogy, however, is taken down to the exile, demonstrating some sustained interest in it, perhaps in the light of the modification or elimination of the Davidic genealogy. Thus the author puts before his audience the catastrophe that resulted from Saul's rule.

David

There is a disproportionate interest in David (1 Chron. 11–29), apart from the genealogical material; in 1 Chronicles 11–19 there are seventy-six references to David. The Chronicler gives the impression that David has communicated directly with Yahweh. Nineteen chapters are devoted to David out of sixty-five. A third of the space that the Chronicler allows from the reign of Saul to the edict of Cyrus (ca. 650 years) is devoted to the thirty-three-year reign of David. Is David a standard for later kings, a paradigm (Riley 1993, 53–58)? Is the picture constructed messianically and eschatologically of the ideal David who will rule? Or is the temple the central Davidic contribution for postexilic Israel? The latter seems to be the case. David dominates the presentation of Chronicles along with the covenant through which the dynasty was established, and, important for the future, through which the temple was built.

Unlike in Samuel, David is presented essentially in cultic terms. The cult becomes the central vehicle through which Israel's relationship to Yahweh is celebrated and presented. David and Aaron are the joint focus of the Chronicler's hope for Israel, and this joint hope of king/priest represents the Chronicler's view of the manner in which theocracy is to be expressed.

It is customarily argued that, in Chronicles, the high priest, who in the postexilic times was ascendant (cf. Sir. 50:1–4), usurps the role of the king. Chronicles, while it points to the Mosaic origin of the institution, and the centrality of the Aaronides within the Levites, submerges priesthood within kingship. Apart, however, from Jehoiada, distinguished for his role in the restoration of the monarchy, the books have little to say about the high priest. The king is the clear patron of the cult (cf. 2 Chron. 24:8 and 2 Kings 12:9). Uzziah, however, who attempts to usurp a priestly role (2 Chron. 26:16–20), is ejected from the temple by the priesthood, not by the high priest. Hilkiah, Josiah's high priest, is subject to Josiah's dictates (2 Chron. 34:20–21). Hezekiah acts like David and Solomon in appointing the divisions of priest and Levites (31:2), and in making provision for the burnt offerings (31:3–7; cf. also 31:11, 13). Chronicles is clear that continuing royal authority is exercised over the cult (2 Chron. 34:8–11).

The cult that centers on the Levitical choral service proclaims (1 Chron. 16:8–36), as was its OT purpose, Yahweh's universal kingship and his choice of Israel. In the cult, Yahweh's presence and protection are invoked, and petitions for the covenant people are presented for deliverance from enemies (16:35). The cult expresses a hopeful expectation of salvation (cf. 1 Chron. 16:35) that embraces land, people, and the Davidic line. But all this is due to David, who organizes and appoints the Levitical cultic personnel (1 Chron. 15:16–24).

In 1 Chronicles 11–16, the ark is the major topic; the capture of Jerusalem and the anointing of David are subordinated here to the primary concern of bringing the ark to Jerusalem. In regard to the ark, David is everything that Saul was not, receiving as well the promise of the dynasty (1 Chron. 17:10–14).

Chapters 17–29 discuss the Davidic preparations for the building of the temple. The Chronicler gives a prime indication of David's purpose, in chapter 17, especially verse 14, where the settlement of kingship on Solomon is bound up with the more primary matters of the temple and the kingdom of God. David's reign, which is to be extended through Solomon, is highly commended. God has taken the kingdom away from Saul and given it to David, who has been chosen to build the temple, for which there were plans in writing from the hand of the Lord (28:19).

The dedication of the temple contains many references to the promise made to David, and the deeds done by him, since dynasty and temple were symbiotic. Solomon's temple-building activities are presented, with conscious allusion to David, and thus Solomon's action is perceived as the faithful completion of David's initiative. Thus, David is drawn into the building of the temple and its cultic arrangements, so that the cult becomes a memorial of David's reign. David is the true cult founder, rather than Solomon, who merely carried out his father's instructions. David had established the conditions of rest that permitted temple building, and the Chronicler is more concerned with the Davidic dynasty's relation to the temple than with the dynasty itself.

Thus, the construction of the temple serves to underscore the theocratic note of kingdom. This link between temple building and the kingdom of God finds its theological conclusion in Cyrus's edict to restore the temple, recorded at the end of 2 Chronicles. The Chronicler does not appear to have been interested in the person of David, in terms of any messianic expectations, nor does he glorify Solomon later, individually. The concentration of interest on these two personalities in Chronicles is in connection with their roles as temple builders, so that the Chronicler does not hesitate to use material that discredits David (cf. the reporting of the census and ensuing plague of 2 Sam. 24 in 1 Chron. 21). The remainder of 1 Chronicles, after David is dealt with, concerns the temple personnel and various administrative measures, preparatory to the building of the Solomonic temple—matters of great importance to the community of the fourth century B.C.

The Reign of Solomon (2 Chron. 1–9)

Solomon's royal inauguration took place while David was still reigning (1 Chron. 29:22–23). Solomon and David are considered as a unit in later references (2 Chron. 11:17; 33:7; 35:4). Solomon is the second Joshua, the faithful accomplisher of the Davidic task. In keeping with the Davidic expectations,

Solomon is blessed and promised an everlasting reign (2 Chron. 7:18), but the element of conditionality is there, for the blessing is predicated on the demonstration of obedience.

The most significant event of Solomon's reign is the dedication of the temple. So Solomon visits the high place of Gibeon overnight (2 Chron. 1:3–13), announces his intention to build (2:3–6), procures master builders and materials (2:7–16), finishes the temple according to plan (3:1–5:1), assembles the people (5:2–14), and presides at the dedication (6:1–7:10); as a result, Yahweh manifests his presence in the temple (2 Chron. 5:13–14; 2 Chron. 7). The major moments connected with the temple in the building—the transfer of the ark (chap. 5) and Solomon's prayer of dedication (7:1–3)—are both marked by divine epiphanies. Solomon prays (2 Chron. 6:40–42) that Yahweh will dwell with his people in this place so that their worship be a joyful celebration of the salvation and benefits which his presence brings. If the phrase "the mercies of David" in 2 Chronicles 6:42 does come from Isaiah 55:3, then the Chronicler has transferred Davidic promises from David to the nation. The real promise to David now rests with the Israel gathered at the temple, rather than with the dynasty. Solomon's prayer (2 Chron. 6:40–42) is immediately followed by a fire theophany on the altar of burnt offerings (2 Chron. 7:1). This event is intended to parallel the revelation of Yahweh's glory on Mount Sinai (Exod. 19:18–19; 20:18), and, more specifically, the theophany that answered David's prayer at 1 Chronicles 21:26. So Solomon's prayer had been granted, and just as Solomon had completed Yahweh's house, so Yahweh had affirmed David's dynasty. Second Chronicles 7:12–22 expresses an intensified interest in the Davidic covenant. Solomon is faultless in Chronicles because he has the temple-building task laid on him. He thus receives cities and secures land (2 Chron. 8:1–6); foreign monarchs increase his wealth (8:17–9:12). But there is the recognition of the conditionality of particular kingships, at 2 Chronicles 6:15–17; 7:17–18, even if the future of the line is ensured.

The temple also testifies to the covenant. The accounts show that Davidic dynasty and temple are mutually related. The dynastic covenant with David is eternal, so that the statement that the ruler will be chastised for sin is omitted (cf. 2 Sam. 7:12b and 2 Chron. 7:12–22). The author is aware of Solomon's decline, but this is not germane to his purposes (cf. 1 Chron. 28:7 and 22:13; 2 Chron. 13:6; 21:7). The function of the Davidic-Solomonic narratives in Chronicles is theocratic, emphasizing the kingdom of God, and not messianic. In the exilic and postexilic writings, there is an absence of any particularly messianic emphasis, other than what is supposedly found in Chronicles. The restoration prophecies of Isaiah 40–55 do not endorse the Davidic dynasty, nor does the Book of Ezekiel, which emphasizes God's kingship (e.g., Ezek. 20:33). Nor can Haggai and Zechariah be drawn into this debate with any real conviction. The evidence for messianism from Zechariah is likewise very slender. Of course, Zerubbabel, venerated in both Haggai and Zechariah, is the temple builder, and in that sense he continues the hopes expressed in the Davidic promises. Overall, there seems to be little real postexilic interest in messianism.

Post-Solomonic Kings to Josiah

In keeping with the theocratic interest to which we have pointed, 2 Chronicles 10–36 emphasizes the prophetic direction to which the southern kingdom was subject after the building of the temple. The direction of the kingdom, through prophecy, had always been a characterizing feature of the period of the united monarchy. Since the southern kingdom is the visible carrier of the Israel concept, 2 Chronicles, unlike the Books of Kings, concentrates almost exclusively on the southern kings. Absolute allegiance to Yahweh on all fronts is demanded, so continuing responsibility for temple maintenance is placed upon the king. Good kings such as Asa, Joash, Hezekiah, and Josiah either make appeals to the north, or reform the temple, or both. The king becomes the figure, not only responsible for the cult, but for the nation as a whole, and for fulfilling the conditions of the covenant.

Important to the Chronicler are his rebukes, administered to Judah for participating in foreign alliances, in military and maritime ventures, and in marriage alliances. Generally, the rebukes entailed some kind of divine chastisement and thus figure within the Chronicler's theory of retribution. Treaties of the post-Solomonic period are condemned as expressions of disloyalty or lack of faith in Yahweh's power to defend his people, and the treaties are said to bring shame on the nation.

A Solomonic-type restoration occurred under Hezekiah, whose reforms to the temple are treated at great length. Hezekiah begins at the cultic center, cleansing the temple. He acts like David and Solomon in appointing the divisions of priests and Levites (31:2) and in making provision for the burnt offerings (31:3–7). The majority of Hezekiah's report deals with his temple measures, the celebration of a great Passover, the eradication of illicit northern and southern sites, the provision of courses for priests and Levites, the institution of regular sacrifice, and the support of cultic personnel. Both Hezekiah and the subsequent Josiah center their reforms on a missionary thrust to the north, aiming at an Israel of twelve tribes united under a Davidic king.

Once again, Israel, by this symbolic cleansing of temple and land, together with the celebration of the Passover under Hezekiah, is restored to an exodus situation: the people of God are fitted for occupancy of the land. For acts of faithfulness detailed in 2 Chronicles 31:2–21, Hezekiah is rewarded with divine protection against Sennacherib as well as with riches and other achievements. But he was proud and had to humble himself to avoid divine wrath, and had to be tested in the incident involving the Babylonian ambassadors.

Chronicles presents Manasseh differently than he is presented in Kings. Second Chronicles 33:1–20 emphasizes the change of heart on Manasseh's part, leading to cultic reform, presenting him as the outstanding paradigm of repentance. Kings, on the other hand, sees him as precipitating inevitable judgment. This difference in point of view is explained by differences in purpose. Through Manasseh, the Chronicler teaches that God is disposed to hear his people and restore their lost blessings, if they will emulate his penitent response and make obedient use of the cult. Restoration after judgment is the message conveyed. Amon, his son, continued the infidelities of his father, Manasseh. Josiah's report concentrates on cultic reform. While Hezekiah becomes a second Solomon, Josiah is the promoter of a Davidic revival. His reforms were followed by a concluding covenant ceremony, and a spectacular Passover was held for both south and north.

From Josiah to the Edict of Cyrus

The treatment of these kings is brief, probably not from lack of interest but simply to underscore what is important to the author and the times. Jehoiakim, Jehoiachin, and Zedekiah are condemned for having done evil; Jehoiakim is said to have been guilty of abomination, and Zedekiah refused to humble himself before Jeremiah (2 Chron. 36:12). During Zedekiah's reign, all the people followed the abomination of the nations. Each king suffers a truncated reign, and none is buried with his fathers. Jehoahaz is carried off to Egypt, Jehoiakim and Jehoiachin to Babylon, and there is no reference to the burial of Zedekiah. Neco of Egypt made Jehoiakim king; Nebuchadnezzar made Zedekiah a vassal.

Cyrus's decree is also the fulfillment of prophecy, and this edict reverses two of the effects of the exile, the destruction of the temple and the exile of the people. For Chronicles, the consequences of past wrongdoing have been requited, and the community now enjoys a new opportunity. Yahweh had warned north and south through his prophets, but such counsel has never been received (36:15–16). Consequently, the symbol of the theocracy, the temple, is finally destroyed and its sacred vessels carried into captivity (36:17–18). These calamities fulfill Jeremiah's prophecy of seventy years of exile (v. 21), a situation that the Cyrus edict is designed to reverse (vv. 22–23).

The Davidic promise of a dynasty is the Chronicler's model for the postexilic community. In 1 Chronicles 3:17–24, the line of David's descendants following the exile begins with Jehoiachin the captive. This anticipates his fate in 2 Chronicles 36:10, but affirms that he will not die childless. This is one of the few portions of Chronicles to continue beyond the exile, possibly down to the writer's own time. The list is further confirmation that the Davidic line has been maintained. The leading tribe, Judah (1 Chron. 3), affirms its continuing significance and the centrality of the Davidic promises in the life of the postexilic community.

The absence of a Davidic king constituted a problem for the postexilic community. In Ezra-Nehemiah, David is a much more peripheral figure, and no mention is made of the eternal covenant. Ezra-Nehemiah retained a vital sense of the importance of the Sinai covenant and the promises to the patriarchs, whereas, for the Chronicler, the Davidic covenant alone points to the fundamental development in the covenantal basis of God's relationship with Israel. This was a shift away from the former emphasis on exodus and Sinai, signaling a distinctively different religious-historical outlook. These represent two complementary reactions, one relating to the historical period, one to eschatological expectations. For Chronicles, David and Solomon become not only types of the normative past, but also indications of the nature of future theocracy. Israel and Judah under the Davidic dynasty are the earthly expression of Yahweh's universal kingdom, embracing the nations and the cosmos (1 Chron. 29:10–19; 2 Chron. 20:6). In the Chronicler's time, although the dynasty had ceased to function, Yahweh's rule is secure, as is Israel's final place. Worship in the temple was designed to remind the community of Yahweh's universal rule.

The edict of Cyrus at the end of 2 Chronicles raises, for us, the particular question of purpose and the eschatological direction of the Books of Chronicles. The Chronicler's theology of retribution has explained the series of punishments and the exile, but his theological direction does not end there. The writer's perception of Yahweh's character demands an eschatology for Israel. The God of Israel is presented as forward looking and merciful, committed to the restoration of God's people, and the Chronicler's interpretation of the Davidic covenant reflects this understanding (1 Chron. 17:9–10; 20–21; 2 Chron. 36:22–23). The language of 2 Chronicles 36:22–23 sustains, for the generation of the Chronicler, the projections of a new exodus set by Isaiah 40–55. This focus is clearly congruent with the second-exodus emphasis of Ezra-Nehemiah. The message of Chronicles is that the kingdom of God will come and that the second exodus will occur. Jerusalem will be the world center to which Gentile kings will come. If the Books of Chronicles were written to introduce the Ezra-Nehemiah reforms, then we might see this work as setting the tone for the second-exodus theology of those books, whose reform movement eventually failed. But if, as is more likely, Chronicles is to be separated from Ezra-Nehemiah, then the Cyrus edict is used as a conclusion, to indicate that the failed Ezra-Nehemiah reforms had set directions that were to be maintained. The temple-centered society of the postexilic period had set a model of divine government. Thus, the tenor of traditional prophetic eschatology (Isa. 2:2–4; Mic. 4:1–5) had been preserved.

Between 400 and 350 B.C., the Chronicler looked back to the program of Isaiah 40–55, to which the decree of Cyrus had called attention. That program had not been implemented, though the exile had historically ended. But this did not mean that the second exodus would not occur. Indeed, the recent efforts of the Ezra-Nehemiah period were attempts to implement the program. Chronicles injects a note of hope into a tired community. In a basic restatement of the older prophetic position, Chronicles represents the notion of an ideal Israel under a theocracy, the model kingdom by which the world will be drawn. God will not withdraw from God's commitment to the world, a commitment given at creation and affirmed through the call of Israel. Accordingly, the disappointments of the present, argues the Chronicler, must spawn a theology of hope. The Chronicler's broad appeal to the community at large, his markedly positive description of the people, and the frequent descriptions of their festive joy all indicate that the writer is interested in the revival and transformation of his community through its participation in temple worship and prayer. In all this activity, Israel may recognize its hope as being established in the ancient covenantal promises to which the temple testifies. Chronicles argued that the covenant constituted Israel as the earthly manifestation of the kingdom of God, in a reality manifested in the temple—appointed for atonement and prayer—and in the Davidic line, the personal expression of God's rule. The Davidic covenant is, for the Chronicler, eternally valid. It continues to mediate Yahweh's promises for the Davidic line, the people, and the land and defines the meaning of the temple as a symbol of the covenant, and as the place of restoration (1 Chron. 17:4–14; 2 Chron. 7:12–22). Chronicles is a call to repentance and hope in Yahweh's restoration. Thus, as the Hebrew Bible in its canonical form concludes by reaffirming the endurance of this promise (2 Chron. 36:23), it issues an invitation to go up (*wayya'al*) and, in so doing, opens trajectories that may take us into the center of New Testament faith.

Bibliography

Ackroyd, P. R. 1968. *Exile and Restoration.* Philadelphia: Westminster.

———. 1978. "Isaiah 1–12: Presentation of a Prophet." *VTSup* 29:16–48.

———. 1987. "The Biblical Interpretation of the Reigns of Ahaz and Hezekiah." In *Studies in the Religious Tradition in the Old Testament,* 181–92. London: SCM.

Albright, W. F. 1942. "King Jehoiachin in Exile." *BA* 5:49–55.

Allen, L. C. 1990. *The Book of Ezekiel.* Waco, Tex.: Word.

Andersen, F. I. 1958. "Who Built the Second Temple?" *ABR* 6:1–35.

———. 1976. *Job: An Introduction and Commentary.* Downers Grove, Ill.: InterVarsity.

Andersen, F. I., and D. N. Freedman. 1980. *Hosea: A New Translation, with Introduction and Commentary.* New York: Doubleday.

———. 1989. *Amos.* New York: Doubleday.

Anderson, R. Dean. 1994. "The Division and Order of the Psalms." *WTJ* 56:219–41.

Ashley, Timothy R. 1997. *The Book of Numbers.* Grand Rapids: Eerdmans.

Baltzer, Klaus. 1971. *The Covenant Formulary in the Old Testament and Jewish and Early Christian Writings.* Oxford: Blackwell.

Barton, J. 1980. *Amos's Oracles against the Nations: A Study of Amos 1:3–2:5.* Cambridge: Cambridge University Press.

Beale, G. K. 1999. *The Book of Revelation: A Commentary on the Greek Text.* NIGTC. Grand Rapids: Eerdmans.

Beckwith, Roger T. 1987. "The Unity and Diversity of God's Covenants." *TynB* 38:92–118

Berg, S. B. 1979. *The Book of Esther.* Missoula, Mont.: Scholars.

Berquist, Jon L. 1993. "Dangerous Waters of Justice and Righteousness, Amos 5:18–20." *BTB* 23:54–67.

Beuken, W. A. M. 1967. *Haggai-Sacharia 1–8.* Assen: Van Gorcum.

———. 1972. "Mispat: The First Servant Song and Its Context." *VT* 22:1–30.

———. 1974. "Isaiah liv: The Multiple Identity of the Person Addressed." *OTS* 19:29–70.

———. 1989. "Servant-Herald of Good Tidings: Isaiah 61 as an Interpretation of Isaiah 40–55." In *The Book of Isaiah,* edited by J. Vermeylen, 412–42. BETL 71. Louvain: Louvain University Press.

———. 1990. "The Main Theme of Trito-Isaiah 'The Servants of Yahweh.'" *JSOT* 47:67–87.

Bird, P. 1981. "'Male and Female He Created Them': Gen. 1:27b in the Context of the Priestly Account of Creation." *HTR* 74:129–59.

Blocher, H. 1977. "The Fear of the Lord as the 'Principle' of Wisdom." *TynB* 28:3–28.

Block, D. I. 1997. *The Book of Ezekiel.* NICOT. Grand Rapids: Eerdmans.

Bolin, Thomas M. 1997. *Freedom beyond Forgiveness: The Book of Jonah Re-examined.* Sheffield: Sheffield Academic Press.

Braulik, G. 1993. "The Sequence of Laws in Deuteronomy 12–16 and in the Decalogue." In *A Song of Power and the Power of a Song,* edited by Duane L. Christensen, 313–35. Winona Lake, Ind.: Eisenbrauns.

Brueggemann, W. 1969. "Amos' Intercessory Formula." *VT* 19:385–99.

———. 1972. "Life and Death in Tenth-Century Israel." *JAAR* 40:96–109.

———. 1990. "1 Samuel 1: A Sense of a Beginning." *ZAW* 102:33–48.

Butler, Trent C. 1983. *Joshua.* Waco, Tex.: Word.

Campbell, A. F. 1975. *The Ark Narrative.* Missoula, Mont.: Scholars.

Campbell, E. F. 1975. *Ruth.* Anchor Bible. New York: Doubleday.

Carlson, R. A. 1964. *David the Chosen King.* Stockholm: Almqvist and Wiksell.

Carroll, Mark D. 1992. *Contexts for Amos: Prophetic Poetics in Latin American Perspective.* JSOTSup 132. Sheffield: Sheffield Academic Press.

Cassuto, U. 1989. *A Commentary on the Book of Genesis.* Vol. 1. Jerusalem: Magnes Press.

Childs, B. S. 1979. *Introduction to the Old Testament as Scripture.* Philadelphia: Fortress.

Christensen, Duane L. 1984. "A Theological Basis for Josiah's Program of Political Expansion." *CBQ* 46:669–82.

———. 2001. *Deuteronomy 1:1–21:9.* 2d ed. Nashville: Nelson.

Clark, W. M. 1969. "A Legal Background to the Yahwist's Use of 'Good and Evil' in Genesis 2–3." *JBL* 88:266–78.

Clifford, R. J. 1983. "Isaiah 55: Invitation to a Feast." In *The Word of the Lord Shall Go Forth: Essays in Honor of David Noel Freedman,* edited by C. L. Meyers and M. O'Connor, 27–35. Winona Lake, Ind.: Eisenbrauns.

———. 1984. *Fair Spoken and Persuading: An Interpretation of Second Isaiah.* New York: Paulist.

Cohn, G. C. 1969. *Das Buch Jona im Lichte der biblischen Erzahlkunst.* Assen: Van Gorcum.

Davies, Eryl W. 1983. "Ruth IV 5 and the Duties of the Go'el." *VT* 33:231–34.

———. 1995. *Numbers.* New Century Bible Commentary. Grand Rapids: Eerdmans.

Davies, John. 2000. "A Royal Priesthood: Literary and Intertextual Perspectives on an Image of Israel in Exodus 19:6." Ph.D. diss., University of Sydney.

Day, John. 1985. *God's Conflict with the Dragon and the Sea: Echoes of a Canaanite Myth in the Old Testament.* Cambridge: Cambridge University Press.

de Vaux, R. 1970. "The Revelation of the Divine Name YHWH." In *Proclamation and Presence: Old Testament Essays in Honour of G. H. Davies,* edited by J. I. Durham and J. R. Porter, 48–75. London: SCM.

de Waard, J. 1977. "The Chiastic Spirit of Amos 5:1–17." *VT* 27:170–77.

Dorsey, David. 1990. "Literary Structures in the Song of Songs." *JSOT* 46:81–96.

Duhm, B. 1892. *Das Buch Jesaia übersetzt und erklärt.* Göttingen: Vandenhoeck & Ruprecht.

Dumbrell, W. J. 1974. "Spirit and Kingdom in the Old Testament." *RTR* 33:1–10.

———. 1977. "Some Observations on the Political Origin of Israel's Eschatology." *RTR* 36:33–41.

———. 1984. *Covenant and Creation: A Theology of Old Testament Covenants.* Exeter, England: Paternoster.

———. 1994. *Search for Order.* Grand Rapids: Baker.

Erlandsson, S. 1970. *The Burden of Babylon.* ConBOT 4. Lund: Gleerup.

Eskenasi, Tamara C. 1988. *In an Age of Prose: A Literary Approach to Ezra-Nehemiah.* SBLMS 36. Atlanta: Scholars.

Eybers, I. H. 1976. "Chronological Problems in Ezra-Nehemiah." *OTWSA* 19:10–29.

Falk, M. 1982. *Love Lyrics from the Bible.* Sheffield: Almond.

Fewell, D. A. 1988. *Circle of Sovereignty: A Story of Stories in Daniel 1–6.* Sheffield: Sheffield Academic Press.

Fishbane, Michael. 1975a. "Composition and Structure in the Jacob Cycle (Gen 25:19–35:22)." *JJS* 26:15–28.

———. 1975b. "The Sacred Centre: The Symbolic Structure of the Bible." In *Texts and Responses,* edited by Michael Fishbane and P. A. Flohr, 24–43. Leiden: Brill.

———. 1979. *Text and Texture.* New York: Schocken.

Fokkelman, J. P. 1975. *Narrative Art in Genesis.* Assen: Van Gorcum.

Fox, Michael V. 1977. "Frame-Narrative and Composition in the Book of Qohelet." *HUCA* 48:83–106.

———. 1986. "Egyptian Onomastica and Biblical Wisdom." *VT* 36:302–10.

———. 1989. *Qohelet and his Contradictions.* JSOTSup 71. Sheffield: Almond.

———. 1991. *Character and Ideology in the Book of Esther.* Columbia: University of South Carolina Press.

———. 1997. "Ideas of Wisdom in Proverbs 1–9." *JBL* 116:613–37.

Fretheim, T. E. 1978. "Jonah and Theodicy." *ZAW* 90:227–37.

Futato, Mark D. 1998. "Because It Had Not Rained: A Study of Gen 2:5–7 with Implications for Gen 2:4–25 and Gen 1:1–2:3." *WTJ* 60:1–21.

Gibson, J. C. L. 1981. *Genesis.* Daily Study Bible 1. Philadelphia: Westminster.

Gitay, Y. 1980. "A Study of Amos's Art of Speech: A Rhetorical Analysis of Amos 3:1–15." *CBQ* 42:293–309.

———. 1981. *Prophecy and Persuasion: A Study of Isaiah 40–48.* Bonn: Linguistica Biblica.

Greenberg, Moshe. 1972. "The Plagues of Egypt." *EvJ* 13:604–13.

———. 1984. "The Design and Theme of Ezekiel's Program of Restoration." *Int* 38:181–204.

Gunkel, Hermann. 1998. *An Introduction to the Psalms.* Translated by James D. Nogalski. Macon, Ga.: Mercer University Press.

Halpern, B. 1974. "Sectionalism and Schism." *JBL* 93:519–32.

———. 1978. "The Ritual Background of Zechariah's Temple Song." *CBQ* 40:167–90.

Hamlin, E. J. 1983. *Joshua: Inheriting the Land.* Grand Rapids: Eerdmans.

Hanson, P. D. 1975. *The Dawn of Apocalyptic.* Philadelphia: Fortress.

Haran, M. 1978. *Temples and Temple-Service in Ancient Israel.* Oxford: Clarendon.

Heidel, A. 1961. *The Babylonian Genesis: The Story of Creation.* 6th ed. Chicago: University of Chicago Press.

Hess, Richard. 1996. *Joshua.* Leicester, England: InterVarsity.

Houser, M. K. 1978. "Holiness in the Book of Leviticus." Master's thesis, Regent College, Vancouver.

Hunter, A. V. 1980. *Seek the Lord! A Study of the Meaning and Function of the Exhortation in Amos, Hosea, Isaiah, Micah, and Zephaniah.* Baltimore: St. Mary's Seminary and University.

Hutter, M. 1986. "Adam als Gaertner und Koenig (Gen 2,8.15)." *BZ* 30:258–62.

Jamieson-Drake, David W. 1991. *Scribes and Schools in Monarchic Israel: A Socio-archeological Approach.* Sheffield: Almond.

Janzen, J. G. 1983. "Samuel Opened the Doors of the House of YHWH." *JSOT* 26:89–96.

Japhet, Sarah. 1983. "People and Land in the Restoration Period." In *Das Land Israel im biblischer Zeit,* edited by N. Kamp and G. Strecker, 103–25. Göttingen: Vandenhoeck & Ruprecht.

Jensen, J. 1979. "The Age of Immanuel." *CBQ* 41:220–39.

Jeremias, Jorg. 1972. "MŠPT im ersten Gottesknechtslied (Jes 42:1–41)." *VT* 22:31–42.

Johnson, B. 1985. "Form and Message in Lamentations." *ZAW* 97:58–73.

Jones, B. W. 1978. "The So-Called Appendix to the Book of Esther." *Semitics* 6:36–43.

Kaiser, W. C., Jr. 1974. "The Blessing of David: The Charter for Humanity." In *The Law and the Prophet: Old Testament Studies in Honor of O. T. Allis,* edited by J. H. Skilton, 298–318. Nutley, N.J.: Presbyterian and Reformed.

Keil, C. F., and F. Delitzsch. 1975. *A Commentary on the Old Testament in Ten Volumes.* Vol. 1, *The Pentateuch.* Grand Rapids: Eerdmans.

Kelly, Brian E. 1996. *Retribution and Eschatology in Chronicles.* JSOTSup 211. Sheffield: Sheffield Academic Press.

Kiuchi, N. 1987. *The Purification Offering in the Priestly Literature: Its Meaning and Function.* JSOTSup 56. Sheffield: Sheffield Academic Press.

Knierim, R. 1968. "The Messianic Concept in the First Book of Samuel." In *Jesus and the Historian: Written in Honor of E. C. Colwell,* edited by F. T. Trotter, 20–51. Philadelphia: Westminster.

Knoppers, Gary N. 1994. *Two Nations under God: The Deuteronomic History of Salvation and the Dual Monarchies.* 2 vols. HSM 52–53. Atlanta: Scholars.

Koch, K. 1974. "Ezra and the Origins of Judaism." *JSS* 19:173–97.

Koehler, L., and W. Baumgartner. 1958. *Lexicon in Veteris Testamenti Libros.* Leiden: Brill.

Kooy, V. H. 1975. "The Fear and Love of God in Deuteronomy." In *Grace upon Grace: Essays in Honor of L. J. Kuyper,* edited by J. I. Cook, 106–16. Grand Rapids: Eerdmans.

Kraus, H.-J. 1966. *Worship in Israel.* Oxford: Blackwell.

Landy, F. 1983. *Paradoxes of Paradise: Identity and Difference in the Song of Songs.* Sheffield: Almond.

Leder, Arie C. A. 1999. "Reading Exodus to Learn and Learning to Read Exodus." *Calvin Theological Journal* 34, no. 1: 11–35.

Levenson, Jon R. 1976. *The Theology of the Program of Restoration of Ezekiel 40–48.* Missoula, Mont.: Scholars.

———. 1985. *Sinai and Zion: An Entry into the Jewish Bible.* Minneapolis: Winston.

Loader, J. A. 1978. "Esther as Novel with Different Levels of Meaning." *ZAW* 90:417–21.

———. 1979. *Polar Structures in the Book of Qohelet.* Berlin: de Gruyter.

Lohfink, N. 1969. *Christian Meaning of the Old Testament.* London: Burns and Oates.

Lundbom, J. R. 1975. *Jeremiah—A Study in Ancient Hebrew Rhetoric.* Missoula, Mont.: Scholars.

Magonet, J. 1983. *Form and Meaning: Studies in Literary Techniques in the Book of Jonah.* Sheffield: Almond.

Maio, A. W. T. 1998. "The Concept of Holiness in the Book of Ezekiel." Ph.D. diss., Cambridge University.

Malamat, A. 1968. "The Last Kings of Judah and the Fall of Jerusalem." *IEJ* 18:137–56.

———. 1976. "Charismatic Leadership in the Book of Judges." In *Magnalia Dei, the Mighty Acts of God: Essays on the Bible and Archeology in Memory of G. Ernest Wright,* edited by F. M. Cross et al., 152–68. New York: Doubleday.

Martin, James D. 1995. *Proverbs.* Sheffield: Sheffield Academic Press.

McBride, Dean. 1987. "The Polity of the Covenant People: The Book of Deuteronomy." *Int* 41:229–44.

McCarter, P. K. 1980. "The Apology of David." *JBL* 99:489–504.

McConville, J. Gordon. 1979. "God's 'Name' and God's 'Glory.'" *TynB* 30:149–63.

———. 1984. *Chronicles.* Daily Study Bible. Edinburgh: St. Andrews Press.

———. 1993. *Judgment and Promise: An Interpretation of the Book of Jeremiah.* Leicester, England: Apollos.

McCurley, F. R. 1983. *Ancient Myths and the Biblical Faith.* Philadelphia: Fortress.

McKenzie, S. L., and H. N. Wallace. 1983. "Covenant Themes in Malachi." *CBQ* 45:549–63.

Mettinger, T. D. 1974. "Abild oder Urbild? 'Imago Dei' in traditionsgeschichtlicher Sicht." *ZAW* 86:403–24.

———. 1976. *King and Messiah.* ConBOT 8. Lund: Gleerup.

Milgrom, J. 1975. "The Priestly Doctrine of Repentance." *RB* 82:186–205.

Miller, P. D. 1969. "The Gift of God: The Deuteronomic Theology of the Land." *Int* 23:451–65.

———. 1990. *Deuteronomy.* Interpretation. Louisville: Westminster John Knox.

Mitchell, Gordon. 1993. *Together in the Land: A Reading of the Book of Joshua.* Sheffield: Sheffield Academic Press.

Mouser, William E., Jr. 1983. *Walking in Wisdom: Studying the Proverbs of Solomon.* Downers Grove, Ill.: InterVarsity.

Mowinckel, Sigmund. 1967. *The Psalms in Israel's Worship,* Translated by D. R. Ap-Thomas. Oxford: Blackwell.

Nel, P. 1982. *Structure and Ethos of the Wisdom Admonitions in Proverbs.* Berlin: de Gruyter.

Newsom, Carol A. 1984. "Maker of Metaphors in Ezekiel's Oracles against Tyre." *Int* 38:151–64.

Niditch, S. 1986. "Ezekiel 40–48 in a Visionary Context." *CBQ* 48:208–24.

Niehaus, Jeffrey J. 1995. *God at Sinai: Covenant and Theophany in the Bible and Ancient Near East.* Grand Rapids: Zondervan.

O'Connell, Robert H. 1994. *Concentration and Continuity: The Literary Structure of Isaiah.* Sheffield: Sheffield Academic Press.

Ogden, G. S. 1979. "Qoheleth's Use of the 'Nothing Is Better' Form." *JBL* 98:339–50.
———. 1980. "Qoheleth 9:17–10:20: Variations on the Theme of Wisdom's Strength and Vulnerability." *VT* 30:27–37.
———. 1983. "Qoheleth 11:1–6." *VT* 33:222–30.
Olson, D. 1985. *The Death of the Old and the Birth of the New: The Framework of the Book of Numbers and the Pentateuch.* Chico, Calif.: Scholars.
Parunak, H. V. 1979. "Structural Studies in Ezekiel." Ph.D. diss., Harvard University.
———. 1980. "The Literary Architecture of Ezekiel's MAR'OT 'ELOHIM." *JBL* 99:61–74.
Paul, S. M. 1971a. "Amos 1:3–2:3: A Concatenous Literary Pattern." *JBL* 90:397–403.
———. 1971b. "Prophets and Prophecy." *EvJ* 13:1150–75.
Petersen, D. L. 1977. *Late Israelite Prophecy.* Missoula, Mont.: Scholars.
Prinsloo, W. S. 1980. "The Theology of the Book of Ruth." *VT* 30:330–41.
———. 1985. *The Theology of the Book of Joel.* Hawthorne, N.Y.: de Gruyter.
Rainey, A. F. 1970. "The Order of Sacrifices in the Old Testament Ritual Texts." *Bib* 51:485–98.
Riley, William. 1993. *King and Cultus in Chronicles: Worship and the Reinterpretation of History.* JSOTSup 60. Sheffield: Sheffield Academic Press.
Robinson, G. 1980. "The Idea of Rest in the Old Testament and the Search for the Basic Character of the Sabbath." *ZAW* 82:32–42.
Sakenfeld, K. 1975. "The Problem of Divine Forgiveness in Numbers 14." *CBQ* 37:317–30.
Schmidt, W. H. 1973. *Die Schopfungsgeschichte der Priesterschrift.* 3d ed. Neukirchen-Vluyn: Neukirchener.
Schramm, Brooks. 1995. *The Opponents of Third Isaiah: Reconstructing the Cultic History of the Restoration.* Sheffield: Sheffield Academic Press.
Scullion, John J. 1984. *Genesis 1–11.* London: SPCK.
Selman, M. 1994. *Chronicles.* Leicester, England: InterVarsity.
Seow, C. L. 1997. *Ecclesiastes.* Anchor Bible 18c. New York: Doubleday.
———. 1999. "I & II Kings." In *The New Interpreters Bible: A Commentary in Twelve Volumes.* Vol. 3. Nashville: Abingdon.
Shaw, Charles S. 1993. *The Speeches of Micah: A Rhetorical-Historical Analysis.* Sheffield: Sheffield Academic Press.
Shenkel, J. D. 1965. "An Interpretation of Ps 93." *Bib* 46:410–16.
Smith, M. H. 1971. *Palestinian Parties and Politics That Shaped the Old Testament.* New York: Columbia University Press.
Stansell, Gary. 1988. *Micah and Isaiah: A Form and Tradition Historical Comparison.* SBLDS 85. Atlanta: Scholars.
Stenson, K. R. 1996. *The Vision of Transformation.* Atlanta: Scholars.
Sweeney, Marvin A. 1991a. "A Form-Critical Assessment of the Book of Zephaniah." *CBQ* 53:388–408.
———. 1991b. "Structure, Genre, and Intent in the Book of Habakkuk." *VT* 41:63–83.
———. 1996. *Isaiah 1–39 with an Introduction to Prophetic Literature.* FOTL 16. Grand Rapids: Eerdmans.
———. 2000. *The Twelve Prophets.* 2 vols. Collegeville, Minn.: Liturgical Press.
Talmon, S. 1953. "The Sectarian *yahad*—A Biblical Noun." *VT* 3:133–40.

———. 1976. "Ezra and Nehemiah." *IDBSup,* 317–28.

Thompson, J. A. 1980. *The Book of Jeremiah.* Grand Rapids: Eerdmans.

Toombs, L. E. 1965. "Love and Justice in Deuteronomy: A Third Approach to the Law." *Int* 19:339–411.

Van der Woude, A. S. 1969. "Micah in Dispute with the Pseudo-Prophets." *VT* 19:244–60.

Vannoy, J. R. 1978. *Covenant Renewal at Gilgal.* Cherry Hill, N.J.: Mack.

von Rad, Gerhard. 1972. *Wisdom in Israel.* London: SCM.

von Waldow, H. E. 1974. "Israel and Her Land: Some Theological Considerations." In *A Light unto My Path: Old Testament Studies in Honor of J. M. Myers,* edited by H. N. Bream et al., 493–508. Philadelphia: Temple University Press.

Wallace, H. N. 1985. *The Eden Narrative.* Atlanta: Scholars.

Walsh, J. T. 1977. "Genesis 2:4b–3:24: A Synchronic Approach." *JBL* 96:161–77.

———. 1982. " Jonah 2:3–10: A Rhetorical Critical Study." *Bib* 63:219–29.

Waltke, B. K. 1979. "The Book of Proverbs and Ancient Wisdom Literature." *BibSac* 136:221–38.

Ward, J. M. 1978. "The Servant's Knowledge in Isaiah 40–55." In *Israelite Wisdom: Theological and Literary Essays in Honor of Samuel Terrien,* edited by J. G. Gammie et al., 121–36. Missoula, Mont.: Scholars.

Watts, Rikki E. 1990. "Consolation or Confrontation? Isaiah 40–55 and the Delay of the New Exodus." *TynB* 41, no. 1: 31–59.

Webb, Barry G. 1987. *The Book of Judges: An Integrated Reading.* JSOTSup 46. Sheffield: Sheffield Academic Press.

Weeks, S. 1994. *Early Israelite Wisdom.* Oxford: Clarendon.

Weinfeld, M. 1972. *Deuteronomy and the Deuteronomic School.* Oxford: Oxford University Press.

———. 1981. "Sabbath, Temple, and Enthronement of the Lord—The Problem of the *Sitz im Leben* of Gen 1:1–2:3." In *Melanges bibliques et orientaux en l'honneur de M. Henri Cazelles,* AOAT 212, 501–12. Kevelaer, Germany: Butzon et Becker.

Wenham, G. J. 1971. "The Deuteronomic Theology of the Book of Joshua." *JBL* 90:140–48.

———. 1979. *The Book of Leviticus.* NICOT 13. Grand Rapids: Eerdmans.

———. 1986. "Sanctuary Symbolism in the Garden of Eden Story." In *Proceedings of Ninth World Congress of Jewish Studies,* 19–25. Jerusalem: World Union of Jewish Studies.

———. 1987. *Genesis 1–15.* Waco, Tex.: Word.

Westermann, Claus. 1965. *Praise and Lament in the Psalms.* Edinburgh: T. & T. Clark.

———. 1978. *Blessing in the Bible and the Life of the Church.* Philadelphia: Fortress.

Whybray, R. N. 1974. *The Intellectual Tradition.* BZAW 135. Berlin: de Gruyter.

Williamson, H. G. M. 1983. "The Composition of Ezra 1–6." *JTS* 34:1–29.

———. 1988. *Ezra, Nehemiah.* Waco, Tex.: Word.

Williamson, Paul R. 2000. *Abraham, Israel, and the Nations: The Patriarchal Promise and Its Covenantal Development in Genesis.* Sheffield: Sheffield Academic Press.

Willis, J. T. 1969. "The Structure of the Book of Micah." *SEÅ* 34:5–42.

Wilson, A. 1986. *The Nations in Deutero-Isaiah: A Study on Composition and Structure.* Lewiston, N.Y.: Edwin Mellen.

Wilson, G. H. 1985. *The Editing of the Hebrew Psalter.* Chico, Calif.: Scholars.

Wilson, R. R. 1972. "The Interpretation of Ezekiel's Dumbness." *VT* 22:91–104.

Wolters, Al. 1991. "The Riddle of the Scales in Daniel 5." *HUCA* 62:155–77.

Zenger, Erich. 1998. "The Composition and Theology of the Fifth Book of Psalms, Psalms 107–145." *JSOT* 80:77–102

Zimmerli, W. 1979. *Ezekiel I: A Commentary upon the Book of the Prophet Ezekiel, Chapters 1–24*. Philadelphia: Fortress.

———. 1980. *Ezekiel II: A Commentary upon the Book of the Prophet Ezekiel, Chapters 25–48*. Philadelphia: Fortress.

———. 1982. *I Am Yahweh*. Atlanta: John Knox.

Index